Created by Spike Chunsoft   Manga by Kyousuke Suga

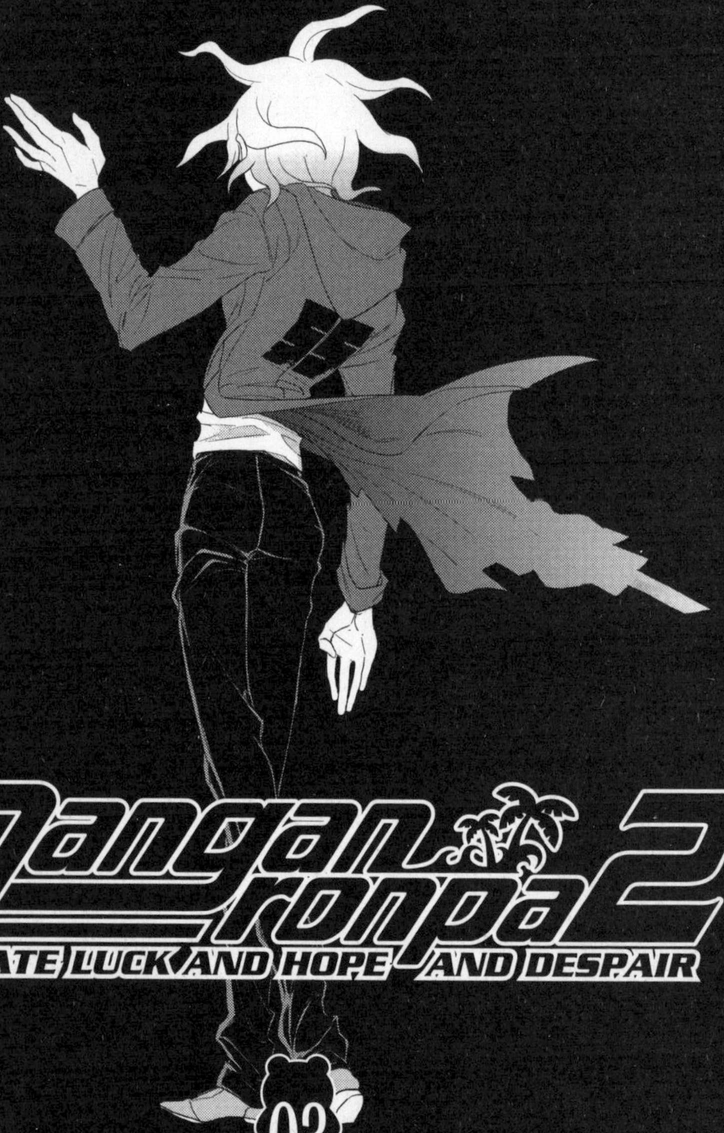

Danganronpa 2

ULTIMATE LUCK AND HOPE AND DESPAIR

03

DARK HORSE MANGA

CONTENTS

Ep.14 ····· ◇◇3

Ep.15 ····· ◇◇49

Ep.16 ····· ◇◇45

Ep.17 ····· ◇◇57

Ep.18 ····· ◇71

Ep.19 ····· ◇◇89

Ep.20 ····· ◇◇95

Ep.21 ····· ◇◇9

Ep.22 ····· 151

Ep.23 ····· ◇65

Translation by **Jackie McClure**
Lettering and touchup by **John Clark**
Edited by **Carl Gustav Horn**

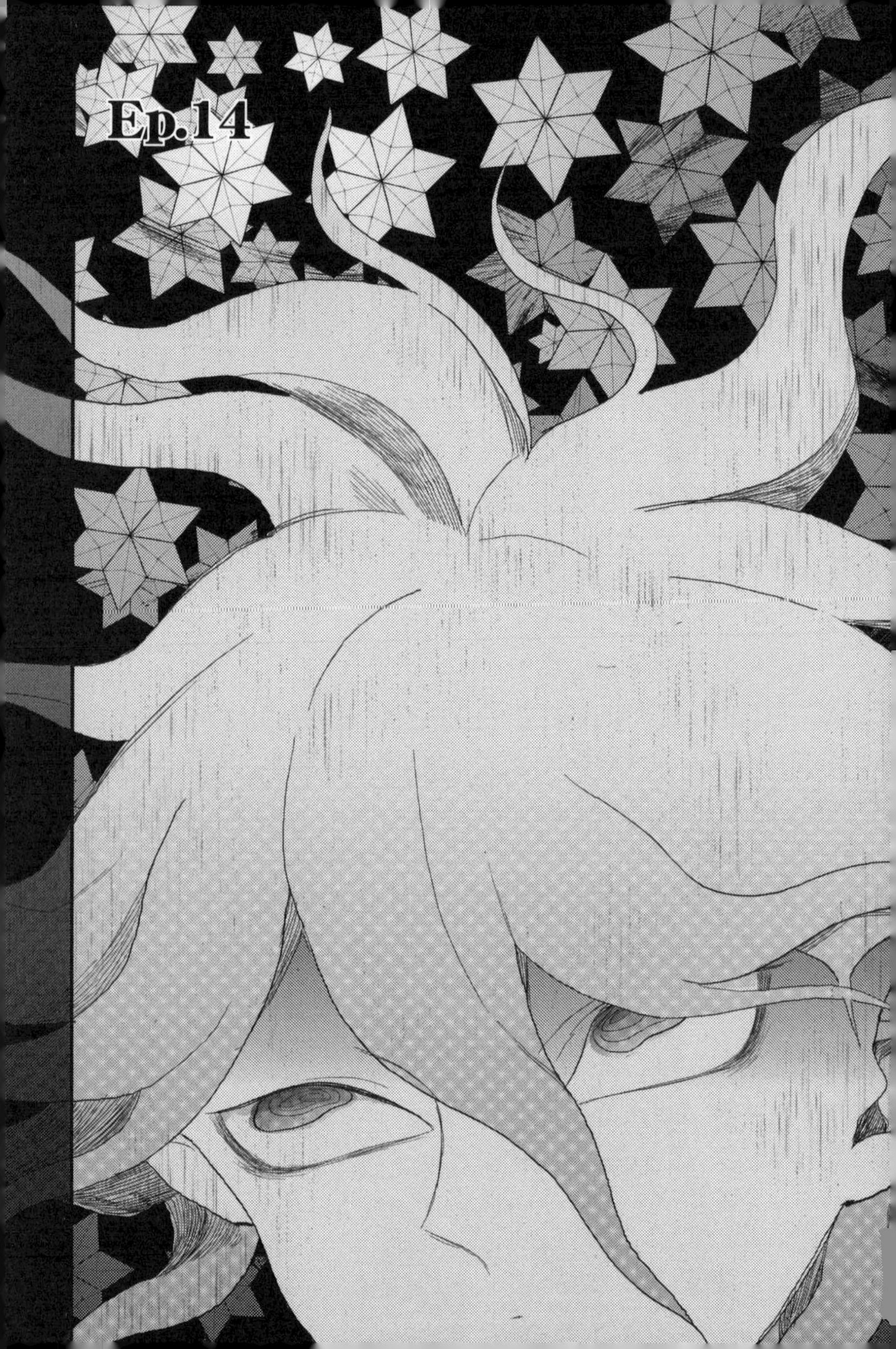
Ep.14

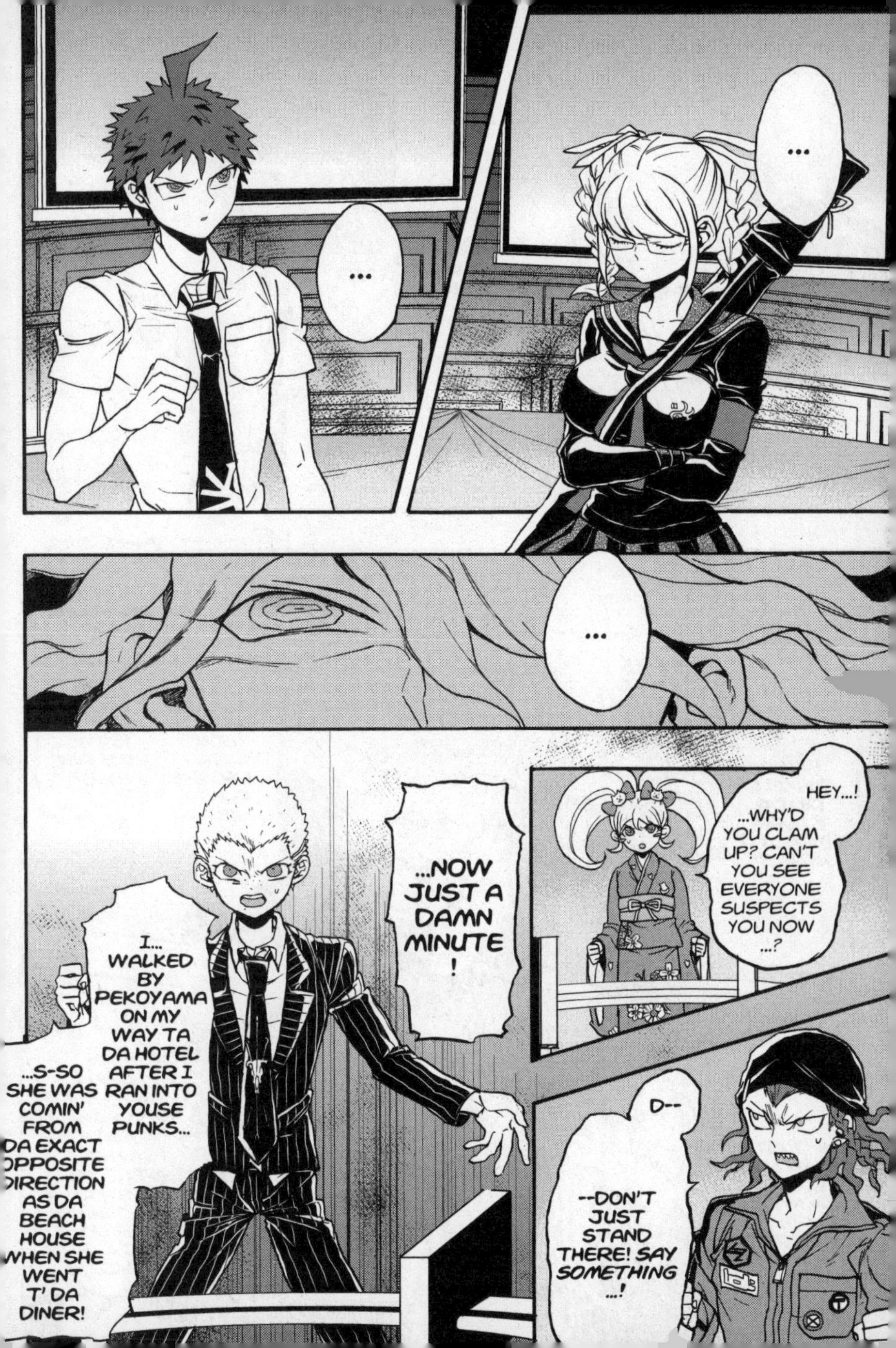
...
...
...
HEY...! ...WHY'D YOU CLAM UP? CAN'T YOU SEE EVERYONE SUSPECTS YOU NOW ...?
D--
--DON'T JUST STAND THERE! SAY SOMETHING ...!
...NOW JUST A DAMN MINUTE !
I... WALKED BY PEKOYAMA ON MY WAY TA DA HOTEL AFTER I RAN INTO YOUSE PUNKS...
...S-SO SHE WAS COMIN' FROM DA EXACT OPPOSITE DIRECTION AS DA BEACH HOUSE WHEN SHE WENT T' DA DINER!

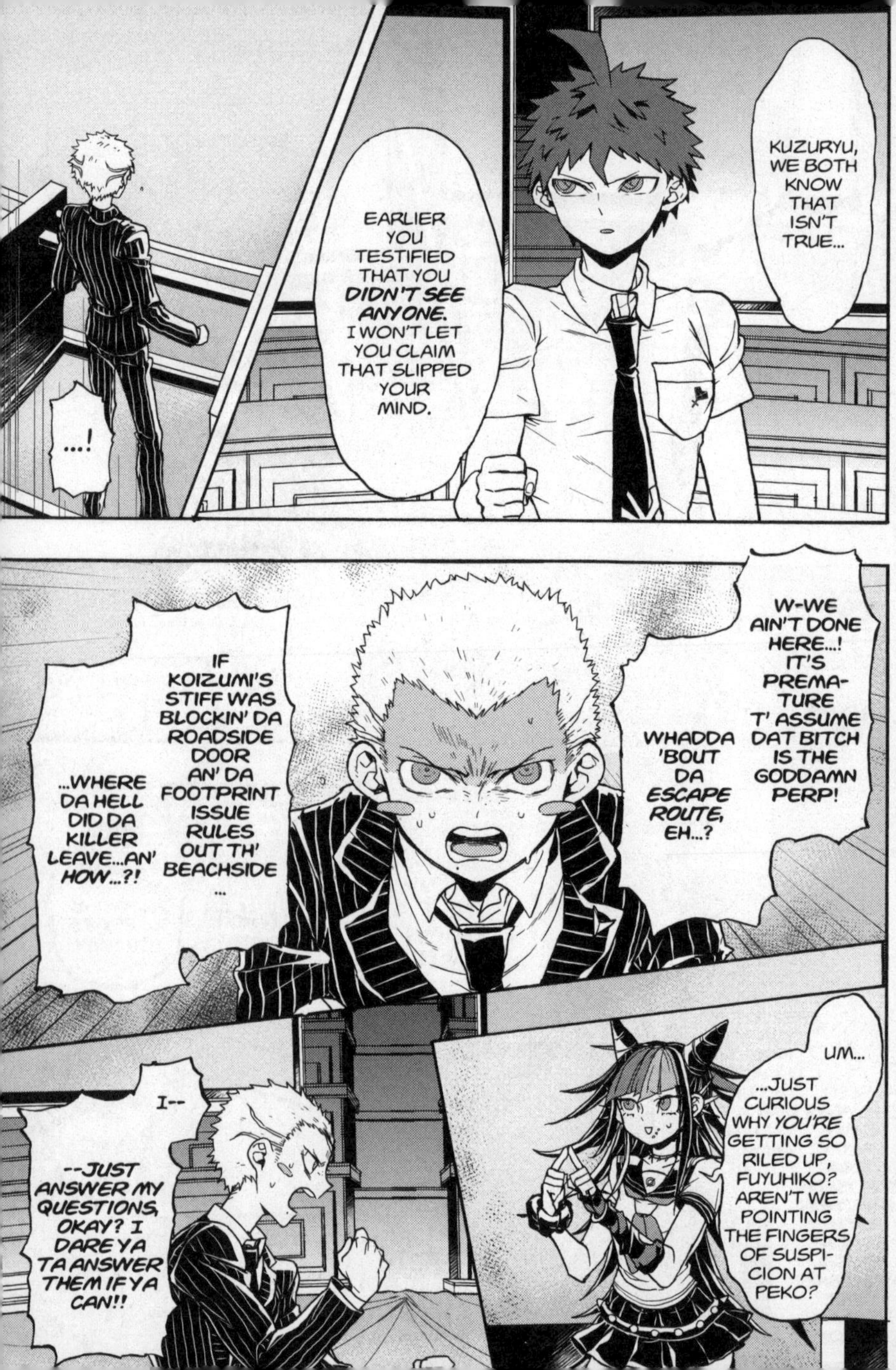
KUZURYU, WE BOTH KNOW THAT ISN'T TRUE...
EARLIER YOU TESTIFIED THAT YOU *DIDN'T SEE ANYONE.* I WON'T LET YOU CLAIM THAT SLIPPED YOUR MIND.
...!
W-WE AIN'T DONE HERE...! IT'S PREMA-TURE T' ASSUME DAT BITCH IS THE GODDAMN PERP!
WHADDA 'BOUT DA *ESCAPE ROUTE,* EH...?
IF KOIZUMI'S STIFF WAS BLOCKIN' DA ROADSIDE DOOR AN' DA FOOTPRINT ISSUE RULES OUT TH' BEACHSIDE ...
...WHERE DA HELL DID DA KILLER LEAVE...AN' *HOW*...?!
UM...
...JUST CURIOUS WHY *YOU'RE* GETTING SO RILED UP, FUYUHIKO? AREN'T WE POINTING THE FINGERS OF SUSPI-CION AT PEKO?
I--
--JUST ANSWER MY QUESTIONS, OKAY? I DARE YA TA ANSWER THEM IF YA CAN!!

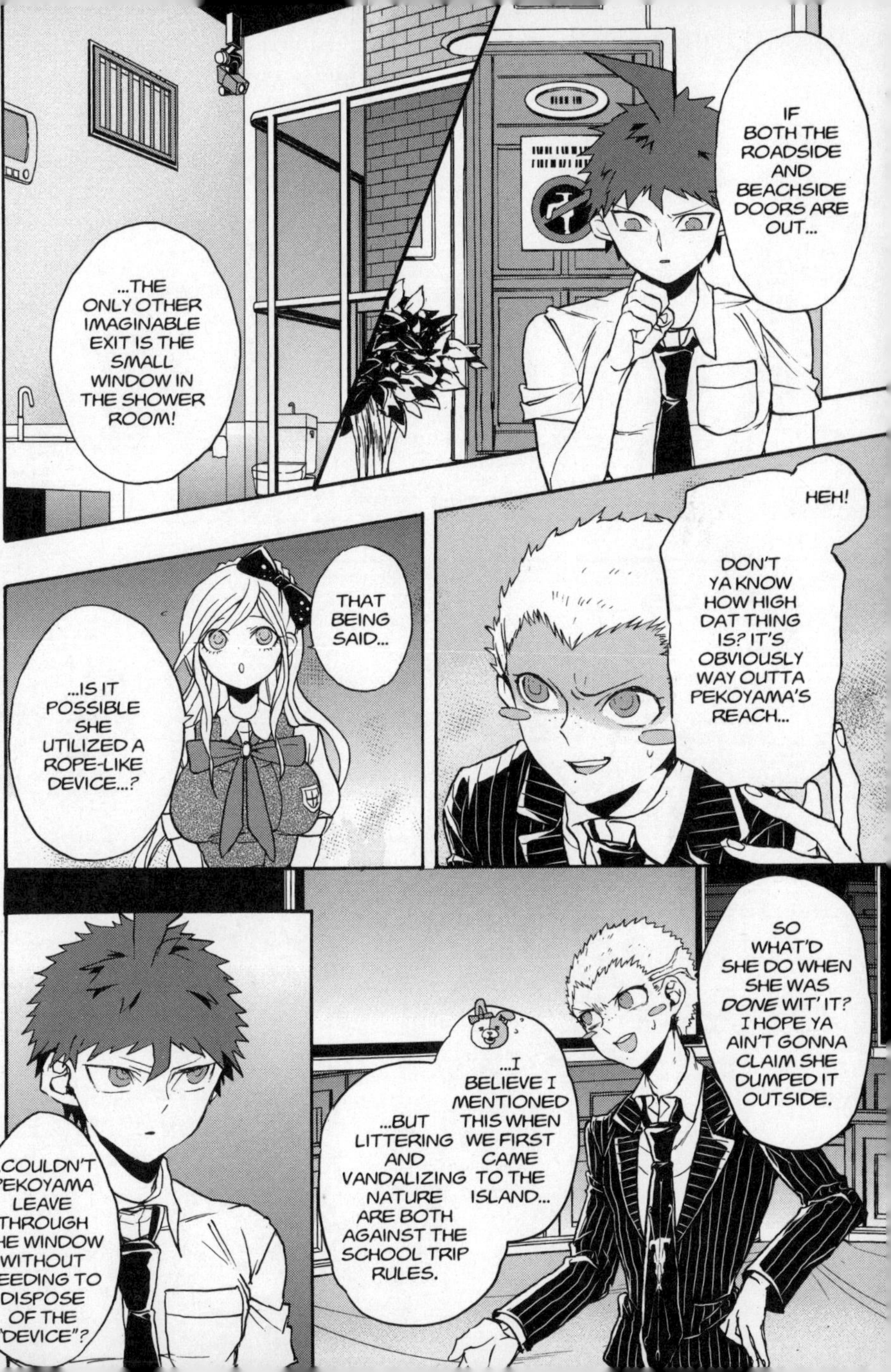
IF BOTH THE ROADSIDE AND BEACHSIDE DOORS ARE OUT...
...THE ONLY OTHER IMAGINABLE EXIT IS THE SMALL WINDOW IN THE SHOWER ROOM!
HEH!
DON'T YA KNOW HOW HIGH DAT THING IS? IT'S OBVIOUSLY WAY OUTTA PEKOYAMA'S REACH...
THAT BEING SAID...
...IS IT POSSIBLE SHE UTILIZED A ROPE-LIKE DEVICE...?
SO WHAT'D SHE DO WHEN SHE WAS *DONE* WIT' IT? I HOPE YA AIN'T GONNA CLAIM SHE DUMPED IT OUTSIDE.
...I BELIEVE I MENTIONED THIS WHEN WE FIRST CAME TO THE ISLAND...
...BUT LITTERING AND VANDALIZING NATURE ARE BOTH AGAINST THE SCHOOL TRIP RULES.
...COULDN'T PEKOYAMA LEAVE THROUGH THE WINDOW WITHOUT NEEDING TO DISPOSE OF THE "DEVICE"?

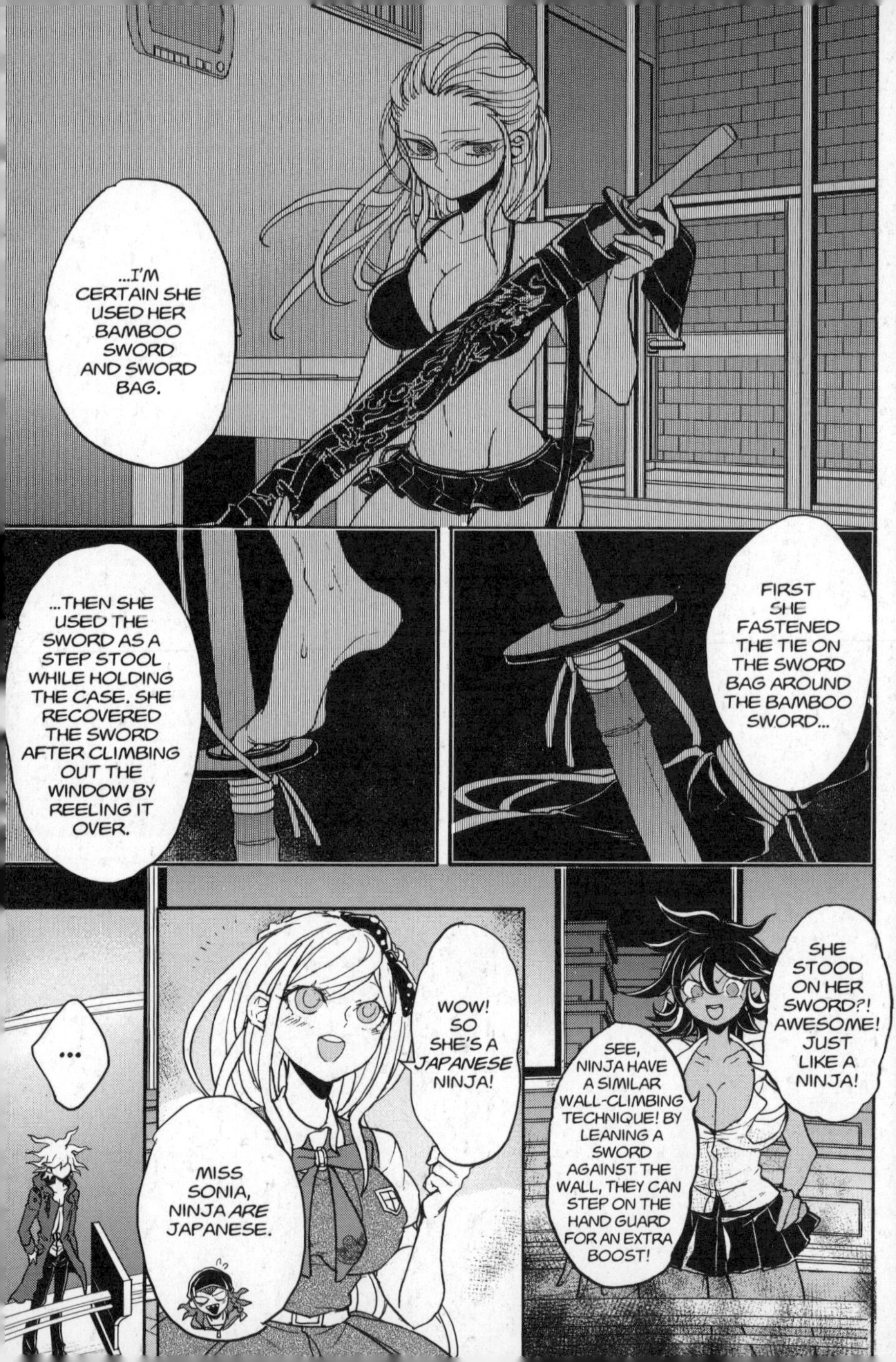
...I'M CERTAIN SHE USED HER BAMBOO SWORD AND SWORD BAG.
FIRST SHE FASTENED THE TIE ON THE SWORD BAG AROUND THE BAMBOO SWORD...
...THEN SHE USED THE SWORD AS A STEP STOOL WHILE HOLDING THE CASE. SHE RECOVERED THE SWORD AFTER CLIMBING OUT THE WINDOW BY REELING IT OVER.
SHE STOOD ON HER SWORD?! AWESOME! JUST LIKE A NINJA!
SEE, NINJA HAVE A SIMILAR WALL-CLIMBING TECHNIQUE! BY LEANING A SWORD AGAINST THE WALL, THEY CAN STEP ON THE HAND GUARD FOR AN EXTRA BOOST!
WOW! SO SHE'S A *JAPANESE* NINJA!
MISS SONIA, NINJA *ARE* JAPANESE.
...

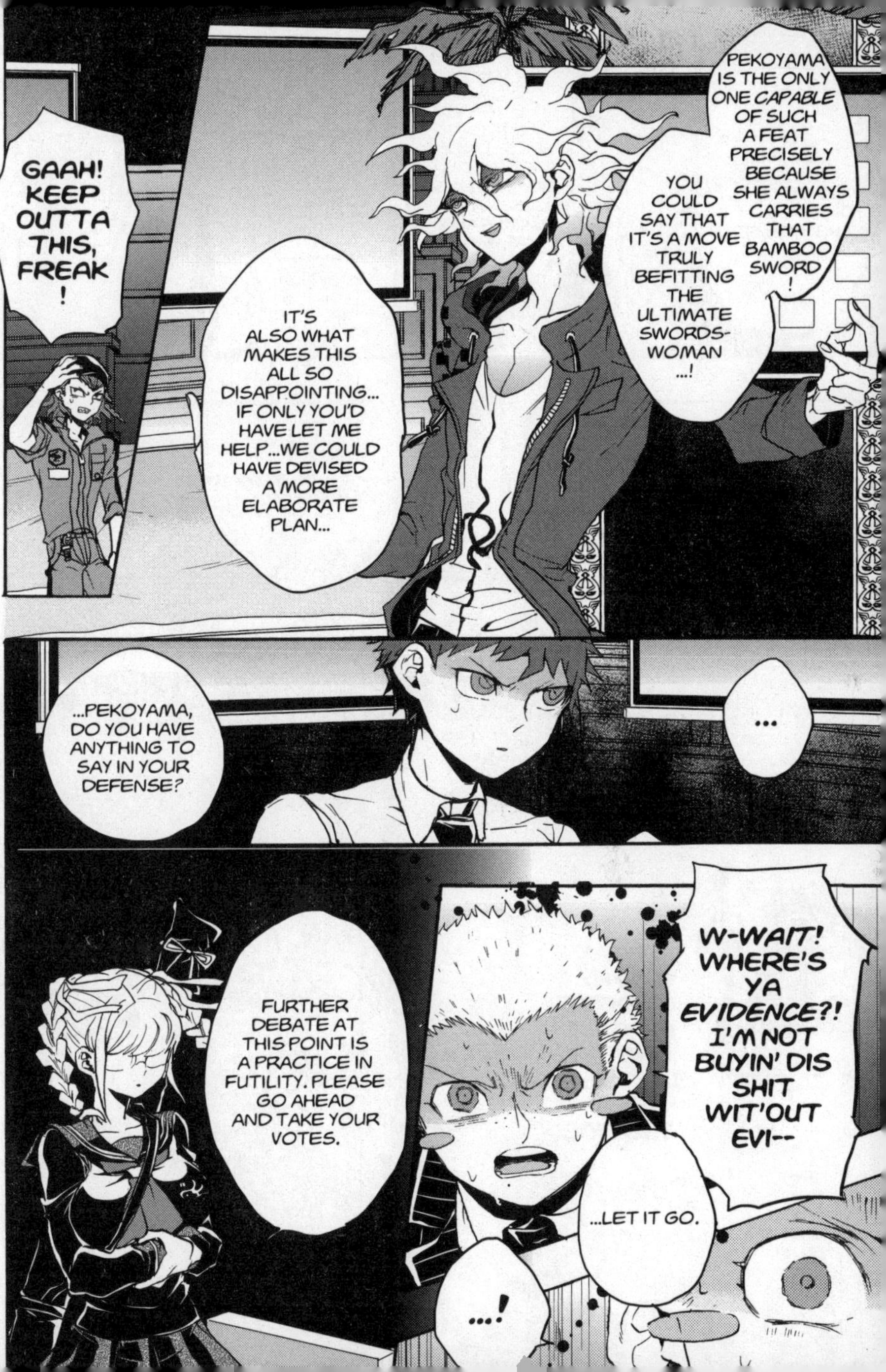

PEKOYAMA IS THE ONLY ONE *CAPABLE* OF SUCH A FEAT PRECISELY BECAUSE SHE ALWAYS CARRIES THAT BAMBOO SWORD!
YOU COULD SAY THAT IT'S A MOVE TRULY BEFITTING THE ULTIMATE SWORDSWOMAN...!
IT'S ALSO WHAT MAKES THIS ALL SO DISAPPOINTING... IF ONLY YOU'D HAVE LET ME HELP...WE COULD HAVE DEVISED A MORE ELABORATE PLAN...
GAAH! KEEP OUTTA THIS, FREAK!
...PEKOYAMA, DO YOU HAVE ANYTHING TO SAY IN YOUR DEFENSE?
...
W-WAIT! WHERE'S YA *EVIDENCE*?! I'M NOT BUYIN' DIS SHIT WIT'OUT EVI--
FURTHER DEBATE AT THIS POINT IS A PRACTICE IN FUTILITY. PLEASE GO AHEAD AND TAKE YOUR VOTES.
...LET IT GO.
...!

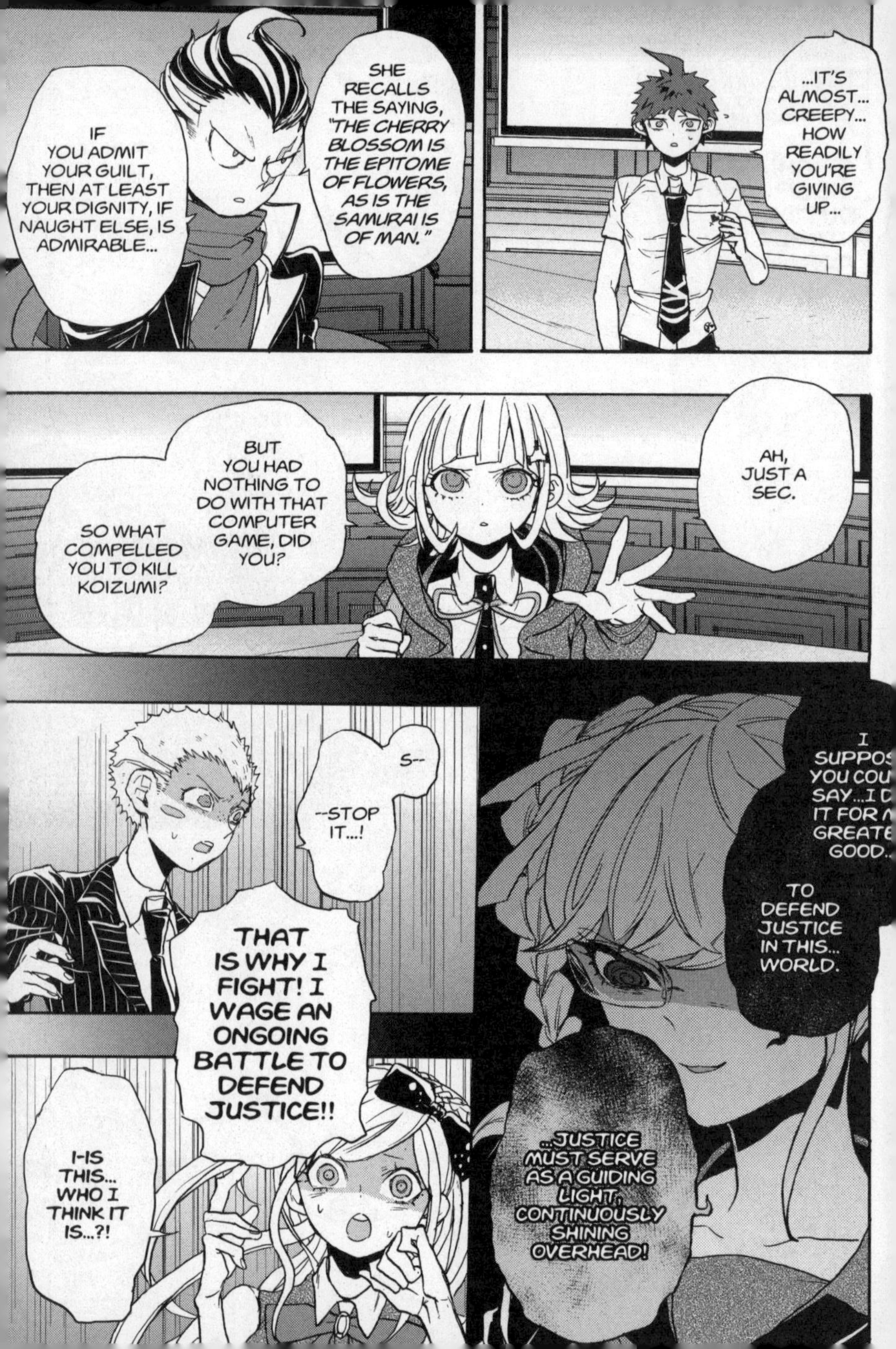
...IT'S ALMOST... CREEPY... HOW READILY YOU'RE GIVING UP...
SHE RECALLS THE SAYING, "THE CHERRY BLOSSOM IS THE EPITOME OF FLOWERS, AS IS THE SAMURAI IS OF MAN."
IF YOU ADMIT YOUR GUILT, THEN AT LEAST YOUR DIGNITY, IF NAUGHT ELSE, IS ADMIRABLE...
AH, JUST A SEC.
BUT YOU HAD NOTHING TO DO WITH THAT COMPUTER GAME, DID YOU?
SO WHAT COMPELLED YOU TO KILL KOIZUMI?
I SUPPOS YOU COU SAY...I D IT FOR A GREATE GOOD.
TO DEFEND JUSTICE IN THIS... WORLD.
...JUSTICE MUST SERVE AS A GUIDING LIGHT, CONTINUOUSLY SHINING OVERHEAD!
S--
--STOP IT...!
THAT IS WHY I FIGHT! I WAGE AN ONGOING BATTLE TO DEFEND JUSTICE!!
I-IS THIS... WHO I THINK IT IS...?!

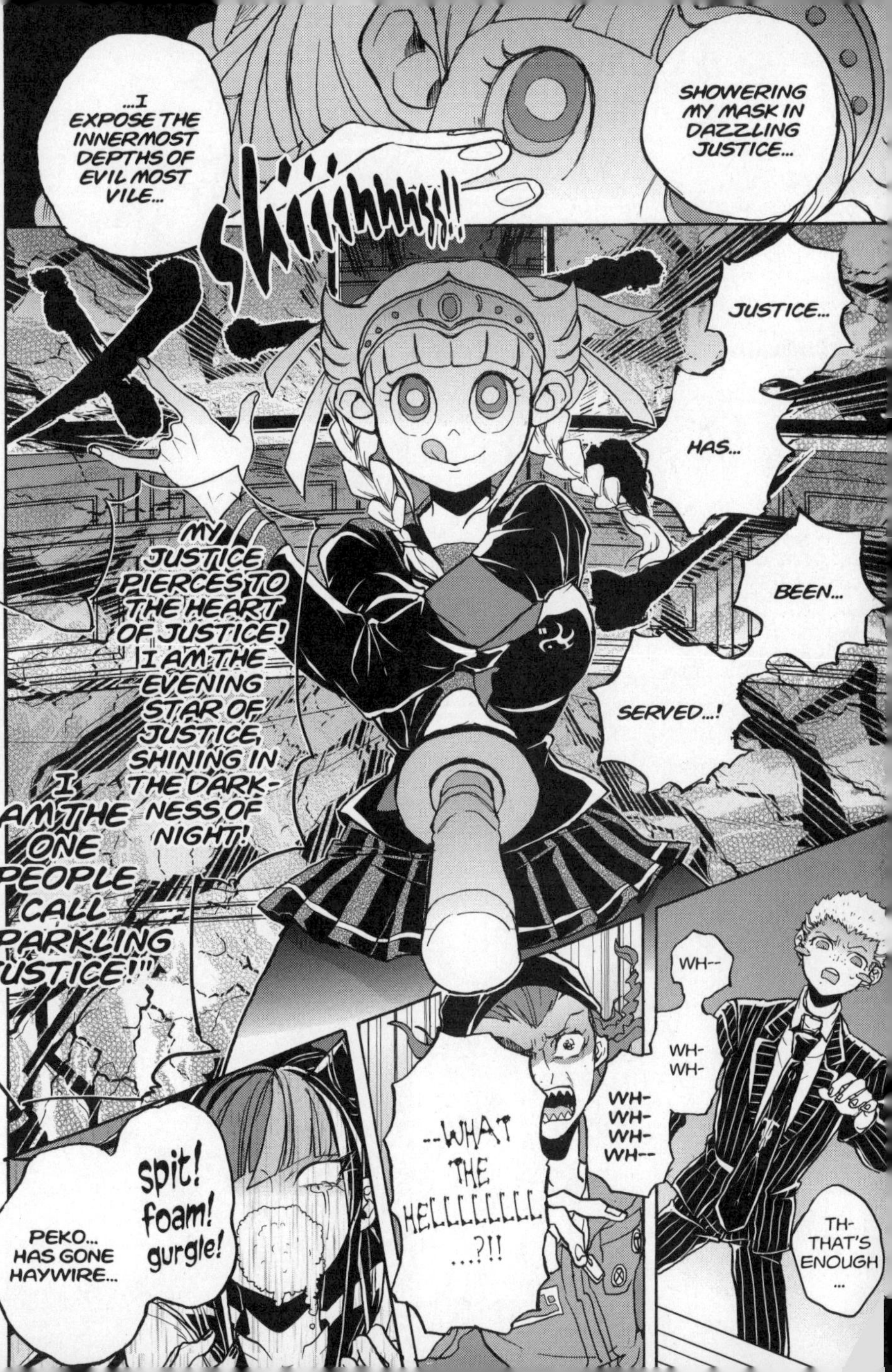
SHOWERING MY MASK IN DAZZLING JUSTICE...
...I EXPOSE THE INNERMOST DEPTHS OF EVIL MOST VILE...
SHIIIINNNNSS!!
JUSTICE...
HAS...
BEEN...
SERVED...!
MY JUSTICE PIERCES TO THE HEART OF JUSTICE! I AM THE EVENING STAR OF JUSTICE, SHINING IN THE DARKNESS OF NIGHT!
I AM THE ONE PEOPLE CALL SPARKLING JUSTICE!!"
WH--
WH-WH-
WH-WH-WH-WH--
TH-THAT'S ENOUGH...
--WHAT THE HELLLLLLLLL...?!!
spit! foam! gurgle!
PEKO... HAS GONE HAYWIRE...

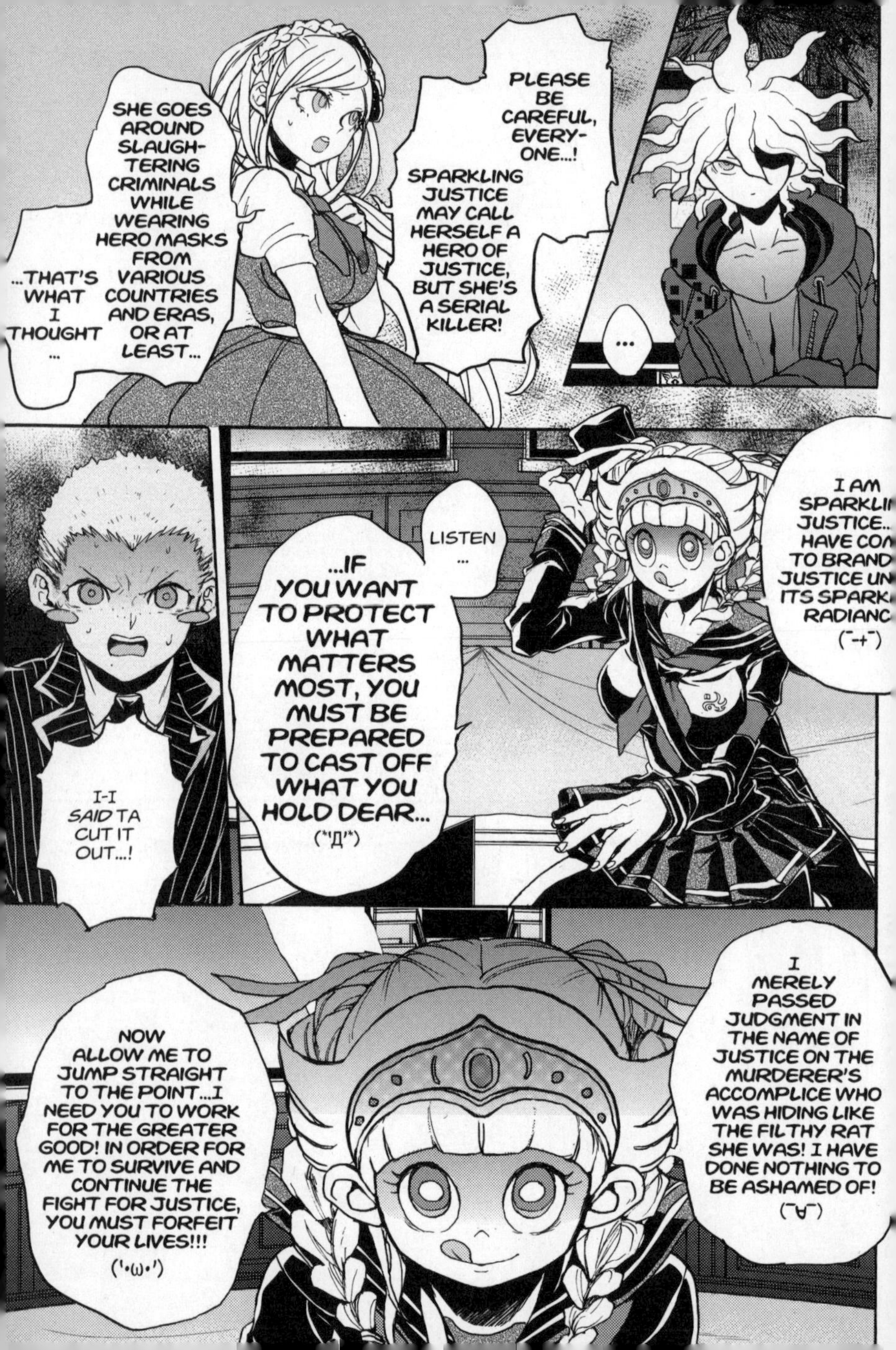
...
PLEASE BE CAREFUL, EVERYONE...!
SPARKLING JUSTICE MAY CALL HERSELF A HERO OF JUSTICE, BUT SHE'S A SERIAL KILLER!
SHE GOES AROUND SLAUGHTERING CRIMINALS WHILE WEARING HERO MASKS FROM VARIOUS COUNTRIES AND ERAS, OR AT LEAST...
...THAT'S WHAT I THOUGHT...
I AM SPARKLI JUSTICE.. HAVE CO TO BRAND JUSTICE UN ITS SPARK RADIANC (¯+¯)
LISTEN...
...IF YOU WANT TO PROTECT WHAT MATTERS MOST, YOU MUST BE PREPARED TO CAST OFF WHAT YOU HOLD DEAR... (*'Д'*)
I-I SAID TA CUT IT OUT...!
I MERELY PASSED JUDGMENT IN THE NAME OF JUSTICE ON THE MURDERER'S ACCOMPLICE WHO WAS HIDING LIKE THE FILTHY RAT SHE WAS! I HAVE DONE NOTHING TO BE ASHAMED OF! (¯∀¯)
NOW ALLOW ME TO JUMP STRAIGHT TO THE POINT...I NEED YOU TO WORK FOR THE GREATER GOOD! IN ORDER FOR ME TO SURVIVE AND CONTINUE THE FIGHT FOR JUSTICE, YOU MUST FORFEIT YOUR LIVES!!! ('•ω•')

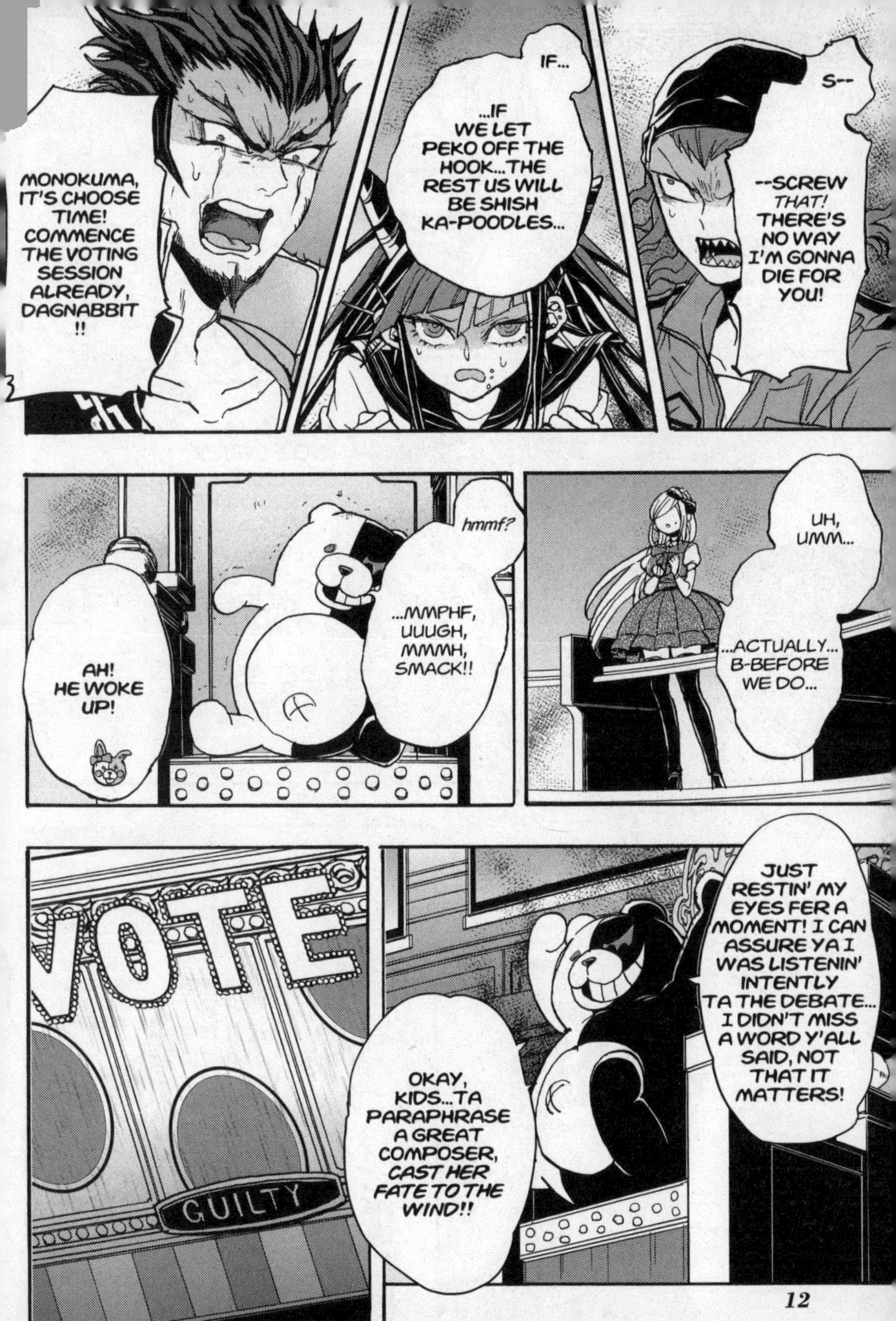
S--
--SCREW THAT! THERE'S NO WAY I'M GONNA DIE FOR YOU!
IF...
...IF WE LET PEKO OFF THE HOOK...THE REST US WILL BE SHISH KA-POODLES...
MONOKUMA, IT'S CHOOSE TIME! COMMENCE THE VOTING SESSION ALREADY, DAGNABBIT!!
UH, UMM...
...ACTUALLY... B-BEFORE WE DO...
hmmf?
...MMPHF, UUUGH, MMMH, SMACK!!
AH! HE WOKE UP!
JUST RESTIN' MY EYES FER A MOMENT! I CAN ASSURE YA I WAS LISTENIN' INTENTLY TA THE DEBATE... I DIDN'T MISS A WORD Y'ALL SAID, NOT THAT IT MATTERS!
OKAY, KIDS...TA PARAPHRASE A GREAT COMPOSER, CAST HER FATE TO THE WIND!!
VOTE
GUILTY

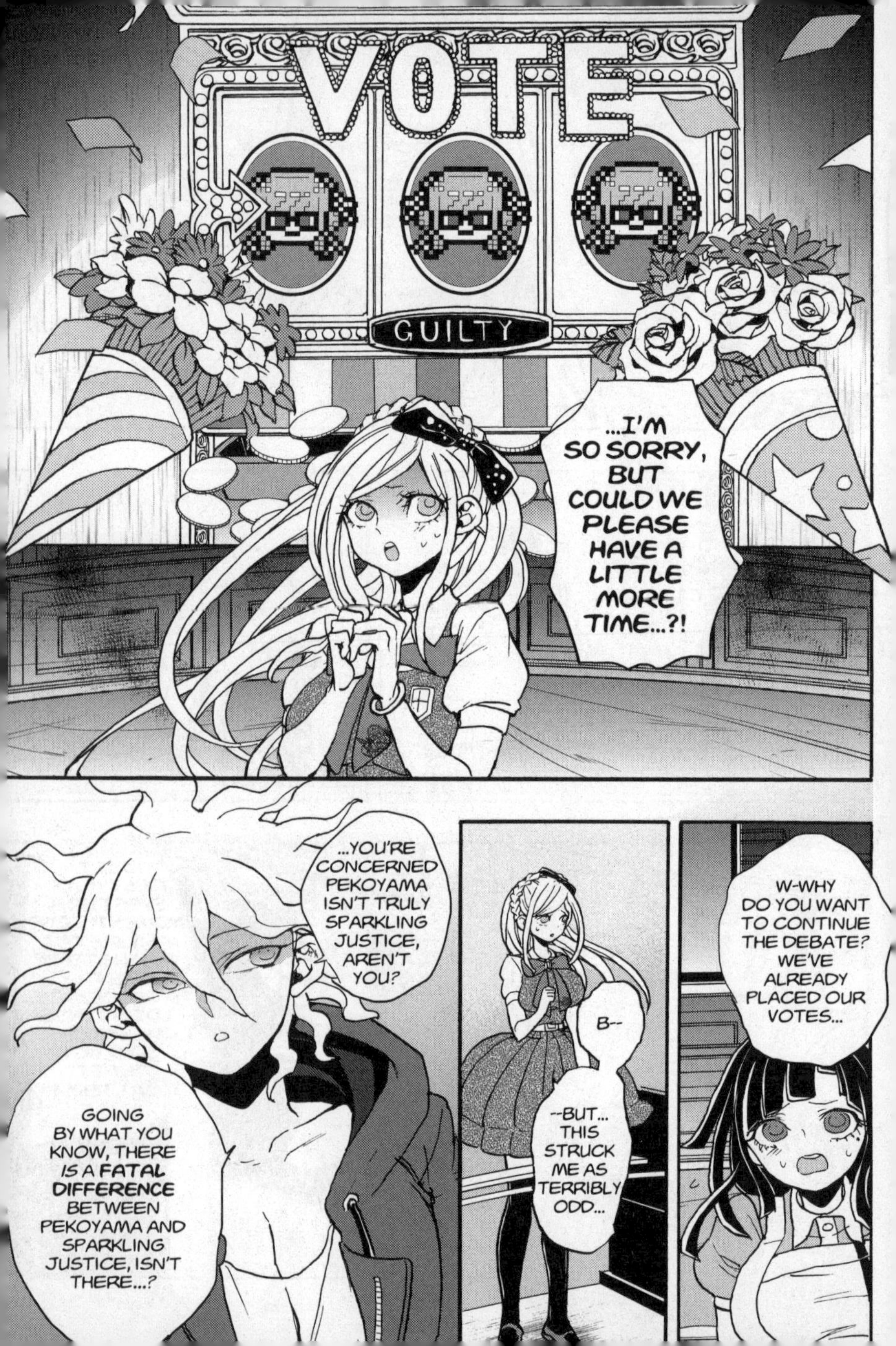
VOTE
GUILTY
...I'M SO SORRY, BUT COULD WE PLEASE HAVE A LITTLE MORE TIME...?!
W-WHY DO YOU WANT TO CONTINUE THE DEBATE? WE'VE ALREADY PLACED OUR VOTES...
B--
--BUT... THIS STRUCK ME AS TERRIBLY ODD...
...YOU'RE CONCERNED PEKOYAMA ISN'T TRULY SPARKLING JUSTICE, AREN'T YOU?
GOING BY WHAT YOU KNOW, THERE IS A **FATAL DIFFERENCE** BETWEEN PEKOYAMA AND SPARKLING JUSTICE, ISN'T THERE...?

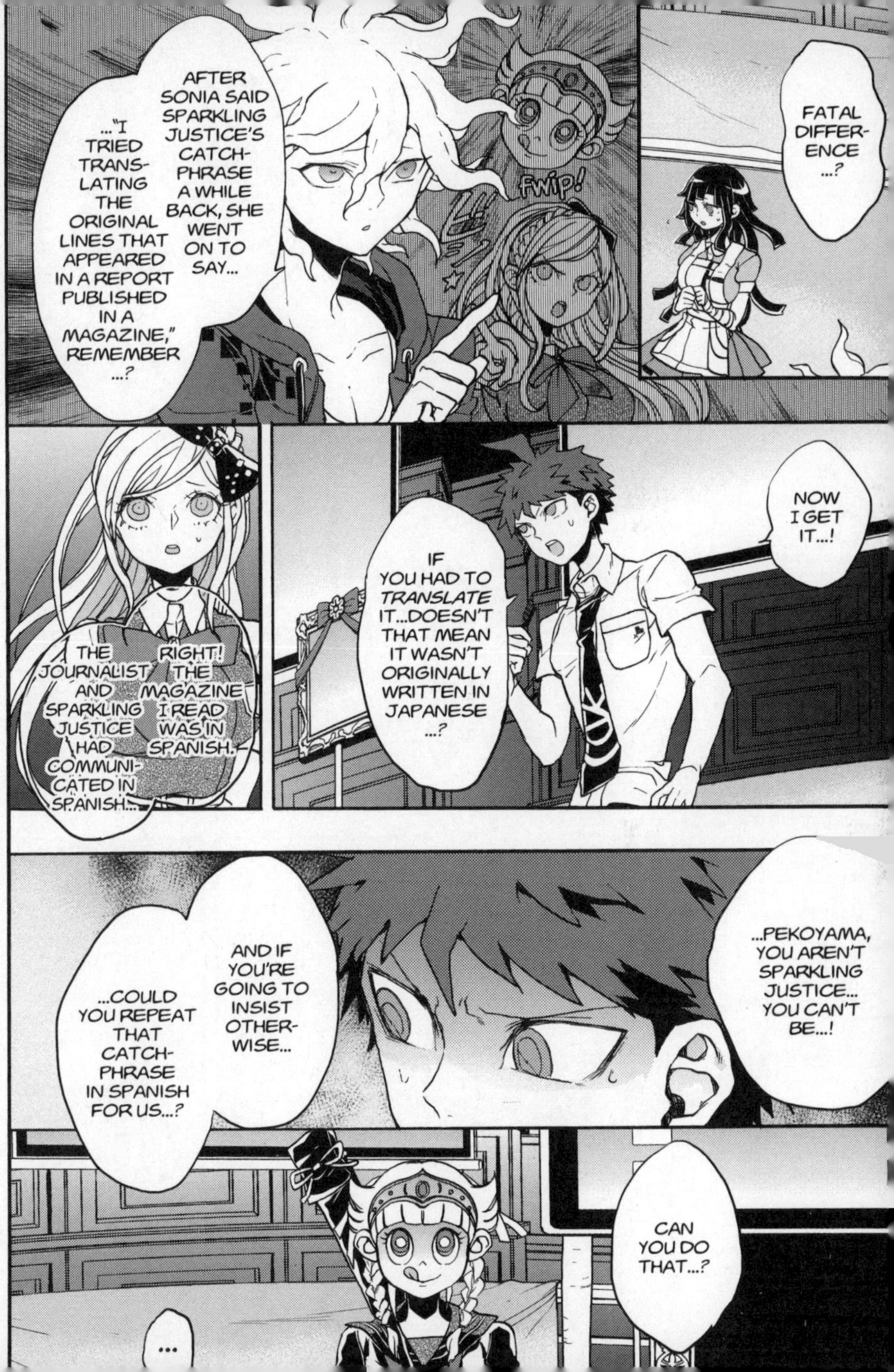
FATAL DIFFERENCE...?
AFTER SONIA SAID SPARKLING JUSTICE'S CATCHPHRASE A WHILE BACK, SHE WENT ON TO SAY...
..."I TRIED TRANSLATING THE ORIGINAL LINES THAT APPEARED IN A REPORT PUBLISHED IN A MAGAZINE," REMEMBER...?
FWIP!
NOW I GET IT...!
IF YOU HAD TO *TRANSLATE* IT...DOESN'T THAT MEAN IT WASN'T ORIGINALLY WRITTEN IN JAPANESE...?
RIGHT! THE MAGAZINE I READ WAS IN SPANISH.
THE JOURNALIST AND SPARKLING JUSTICE HAD COMMUNICATED IN SPANISH...
...PEKOYAMA, YOU AREN'T SPARKLING JUSTICE... YOU CAN'T BE...!
AND IF YOU'RE GOING TO INSIST OTHERWISE...
...COULD YOU REPEAT THAT CATCHPHRASE IN SPANISH FOR US...?
CAN YOU DO THAT...?
...

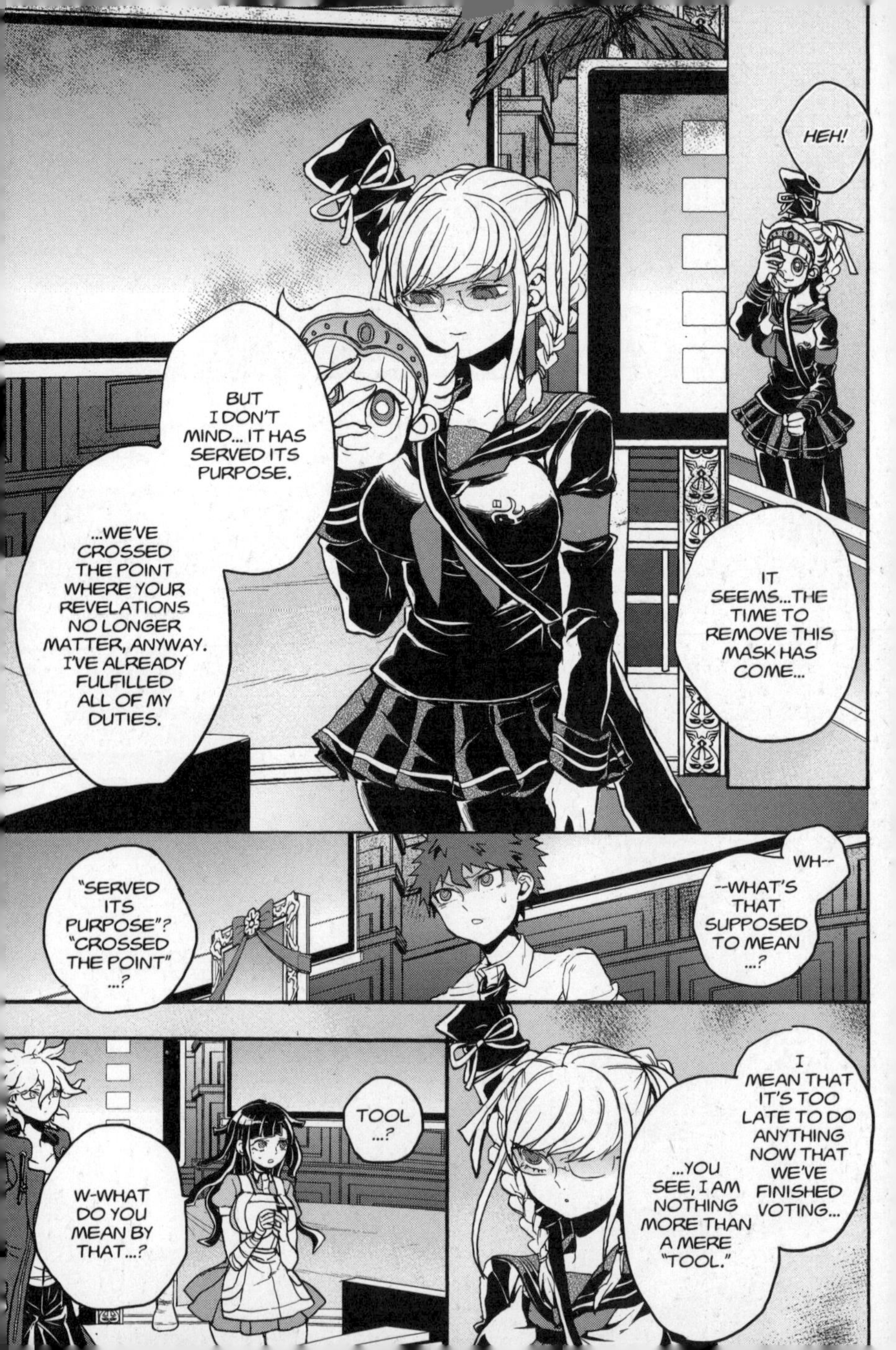
HEH!
IT SEEMS...THE TIME TO REMOVE THIS MASK HAS COME...
BUT I DON'T MIND... IT HAS SERVED ITS PURPOSE.
...WE'VE CROSSED THE POINT WHERE YOUR REVELATIONS NO LONGER MATTER, ANYWAY. I'VE ALREADY FULFILLED ALL OF MY DUTIES.
WH-- --WHAT'S THAT SUPPOSED TO MEAN...?
"SERVED ITS PURPOSE"? "CROSSED THE POINT"...?
I MEAN THAT IT'S TOO LATE TO DO ANYTHING NOW THAT WE'VE FINISHED VOTING...
...YOU SEE, I AM NOTHING MORE THAN A MERE "TOOL."
TOOL...?
W-WHAT DO YOU MEAN BY THAT...?

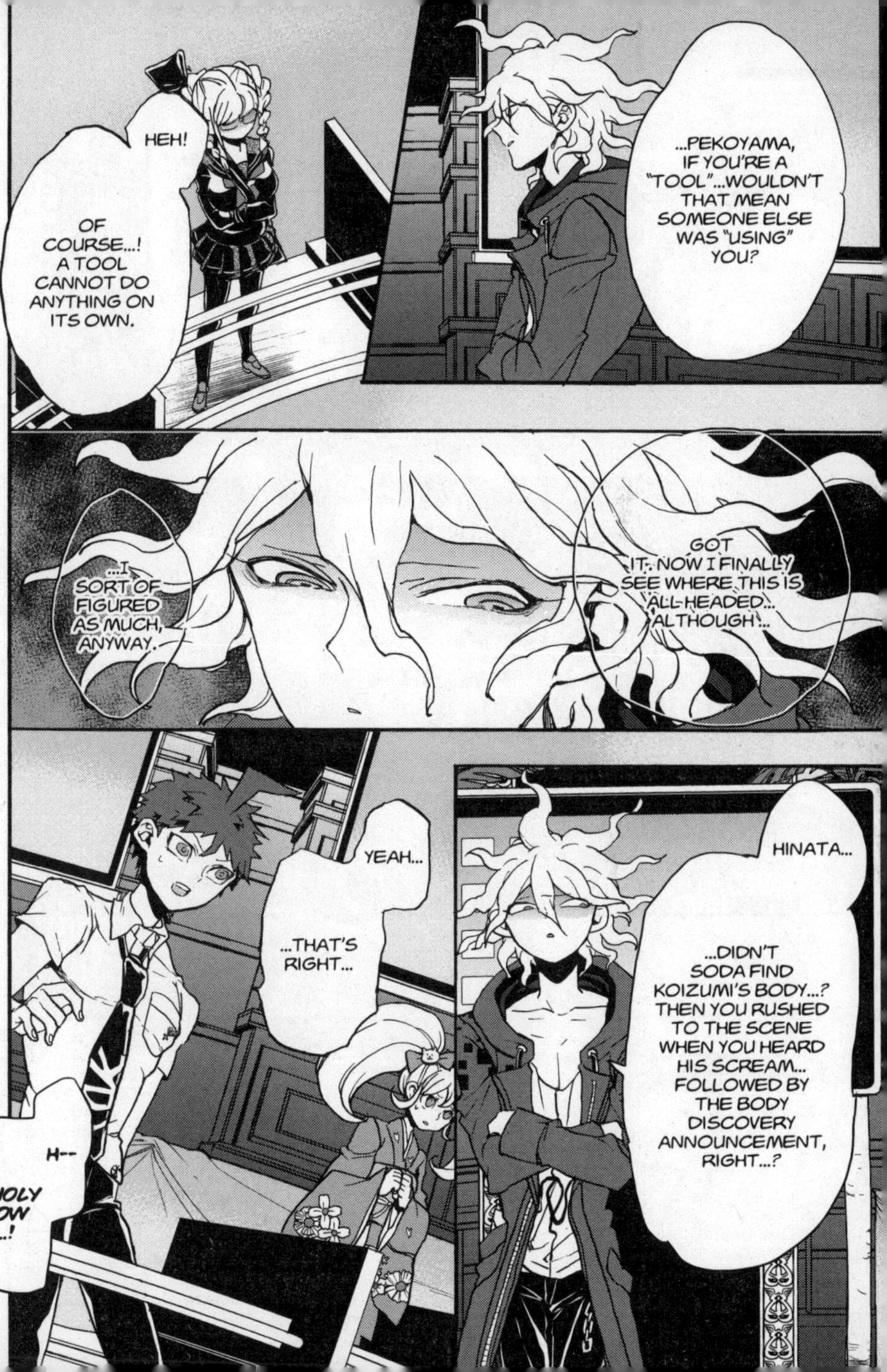
...PEKOYAMA, IF YOU'RE A "TOOL"...WOULDN'T THAT MEAN SOMEONE ELSE WAS "USING" YOU?
HEH!
OF COURSE...! A TOOL CANNOT DO ANYTHING ON ITS OWN.
GOT IT. NOW I FINALLY SEE WHERE THIS IS ALL HEADED... ALTHOUGH...
...I SORT OF FIGURED AS MUCH, ANYWAY.
HINATA...
...DIDN'T SODA FIND KOIZUMI'S BODY...? THEN YOU RUSHED TO THE SCENE WHEN YOU HEARD HIS SCREAM... FOLLOWED BY THE BODY DISCOVERY ANNOUNCEMENT, RIGHT...?
YEAH...
...THAT'S RIGHT...
H--
-HOLY COW ...!

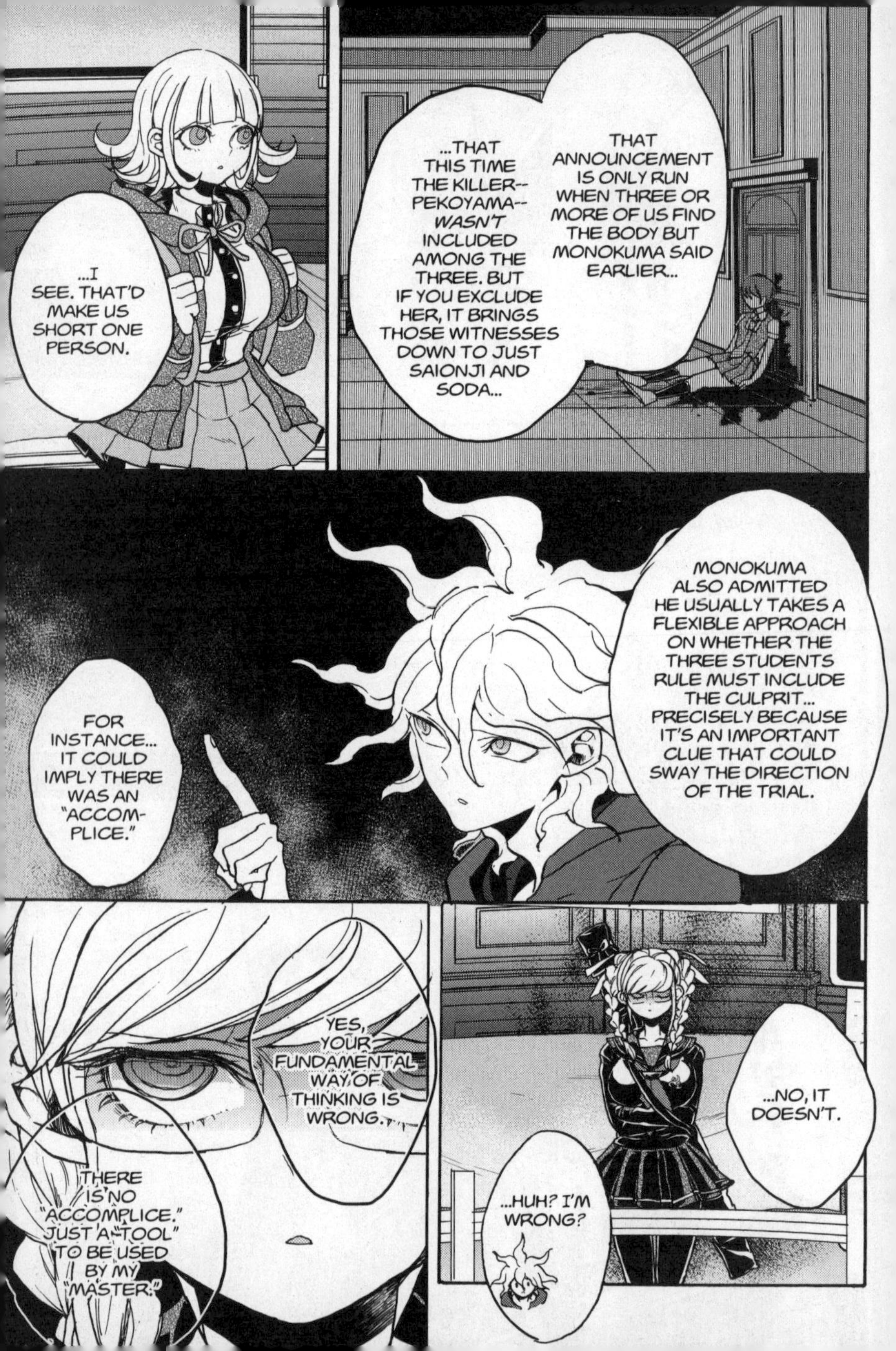
THAT ANNOUNCEMENT IS ONLY RUN WHEN THREE OR MORE OF US FIND THE BODY BUT MONOKUMA SAID EARLIER...
...THAT THIS TIME THE KILLER--PEKOYAMA--WASN'T INCLUDED AMONG THE THREE. BUT IF YOU EXCLUDE HER, IT BRINGS THOSE WITNESSES DOWN TO JUST SAIONJI AND SODA...
...I SEE. THAT'D MAKE US SHORT ONE PERSON.
MONOKUMA ALSO ADMITTED HE USUALLY TAKES A FLEXIBLE APPROACH ON WHETHER THE THREE STUDENTS RULE MUST INCLUDE THE CULPRIT... PRECISELY BECAUSE IT'S AN IMPORTANT CLUE THAT COULD SWAY THE DIRECTION OF THE TRIAL.
FOR INSTANCE... IT COULD IMPLY THERE WAS AN "ACCOMPLICE."
...NO, IT DOESN'T.
...HUH? I'M WRONG?
YES, YOUR FUNDAMENTAL WAY OF THINKING IS WRONG.
THERE IS NO "ACCOMPLICE." JUST A "TOOL" TO BE USED BY MY "MASTER."

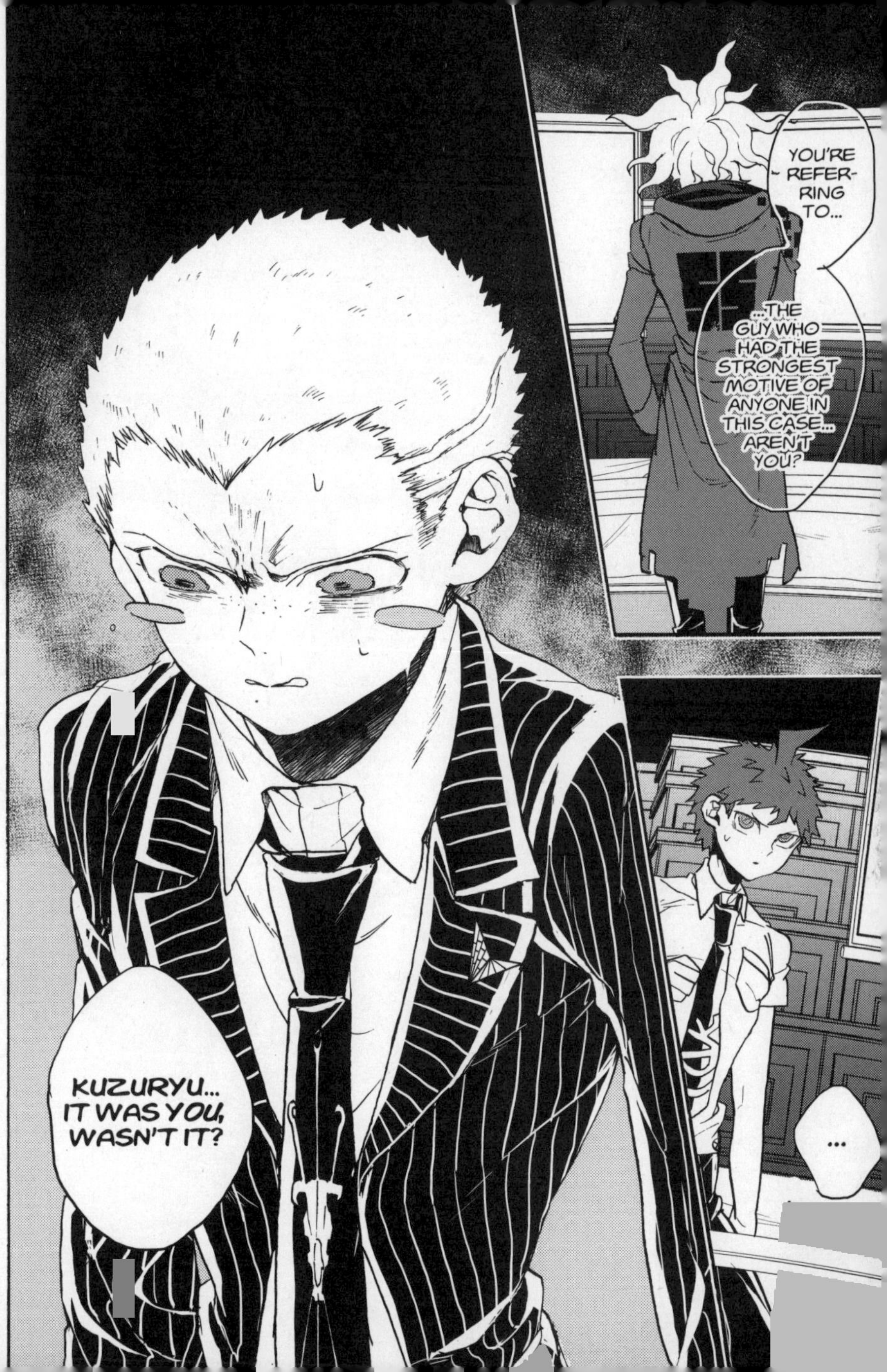
YOU'RE REFERRING TO...
...THE GUY WHO HAD THE STRONGEST MOTIVE OF ANYONE IN THIS CASE... AREN'T YOU?
...
KUZURYU... IT WAS YOU, WASN'T IT?

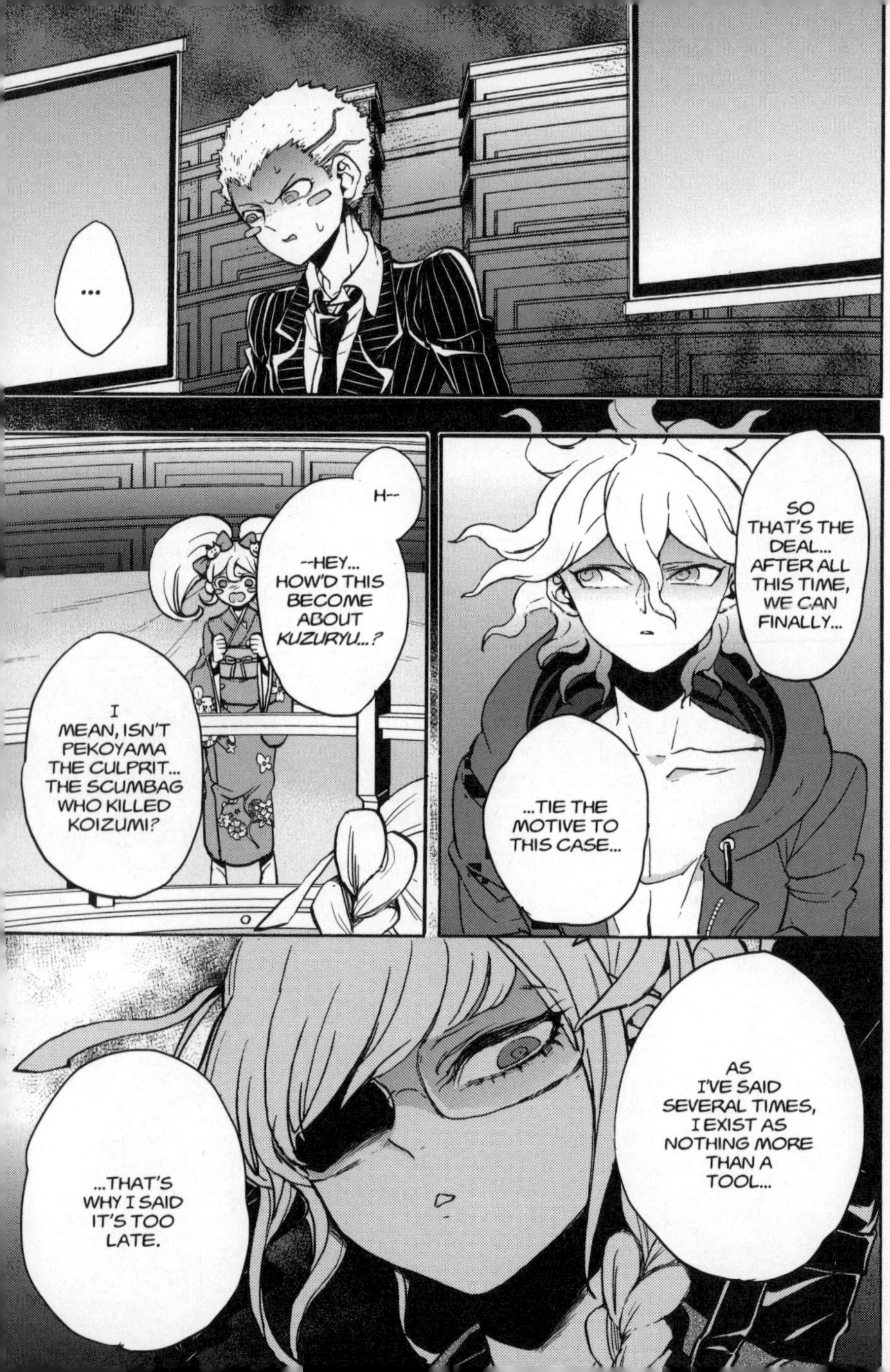
...
SO THAT'S THE DEAL... AFTER ALL THIS TIME, WE CAN FINALLY...
...TIE THE MOTIVE TO THIS CASE...
H--
--HEY... HOW'D THIS BECOME ABOUT KUZURYU...?
I MEAN, ISN'T PEKOYAMA THE CULPRIT... THE SCUMBAG WHO KILLED KOIZUMI?
AS I'VE SAID SEVERAL TIMES, I EXIST AS NOTHING MORE THAN A TOOL...
...THAT'S WHY I SAID IT'S TOO LATE.

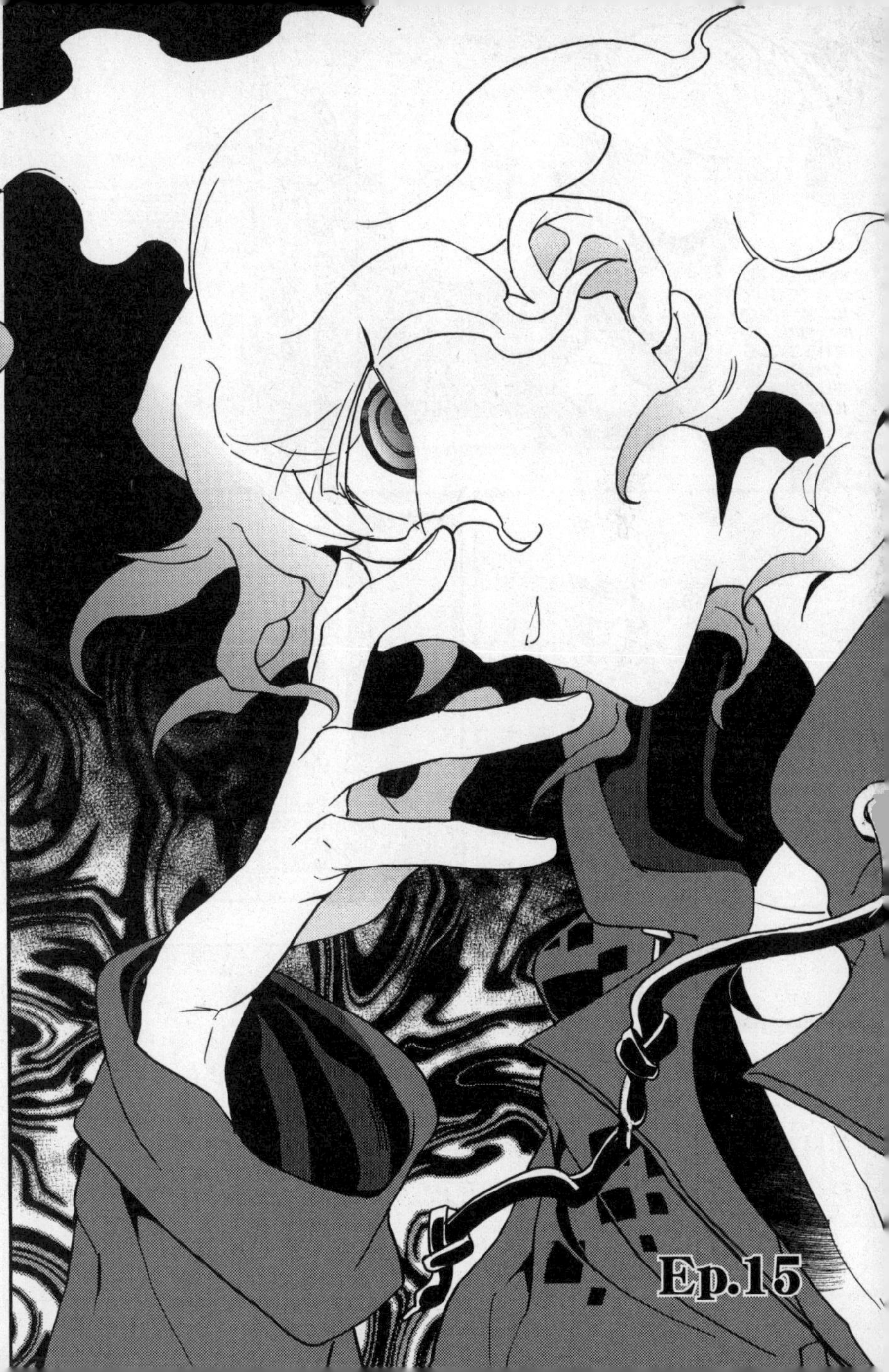
Ep.15

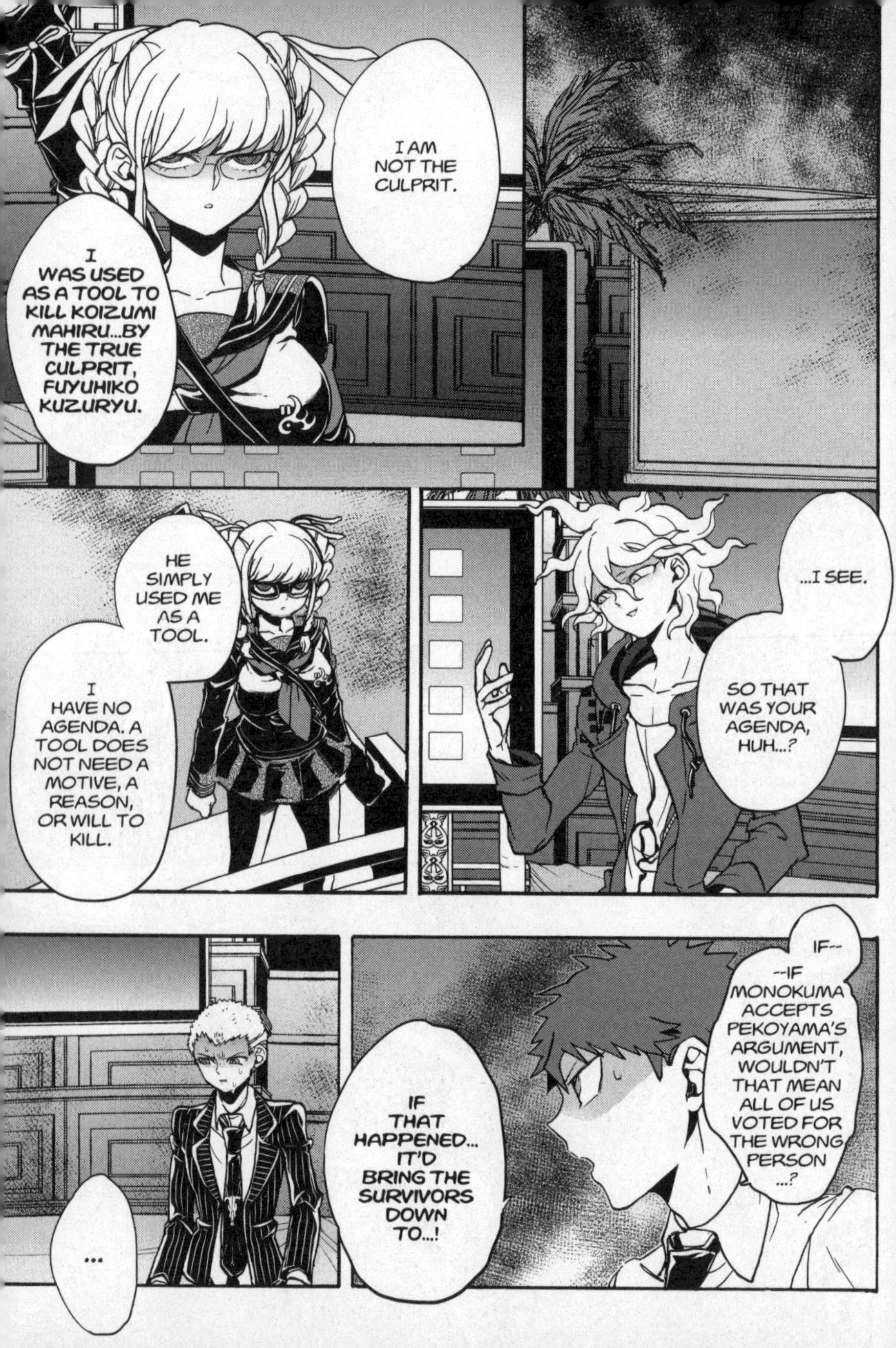
I AM NOT THE CULPRIT.
I WAS USED AS A TOOL TO KILL KOIZUMI MAHIRU...BY THE TRUE CULPRIT, FUYUHIKO KUZURYU.
...I SEE.
SO THAT WAS YOUR AGENDA, HUH...?
HE SIMPLY USED ME AS A TOOL.
I HAVE NO AGENDA. A TOOL DOES NOT NEED A MOTIVE, A REASON, OR WILL TO KILL.
IF--
--IF MONOKUMA ACCEPTS PEKOYAMA'S ARGUMENT, WOULDN'T THAT MEAN ALL OF US VOTED FOR THE WRONG PERSON ...?
IF THAT HAPPENED... IT'D BRING THE SURVIVORS DOWN TO...!
...

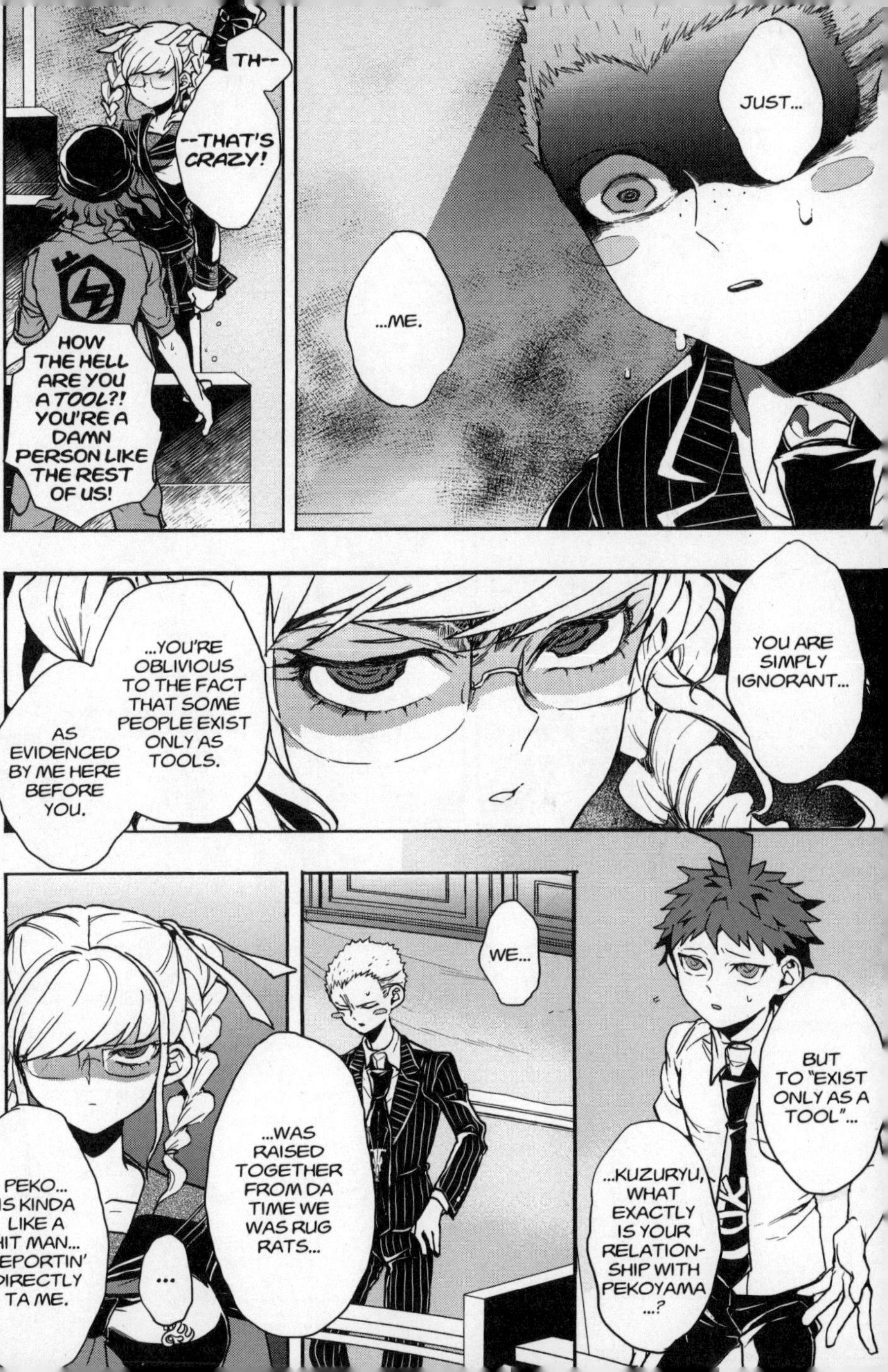
JUST...
...ME.
TH--
--THAT'S CRAZY!
HOW THE HELL ARE YOU A TOOL?! YOU'RE A DAMN PERSON LIKE THE REST OF US!
YOU ARE SIMPLY IGNORANT...
...YOU'RE OBLIVIOUS TO THE FACT THAT SOME PEOPLE EXIST ONLY AS TOOLS.
AS EVIDENCED BY ME HERE BEFORE YOU.
BUT TO "EXIST ONLY AS A TOOL"...
...KUZURYU, WHAT EXACTLY IS YOUR RELATION-SHIP WITH PEKOYAMA...?
WE...
...WAS RAISED TOGETHER FROM DA TIME WE WAS RUG RATS...
PEKO... IS KINDA LIKE A HIT MAN... REPORTIN' DIRECTLY TA ME.
...

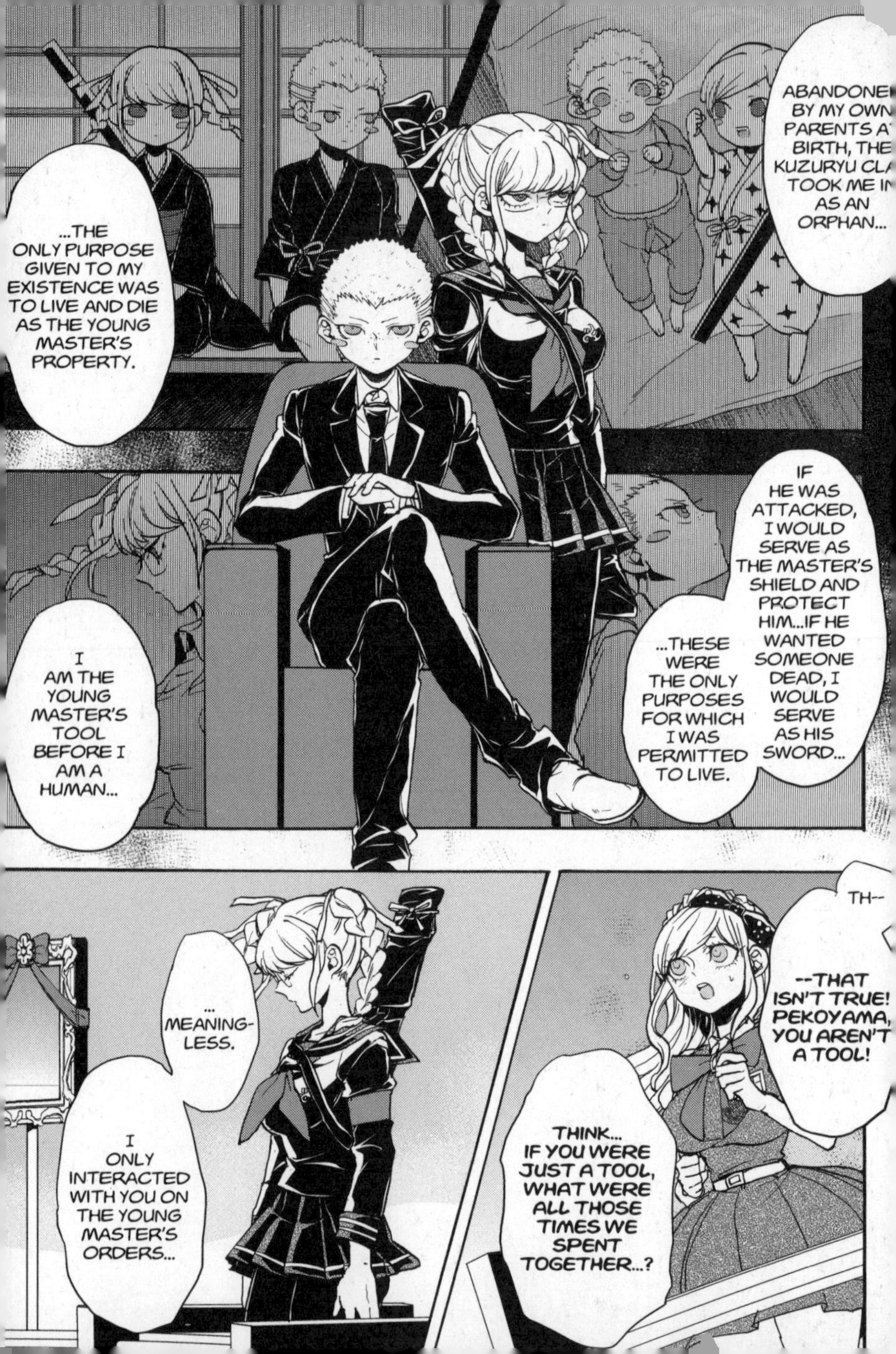
ABANDONE BY MY OWN PARENTS A BIRTH, THE KUZURYU CLA TOOK ME I AS AN ORPHAN...
...THE ONLY PURPOSE GIVEN TO MY EXISTENCE WAS TO LIVE AND DIE AS THE YOUNG MASTER'S PROPERTY.
IF HE WAS ATTACKED, I WOULD SERVE AS THE MASTER'S SHIELD AND PROTECT HIM...IF HE WANTED SOMEONE DEAD, I WOULD SERVE AS HIS SWORD...
...THESE WERE THE ONLY PURPOSES FOR WHICH I WAS PERMITTED TO LIVE.
I AM THE YOUNG MASTER'S TOOL BEFORE I AM A HUMAN...
TH--
--THAT ISN'T TRUE! PEKOYAMA, YOU AREN'T A TOOL!
THINK... IF YOU WERE JUST A TOOL, WHAT WERE ALL THOSE TIMES WE SPENT TOGETHER...?
... MEANING-LESS.
I ONLY INTERACTED WITH YOU ON THE YOUNG MASTER'S ORDERS...

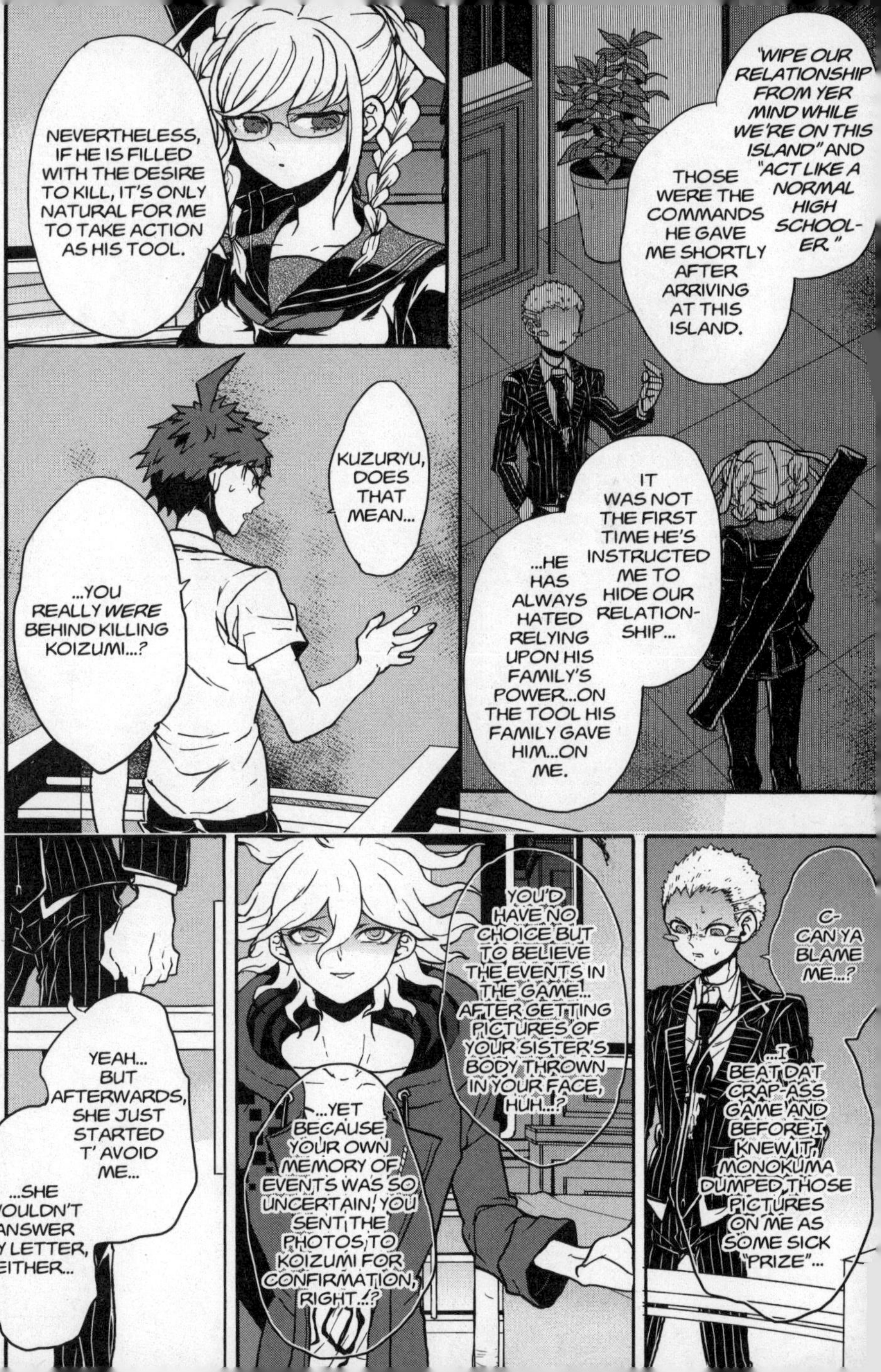
"WIPE OUR RELATIONSHIP FROM YER MIND WHILE WE'RE ON THIS ISLAND" AND "ACT LIKE A NORMAL HIGH SCHOOLER."
THOSE WERE THE COMMANDS HE GAVE ME SHORTLY AFTER ARRIVING AT THIS ISLAND.
IT WAS NOT THE FIRST TIME HE'S INSTRUCTED ME TO HIDE OUR RELATIONSHIP...
...HE HAS ALWAYS HATED RELYING UPON HIS FAMILY'S POWER...ON THE TOOL HIS FAMILY GAVE HIM...ON ME.
NEVERTHELESS, IF HE IS FILLED WITH THE DESIRE TO KILL, IT'S ONLY NATURAL FOR ME TO TAKE ACTION AS HIS TOOL.
KUZURYU, DOES THAT MEAN...
...YOU REALLY *WERE* BEHIND KILLING KOIZUMI...?
C-CAN YA BLAME ME...?
...I BEAT DAT CRAP-ASS GAME AND BEFORE I KNEW IT, MONOKUMA DUMPED THOSE PICTURES ON ME AS SOME SICK "PRIZE"...
YOU'D HAVE NO CHOICE BUT TO BELIEVE THE EVENTS IN THE GAME... AFTER GETTING PICTURES OF YOUR SISTER'S BODY THROWN IN YOUR FACE, HUH...?
...YET BECAUSE YOUR OWN MEMORY OF EVENTS WAS SO UNCERTAIN, YOU SENT THE PHOTOS TO KOIZUMI FOR CONFIRMATION, RIGHT...?
YEAH... BUT AFTERWARDS, SHE JUST STARTED T' AVOID ME...
...SHE WOULDN'T ANSWER MY LETTER, EITHER...

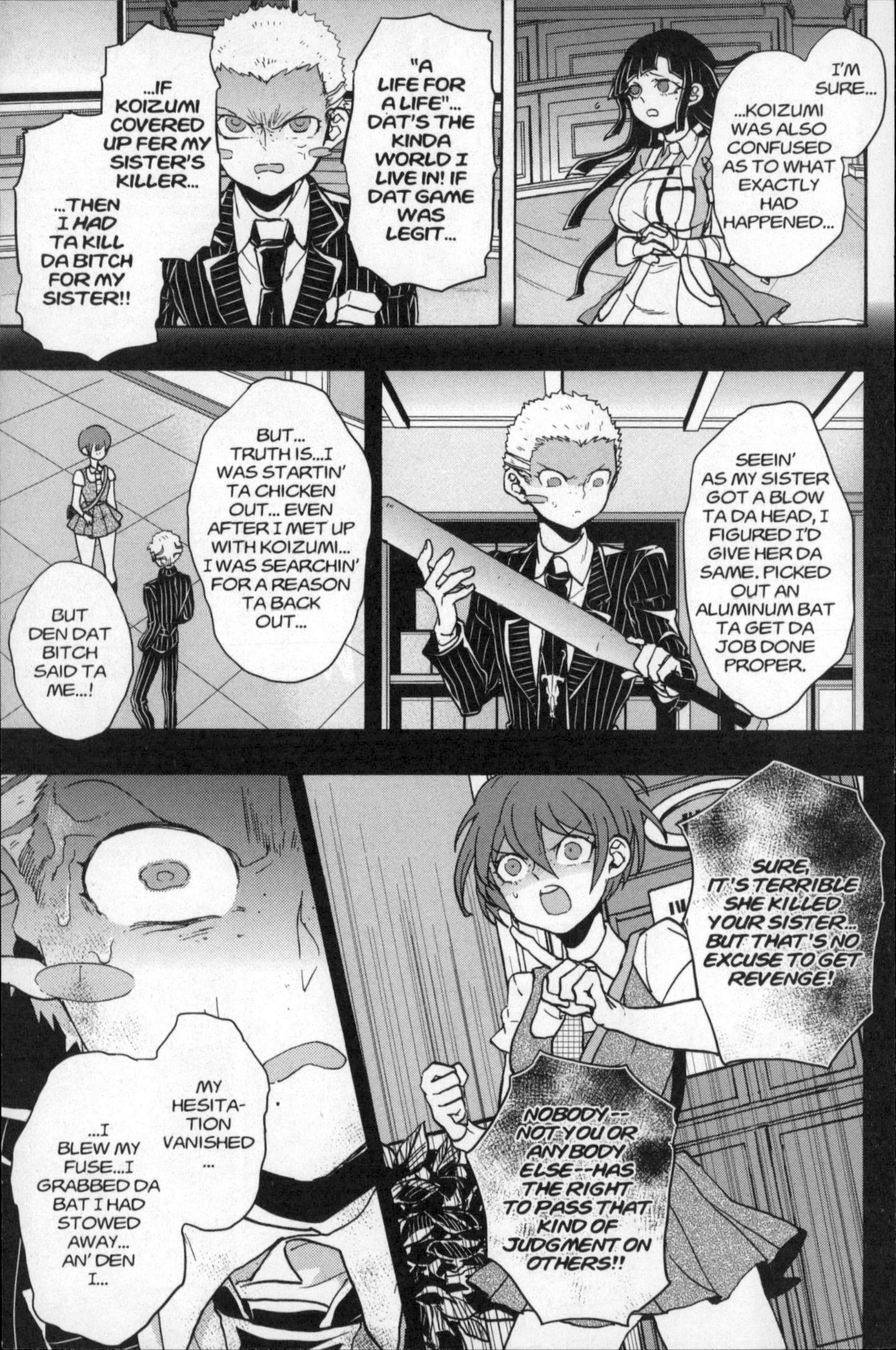
I'M SURE... ...KOIZUMI WAS ALSO CONFUSED AS TO WHAT EXACTLY HAD HAPPENED...
"A LIFE FOR A LIFE"... DAT'S THE KINDA WORLD I LIVE IN! IF DAT GAME WAS LEGIT...
...IF KOIZUMI COVERED UP FER MY SISTER'S KILLER...
...THEN I *HAD* TA KILL DA BITCH FOR MY SISTER!!
SEEIN' AS MY SISTER GOT A BLOW TA DA HEAD, I FIGURED I'D GIVE HER DA SAME. PICKED OUT AN ALUMINUM BAT TA GET DA JOB DONE PROPER.
BUT... TRUTH IS...I WAS STARTIN' TA CHICKEN OUT... EVEN AFTER I MET UP WITH KOIZUMI... I WAS SEARCHIN' FOR A REASON TA BACK OUT...
BUT DEN DAT BITCH SAID TA ME...!
SURE, IT'S TERRIBLE SHE KILLED YOUR SISTER... BUT THAT'S NO EXCUSE TO GET REVENGE!
NOBODY-- NOT YOU OR ANYBODY ELSE--HAS THE RIGHT TO PASS THAT KIND OF JUDGMENT ON OTHERS!!
MY HESITATION VANISHED...
...I BLEW MY FUSE...I GRABBED DA BAT I HAD STOWED AWAY... AN' DEN I...

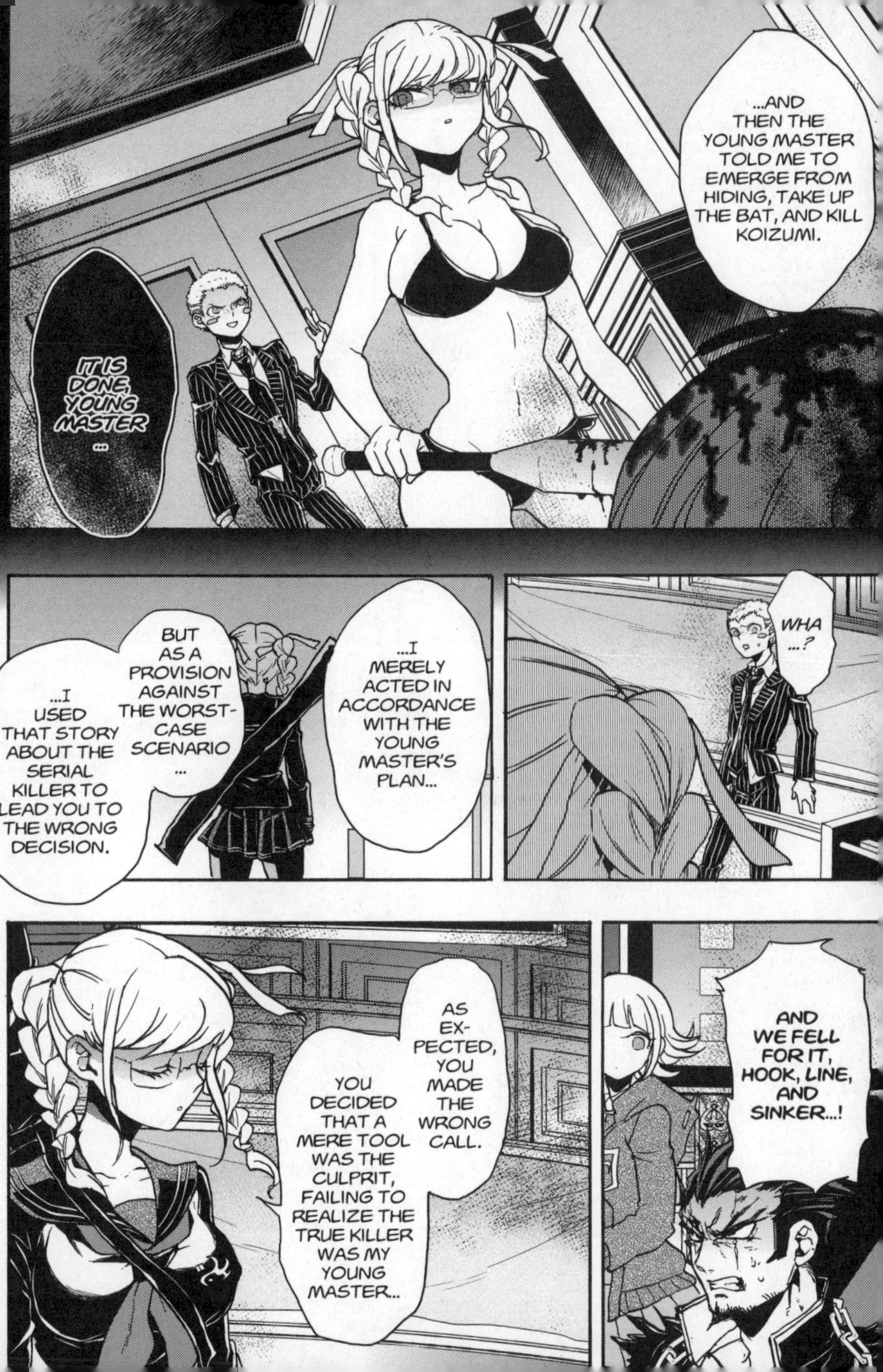
...AND THEN THE YOUNG MASTER TOLD ME TO EMERGE FROM HIDING, TAKE UP THE BAT, AND KILL KOIZUMI.
IT IS DONE, YOUNG MASTER...
WHA...?
...I MERELY ACTED IN ACCORDANCE WITH THE YOUNG MASTER'S PLAN...
BUT AS A PROVISION AGAINST THE WORST-CASE SCENARIO...
...I USED THAT STORY ABOUT THE SERIAL KILLER TO LEAD YOU TO THE WRONG DECISION.
AND WE FELL FOR IT, HOOK, LINE, AND SINKER...!
AS EXPECTED, YOU MADE THE WRONG CALL.
YOU DECIDED THAT A MERE TOOL WAS THE CULPRIT, FAILING TO REALIZE THE TRUE KILLER WAS MY YOUNG MASTER...

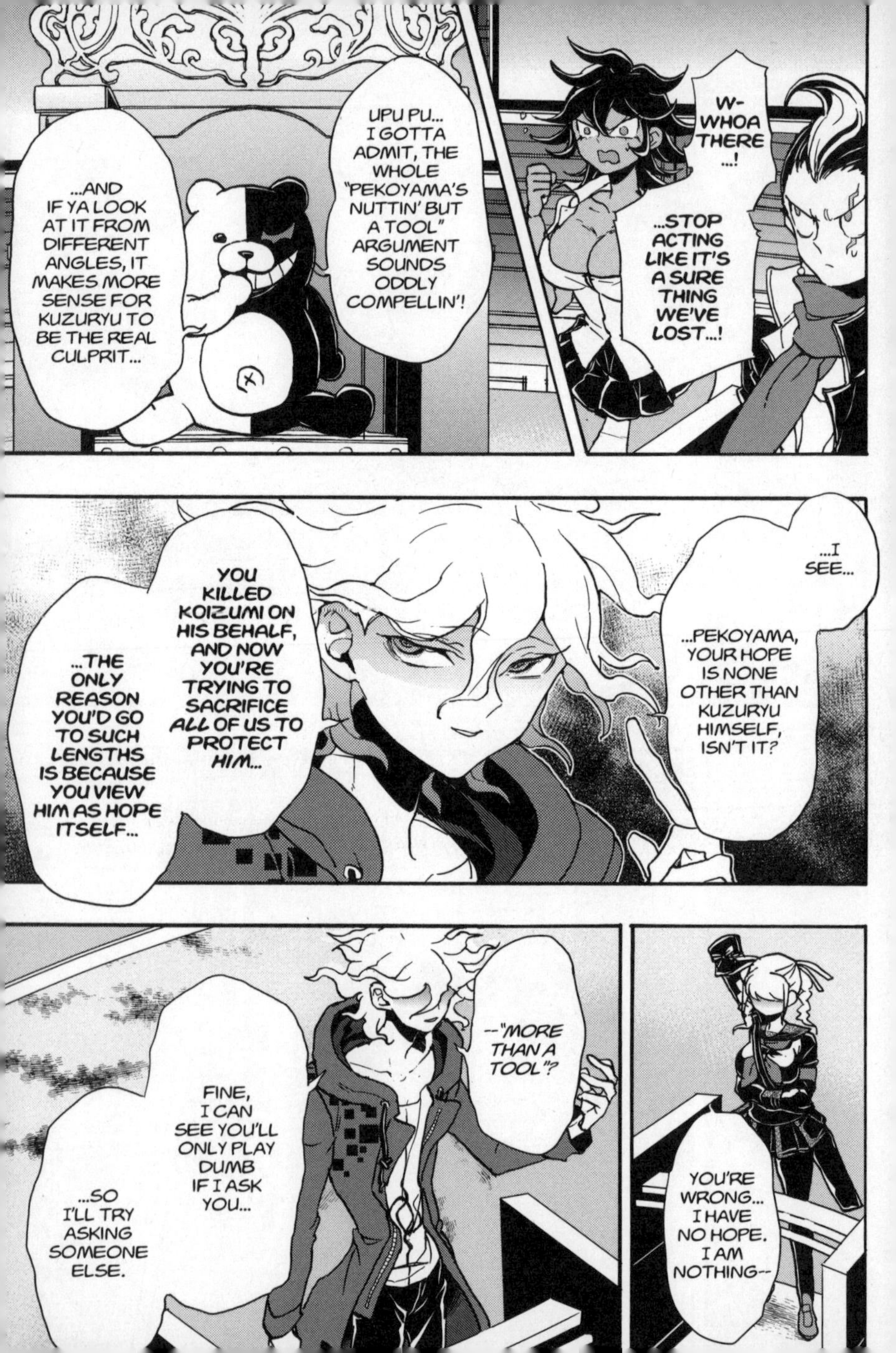
W-WHOA THERE ...!
...STOP ACTING LIKE IT'S A SURE THING WE'VE LOST...!
UPU PU... I GOTTA ADMIT, THE WHOLE "PEKOYAMA'S NUTTIN' BUT A TOOL" ARGUMENT SOUNDS ODDLY COMPELLIN'!
...AND IF YA LOOK AT IT FROM DIFFERENT ANGLES, IT MAKES MORE SENSE FOR KUZURYU TO BE THE REAL CULPRIT...
...I SEE...
...PEKOYAMA, YOUR HOPE IS NONE OTHER THAN KUZURYU HIMSELF, ISN'T IT?
YOU KILLED KOIZUMI ON HIS BEHALF, AND NOW YOU'RE TRYING TO SACRIFICE ALL OF US TO PROTECT HIM...
...THE ONLY REASON YOU'D GO TO SUCH LENGTHS IS BECAUSE YOU VIEW HIM AS HOPE ITSELF...
YOU'RE WRONG... I HAVE NO HOPE. I AM NOTHING--
--"MORE THAN A TOOL"?
FINE, I CAN SEE YOU'LL ONLY PLAY DUMB IF I ASK YOU...
...SO I'LL TRY ASKING SOMEONE ELSE.

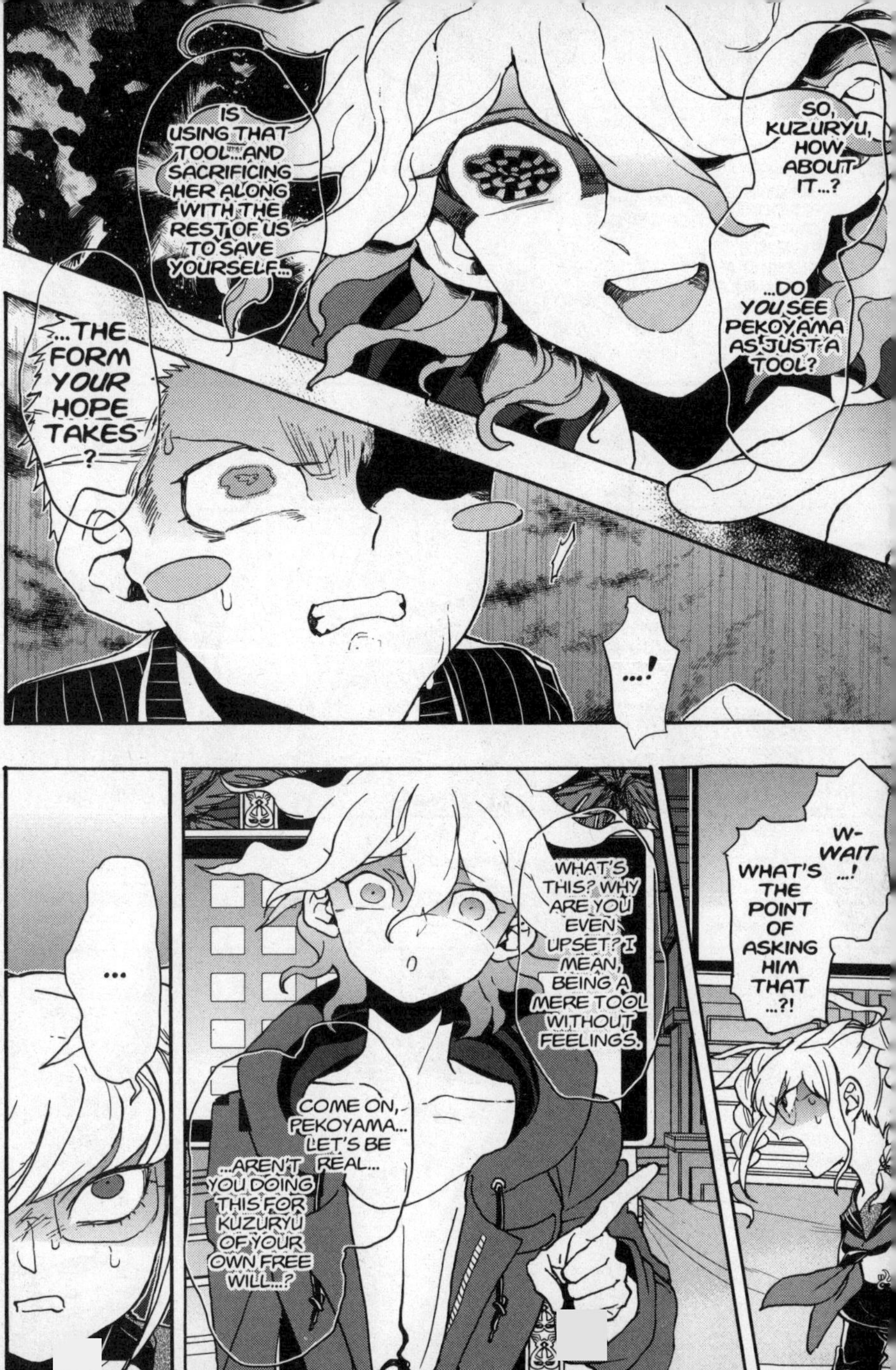
SO, KUZURYU, HOW ABOUT IT...?
...DO YOU SEE PEKOYAMA AS JUST A TOOL?
IS USING THAT TOOL...AND SACRIFICING HER ALONG WITH THE REST OF US TO SAVE YOURSELF...
...THE FORM YOUR HOPE TAKES?
...!
W-WAIT...!
WHAT'S THE POINT OF ASKING HIM THAT...?!
WHAT'S THIS? WHY ARE YOU EVEN UPSET? I MEAN, BEING A MERE TOOL WITHOUT FEELINGS.
COME ON, PEKOYAMA... LET'S BE REAL...
...AREN'T YOU DOING THIS FOR KUZURYU OF YOUR OWN FREE WILL...?
...

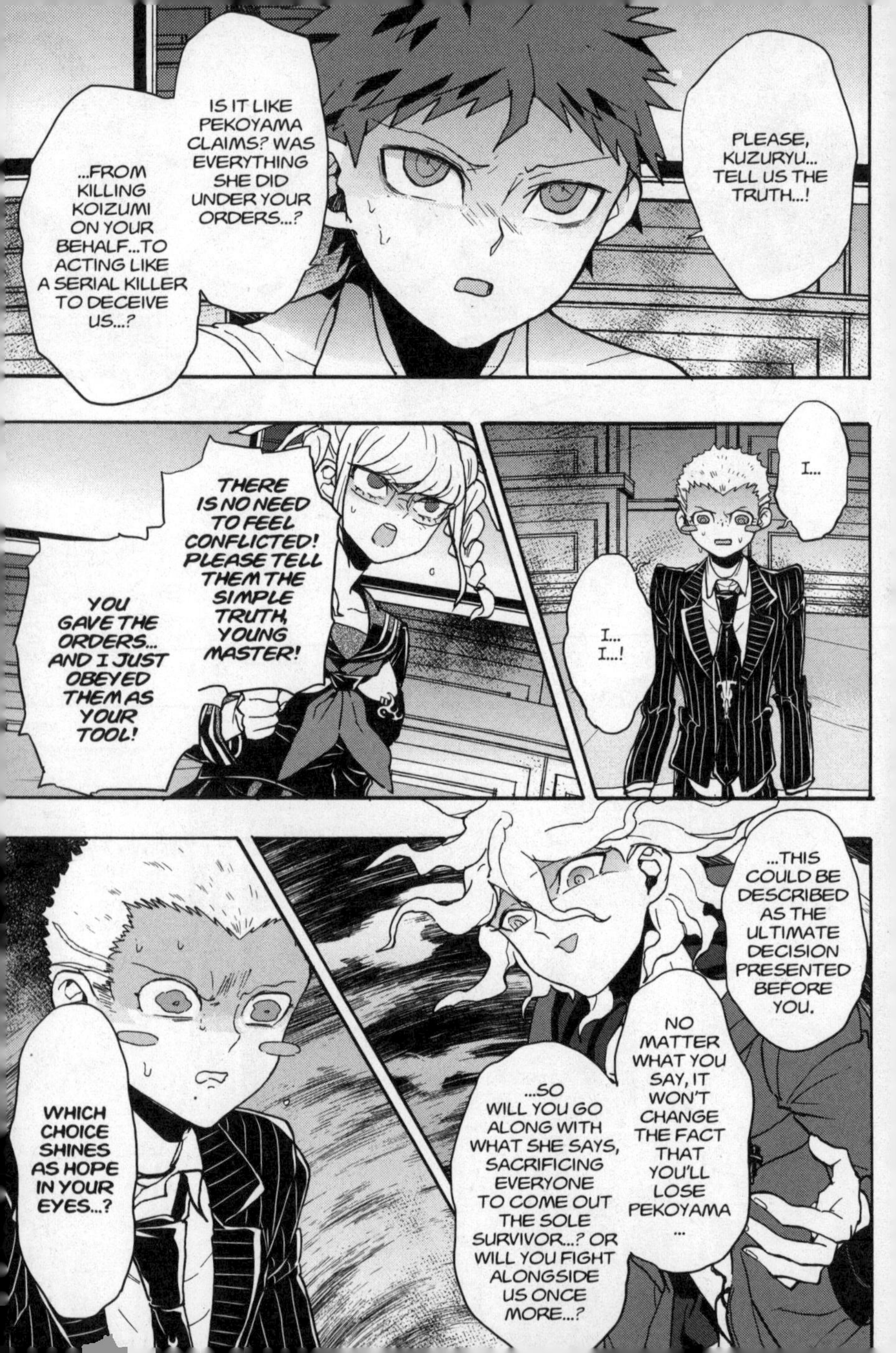
PLEASE, KUZURYU... TELL US THE TRUTH...!
IS IT LIKE PEKOYAMA CLAIMS? WAS EVERYTHING SHE DID UNDER YOUR ORDERS...?
...FROM KILLING KOIZUMI ON YOUR BEHALF...TO ACTING LIKE A SERIAL KILLER TO DECEIVE US...?
I...
I... I...!
THERE IS NO NEED TO FEEL CONFLICTED! PLEASE TELL THEM THE SIMPLE TRUTH, YOUNG MASTER!
YOU GAVE THE ORDERS... AND I JUST OBEYED THEM AS YOUR TOOL!
...THIS COULD BE DESCRIBED AS THE ULTIMATE DECISION PRESENTED BEFORE YOU.
NO MATTER WHAT YOU SAY, IT WON'T CHANGE THE FACT THAT YOU'LL LOSE PEKOYAMA...
...SO WILL YOU GO ALONG WITH WHAT SHE SAYS, SACRIFICING EVERYONE TO COME OUT THE SOLE SURVIVOR...? OR WILL YOU FIGHT ALONGSIDE US ONCE MORE...?
WHICH CHOICE SHINES AS HOPE IN YOUR EYES...?

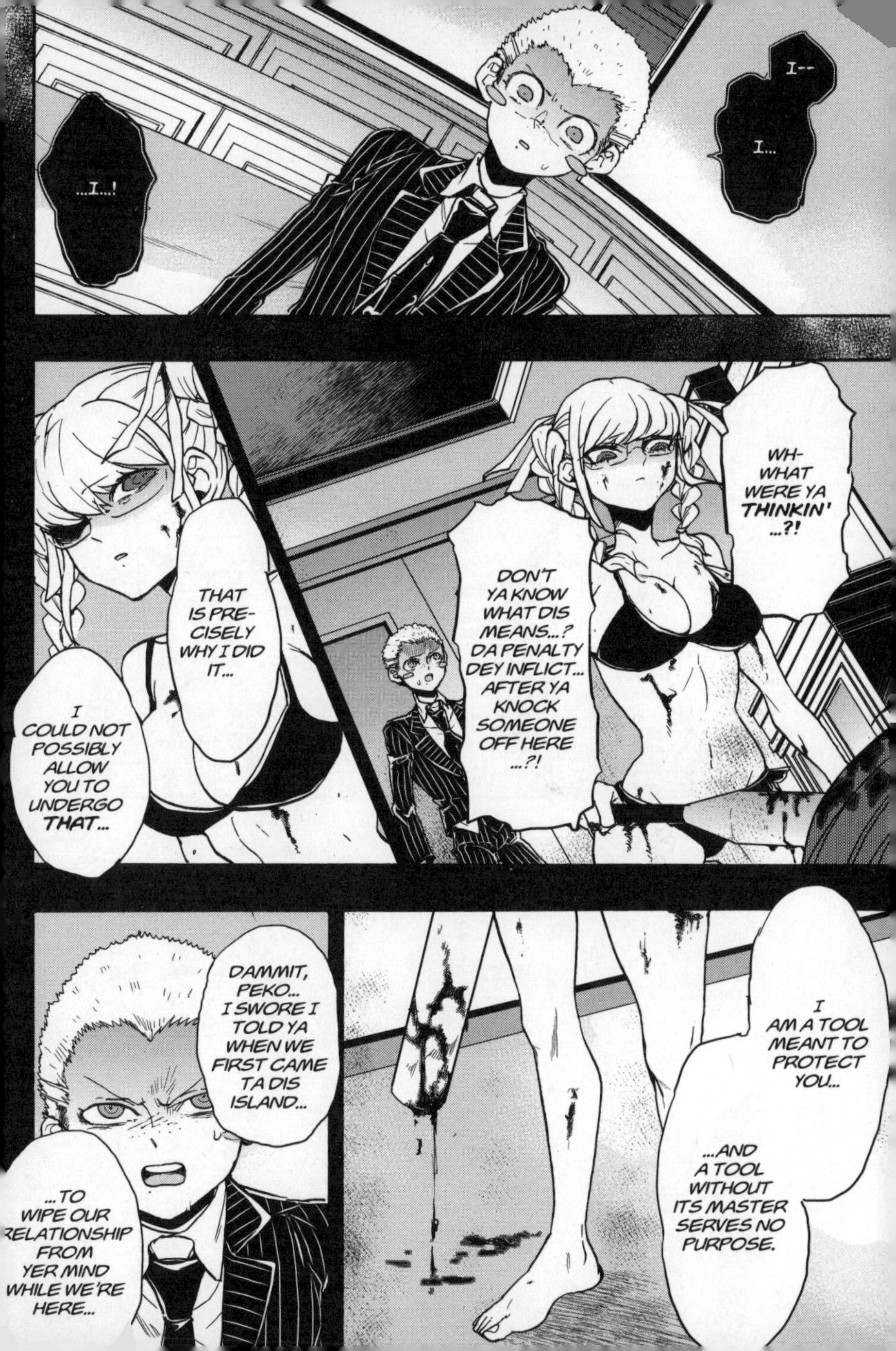
I--
I...
...I...!
WH- WHAT WERE YA THINKIN' ...?!
DON'T YA KNOW WHAT DIS MEANS...? DA PENALTY DEY INFLICT... AFTER YA KNOCK SOMEONE OFF HERE ...?!
THAT IS PRECISELY WHY I DID IT...
I COULD NOT POSSIBLY ALLOW YOU TO UNDERGO THAT...
I AM A TOOL MEANT TO PROTECT YOU...
...AND A TOOL WITHOUT ITS MASTER SERVES NO PURPOSE.
DAMMIT, PEKO... I SWORE I TOLD YA WHEN WE FIRST CAME TA DIS ISLAND...
...TO WIPE OUR RELATIONSHIP FROM YER MIND WHILE WE'RE HERE...

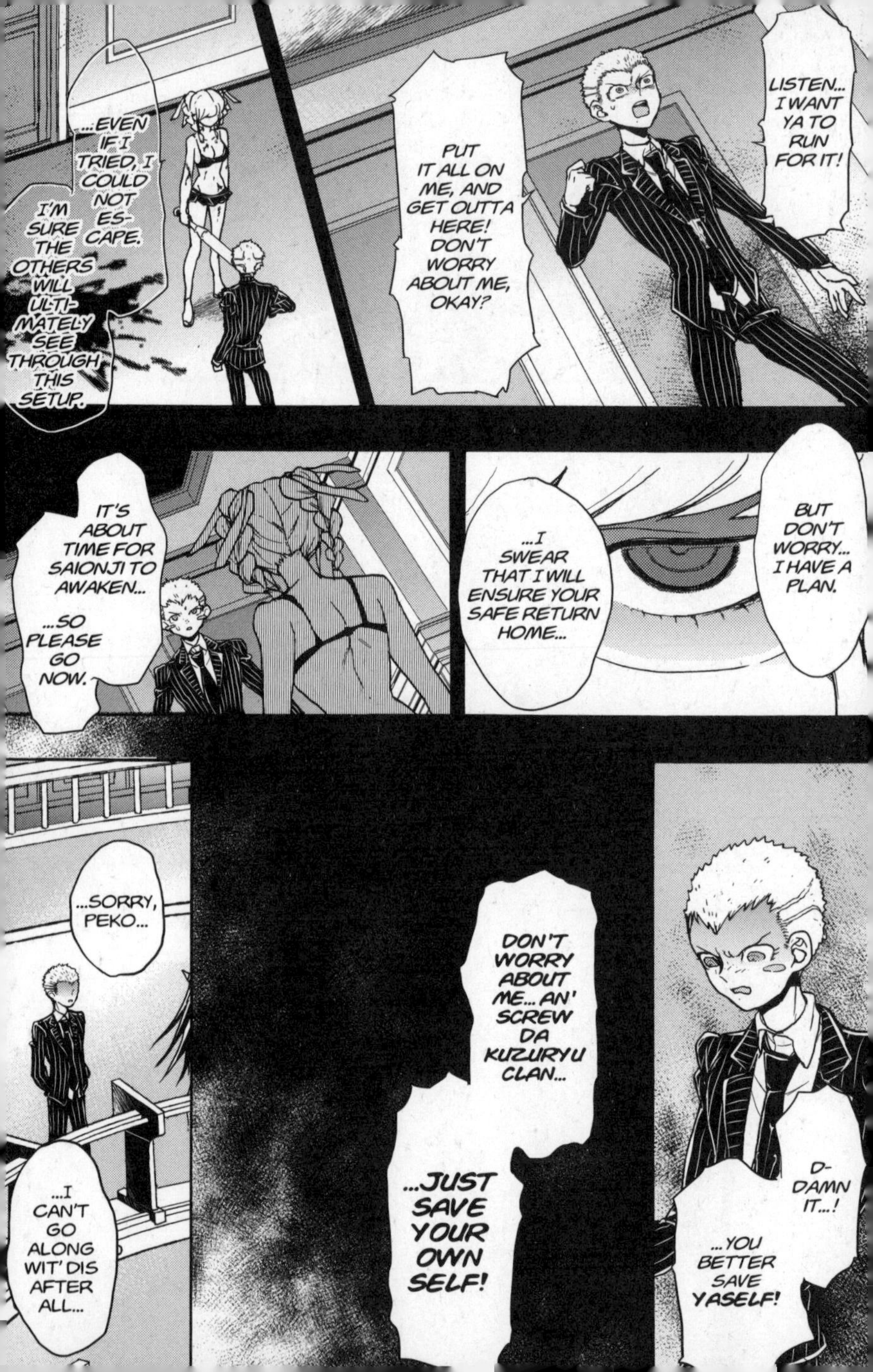

LISTEN... I WANT YA TO RUN FOR IT!
PUT IT ALL ON ME, AND GET OUTTA HERE! DON'T WORRY ABOUT ME, OKAY?
...EVEN IF I TRIED, I COULD NOT ES-CAPE.
I'M SURE THE OTHERS WILL ULTI-MATELY SEE THROUGH THIS SETUP.
BUT DON'T WORRY... I HAVE A PLAN.
...I SWEAR THAT I WILL ENSURE YOUR SAFE RETURN HOME...
IT'S ABOUT TIME FOR SAIONJI TO AWAKEN...
...SO PLEASE GO NOW.
D-DAMN IT...!
...YOU BETTER SAVE YASELF!
DON'T WORRY ABOUT ME... AN' SCREW DA KUZURYU CLAN...
...JUST SAVE YOUR OWN SELF!
...SORRY, PEKO...
...I CAN'T GO ALONG WIT' DIS AFTER ALL...

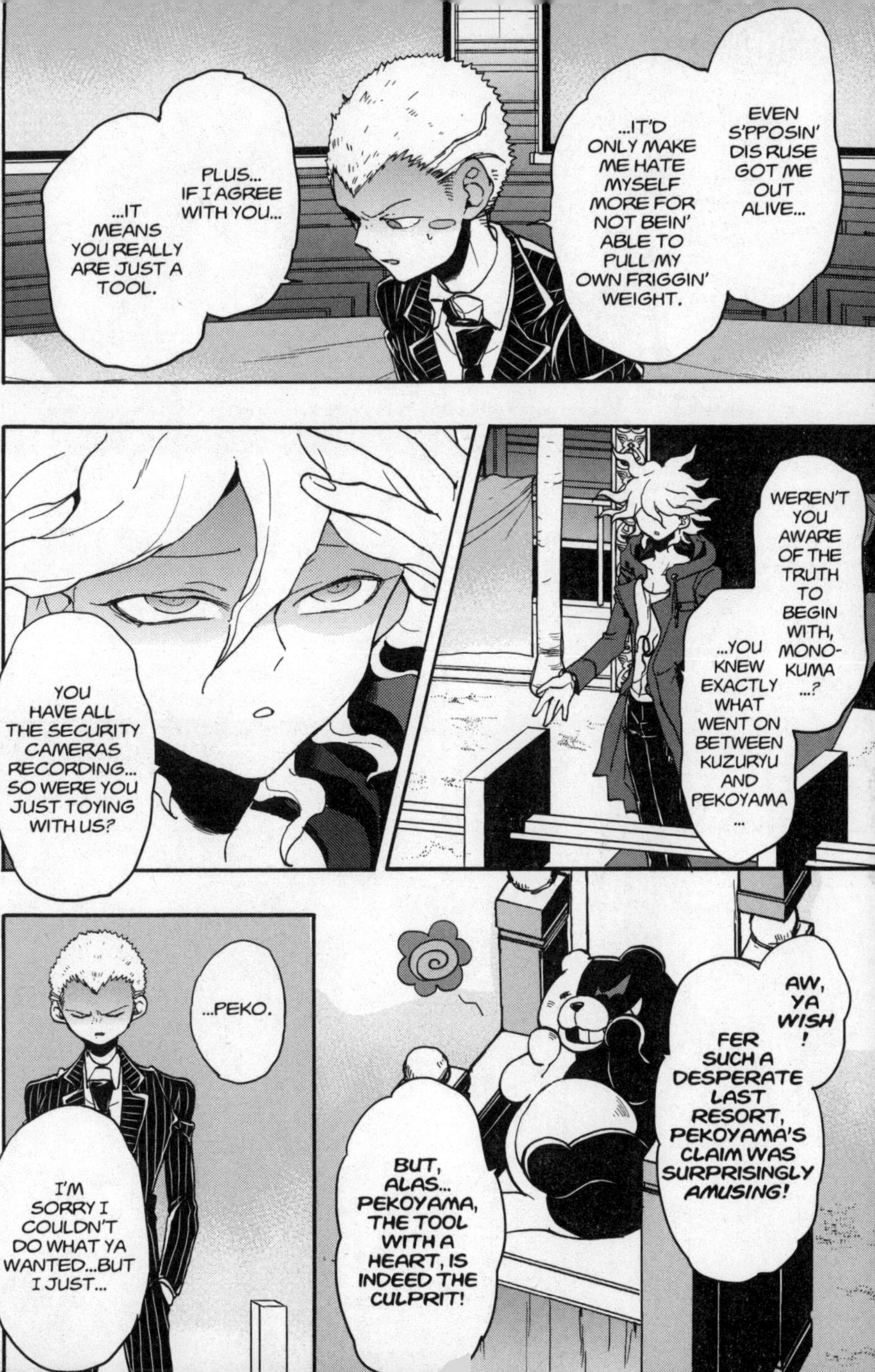
EVEN S'PPOSIN' DIS RUSE GOT ME OUT ALIVE...
...IT'D ONLY MAKE ME HATE MYSELF MORE FOR NOT BEIN' ABLE TO PULL MY OWN FRIGGIN' WEIGHT.
PLUS... IF I AGREE WITH YOU...
...IT MEANS YOU REALLY ARE JUST A TOOL.
WEREN'T YOU AWARE OF THE TRUTH TO BEGIN WITH, MONOKUMA...?
...YOU KNEW EXACTLY WHAT WENT ON BETWEEN KUZURYU AND PEKOYAMA...
YOU HAVE ALL THE SECURITY CAMERAS RECORDING... SO WERE YOU JUST TOYING WITH US?
AW, YA *WISH*!
FER SUCH A DESPERATE LAST RESORT, PEKOYAMA'S CLAIM WAS SURPRISINGLY *AMUSING*!
BUT, ALAS... PEKOYAMA, THE TOOL WITH A HEART, IS INDEED THE CULPRIT!
...PEKO.
I'M SORRY I COULDN'T DO WHAT YA WANTED...BUT I JUST...

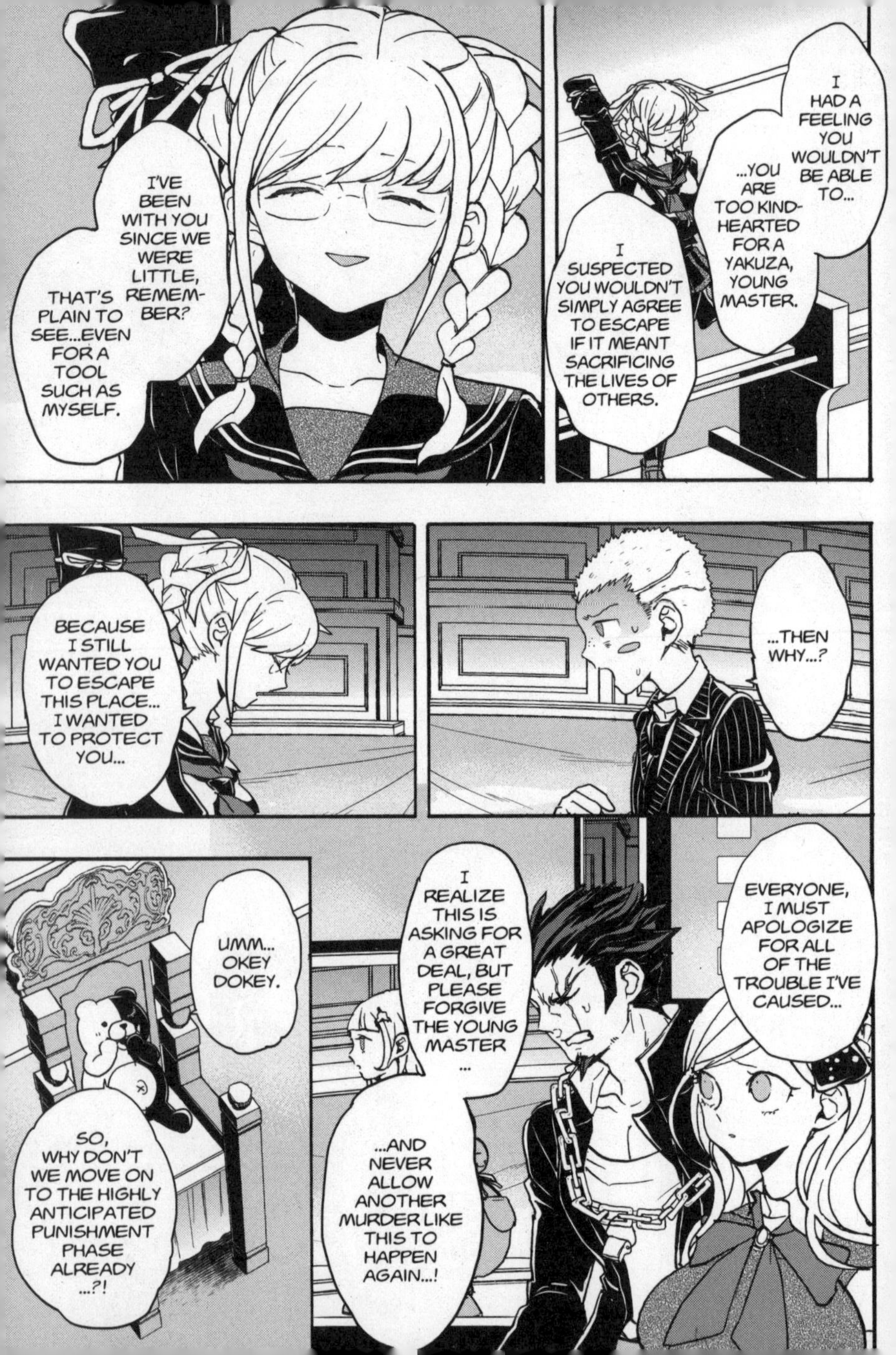
I HAD A FEELING YOU WOULDN'T BE ABLE TO...
...YOU ARE TOO KIND-HEARTED FOR A YAKUZA, YOUNG MASTER.
I SUSPECTED YOU WOULDN'T SIMPLY AGREE TO ESCAPE IF IT MEANT SACRIFICING THE LIVES OF OTHERS.
I'VE BEEN WITH YOU SINCE WE WERE LITTLE, REMEMBER?
THAT'S PLAIN TO SEE...EVEN FOR A TOOL SUCH AS MYSELF.
...THEN WHY...?
BECAUSE I STILL WANTED YOU TO ESCAPE THIS PLACE... I WANTED TO PROTECT YOU...
EVERYONE, I MUST APOLOGIZE FOR ALL OF THE TROUBLE I'VE CAUSED...
I REALIZE THIS IS ASKING FOR A GREAT DEAL, BUT PLEASE FORGIVE THE YOUNG MASTER...
...AND NEVER ALLOW ANOTHER MURDER LIKE THIS TO HAPPEN AGAIN...!
UMM... OKEY DOKEY.
SO, WHY DON'T WE MOVE ON TO THE HIGHLY ANTICIPATED PUNISHMENT PHASE ALREADY...?!

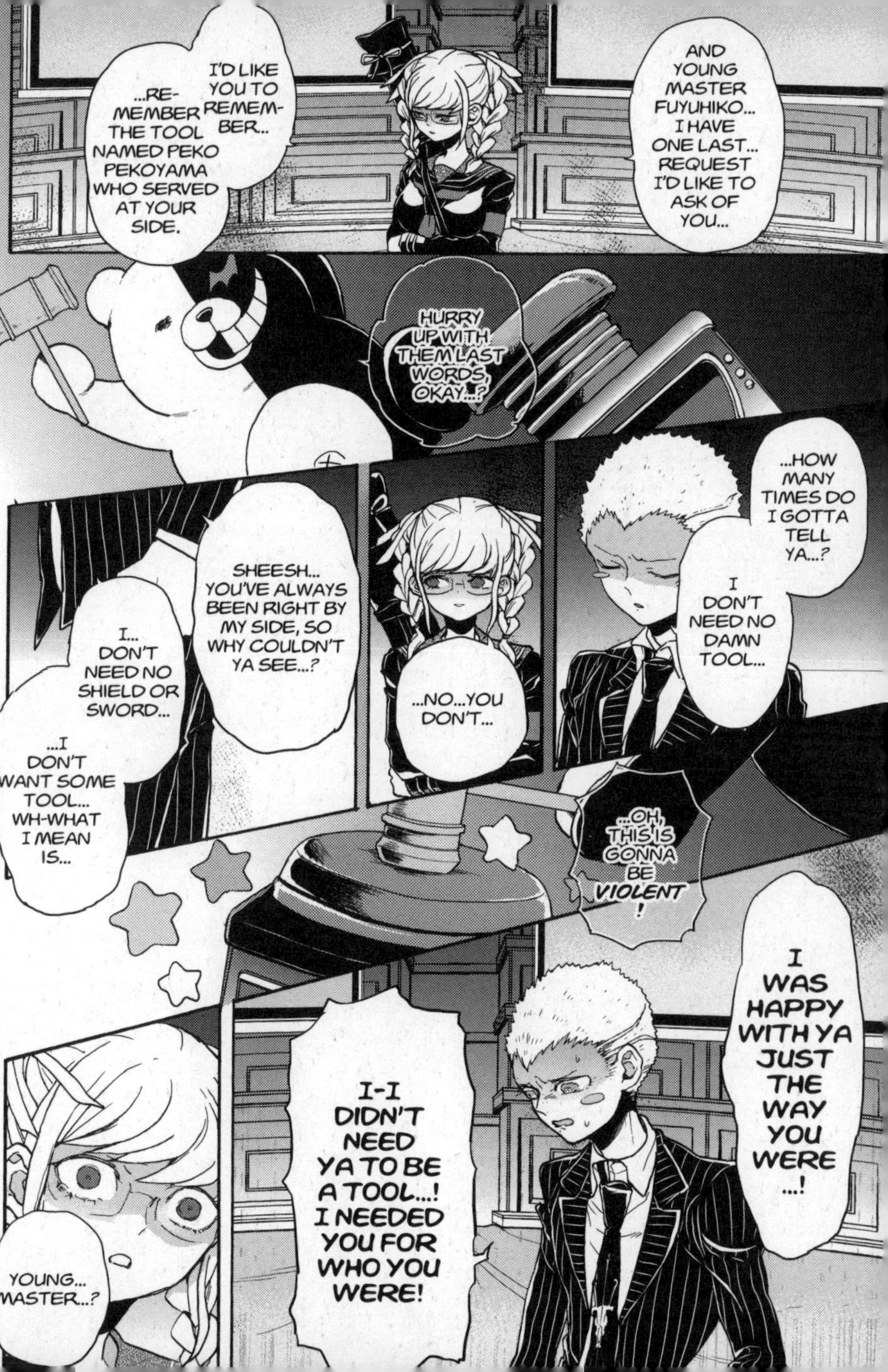
AND YOUNG MASTER FUYUHIKO... I HAVE ONE LAST... REQUEST I'D LIKE TO ASK OF YOU...
I'D LIKE YOU TO REMEMBER...
...REMEMBER THE TOOL NAMED PEKO PEKOYAMA WHO SERVED AT YOUR SIDE.
HURRY UP WITH THEM LAST WORDS, OKAY...?
...HOW MANY TIMES DO I GOTTA TELL YA...?
I DON'T NEED NO DAMN TOOL...
...NO...YOU DON'T...
SHEESH... YOU'VE ALWAYS BEEN RIGHT BY MY SIDE, SO WHY COULDN'T YA SEE...?
I... DON'T NEED NO SHIELD OR SWORD...
...I DON'T WANT SOME TOOL... WH-WHAT I MEAN IS...
...OH, THIS IS GONNA BE VIOLENT!
I WAS HAPPY WITH YA JUST THE WAY YOU WERE...!
I-I DIDN'T NEED YA TO BE A TOOL...! I NEEDED YOU FOR WHO YOU WERE!
YOUNG... MASTER...?

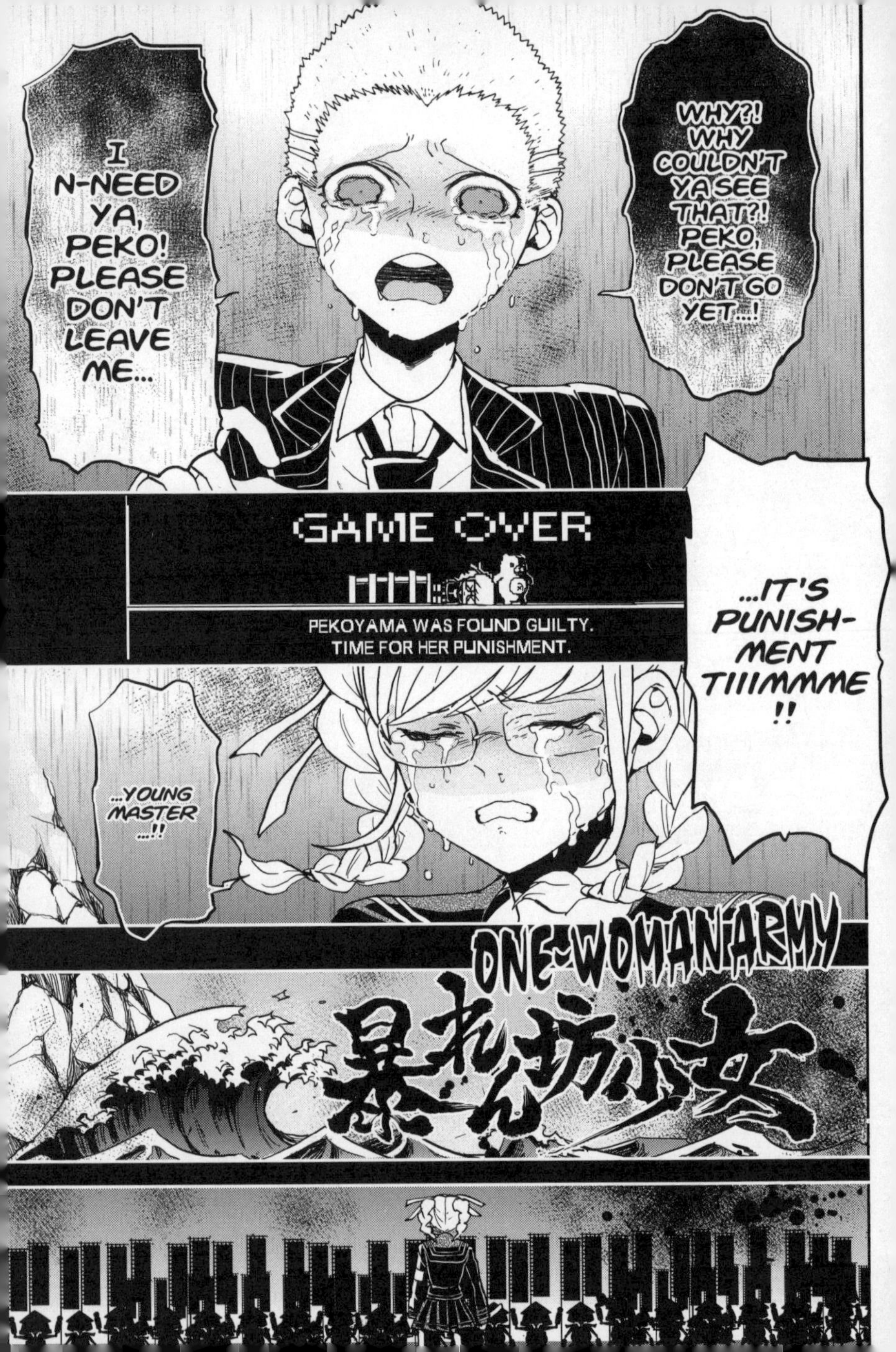
WHY?! WHY COULDN'T YA SEE THAT?! PEKO, PLEASE DON'T GO YET...!
I N-NEED YA, PEKO! PLEASE DON'T LEAVE ME...
GAME OVER
PEKOYAMA WAS FOUND GUILTY. TIME FOR HER PUNISHMENT.
...IT'S PUNISHMENT TIIIMMME!!
...YOUNG MASTER...!!
ONE-WOMAN ARMY
暴れん坊少女

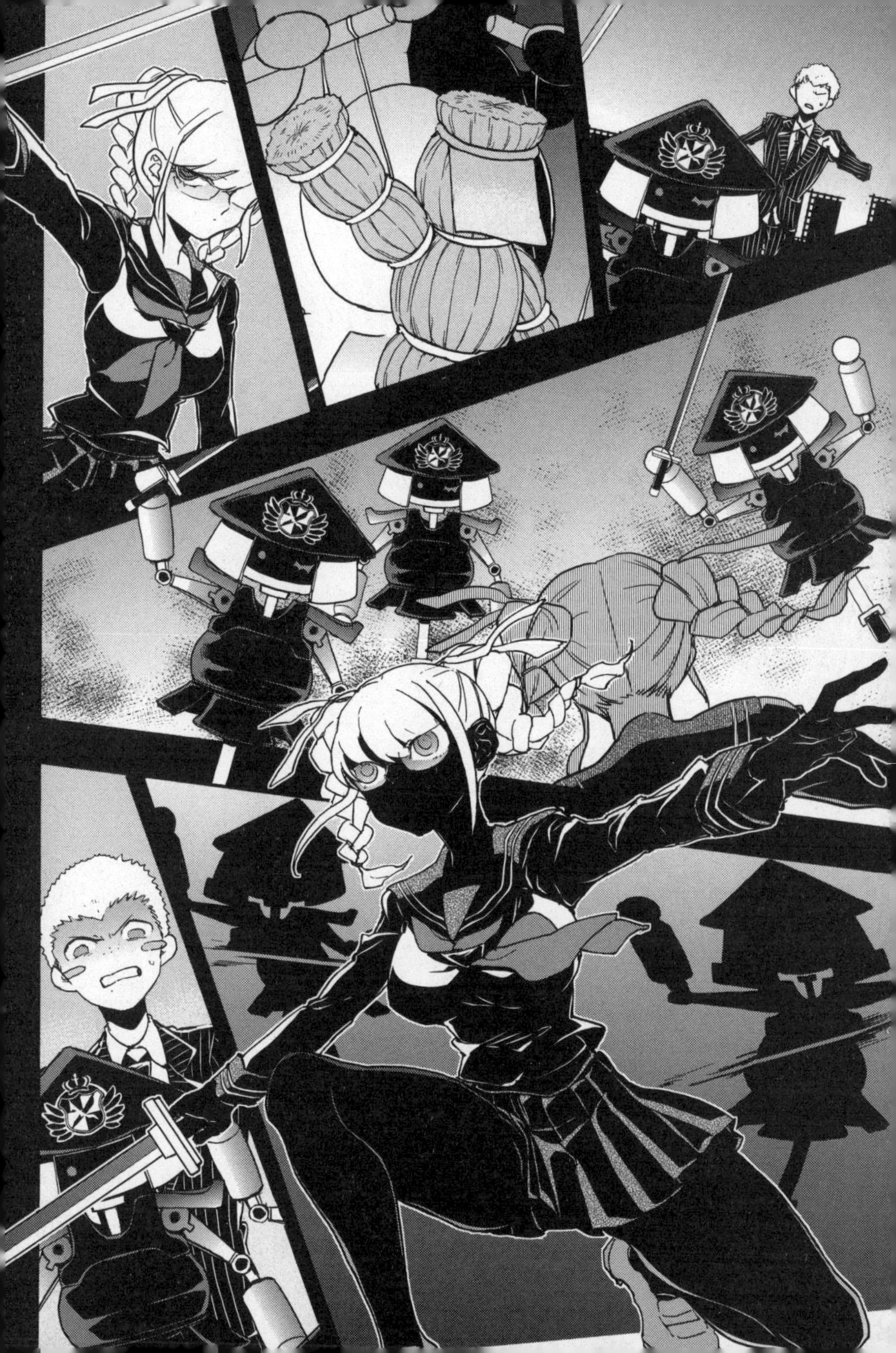

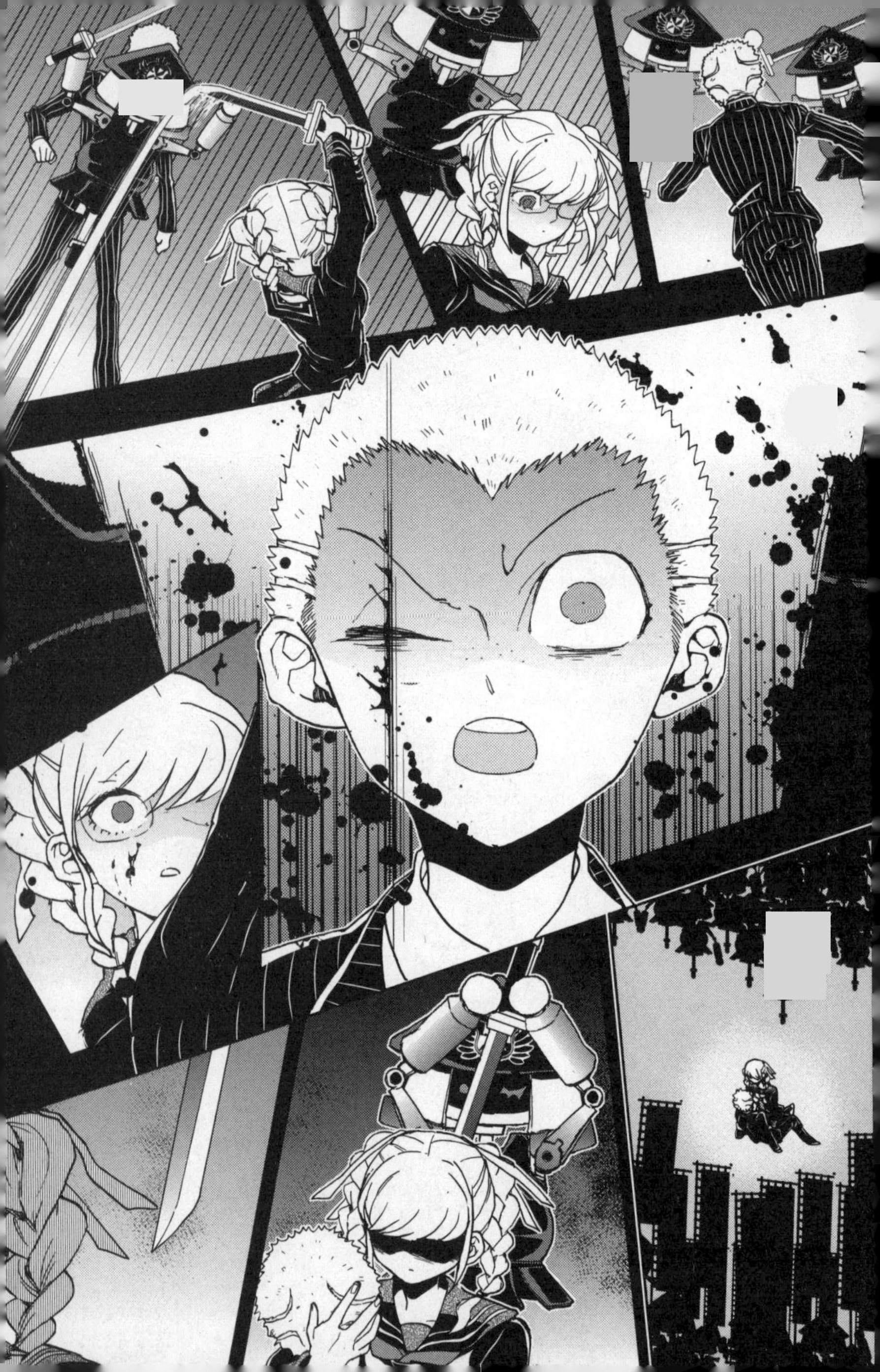

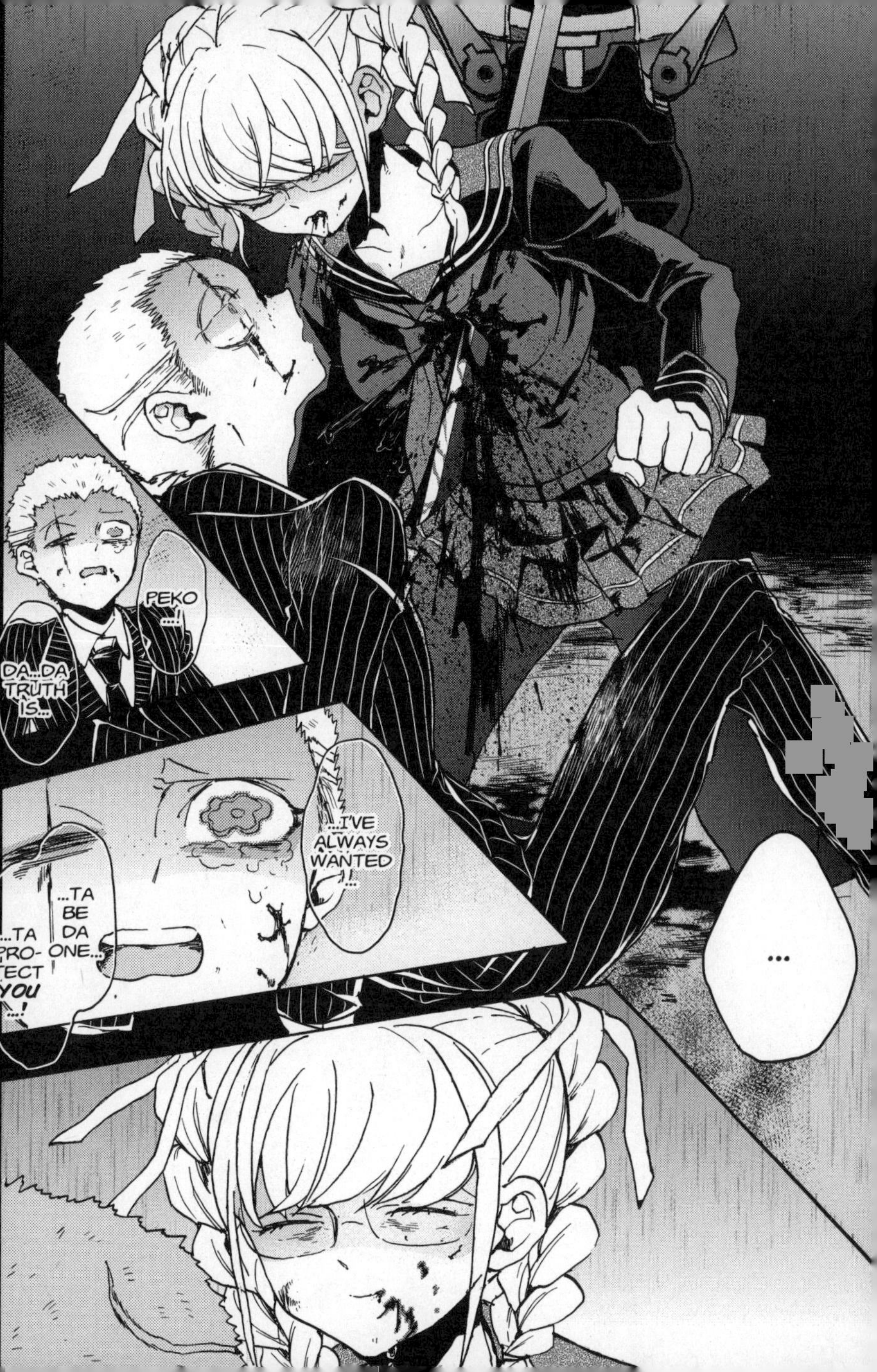
PEKO ...!
DA...DA TRUTH IS...
...I'VE ALWAYS WANTED ...
...TA BE DA ONE...
...TA PRO-TECT YOU ...!
...

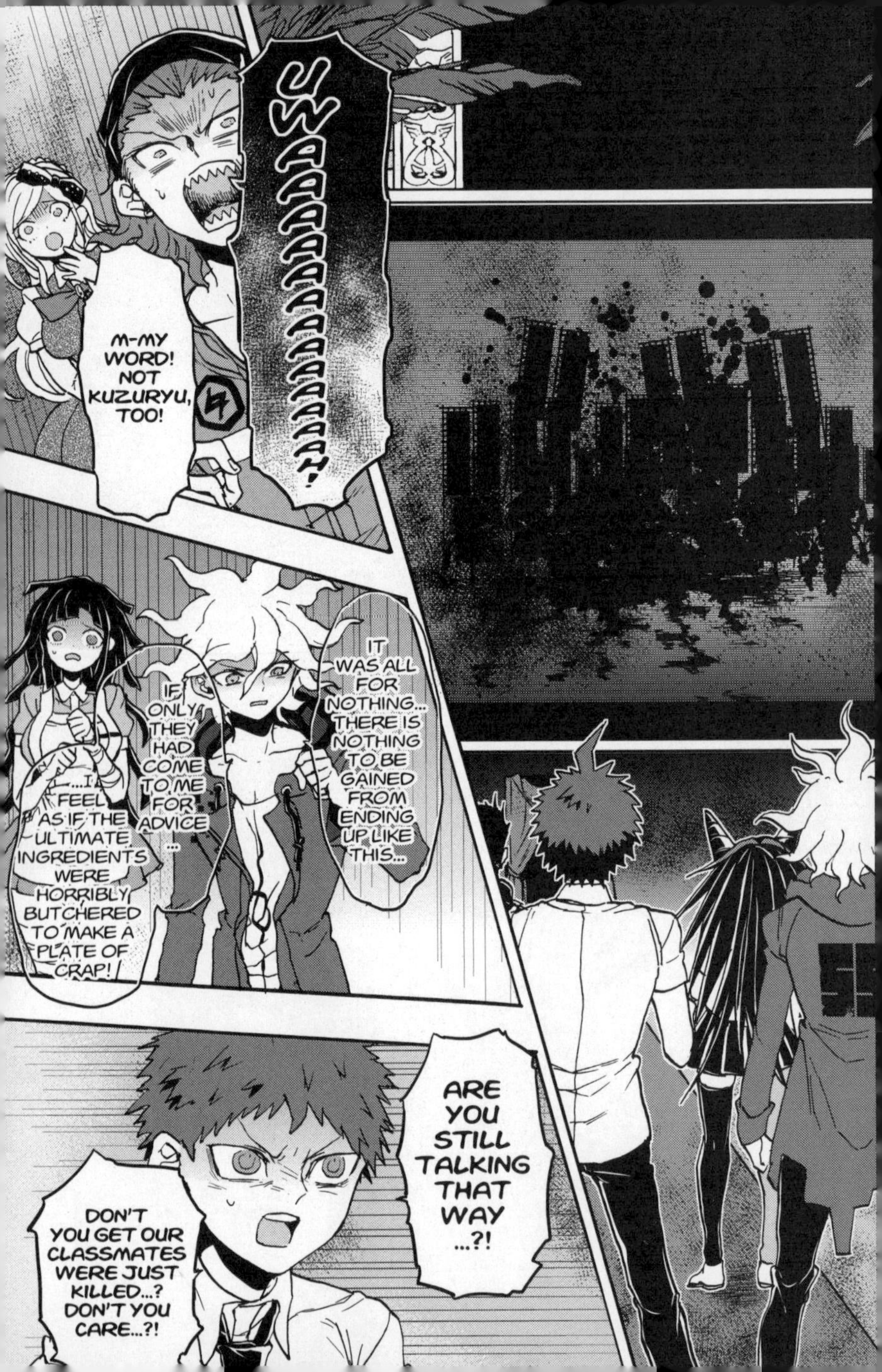
UWAAAAAAAAAAAAAAAAAAH!
M-MY WORD! NOT KUZURYU, TOO!
IT WAS ALL FOR NOTHING... THERE IS NOTHING TO BE GAINED FROM ENDING UP LIKE THIS...
IF ONLY THEY HAD COME TO ME FOR ADVICE...
...I FEEL AS IF THE ULTIMATE INGREDIENTS WERE HORRIBLY BUTCHERED TO MAKE A PLATE OF CRAP!
ARE YOU STILL TALKING THAT WAY ...?!
DON'T YOU GET OUR CLASSMATES WERE JUST KILLED...? DON'T YOU CARE...?!

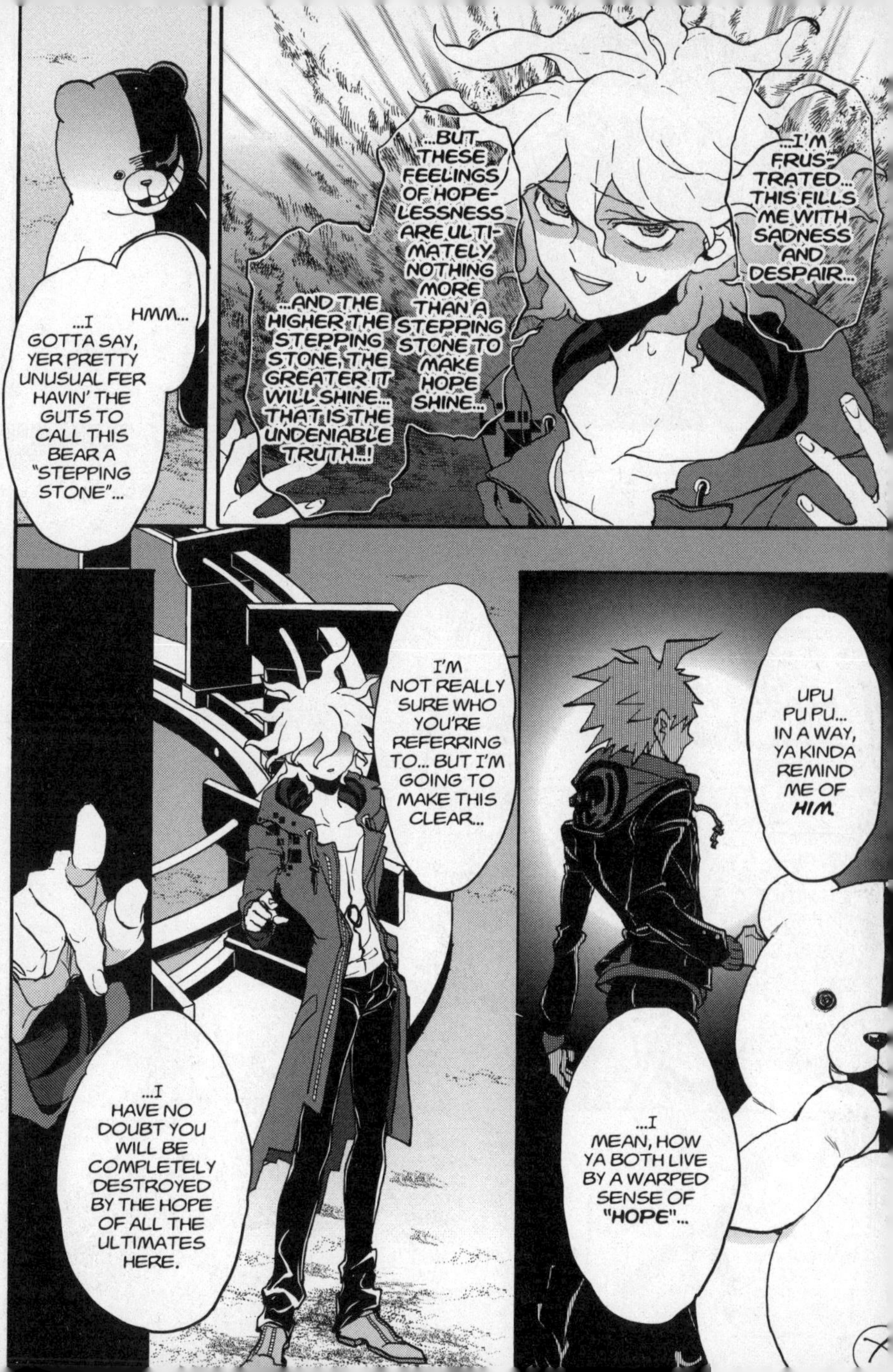
...I'M FRUSTRATED... THIS FILLS ME WITH SADNESS AND DESPAIR...
...BUT THESE FEELINGS OF HOPELESSNESS ARE ULTIMATELY NOTHING MORE THAN A STEPPING STONE TO MAKE HOPE SHINE...
...AND THE HIGHER THE STEPPING STONE, THE GREATER IT WILL SHINE... THAT IS THE UNDENIABLE TRUTH...!
HMM...
...I GOTTA SAY, YER PRETTY UNUSUAL FER HAVIN' THE GUTS TO CALL THIS BEAR A "STEPPING STONE"...
UPU PU PU... IN A WAY, YA KINDA REMIND ME OF **HIM**.
...I MEAN, HOW YA BOTH LIVE BY A WARPED SENSE OF "**HOPE**"...
I'M NOT REALLY SURE WHO YOU'RE REFERRING TO... BUT I'M GOING TO MAKE THIS CLEAR...
...I HAVE NO DOUBT YOU WILL BE COMPLETELY DESTROYED BY THE HOPE OF ALL THE ULTIMATES HERE.

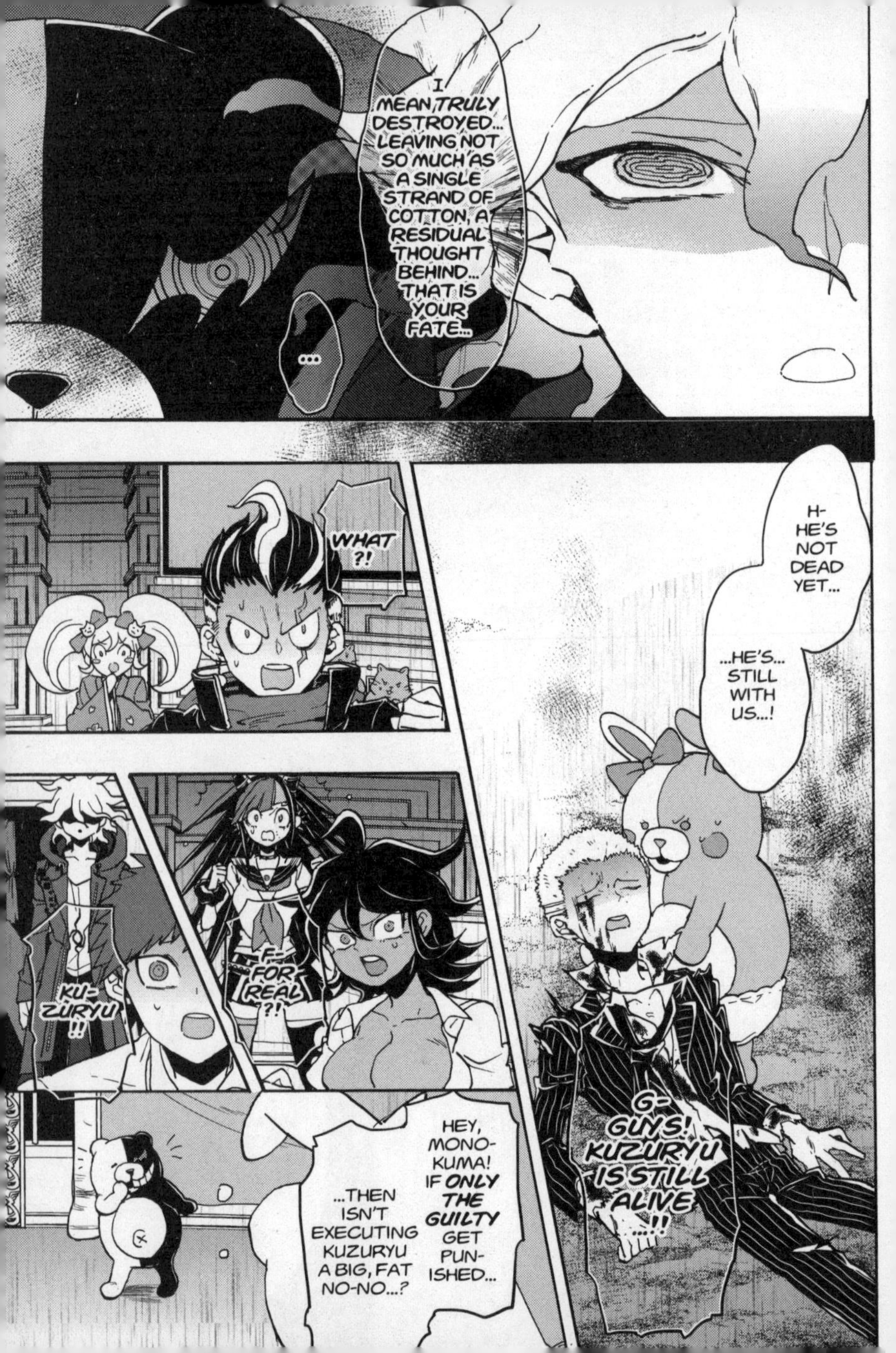
I MEAN, TRULY DESTROYED... LEAVING NOT SO MUCH AS A SINGLE STRAND OF COTTON, A RESIDUAL THOUGHT BEHIND... THAT IS YOUR FATE...
...
H-HE'S NOT DEAD YET...
...HE'S... STILL WITH US...!
G-GUYS! KUZURYU IS STILL ALIVE...!!
WHAT?!
F-FOR REAL?!
KUZURYU!!
HEY, MONOKUMA! IF ONLY THE GUILTY GET PUNISHED...
...THEN ISN'T EXECUTING KUZURYU A BIG, FAT NO-NO...?

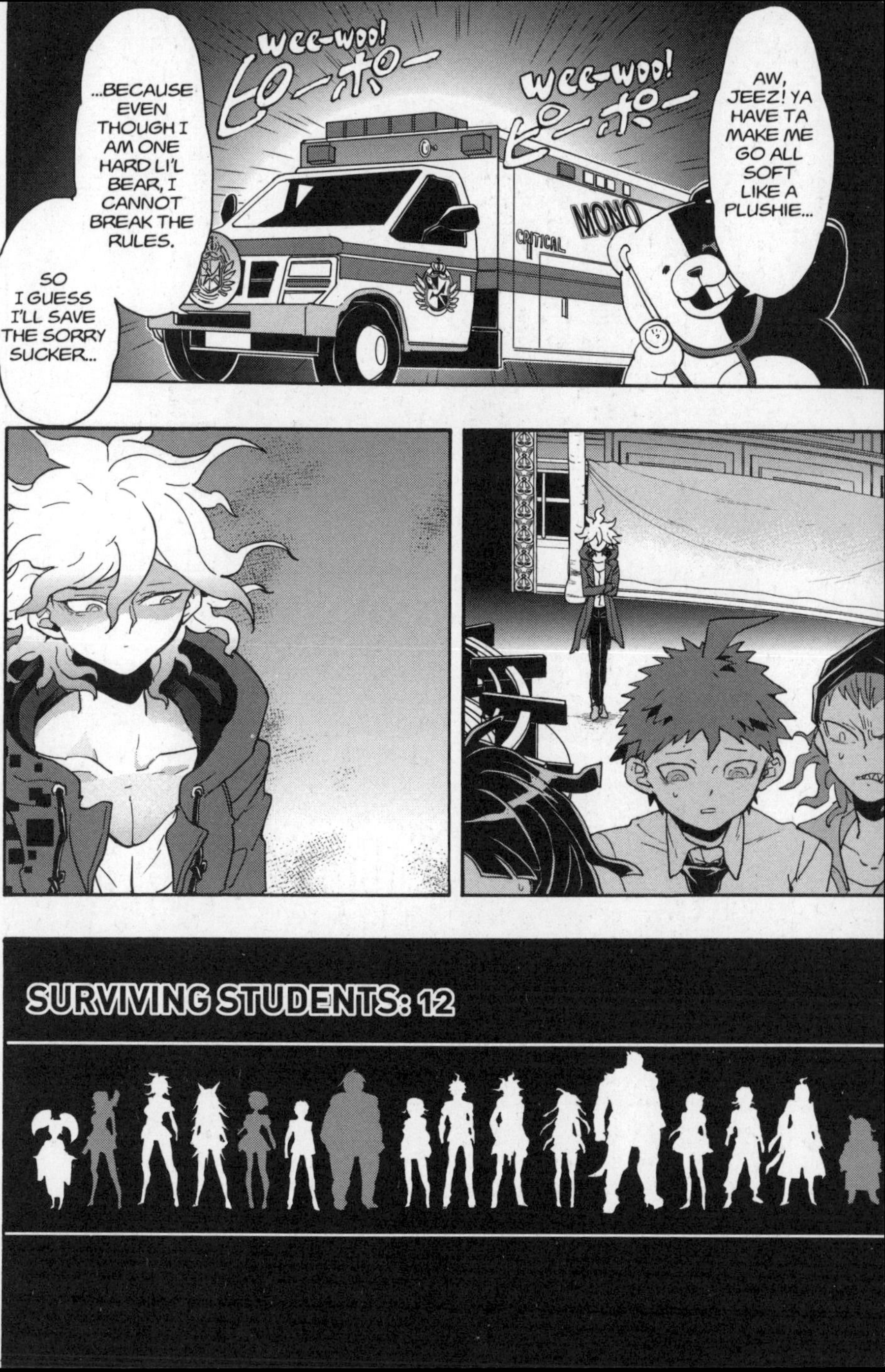
AW, JEEZ! YA HAVE TA MAKE ME GO ALL SOFT LIKE A PLUSHIE...
wee-woo! ピーポー
wee-woo! ピーポー
...BECAUSE EVEN THOUGH I AM ONE HARD LI'L BEAR, I CANNOT BREAK THE RULES.
SO I GUESS I'LL SAVE THE SORRY SUCKER...
MONO
CRITICAL
SURVIVING STUDENTS: 12

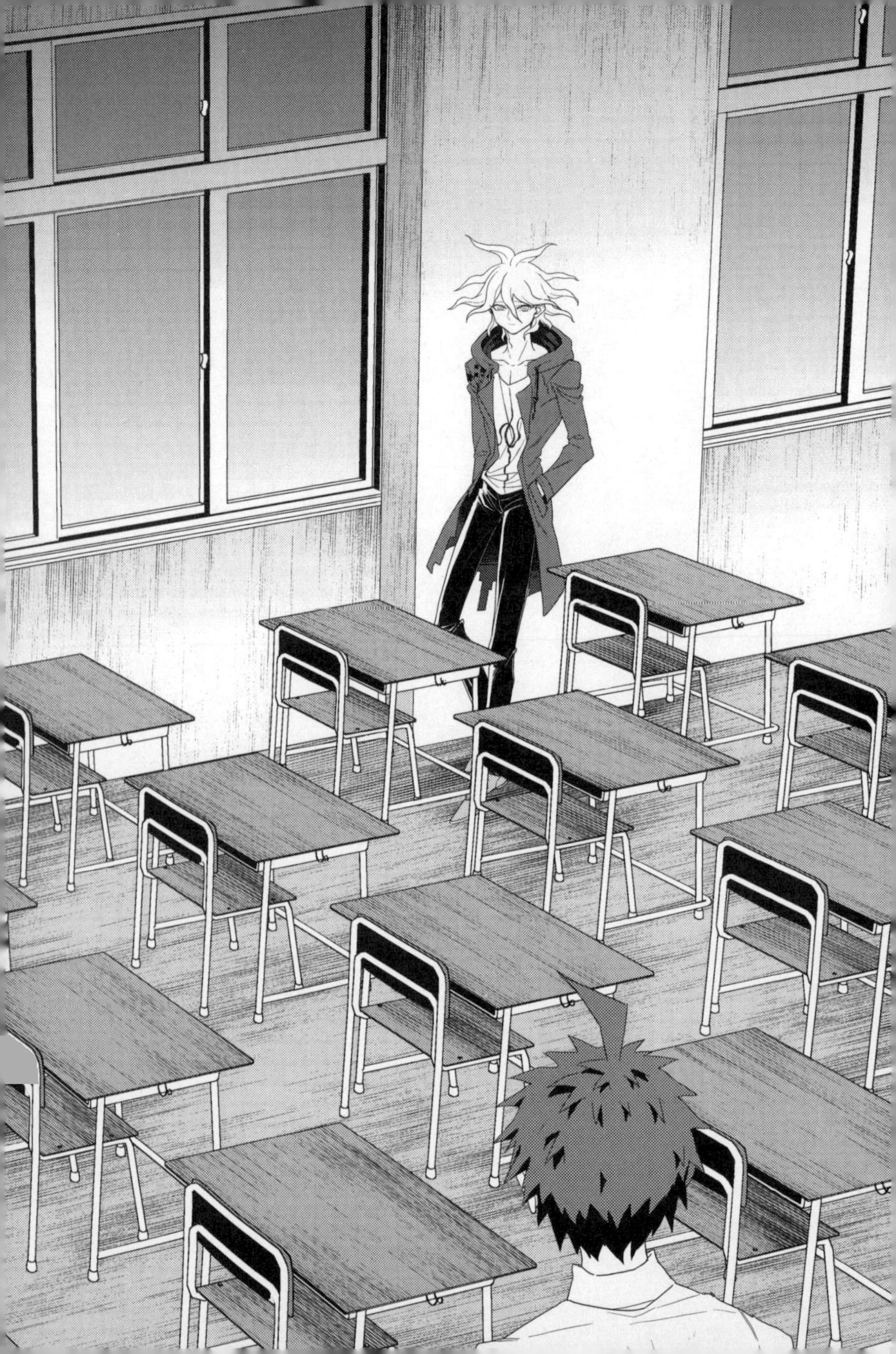

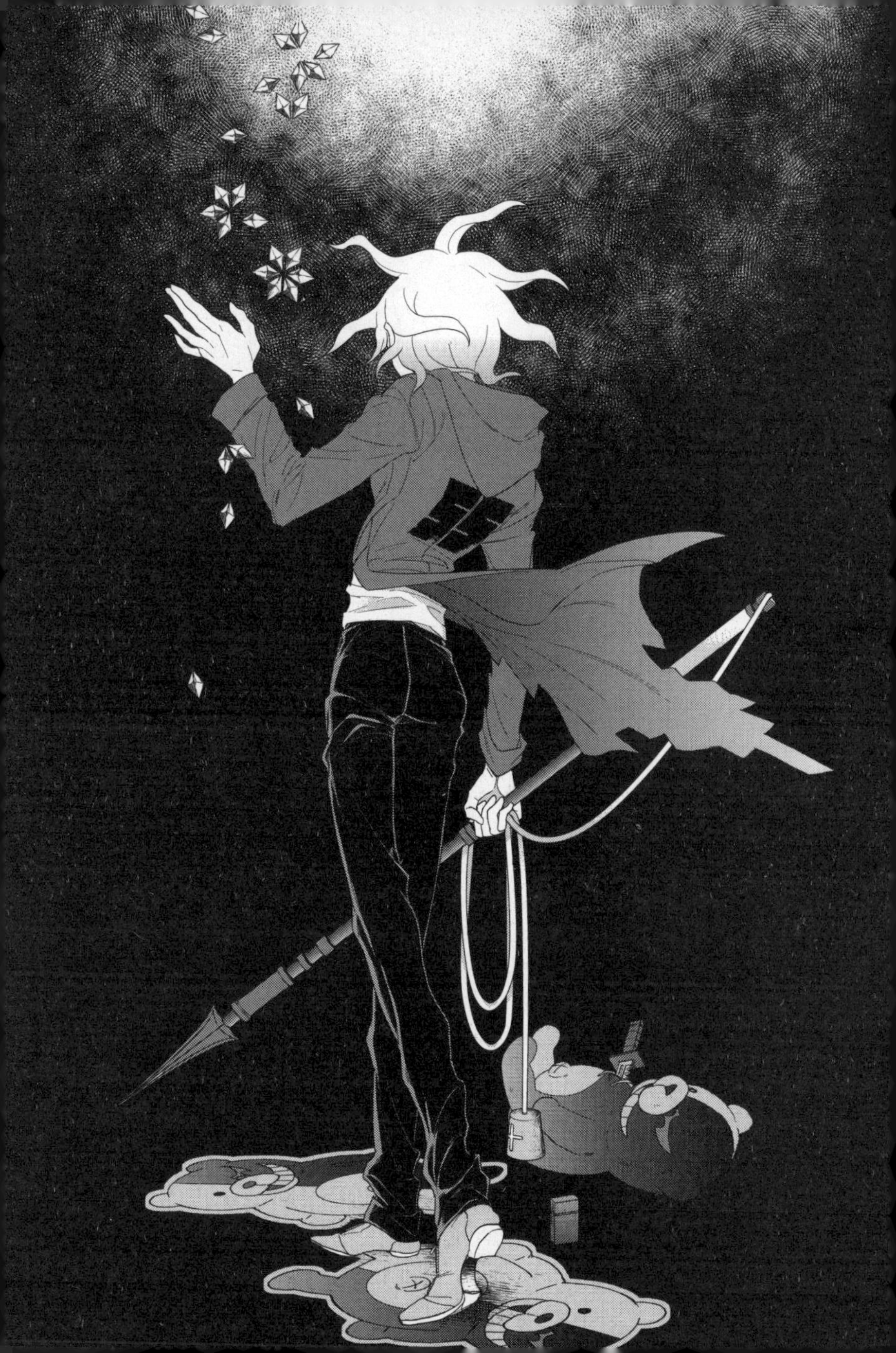

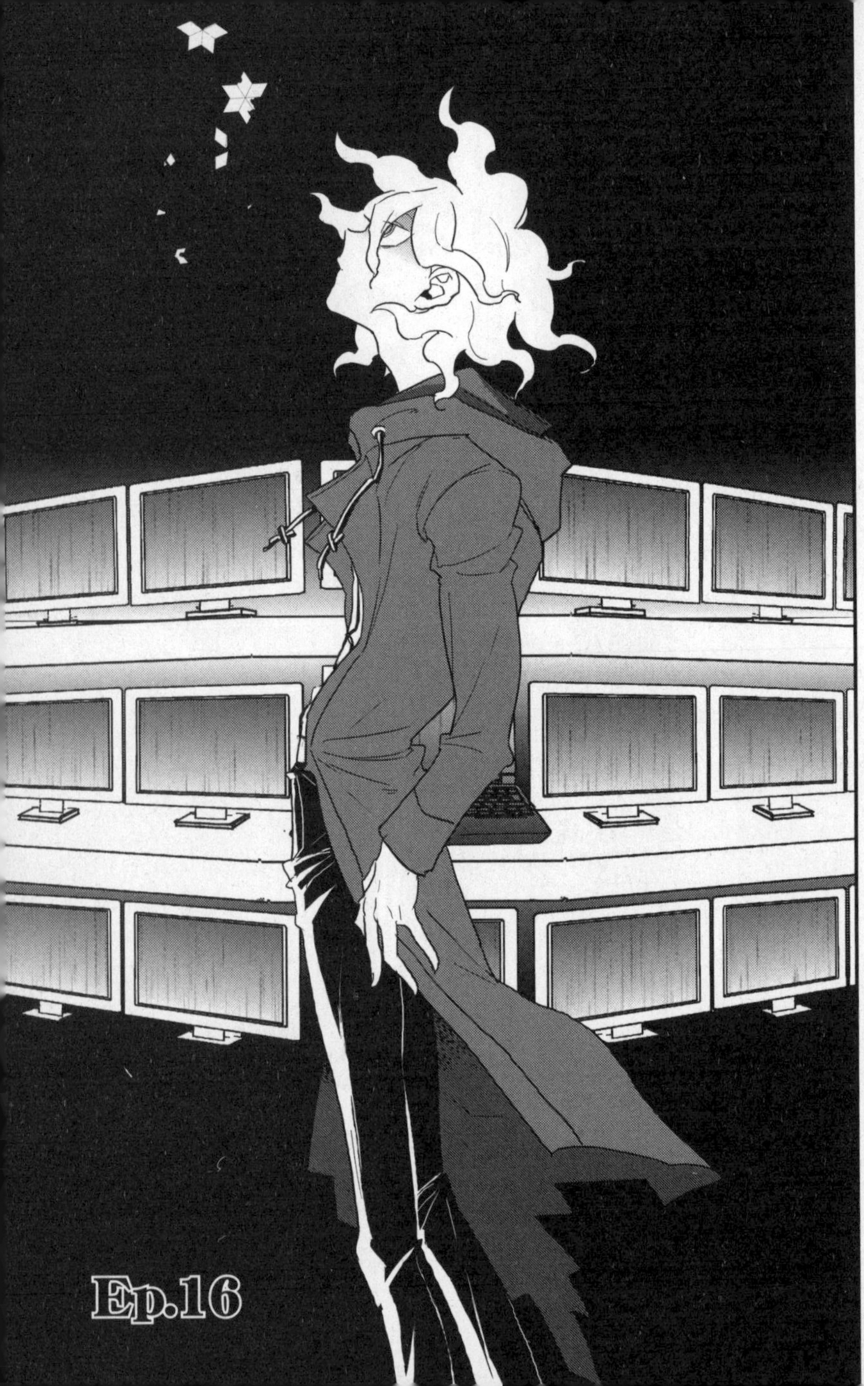
Ep.16

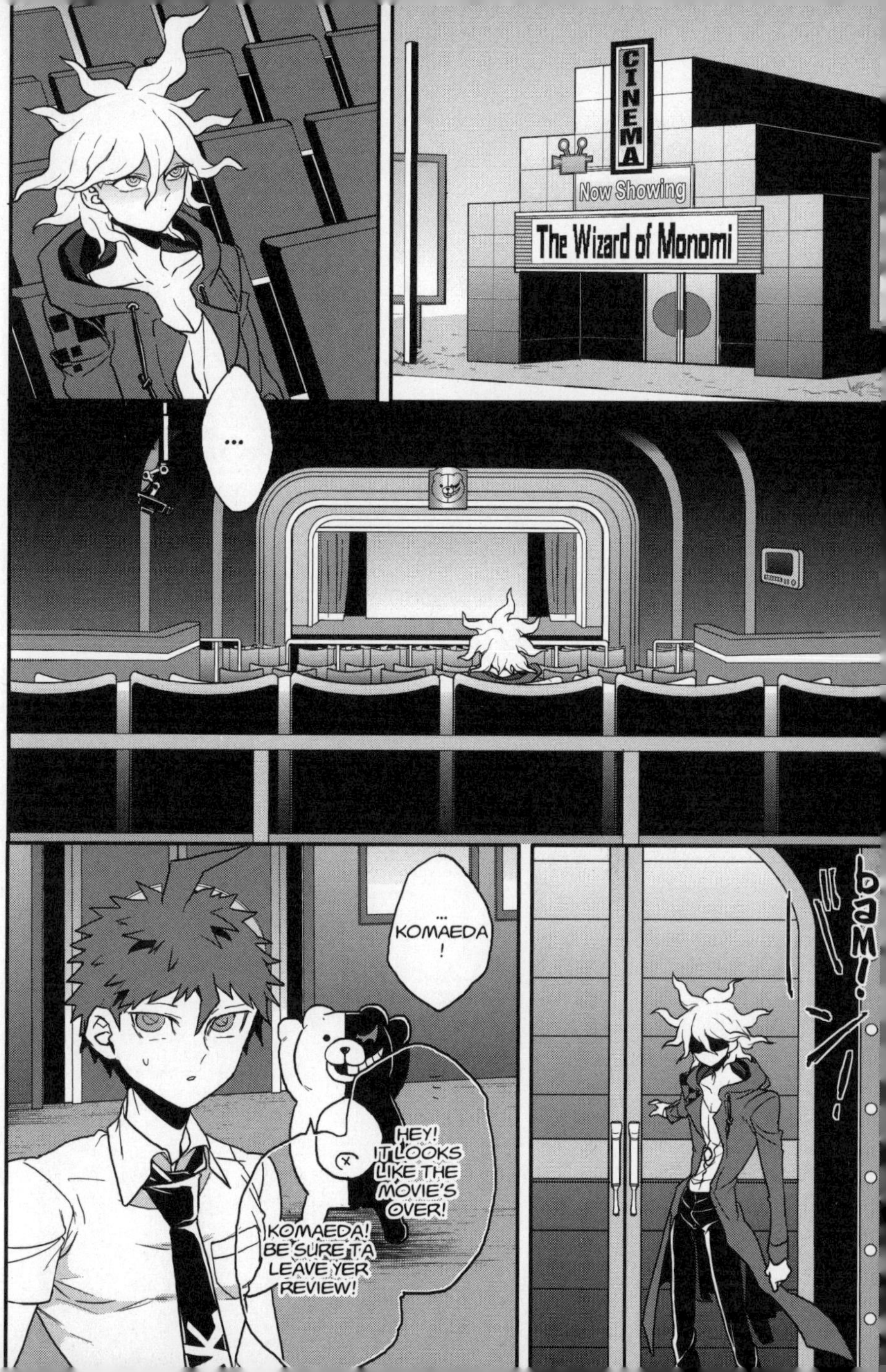
CINEMA
Now Showing
The Wizard of Monomi
...
bam!
...KOMAEDA!
HEY! IT LOOKS LIKE THE MOVIE'S OVER!
KOMAEDA! BE SURE TA LEAVE YER REVIEW!

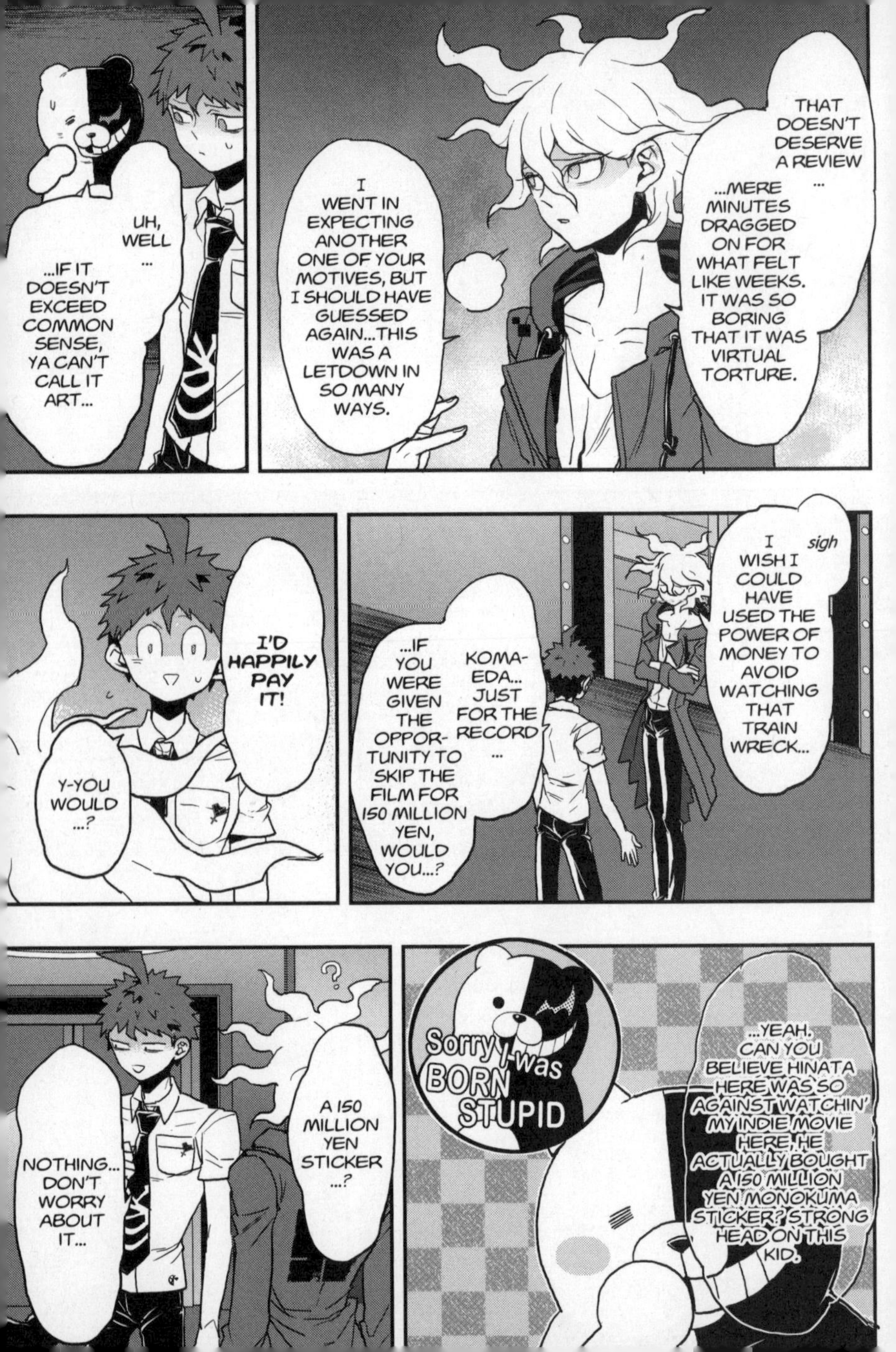
THAT DOESN'T DESERVE A REVIEW ...
...MERE MINUTES DRAGGED ON FOR WHAT FELT LIKE WEEKS. IT WAS SO BORING THAT IT WAS VIRTUAL TORTURE.
I WENT IN EXPECTING ANOTHER ONE OF YOUR MOTIVES, BUT I SHOULD HAVE GUESSED AGAIN...THIS WAS A LETDOWN IN SO MANY WAYS.
UH, WELL ...
...IF IT DOESN'T EXCEED COMMON SENSE, YA CAN'T CALL IT ART...
sigh
I WISH I COULD HAVE USED THE POWER OF MONEY TO AVOID WATCHING THAT TRAIN WRECK...
KOMAEDA... JUST FOR THE RECORD ...
...IF YOU WERE GIVEN THE OPPORTUNITY TO SKIP THE FILM FOR 150 MILLION YEN, WOULD YOU...?
I'D HAPPILY PAY IT!
Y-YOU WOULD ...?
...YEAH. CAN YOU BELIEVE HINATA HERE WAS SO AGAINST WATCHIN' MY INDIE MOVIE HERE, HE ACTUALLY BOUGHT A 150 MILLION YEN MONOKUMA STICKER? STRONG HEAD ON THIS KID.
Sorry I was BORN STUPID
?
A 150 MILLION YEN STICKER ...?
NOTHING... DON'T WORRY ABOUT IT...

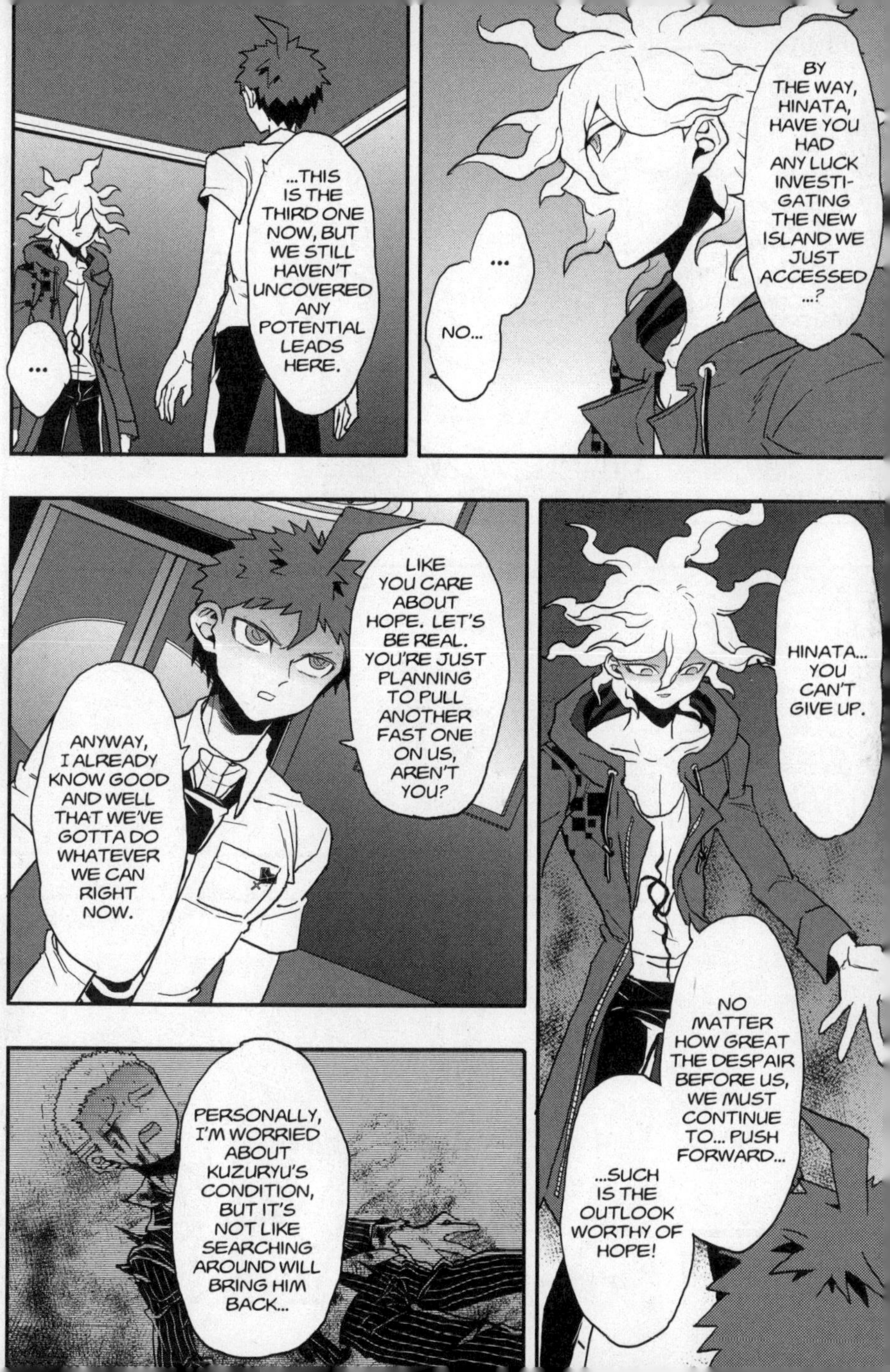
BY THE WAY, HINATA, HAVE YOU HAD ANY LUCK INVESTIGATING THE NEW ISLAND WE JUST ACCESSED...?
...
NO...
...THIS IS THE THIRD ONE NOW, BUT WE STILL HAVEN'T UNCOVERED ANY POTENTIAL LEADS HERE.
...
HINATA... YOU CAN'T GIVE UP.
NO MATTER HOW GREAT THE DESPAIR BEFORE US, WE MUST CONTINUE TO... PUSH FORWARD...
...SUCH IS THE OUTLOOK WORTHY OF HOPE!
LIKE YOU CARE ABOUT HOPE. LET'S BE REAL. YOU'RE JUST PLANNING TO PULL ANOTHER FAST ONE ON US, AREN'T YOU?
ANYWAY, I ALREADY KNOW GOOD AND WELL THAT WE'VE GOTTA DO WHATEVER WE CAN RIGHT NOW.
PERSONALLY, I'M WORRIED ABOUT KUZURYU'S CONDITION, BUT IT'S NOT LIKE SEARCHING AROUND WILL BRING HIM BACK...

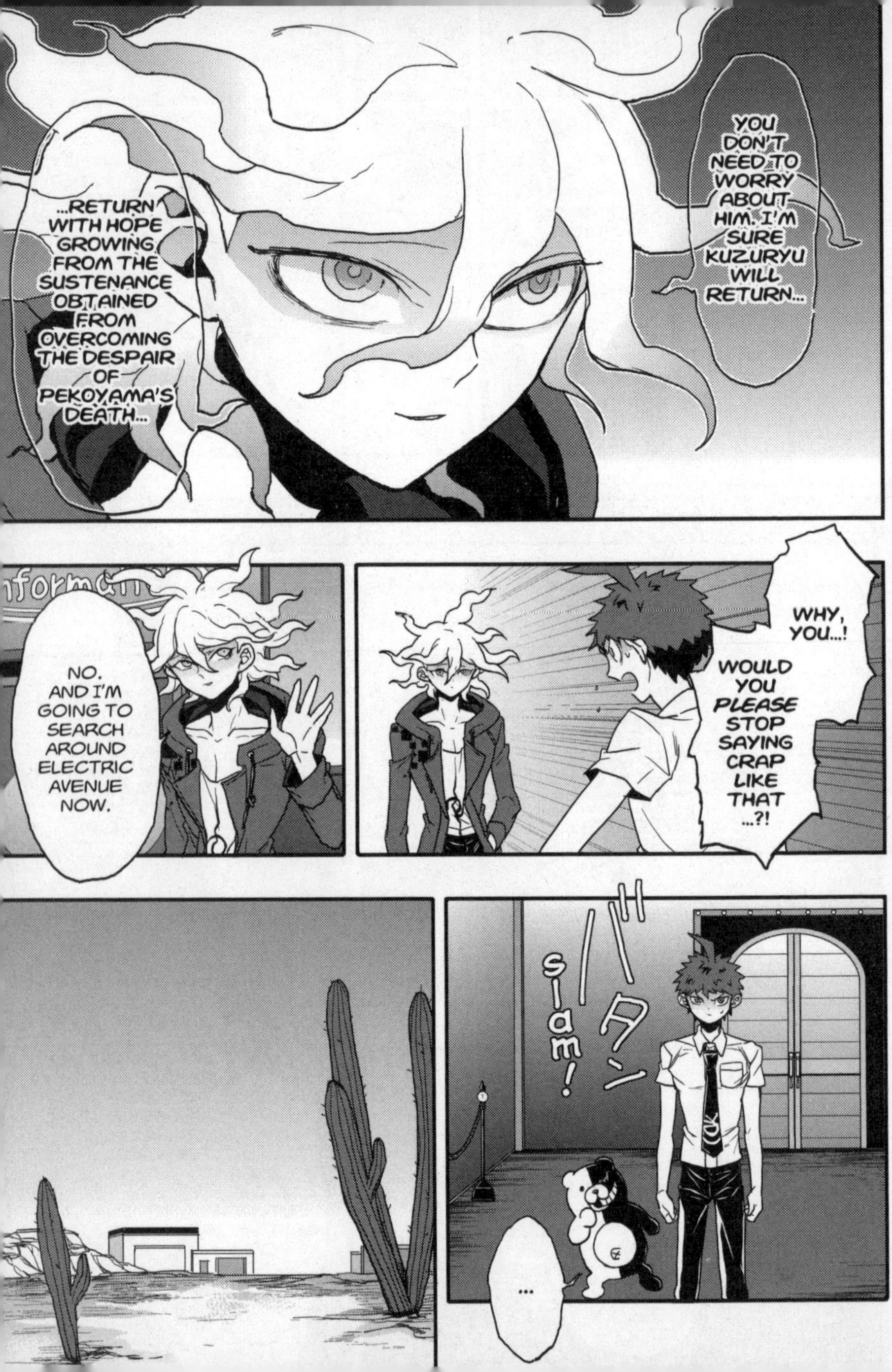
YOU DON'T NEED TO WORRY ABOUT HIM. I'M SURE KUZURYU WILL RETURN...
...RETURN WITH HOPE GROWING FROM THE SUSTENANCE OBTAINED FROM OVERCOMING THE DESPAIR OF PEKOYAMA'S DEATH...
WHY, YOU...!
WOULD YOU *PLEASE* STOP SAYING CRAP LIKE THAT...?!
NO. AND I'M GOING TO SEARCH AROUND ELECTRIC AVENUE NOW.
バタン
slam!
...

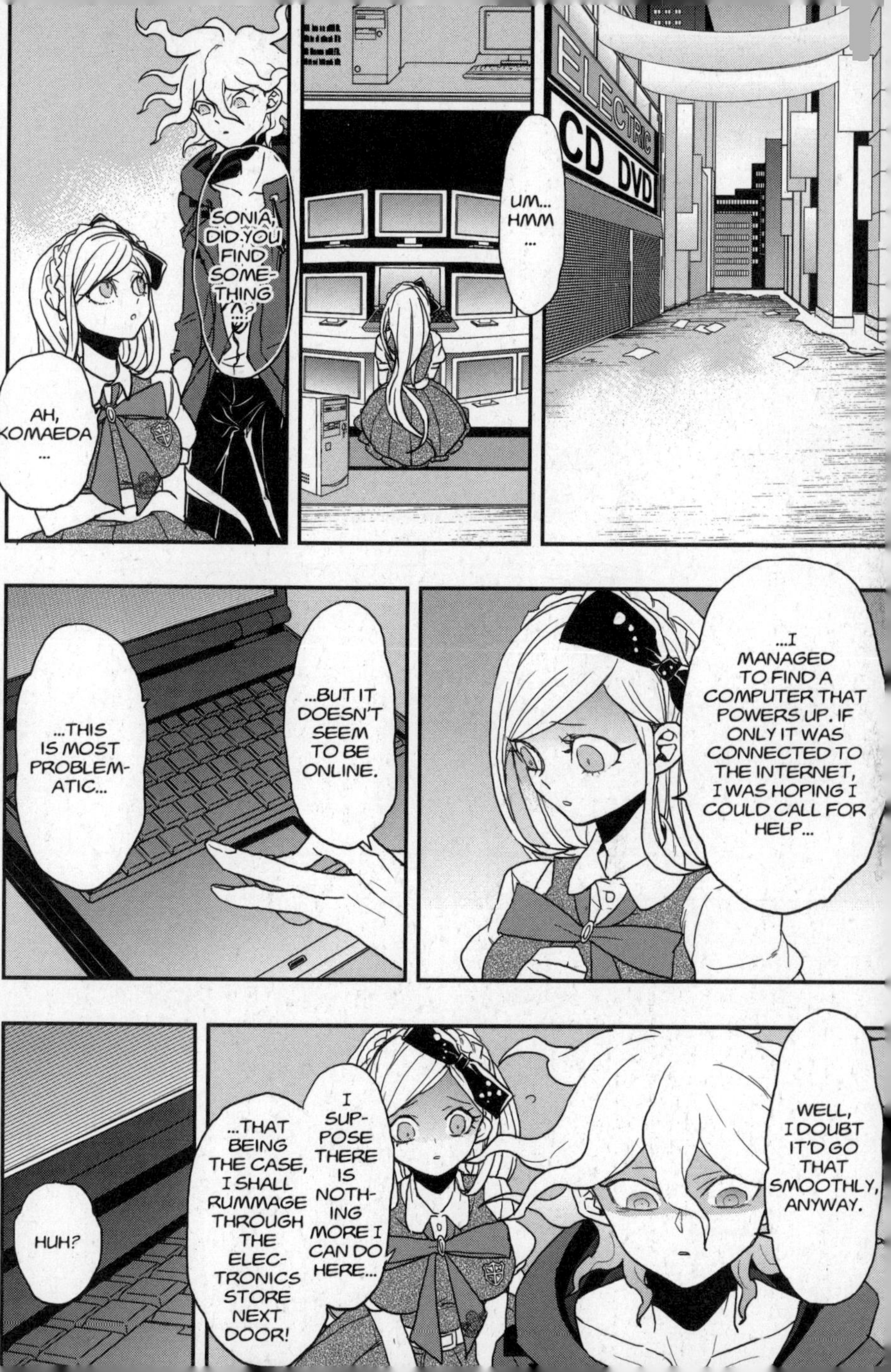
ELECTRIC
CD DVD
UM... HMM...
SONIA, DID YOU FIND SOMETHING...?
AH, KOMAEDA...
...I MANAGED TO FIND A COMPUTER THAT POWERS UP. IF ONLY IT WAS CONNECTED TO THE INTERNET, I WAS HOPING I COULD CALL FOR HELP...
...BUT IT DOESN'T SEEM TO BE ONLINE.
...THIS IS MOST PROBLEMATIC...
WELL, I DOUBT IT'D GO THAT SMOOTHLY, ANYWAY.
I SUPPOSE THERE IS NOTHING MORE I CAN DO HERE...
...THAT BEING THE CASE, I SHALL RUMMAGE THROUGH THE ELECTRONICS STORE NEXT DOOR!
HUH?

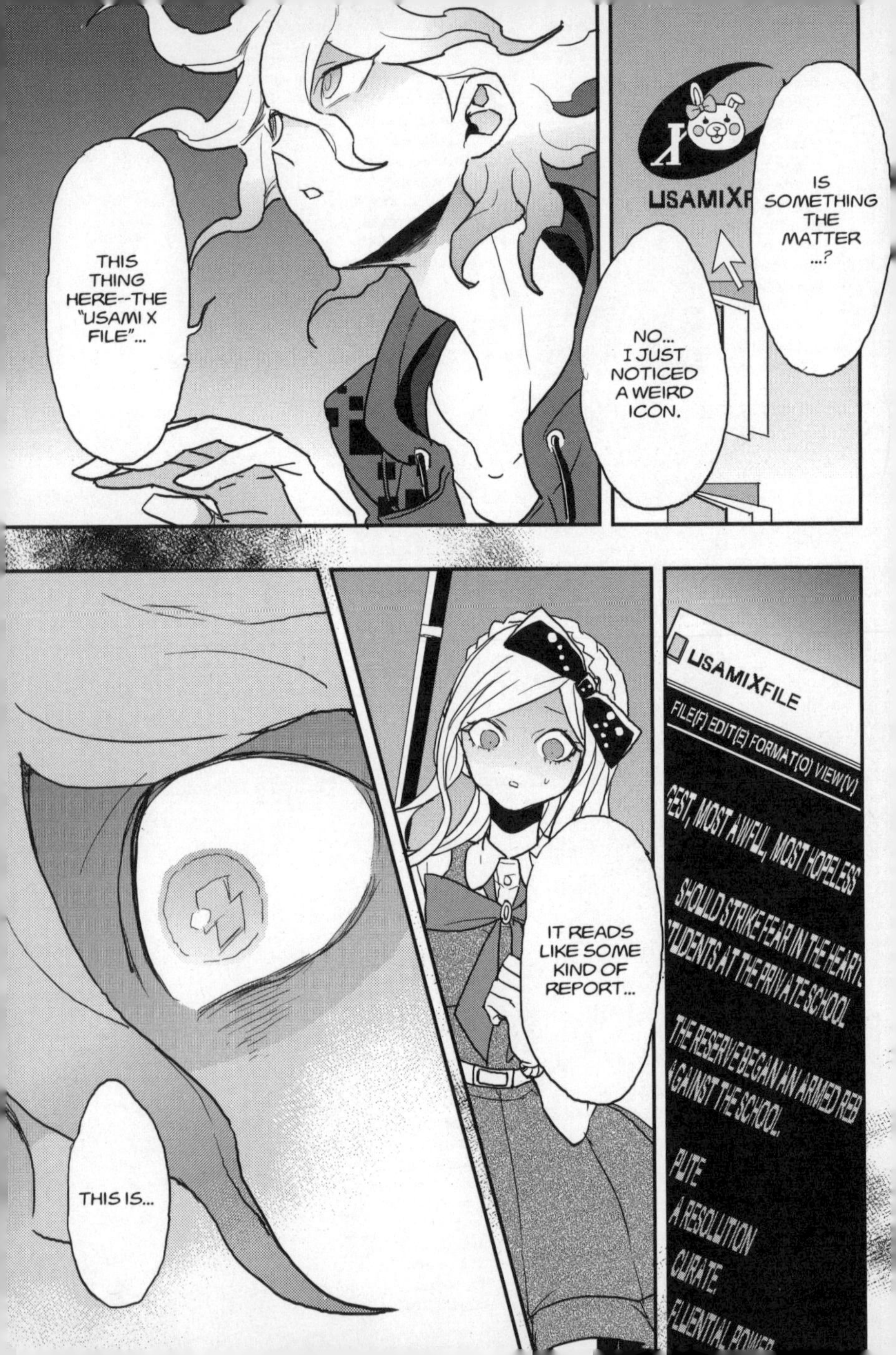
USAMIXF
IS SOMETHING THE MATTER ...?
NO... I JUST NOTICED A WEIRD ICON.
THIS THING HERE--THE "USAMI X FILE"...
USAMIXFILE
FILE(F) EDIT(E) FORMAT(O) VIEW(V)
GEST, MOST AWFUL, MOST HOPELESS
SHOULD STRIKE FEAR IN THE HEART
TUDENTS AT THE PRIVATE SCHOOL
THE RESERVE BEGAN AN ARMED REB
AGAINST THE SCHOOL.
PUTE
A RESOLUTION
CURATE.
FLUENTIAL POWER
IT READS LIKE SOME KIND OF REPORT...
THIS IS...

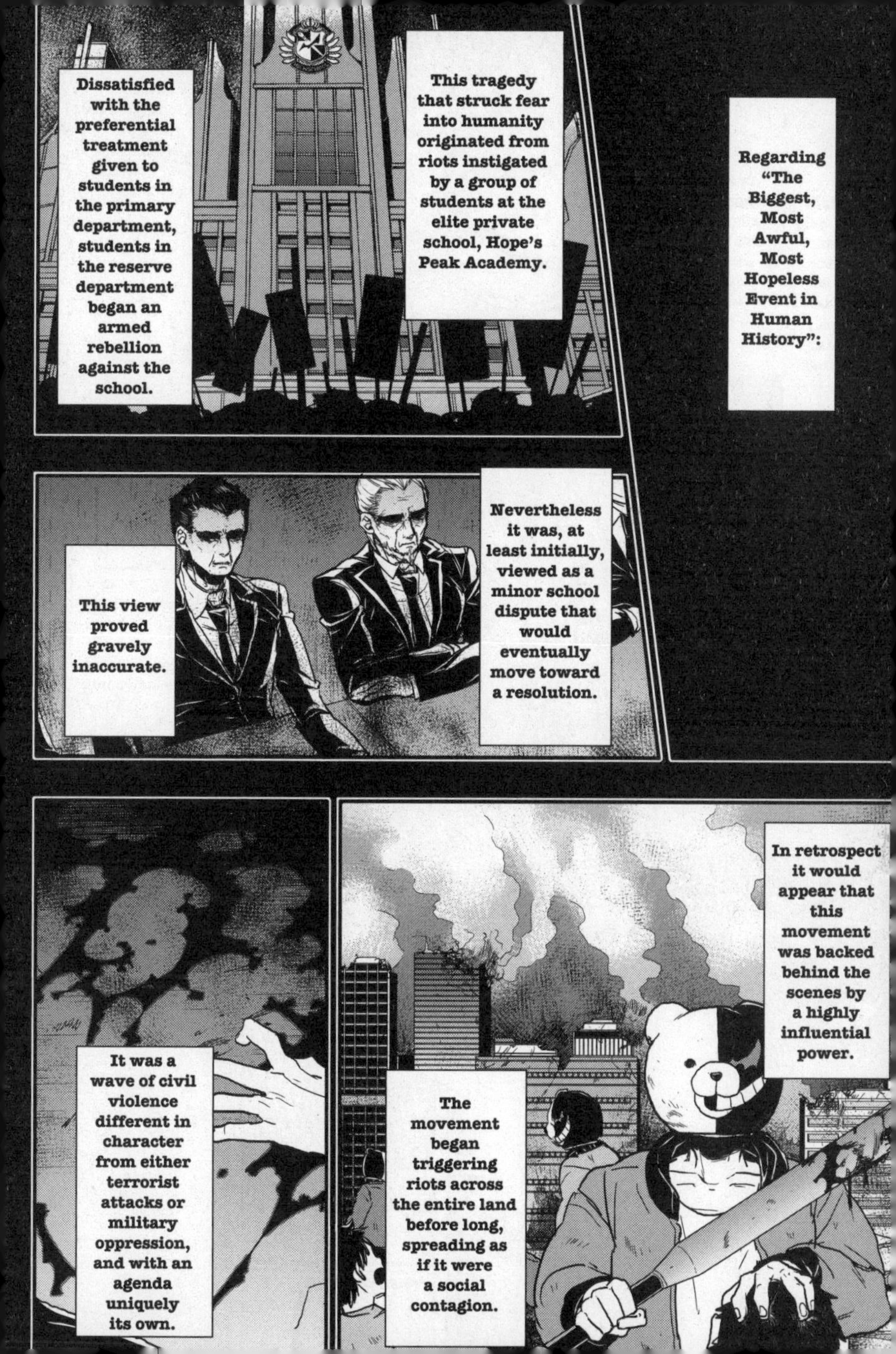
Regarding "The Biggest, Most Awful, Most Hopeless Event in Human History":
This tragedy that struck fear into humanity originated from riots instigated by a group of students at the elite private school, Hope's Peak Academy.
Dissatisfied with the preferential treatment given to students in the primary department, students in the reserve department began an armed rebellion against the school.
Nevertheless it was, at least initially, viewed as a minor school dispute that would eventually move toward a resolution.
This view proved gravely inaccurate.
In retrospect it would appear that this movement was backed behind the scenes by a highly influential power.
The movement began triggering riots across the entire land before long, spreading as if it were a social contagion.
It was a wave of civil violence different in character from either terrorist attacks or military oppression, and with an agenda uniquely its own.

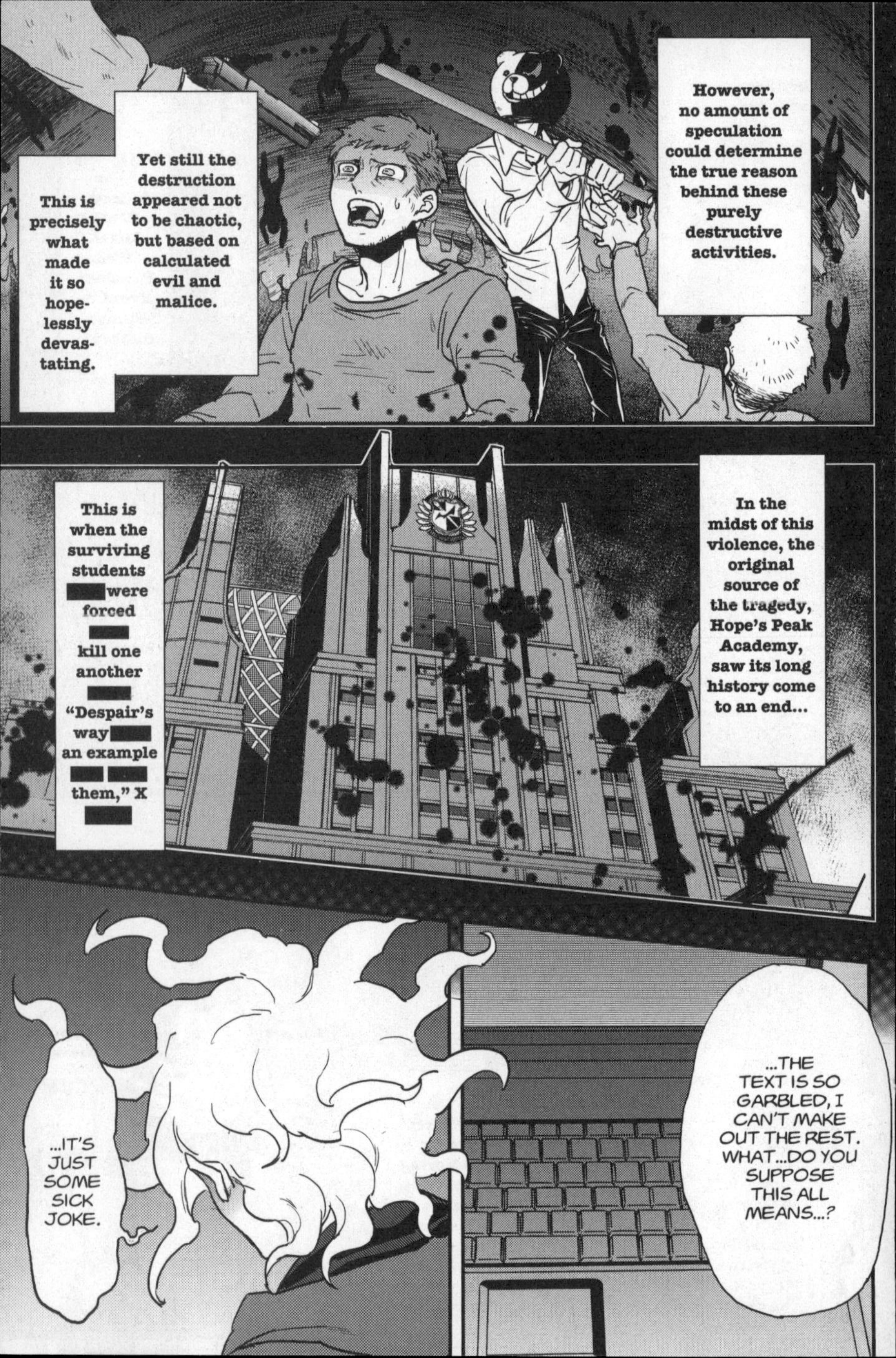
However, no amount of speculation could determine the true reason behind these purely destructive activities.
Yet still the destruction appeared not to be chaotic, but based on calculated evil and malice.
This is precisely what made it so hopelessly devastating.
In the midst of this violence, the original source of the tragedy, Hope's Peak Academy, saw its long history come to an end...
This is when the surviving students [redacted] were forced [redacted] kill one another [redacted] "Despair's way [redacted] an example [redacted] [redacted] them," X [redacted]
...THE TEXT IS SO GARBLED, I CAN'T MAKE OUT THE REST. WHAT...DO YOU SUPPOSE THIS ALL MEANS...?
...IT'S JUST SOME SICK JOKE.

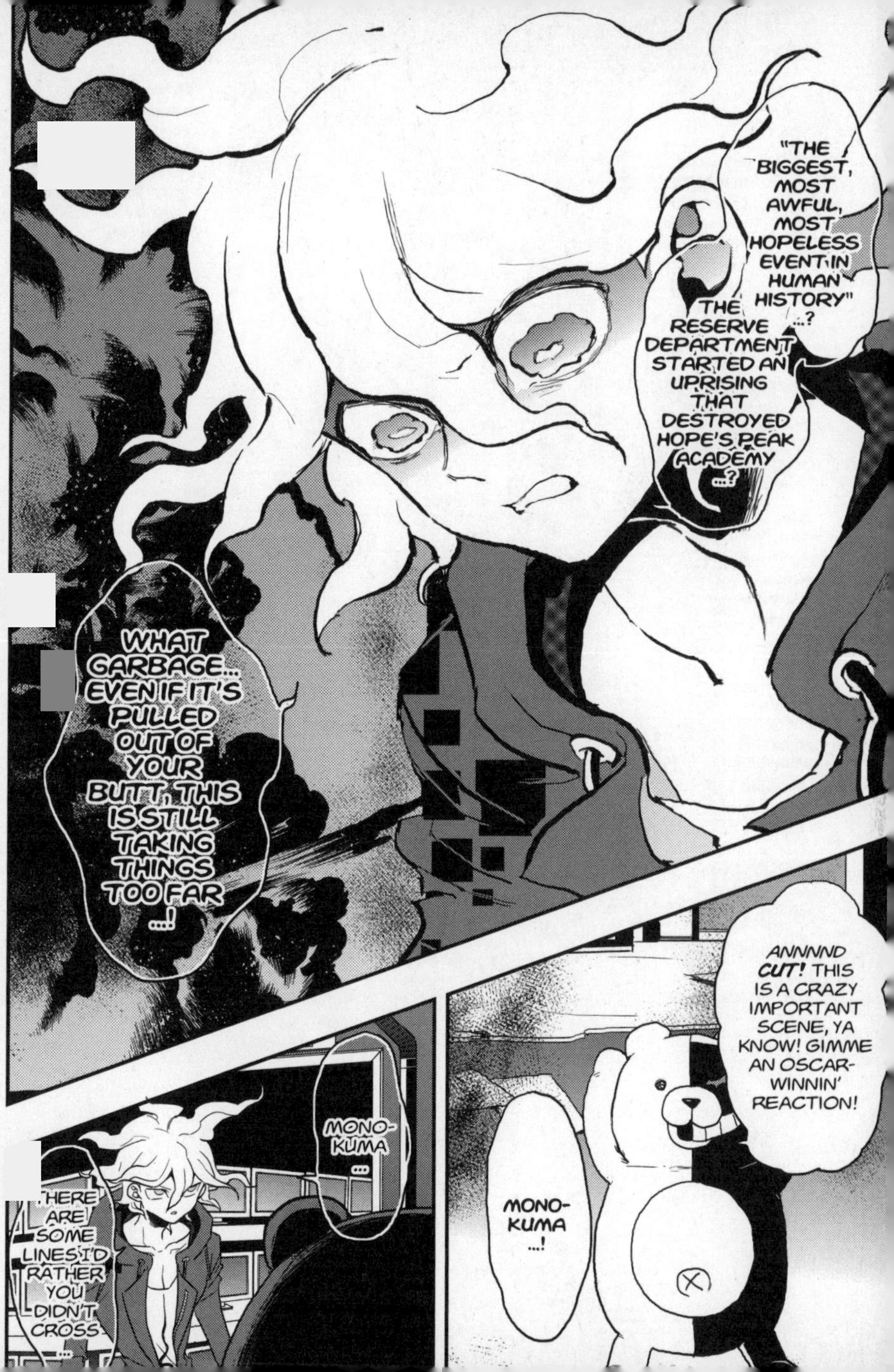
"THE BIGGEST, MOST AWFUL, MOST HOPELESS EVENT IN HUMAN HISTORY" ...?
THE RESERVE DEPARTMENT STARTED AN UPRISING THAT DESTROYED HOPE'S PEAK ACADEMY ...?
WHAT GARBAGE... EVEN IF IT'S PULLED OUT OF YOUR BUTT, THIS IS STILL TAKING THINGS TOO FAR ...!
ANNNND CUT! THIS IS A CRAZY IMPORTANT SCENE, YA KNOW! GIMME AN OSCAR-WINNIN' REACTION!
MONO-KUMA ...!
MONO-KUMA ...
THERE ARE SOME LINES I'D RATHER YOU DIDN'T CROSS ...

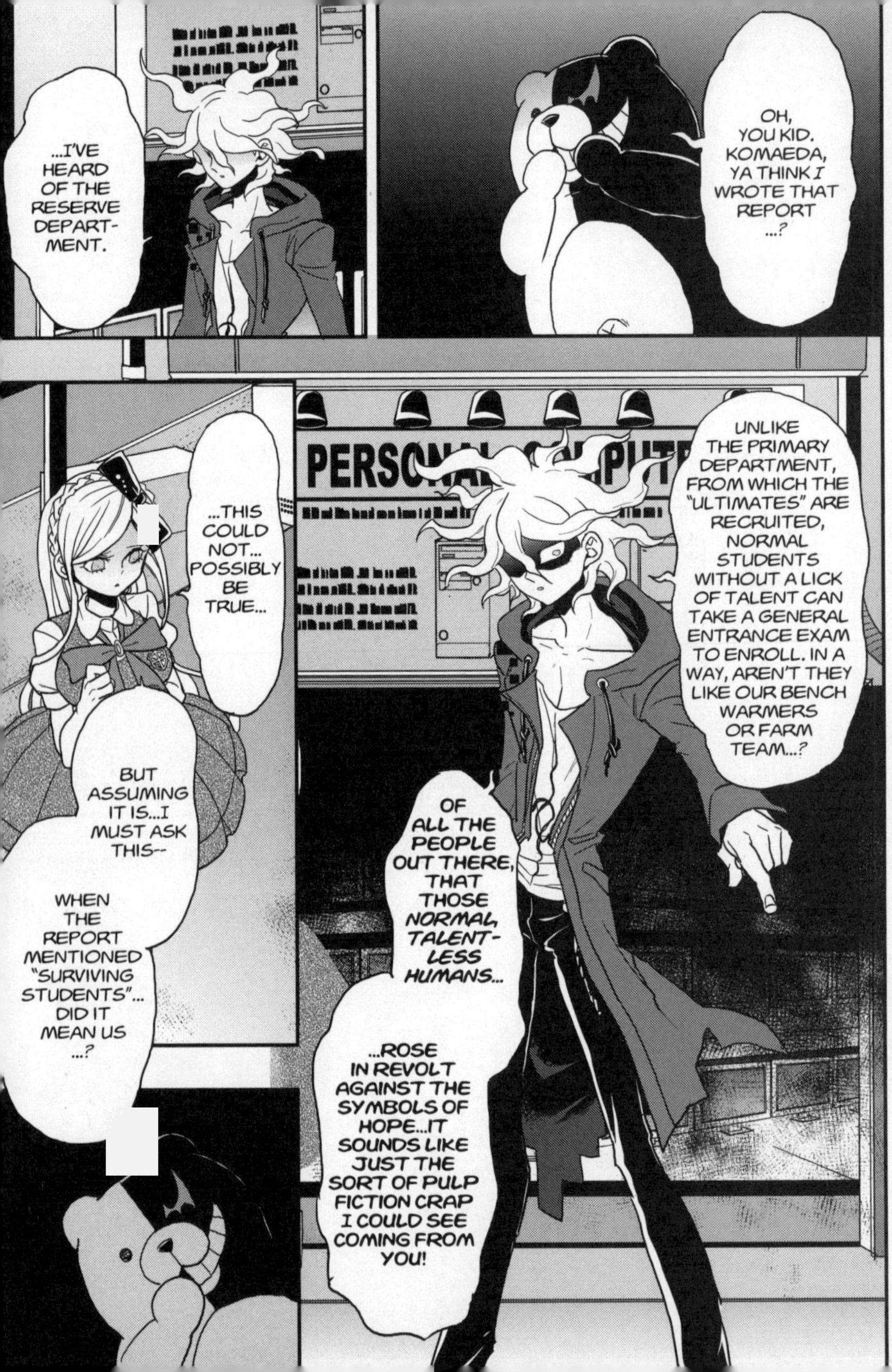
OH, YOU KID. KOMAEDA, YA THINK *I* WROTE THAT REPORT ...?
...I'VE HEARD OF THE RESERVE DEPART-MENT.
PERSONAL
UNLIKE THE PRIMARY DEPARTMENT, FROM WHICH THE "ULTIMATES" ARE RECRUITED, NORMAL STUDENTS WITHOUT A LICK OF TALENT CAN TAKE A GENERAL ENTRANCE EXAM TO ENROLL. IN A WAY, AREN'T THEY LIKE OUR BENCH WARMERS OR FARM TEAM...?
OF ALL THE PEOPLE OUT THERE, THAT THOSE *NORMAL, TALENT-LESS HUMANS*...
...ROSE IN REVOLT AGAINST THE SYMBOLS OF HOPE...IT SOUNDS LIKE JUST THE SORT OF PULP FICTION CRAP I COULD SEE COMING FROM YOU!
...THIS COULD NOT... POSSIBLY BE TRUE...
BUT ASSUMING IT IS...I MUST ASK THIS--
WHEN THE REPORT MENTIONED "SURVIVING STUDENTS"... DID IT MEAN US ...?

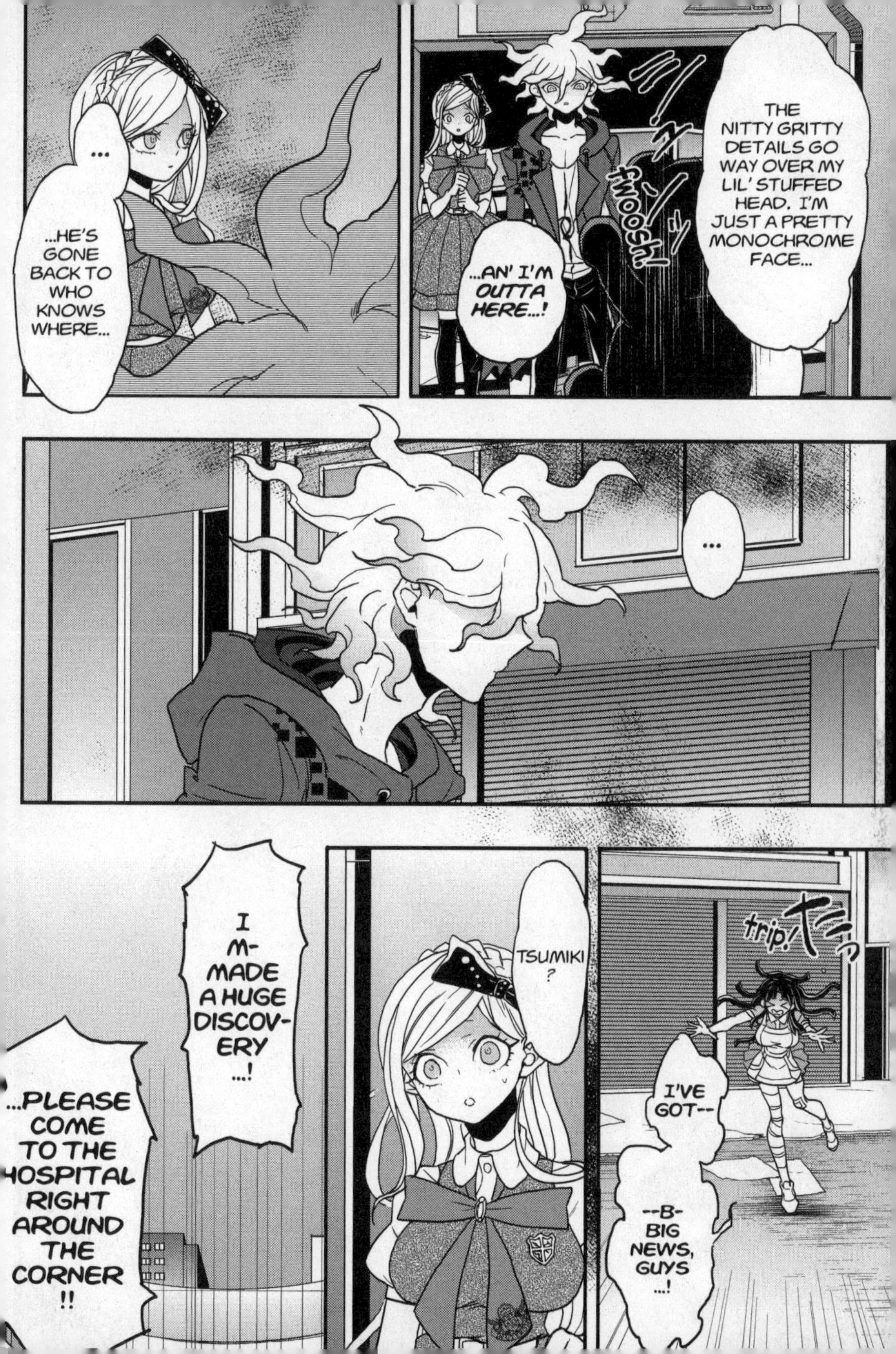
THE NITTY GRITTY DETAILS GO WAY OVER MY LIL' STUFFED HEAD. I'M JUST A PRETTY MONOCHROME FACE...
fwoosh!
...AN' I'M OUTTA HERE...!
...
...HE'S GONE BACK TO WHO KNOWS WHERE...
...
trip!
I'VE GOT--
--B-BIG NEWS, GUYS...!
TSUMIKI?
I M-MADE A HUGE DISCOVERY...!
...PLEASE COME TO THE HOSPITAL RIGHT AROUND THE CORNER!!

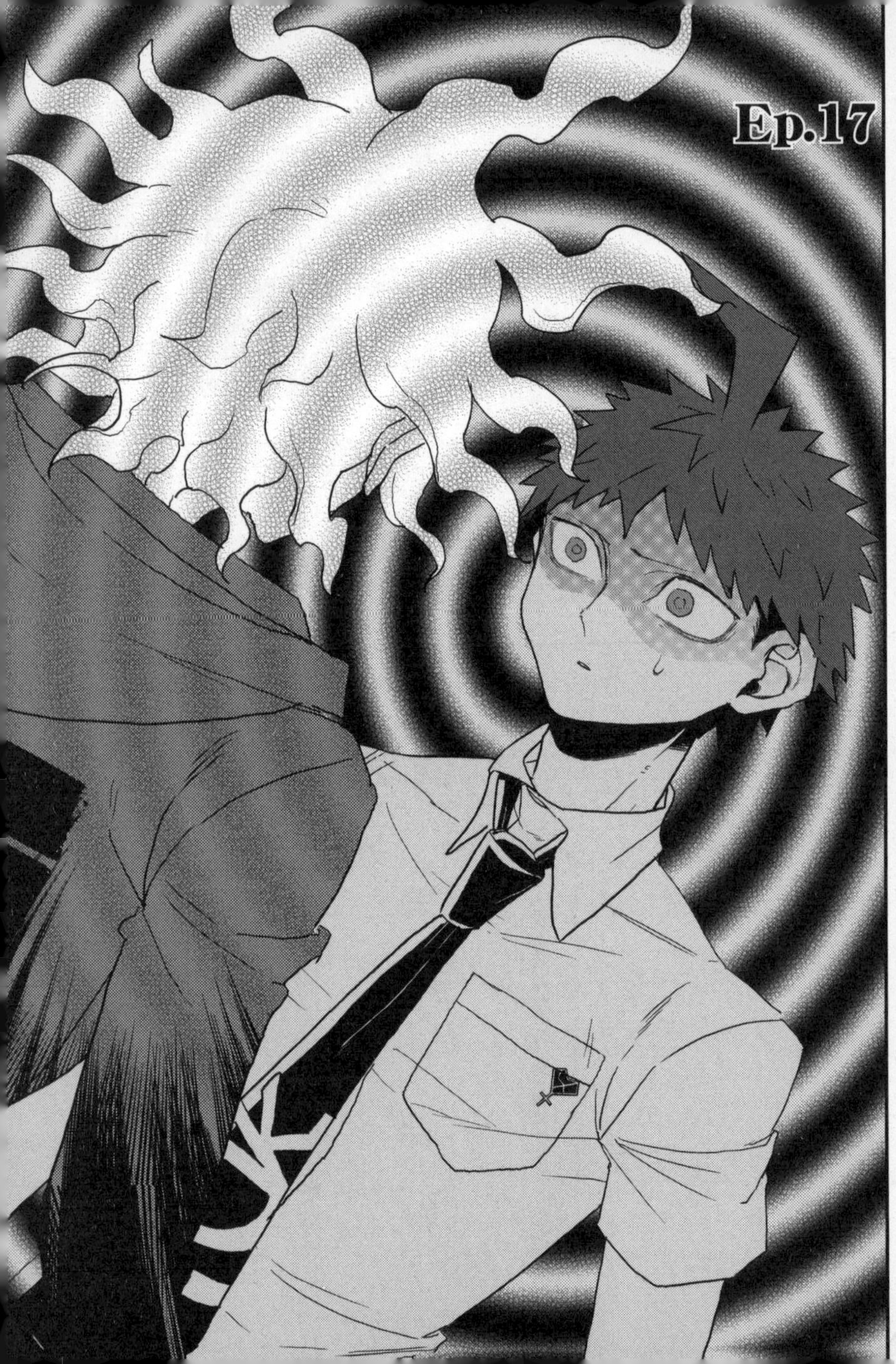
Ep.17

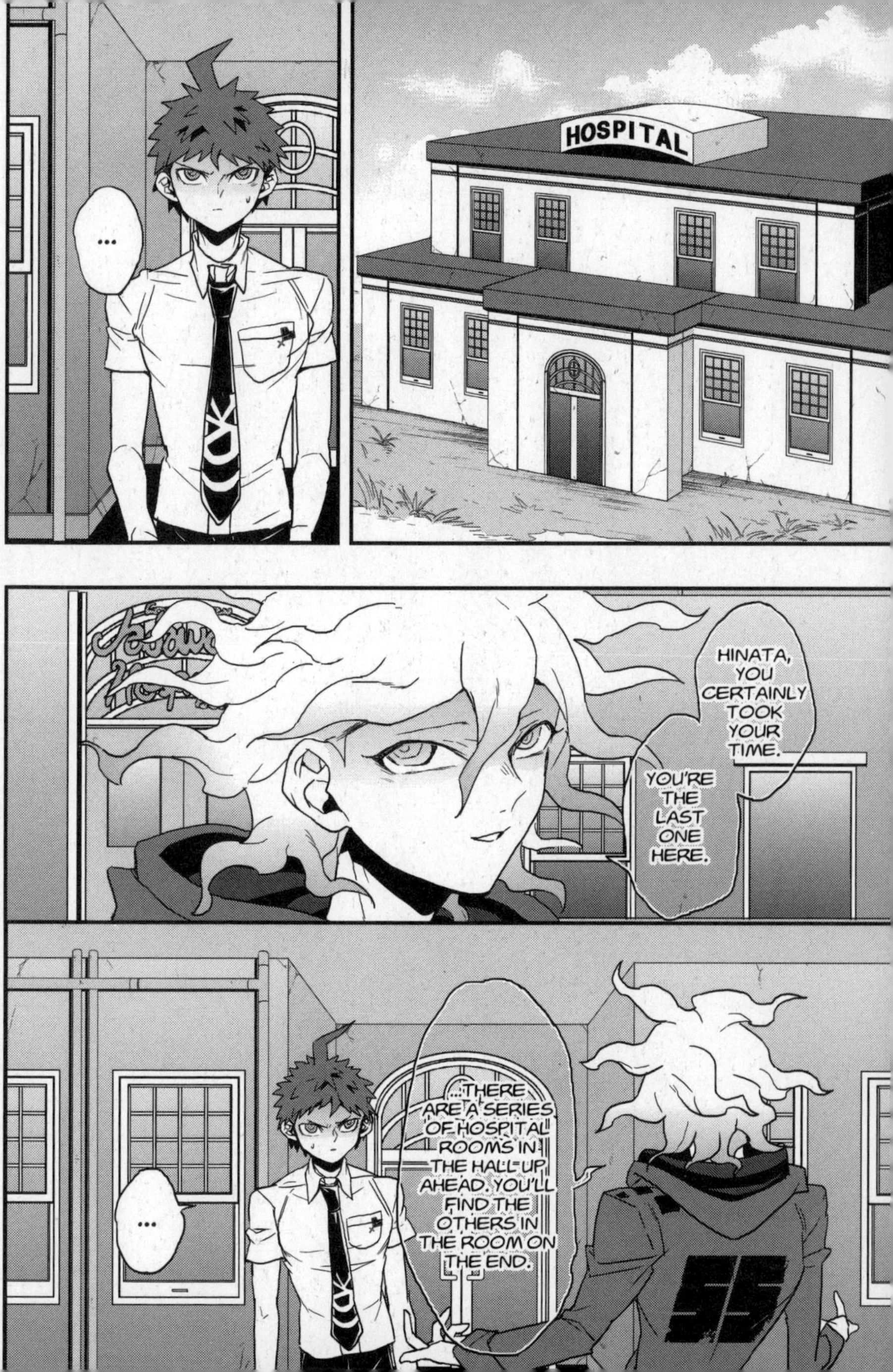
HOSPITAL
...
HINATA, YOU CERTAINLY TOOK YOUR TIME.
YOU'RE THE LAST ONE HERE.
...THERE ARE A SERIES OF HOSPITAL ROOMS IN THE HALL UP AHEAD. YOU'LL FIND THE OTHERS IN THE ROOM ON THE END.
...

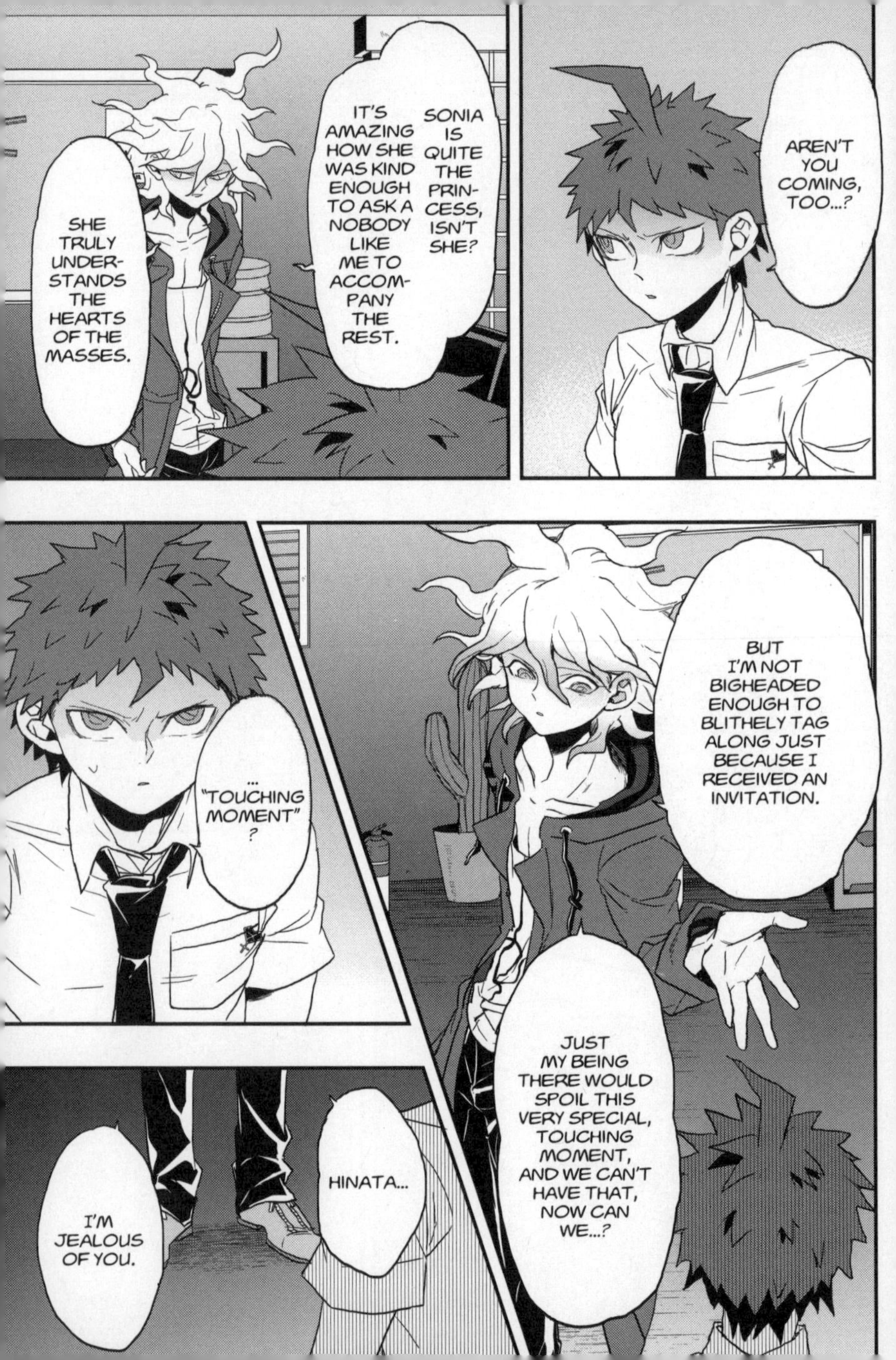
AREN'T YOU COMING, TOO...?
SONIA IS QUITE THE PRINCESS, ISN'T SHE?
IT'S AMAZING HOW SHE WAS KIND ENOUGH TO ASK A NOBODY LIKE ME TO ACCOMPANY THE REST.
SHE TRULY UNDERSTANDS THE HEARTS OF THE MASSES.
BUT I'M NOT BIGHEADED ENOUGH TO BLITHELY TAG ALONG JUST BECAUSE I RECEIVED AN INVITATION.
JUST MY BEING THERE WOULD SPOIL THIS VERY SPECIAL, TOUCHING MOMENT, AND WE CAN'T HAVE THAT, NOW CAN WE...?
... "TOUCHING MOMENT" ?
HINATA...
I'M JEALOUS OF YOU.

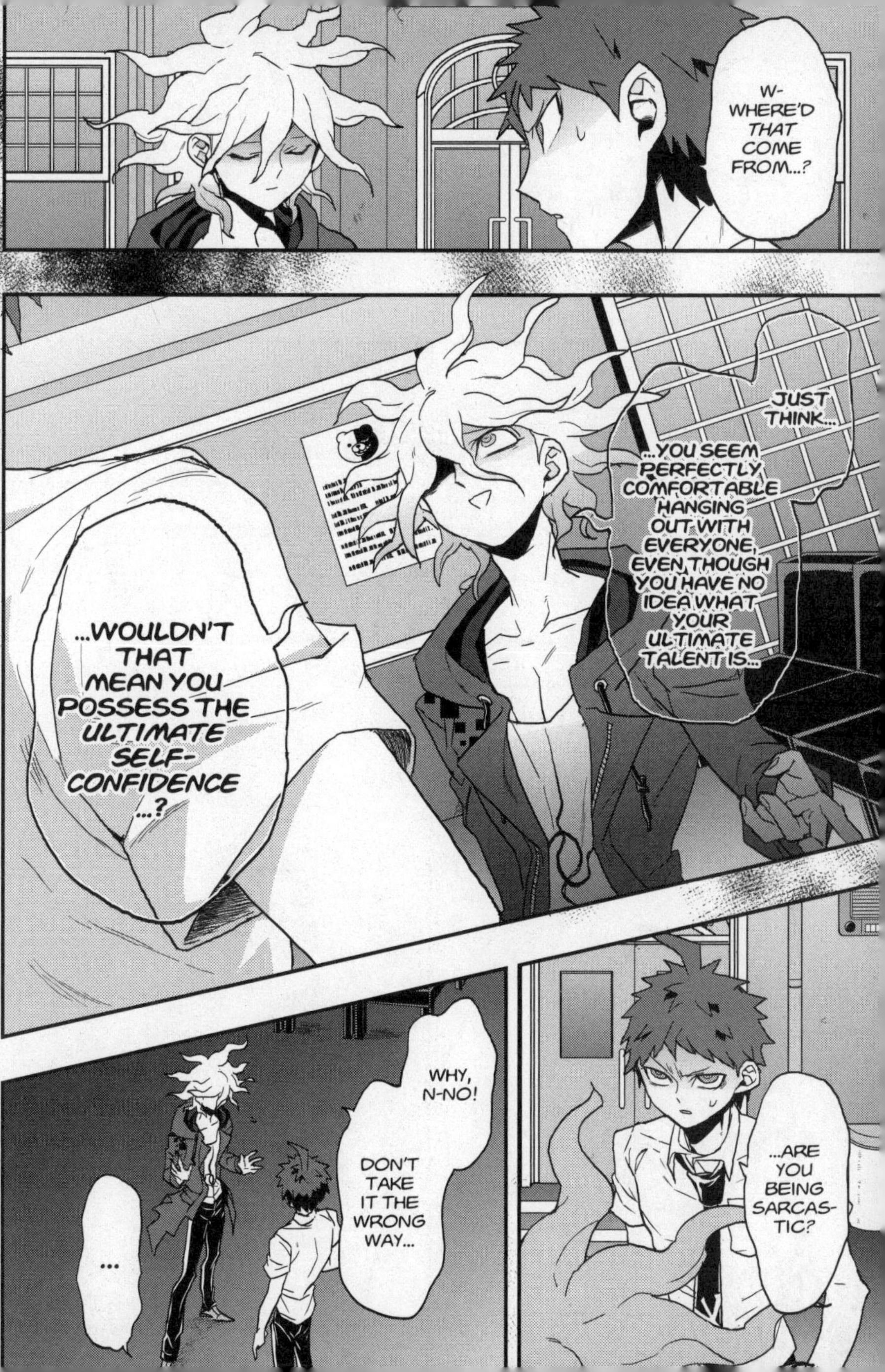
W-WHERE'D THAT COME FROM...?
JUST THINK...
...YOU SEEM PERFECTLY COMFORTABLE HANGING OUT WITH EVERYONE, EVEN THOUGH YOU HAVE NO IDEA WHAT YOUR ULTIMATE TALENT IS...
...WOULDN'T THAT MEAN YOU POSSESS THE ULTIMATE SELF-CONFIDENCE ...?
...ARE YOU BEING SARCASTIC?
WHY, N-NO!
DON'T TAKE IT THE WRONG WAY...
...

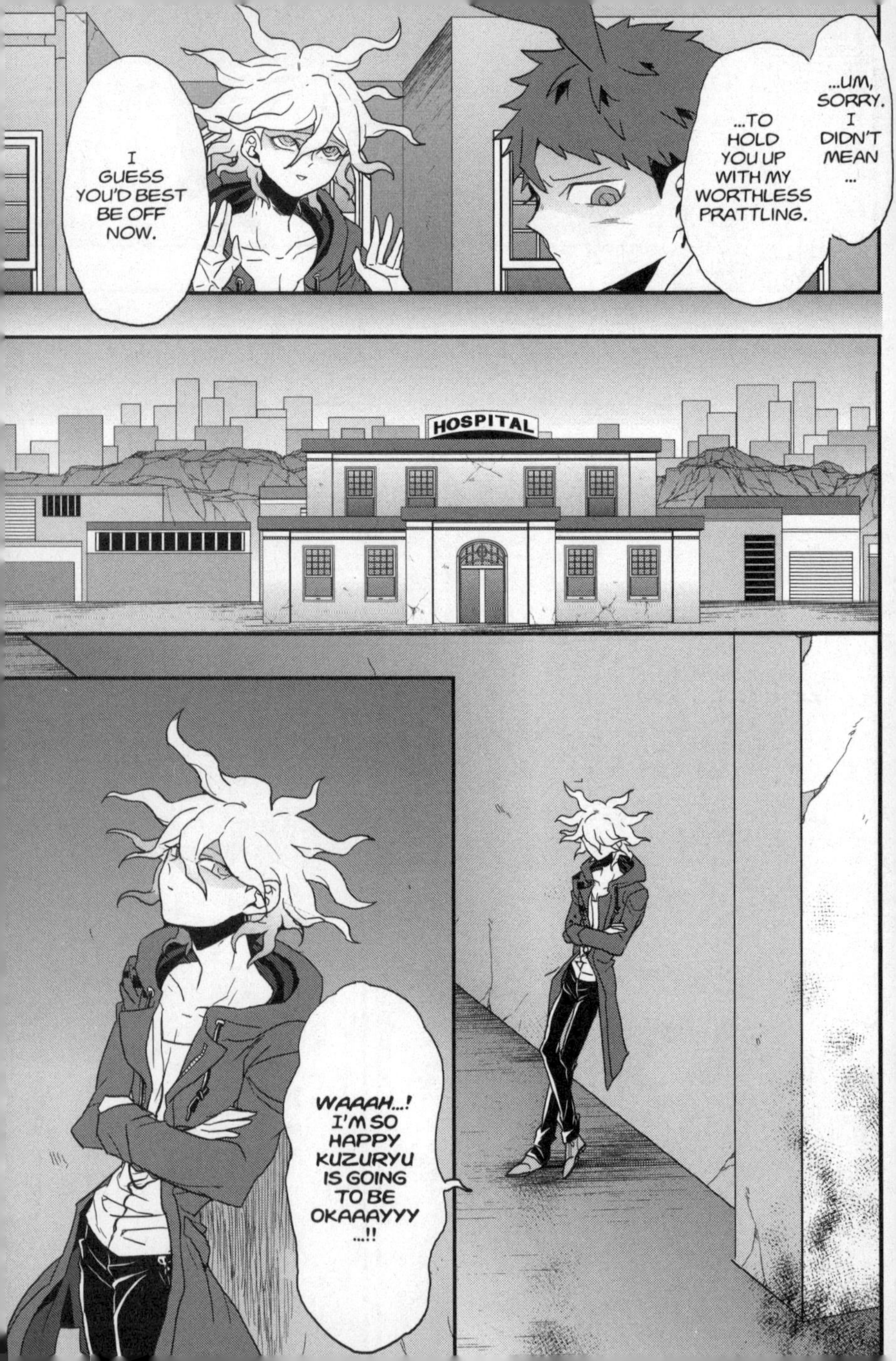
...UM, SORRY. I DIDN'T MEAN ...
...TO HOLD YOU UP WITH MY WORTHLESS PRATTLING.
I GUESS YOU'D BEST BE OFF NOW.
HOSPITAL
WAAAH...! I'M SO HAPPY KUZURYU IS GOING TO BE OKAAAYYY ...!!

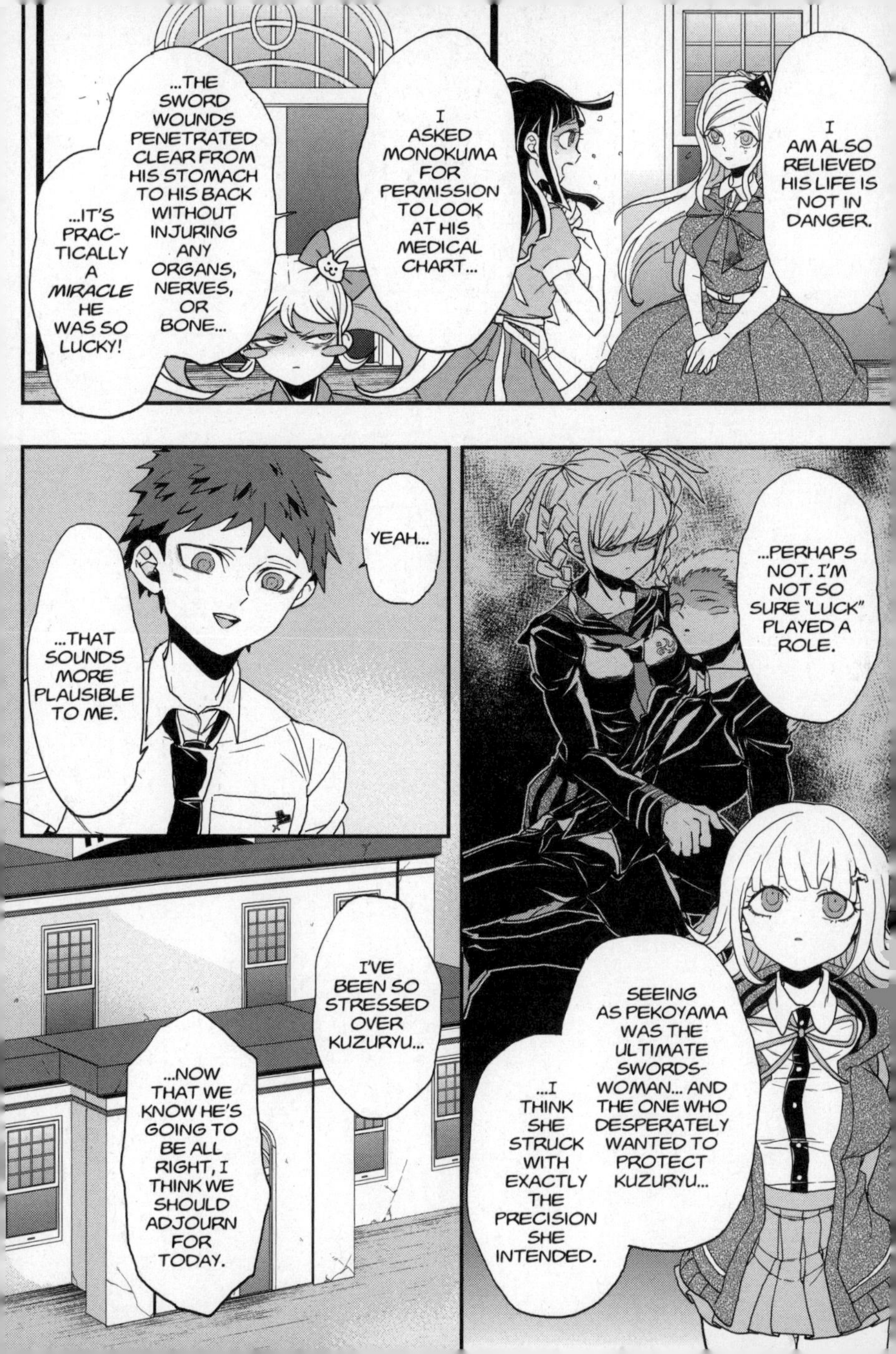
I AM ALSO RELIEVED HIS LIFE IS NOT IN DANGER.
I ASKED MONOKUMA FOR PERMISSION TO LOOK AT HIS MEDICAL CHART...
...THE SWORD WOUNDS PENETRATED CLEAR FROM HIS STOMACH TO HIS BACK WITHOUT INJURING ANY ORGANS, NERVES, OR BONE...
...IT'S PRACTICALLY A *MIRACLE* HE WAS SO LUCKY!
...PERHAPS NOT. I'M NOT SO SURE "LUCK" PLAYED A ROLE.
SEEING AS PEKOYAMA WAS THE ULTIMATE SWORDSWOMAN... AND THE ONE WHO DESPERATELY WANTED TO PROTECT KUZURYU...
...I THINK SHE STRUCK WITH EXACTLY THE PRECISION SHE INTENDED.
YEAH...
...THAT SOUNDS MORE PLAUSIBLE TO ME.
I'VE BEEN SO STRESSED OVER KUZURYU...
...NOW THAT WE KNOW HE'S GOING TO BE ALL RIGHT, I THINK WE SHOULD ADJOURN FOR TODAY.

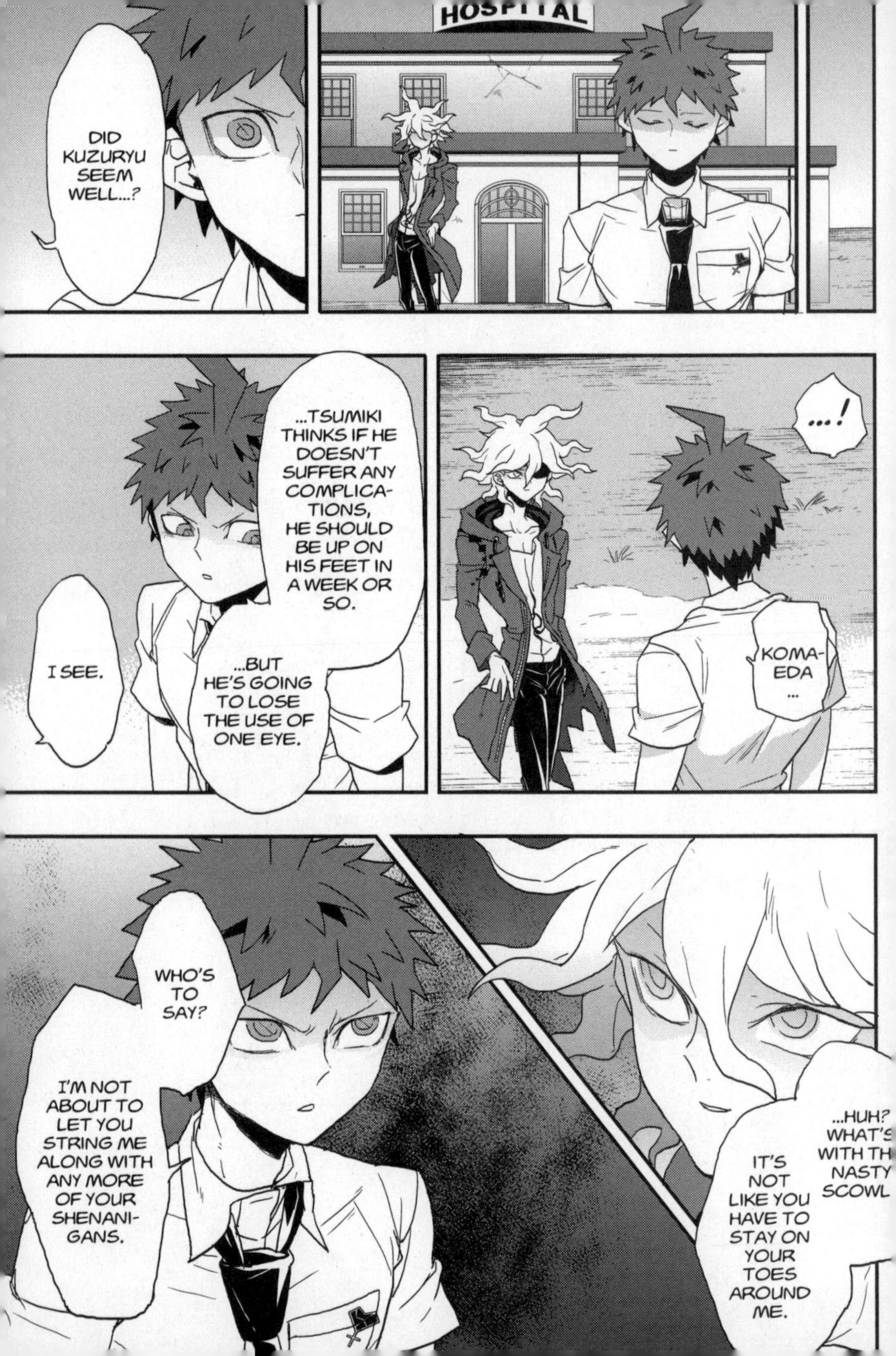
HOSPITAL
DID KUZURYU SEEM WELL...?
...!
KOMA-EDA...
...TSUMIKI THINKS IF HE DOESN'T SUFFER ANY COMPLICA-TIONS, HE SHOULD BE UP ON HIS FEET IN A WEEK OR SO.
...BUT HE'S GOING TO LOSE THE USE OF ONE EYE.
I SEE.
...HUH? WHAT'S WITH TH NASTY SCOWL
IT'S NOT LIKE YOU HAVE TO STAY ON YOUR TOES AROUND ME.
WHO'S TO SAY?
I'M NOT ABOUT TO LET YOU STRING ME ALONG WITH ANY MORE OF YOUR SHENANI-GANS.

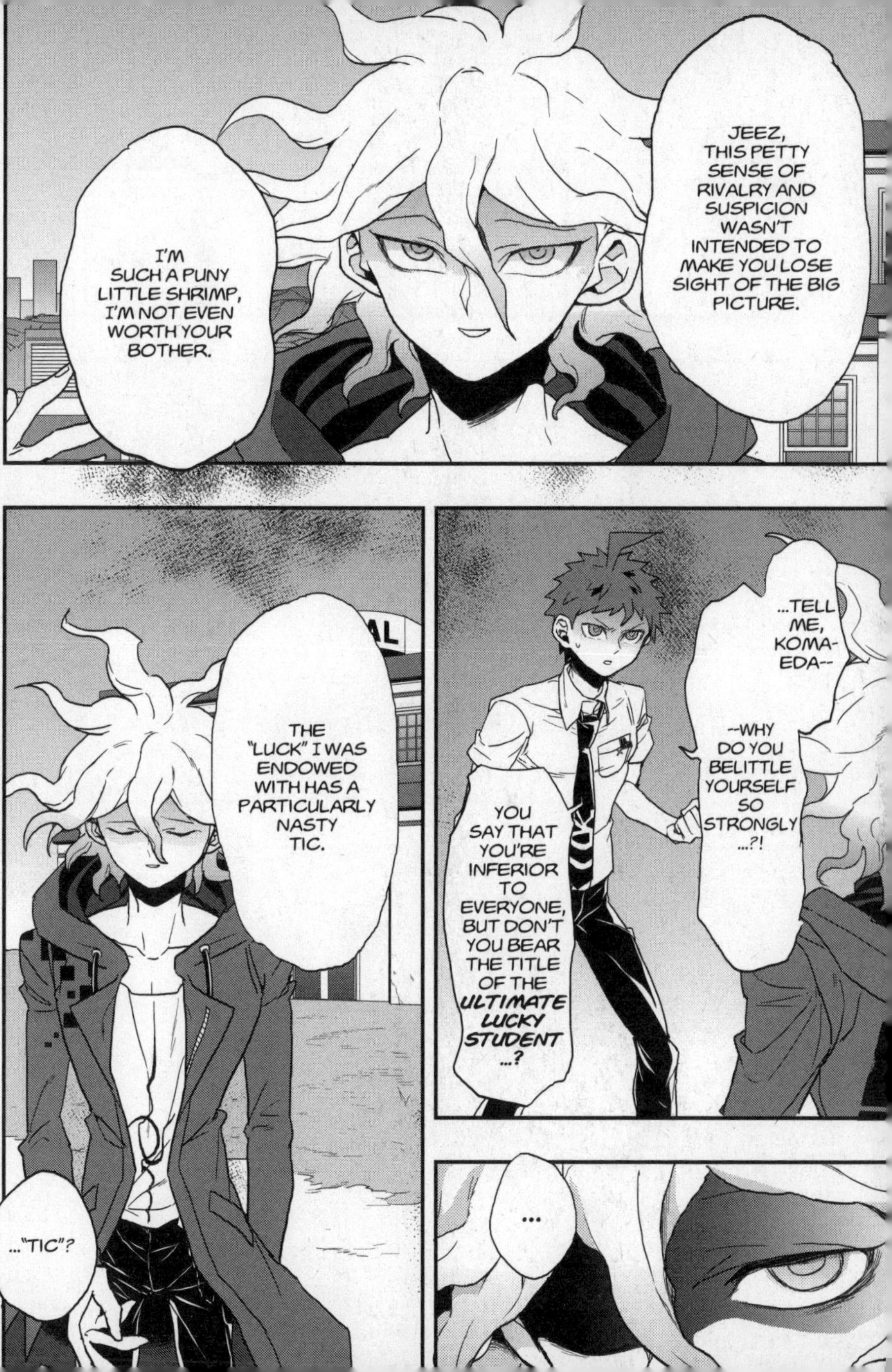
JEEZ, THIS PETTY SENSE OF RIVALRY AND SUSPICION WASN'T INTENDED TO MAKE YOU LOSE SIGHT OF THE BIG PICTURE.
I'M SUCH A PUNY LITTLE SHRIMP, I'M NOT EVEN WORTH YOUR BOTHER.
...TELL ME, KOMA-EDA--
--WHY DO YOU BELITTLE YOURSELF SO STRONGLY ...?!
YOU SAY THAT YOU'RE INFERIOR TO EVERYONE, BUT DON'T YOU BEAR THE TITLE OF THE *ULTIMATE LUCKY STUDENT* ...?
...
THE "LUCK" I WAS ENDOWED WITH HAS A PARTICULARLY NASTY TIC.
..."TIC"?

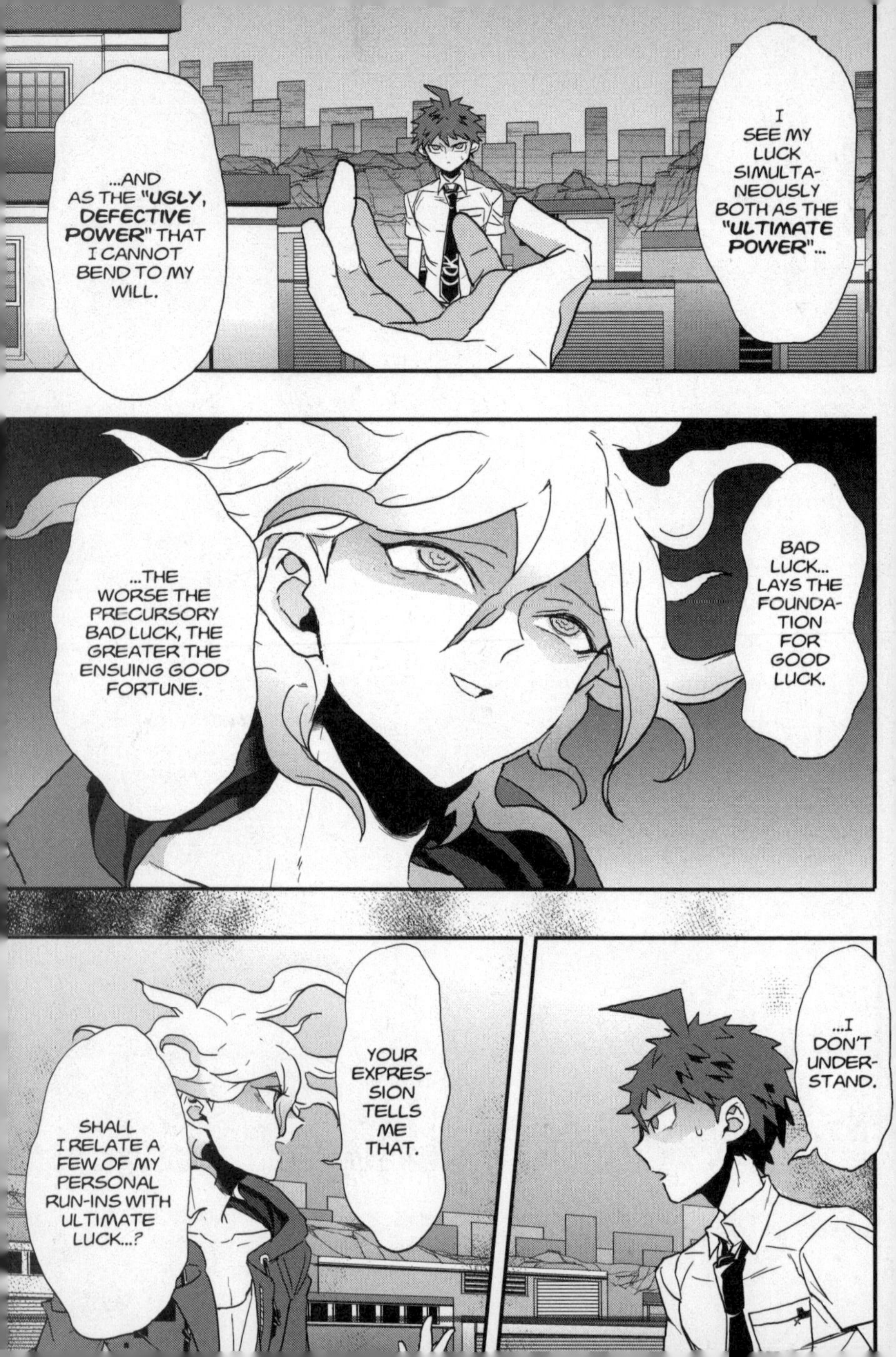
I SEE MY LUCK SIMULTANEOUSLY BOTH AS THE "ULTIMATE POWER"...
...AND AS THE "UGLY, DEFECTIVE POWER" THAT I CANNOT BEND TO MY WILL.
BAD LUCK... LAYS THE FOUNDATION FOR GOOD LUCK.
...THE WORSE THE PRECURSORY BAD LUCK, THE GREATER THE ENSUING GOOD FORTUNE.
...I DON'T UNDERSTAND.
YOUR EXPRESSION TELLS ME THAT.
SHALL I RELATE A FEW OF MY PERSONAL RUN-INS WITH ULTIMATE LUCK...?

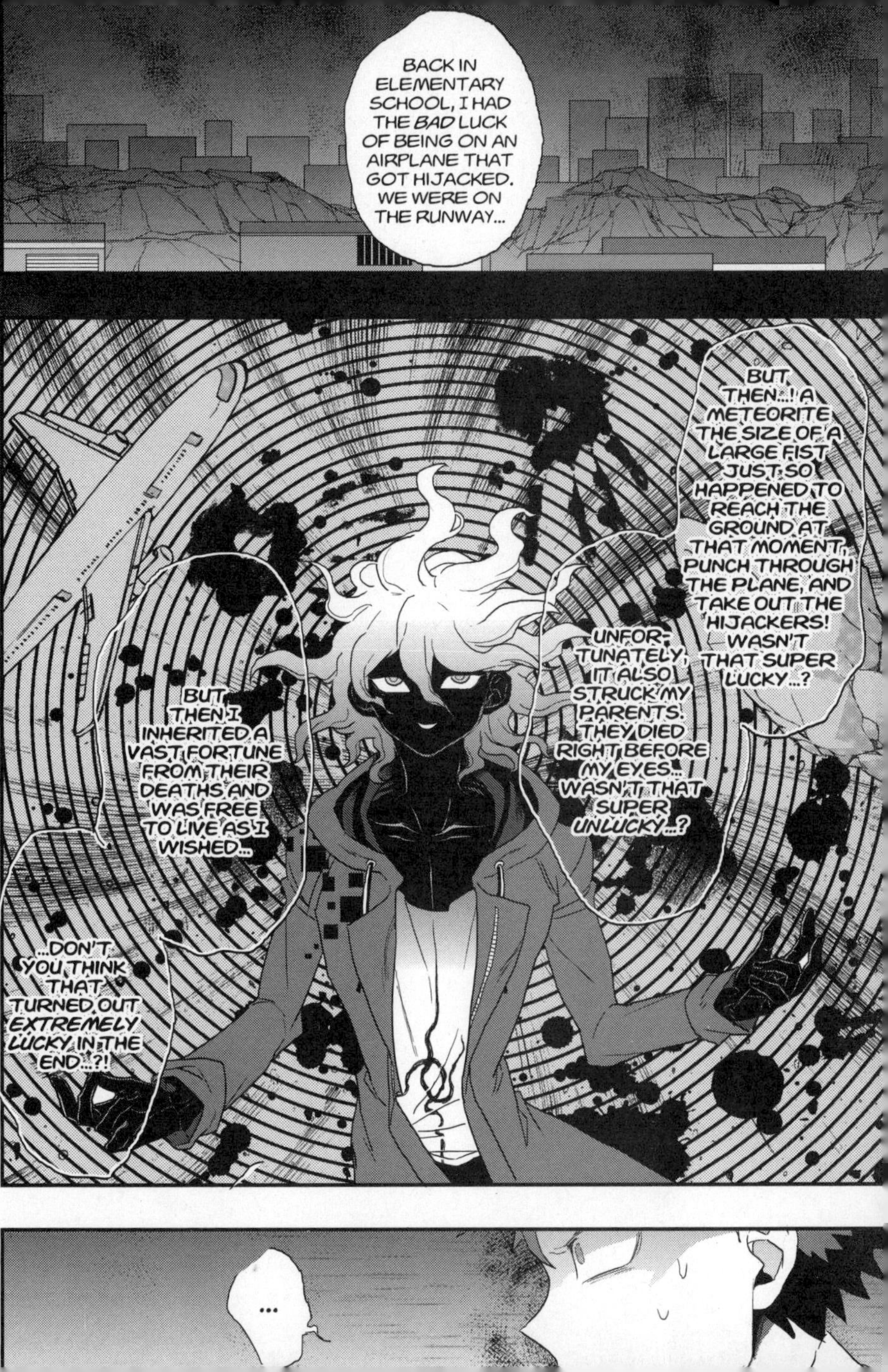
BACK IN ELEMENTARY SCHOOL, I HAD THE *BAD* LUCK OF BEING ON AN AIRPLANE THAT GOT HIJACKED. WE WERE ON THE RUNWAY...
BUT THEN...! A METEORITE THE SIZE OF A LARGE FIST JUST SO HAPPENED TO REACH THE GROUND AT THAT MOMENT, PUNCH THROUGH THE PLANE, AND TAKE OUT THE HIJACKERS! WASN'T THAT SUPER LUCKY...?
UNFORTUNATELY, IT ALSO STRUCK MY PARENTS. THEY DIED RIGHT BEFORE MY EYES... WASN'T THAT SUPER *UNLUCKY*...?
BUT THEN I INHERITED A VAST FORTUNE FROM THEIR DEATHS AND WAS FREE TO LIVE AS I WISHED...
...DON'T YOU THINK THAT TURNED OUT *EXTREMELY LUCKY* IN THE END...?!
...

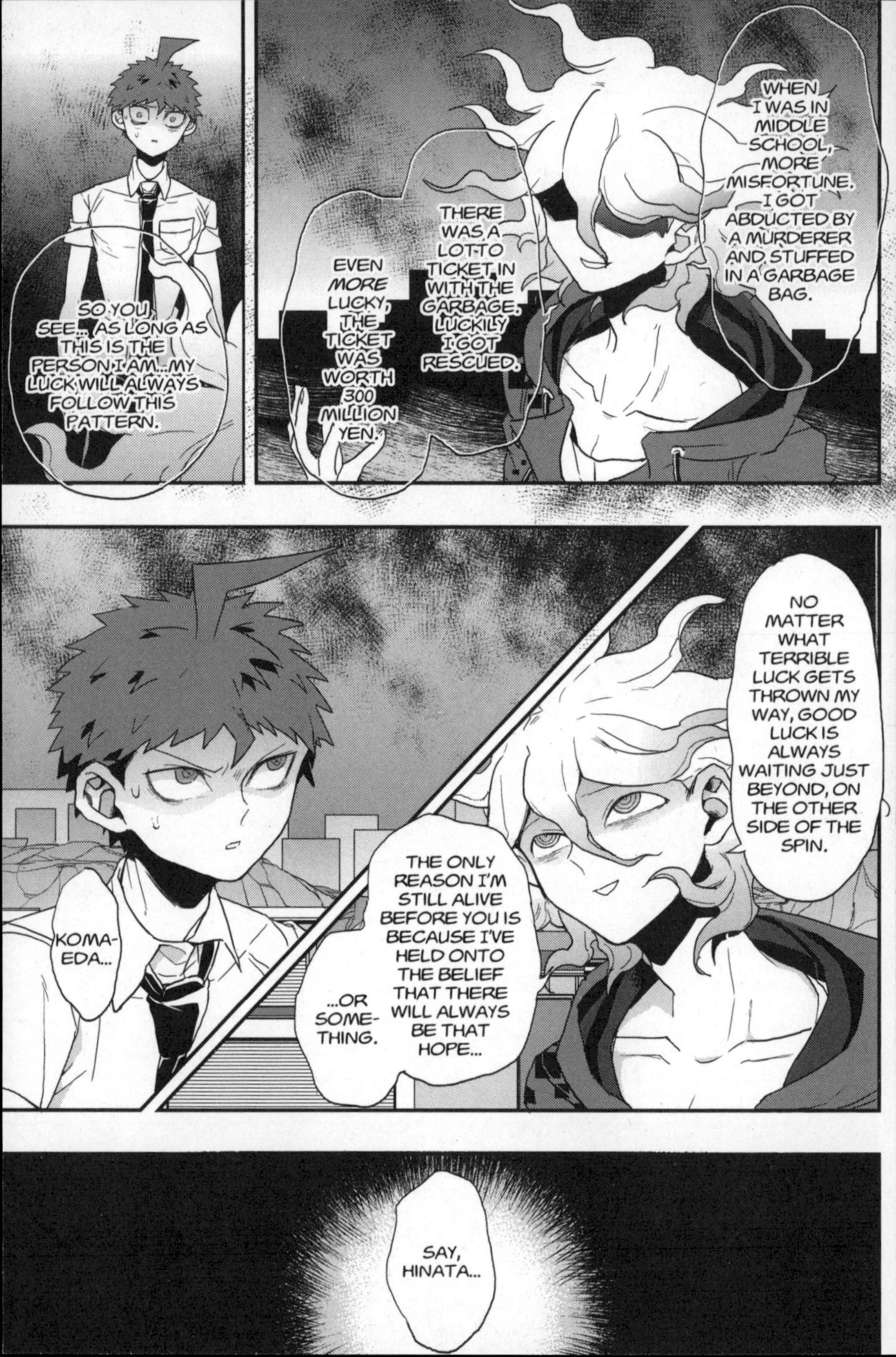
WHEN I WAS IN MIDDLE SCHOOL, MORE MISFORTUNE. I GOT ABDUCTED BY A MURDERER AND STUFFED IN A GARBAGE BAG.
THERE WAS A LOTTO TICKET IN WITH THE GARBAGE. LUCKILY I GOT RESCUED.
EVEN MORE LUCKY, THE TICKET WAS WORTH 300 MILLION YEN.
SO YOU SEE... AS LONG AS THIS IS THE PERSON I AM...MY LUCK WILL ALWAYS FOLLOW THIS PATTERN.
NO MATTER WHAT TERRIBLE LUCK GETS THROWN MY WAY, GOOD LUCK IS ALWAYS WAITING JUST BEYOND, ON THE OTHER SIDE OF THE SPIN.
THE ONLY REASON I'M STILL ALIVE BEFORE YOU IS BECAUSE I'VE HELD ONTO THE BELIEF THAT THERE WILL ALWAYS BE THAT HOPE...
...OR SOME-THING.
KOMA-EDA...
SAY, HINATA...

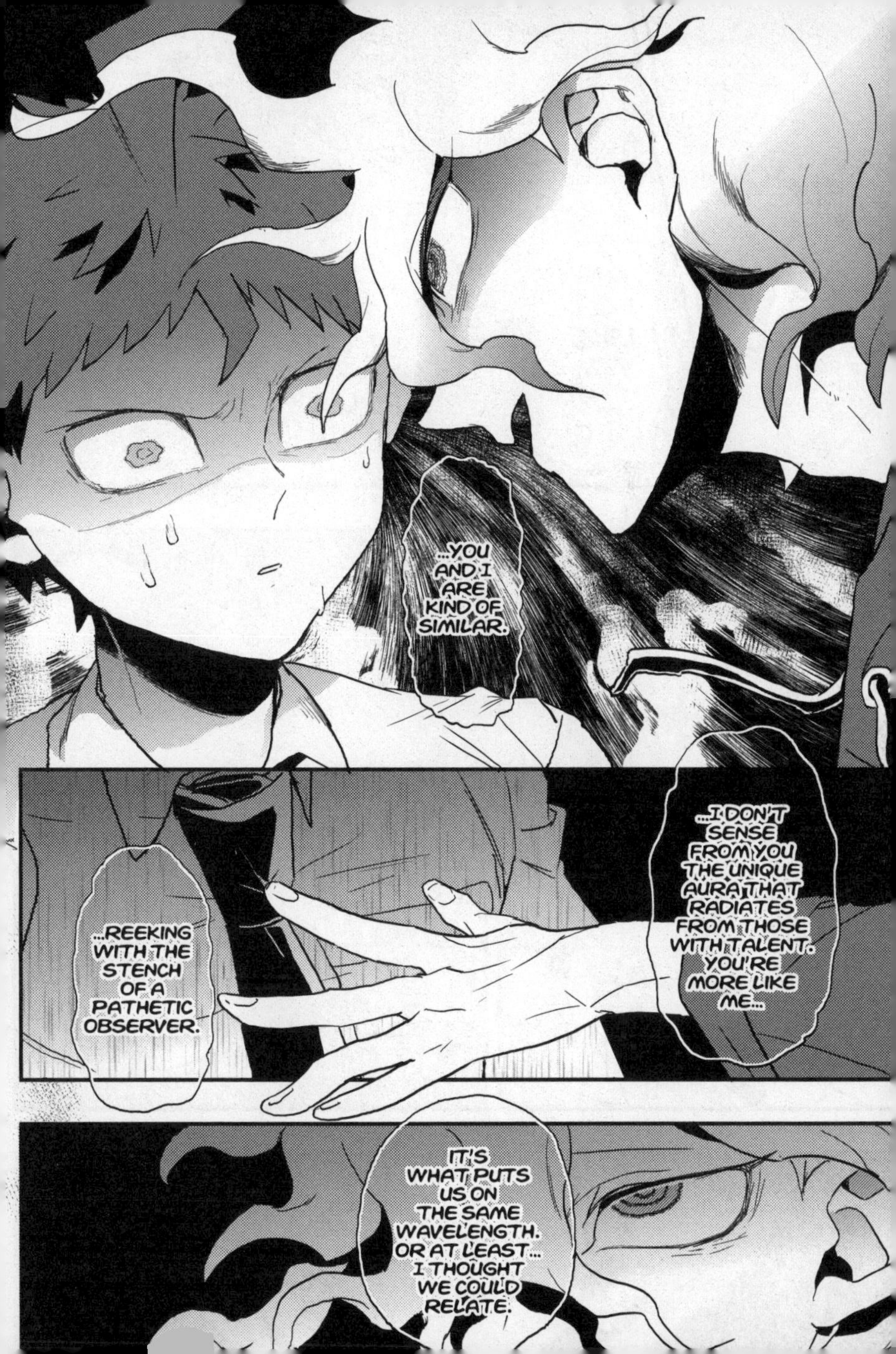
...YOU AND I ARE KIND OF SIMILAR.
...I DON'T SENSE FROM YOU THE UNIQUE AURA THAT RADIATES FROM THOSE WITH TALENT. YOU'RE MORE LIKE ME...
...REEKING WITH THE STENCH OF A PATHETIC OBSERVER.
IT'S WHAT PUTS US ON THE SAME WAVELENGTH. OR AT LEAST... I THOUGHT WE COULD RELATE.

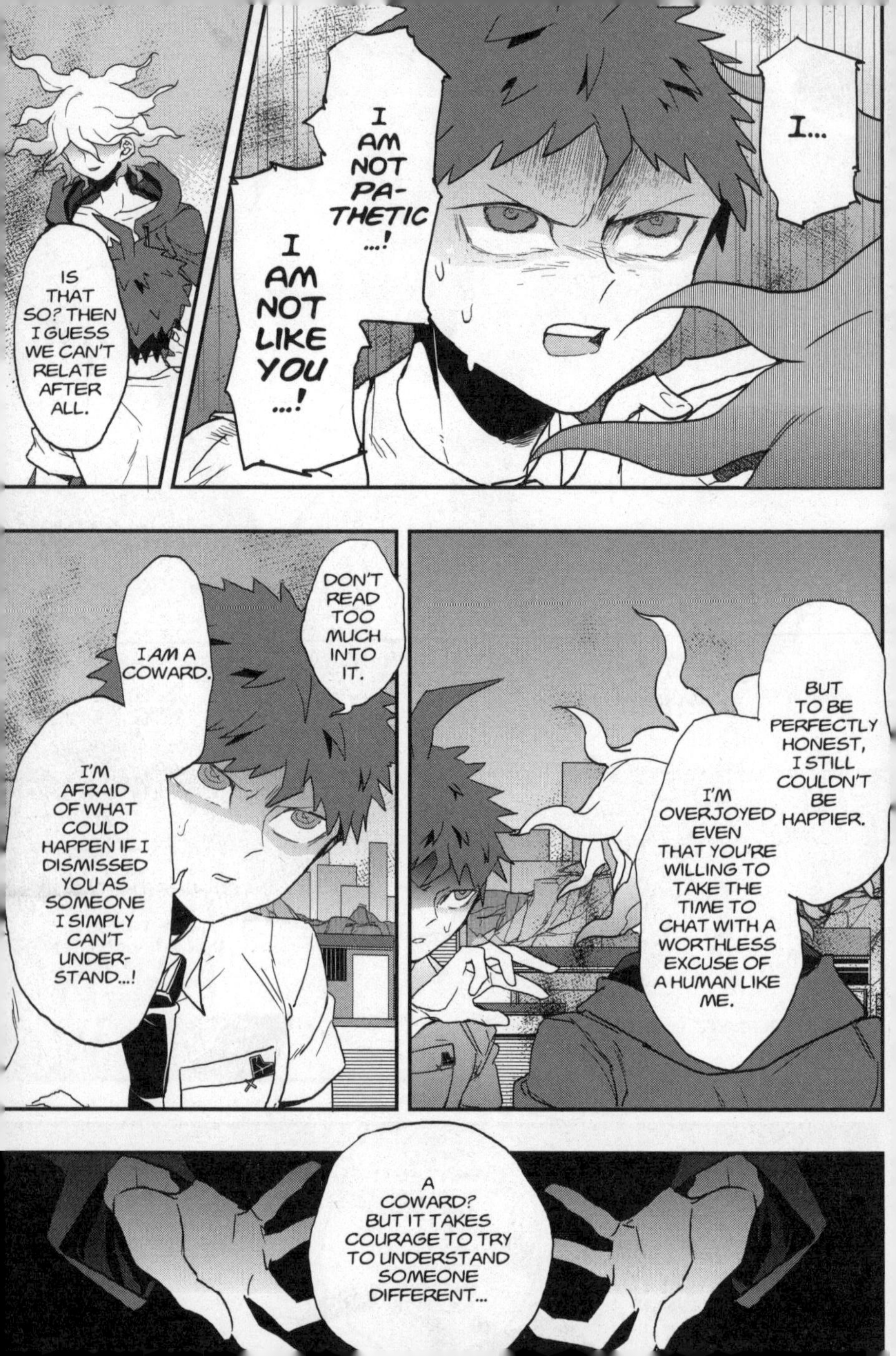
I...
I AM NOT PATHETIC ...!
I AM NOT LIKE YOU ...!
IS THAT SO? THEN I GUESS WE CAN'T RELATE AFTER ALL.
BUT TO BE PERFECTLY HONEST, I STILL COULDN'T BE HAPPIER.
I'M OVERJOYED EVEN THAT YOU'RE WILLING TO TAKE THE TIME TO CHAT WITH A WORTHLESS EXCUSE OF A HUMAN LIKE ME.
DON'T READ TOO MUCH INTO IT.
I AM A COWARD.
I'M AFRAID OF WHAT COULD HAPPEN IF I DISMISSED YOU AS SOMEONE I SIMPLY CAN'T UNDER-STAND...!
A COWARD? BUT IT TAKES COURAGE TO TRY TO UNDERSTAND SOMEONE DIFFERENT...

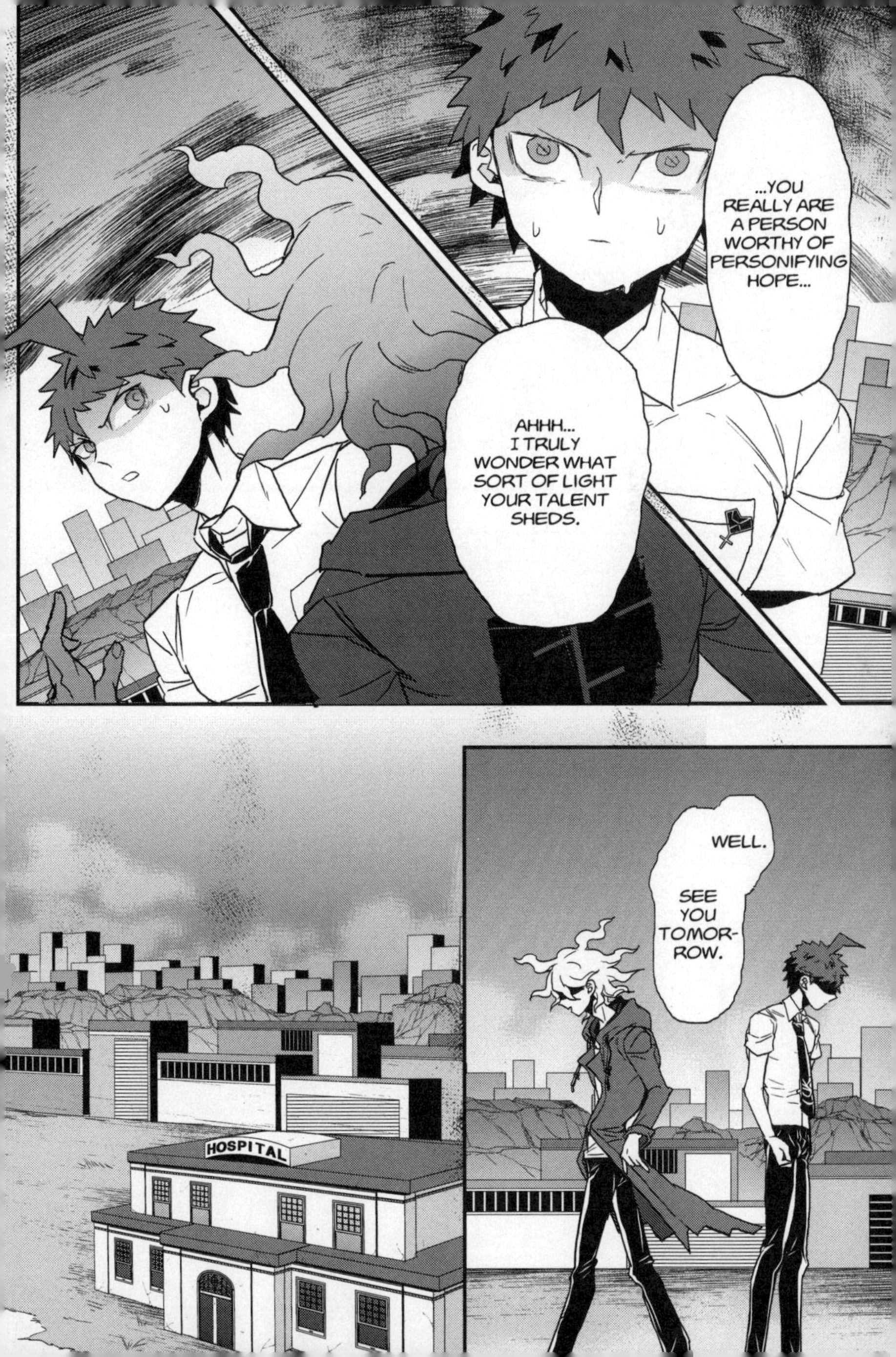
...YOU REALLY ARE A PERSON WORTHY OF PERSONIFYING HOPE...
AHHH... I TRULY WONDER WHAT SORT OF LIGHT YOUR TALENT SHEDS.
WELL.
SEE YOU TOMORROW.
HOSPITAL

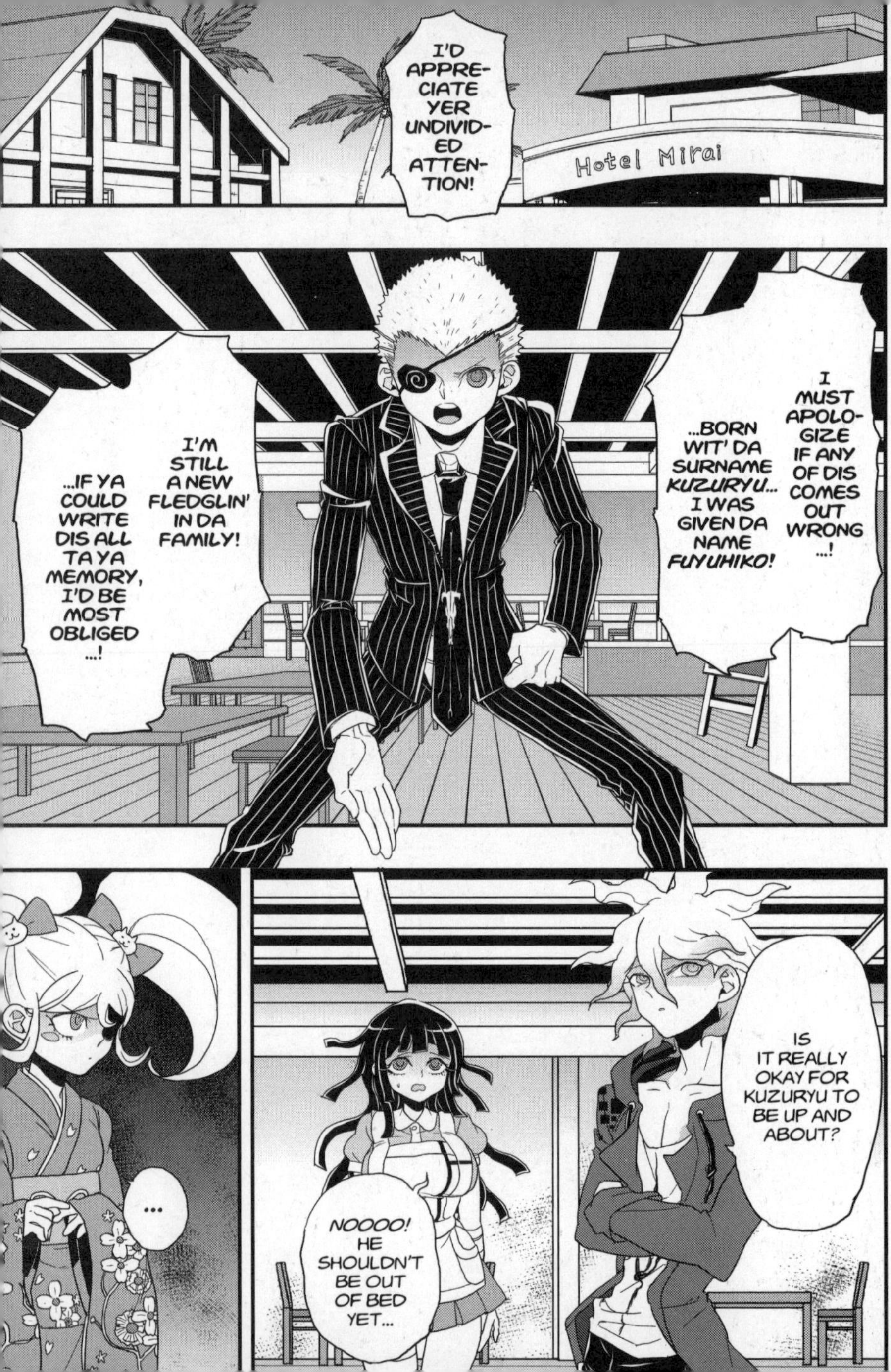

I'D APPRECIATE YER UNDIVIDED ATTENTION!
Hotel Mirai
I MUST APOLOGIZE IF ANY OF DIS COMES OUT WRONG ...!
...BORN WIT' DA SURNAME KUZURYU... I WAS GIVEN DA NAME FUYUHIKO!
I'M STILL A NEW FLEDGLIN' IN DA FAMILY!
...IF YA COULD WRITE DIS ALL TA YA MEMORY, I'D BE MOST OBLIGED ...!
IS IT REALLY OKAY FOR KUZURYU TO BE UP AND ABOUT?
NOOOO! HE SHOULDN'T BE OUT OF BED YET...
...

Ep.18

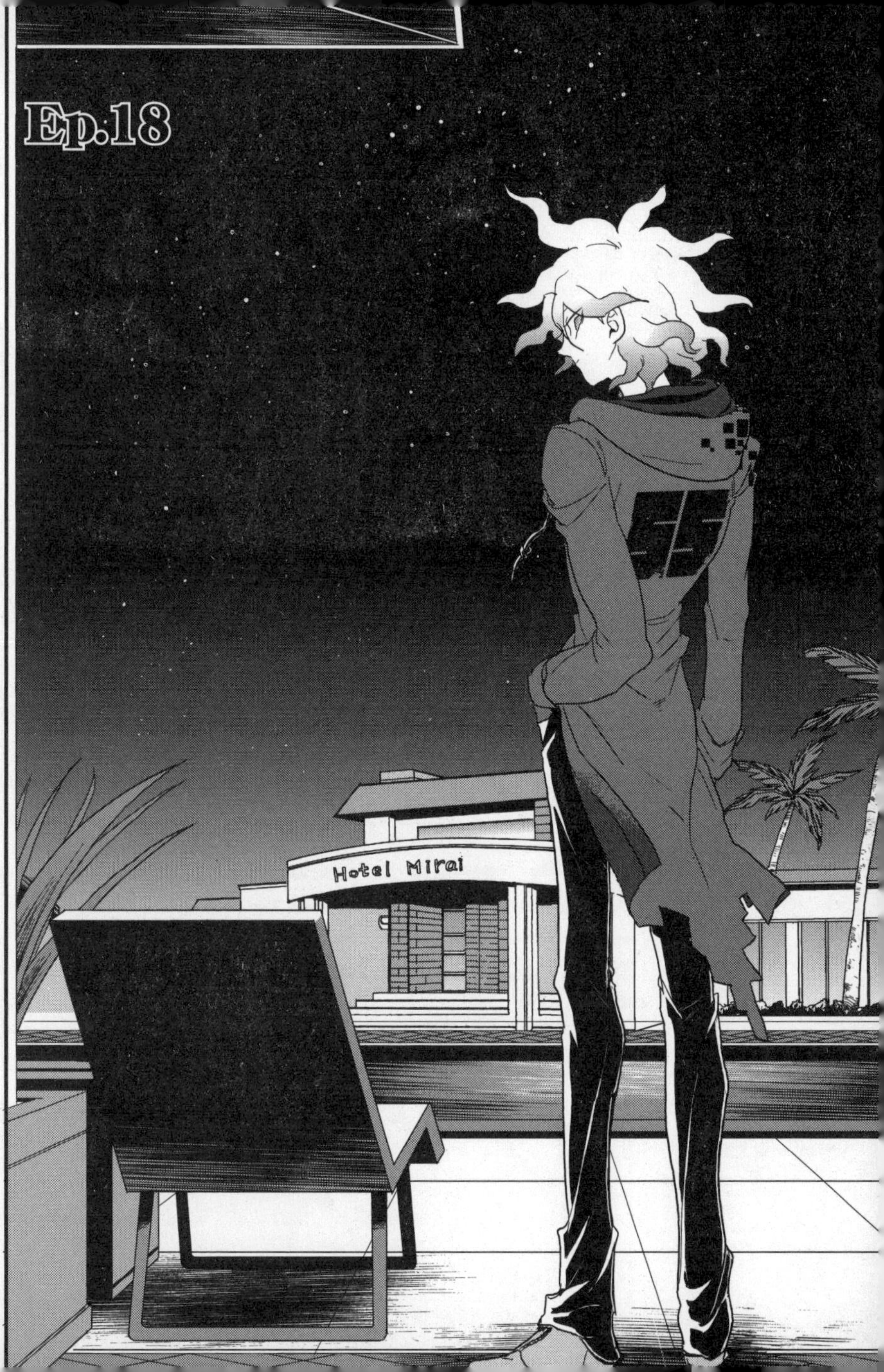
Hotel Mirai

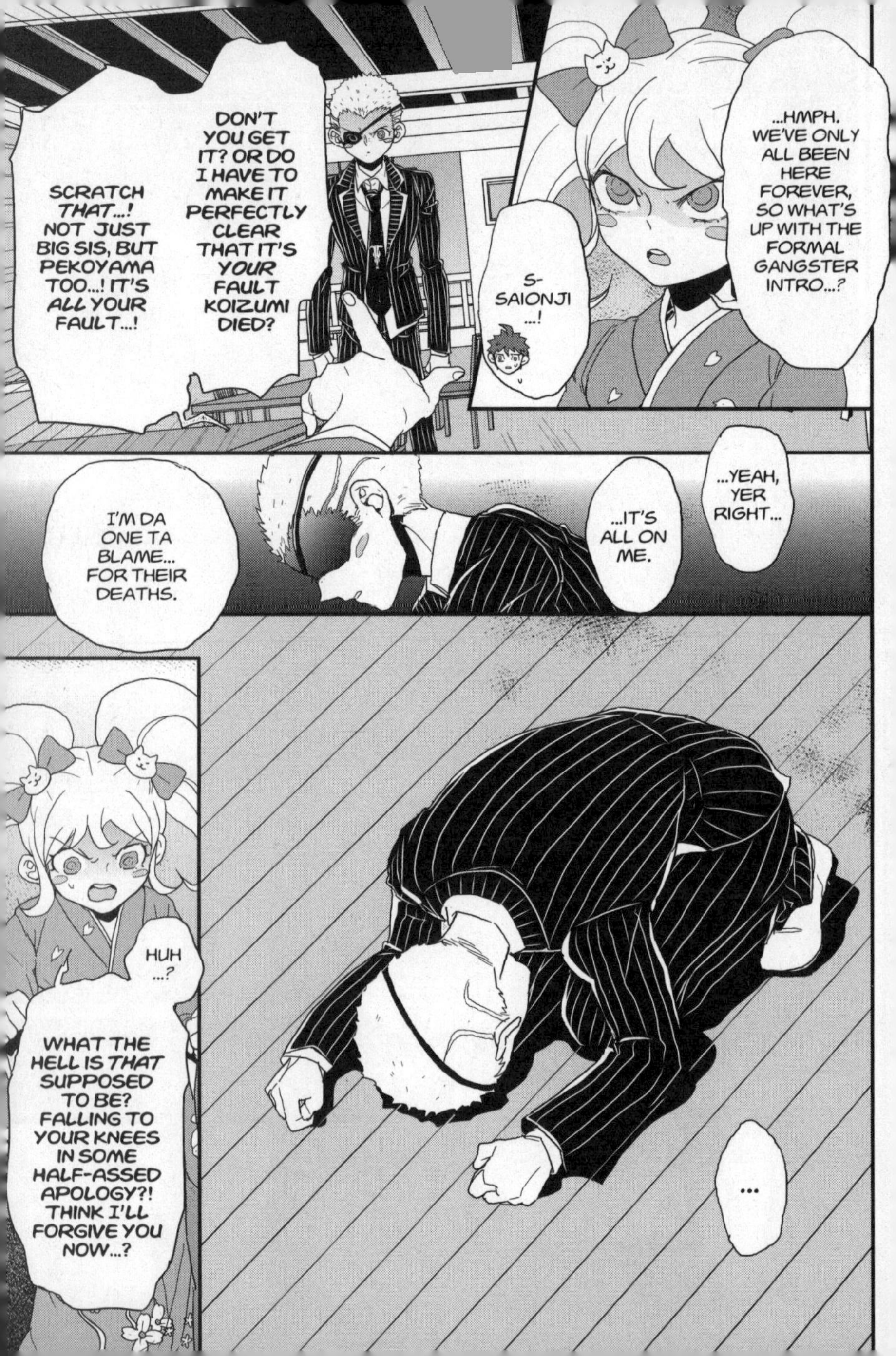
...HMPH. WE'VE ONLY ALL BEEN HERE FOREVER, SO WHAT'S UP WITH THE FORMAL GANGSTER INTRO...?
S-SAIONJI...!
DON'T YOU GET IT? OR DO I HAVE TO MAKE IT PERFECTLY CLEAR THAT IT'S *YOUR* FAULT KOIZUMI DIED?
SCRATCH *THAT*...! NOT JUST BIG SIS, BUT PEKOYAMA TOO...! IT'S *ALL* YOUR FAULT...!
...YEAH, YER RIGHT...
...IT'S ALL ON ME.
I'M DA ONE TA BLAME... FOR THEIR DEATHS.
...
HUH...?
WHAT THE HELL IS *THAT* SUPPOSED TO BE? FALLING TO YOUR KNEES IN SOME HALF-ASSED APOLOGY?! THINK I'LL FORGIVE YOU NOW...?

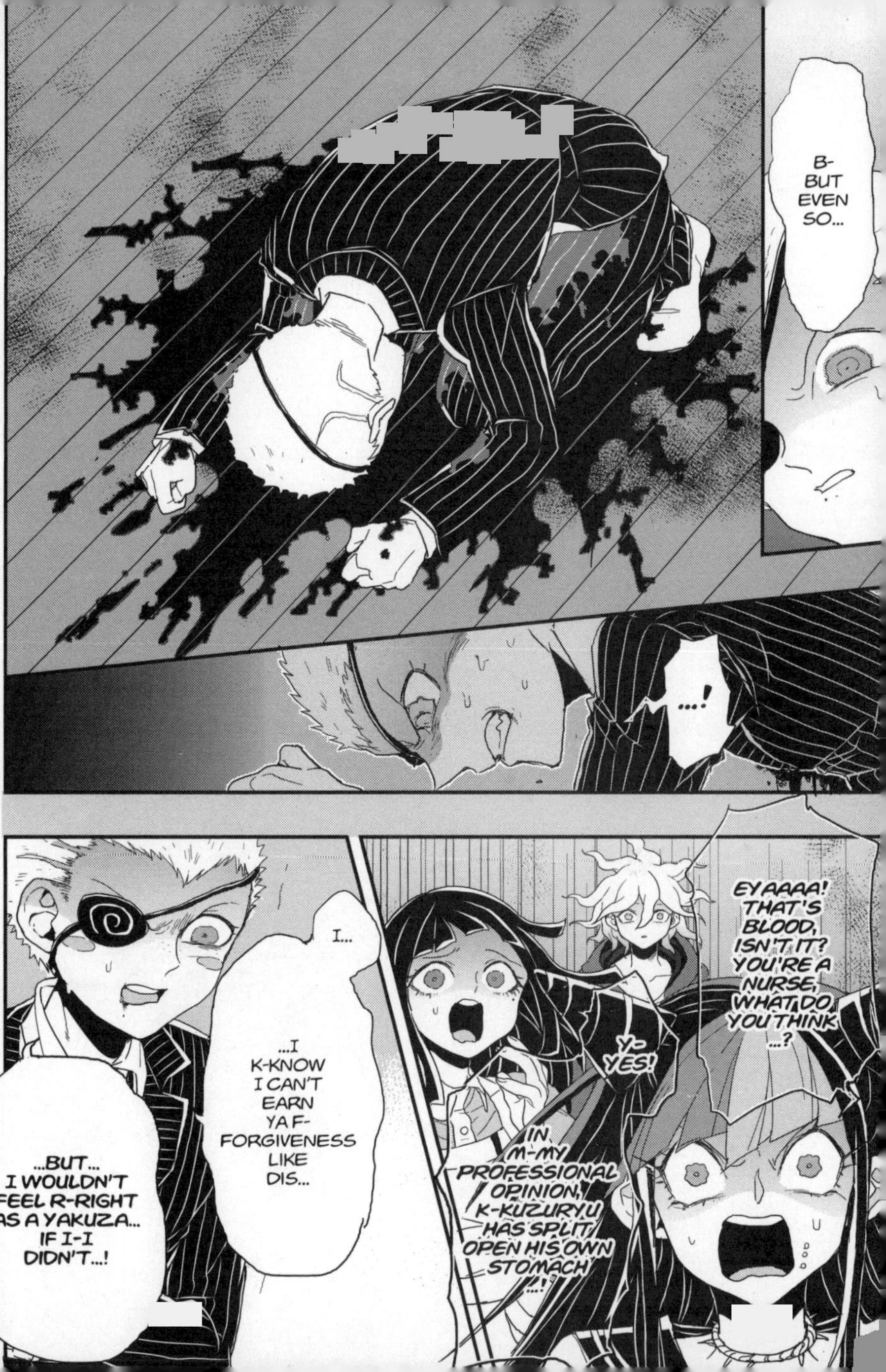
B- BUT EVEN SO...
...!
EYAAAA! THAT'S BLOOD, ISN'T IT? YOU'RE A NURSE, WHAT DO YOU THINK...?
Y- YES!
IN M-MY PROFESSIONAL OPINION, K-KUZURYU HAS SPLIT OPEN HIS OWN STOMACH...!
I...
...I K-KNOW I CAN'T EARN YA F-FORGIVENESS LIKE DIS...
...BUT... I WOULDN'T FEEL R-RIGHT AS A YAKUZA... IF I-I DIDN'T...!

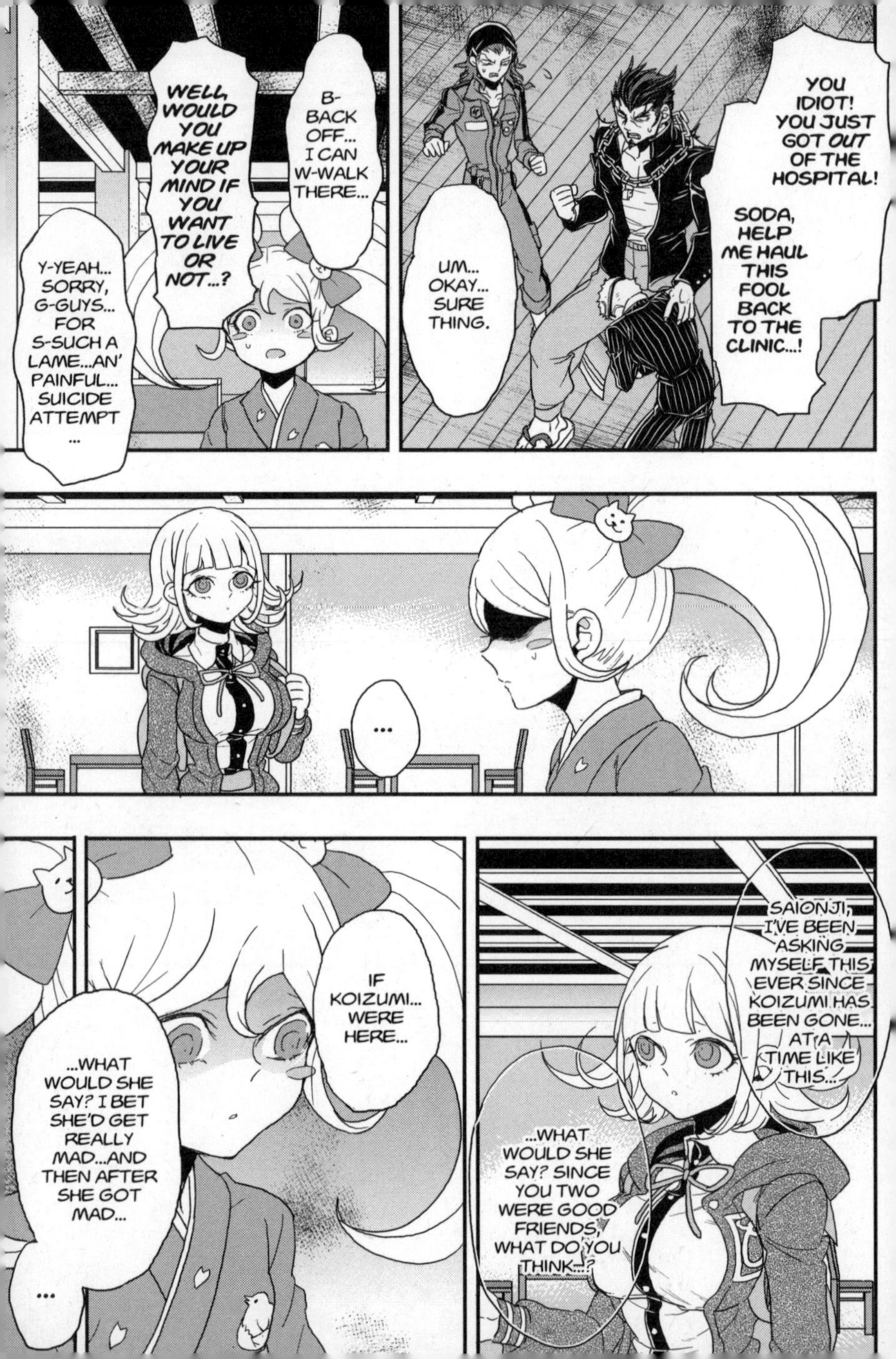
YOU IDIOT! YOU JUST GOT OUT OF THE HOSPITAL!
SODA, HELP ME HAUL THIS FOOL BACK TO THE CLINIC...!
UM... OKAY... SURE THING.
B-BACK OFF... I CAN W-WALK THERE...
WELL, WOULD YOU MAKE UP YOUR MIND IF YOU WANT TO LIVE OR NOT...?
Y-YEAH... SORRY, G-GUYS... FOR S-SUCH A LAME...AN' PAINFUL... SUICIDE ATTEMPT...
...
SAIONJI, I'VE BEEN ASKING MYSELF THIS EVER SINCE KOIZUMI HAS BEEN GONE... AT A TIME LIKE THIS...
...WHAT WOULD SHE SAY? SINCE YOU TWO WERE GOOD FRIENDS, WHAT DO YOU THINK...?
IF KOIZUMI... WERE HERE...
...WHAT WOULD SHE SAY? I BET SHE'D GET REALLY MAD...AND THEN AFTER SHE GOT MAD...
...

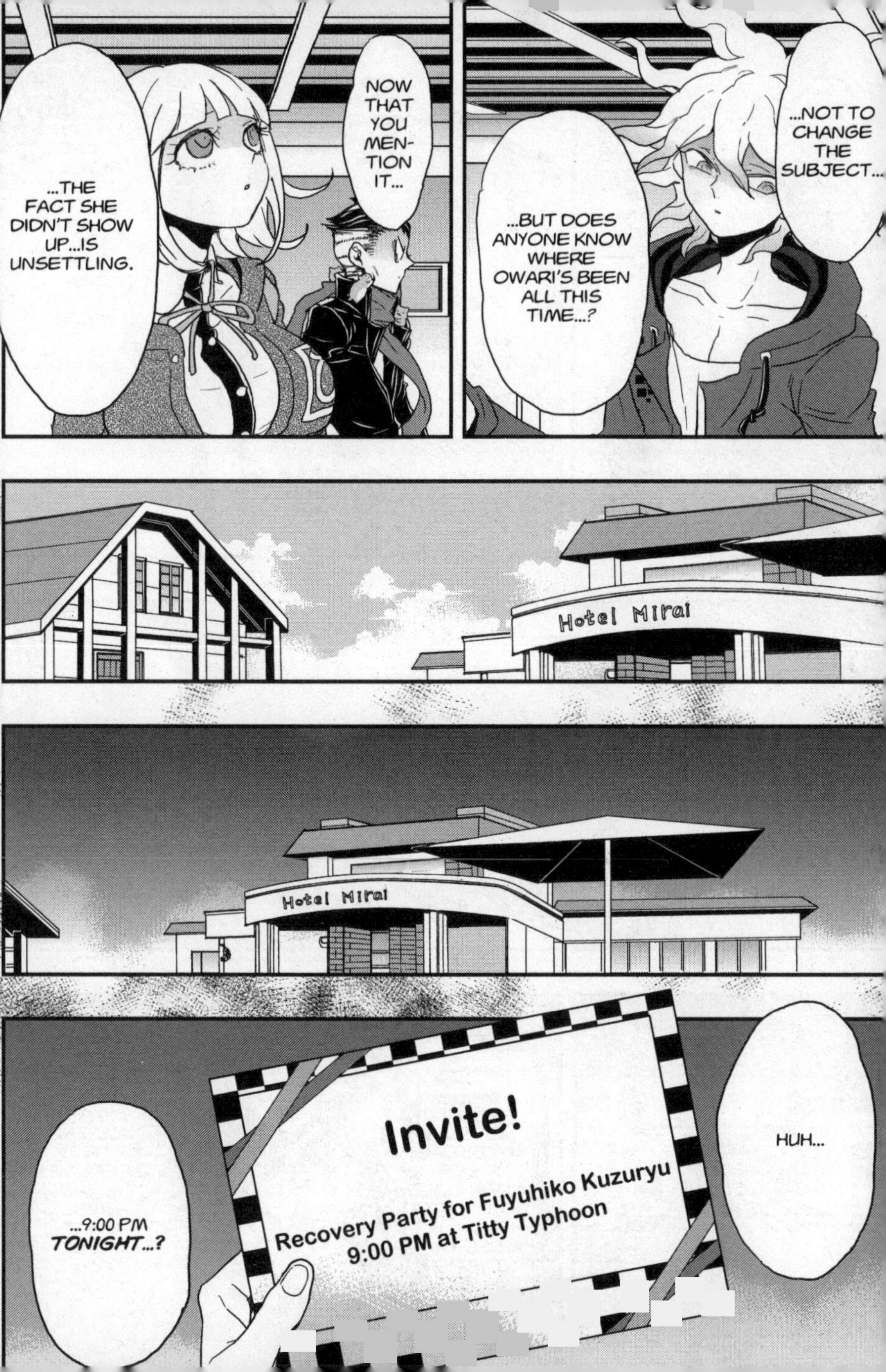
...NOT TO CHANGE THE SUBJECT...
...BUT DOES ANYONE KNOW WHERE OWARI'S BEEN ALL THIS TIME...?
NOW THAT YOU MEN-TION IT...
...THE FACT SHE DIDN'T SHOW UP...IS UNSETTLING.
Hotel Mirai
Hotel Mirai
HUH...
Invite!
Recovery Party for Fuyuhiko Kuzuryu
9:00 PM at Titty Typhoon
...9:00 PM TONIGHT...?

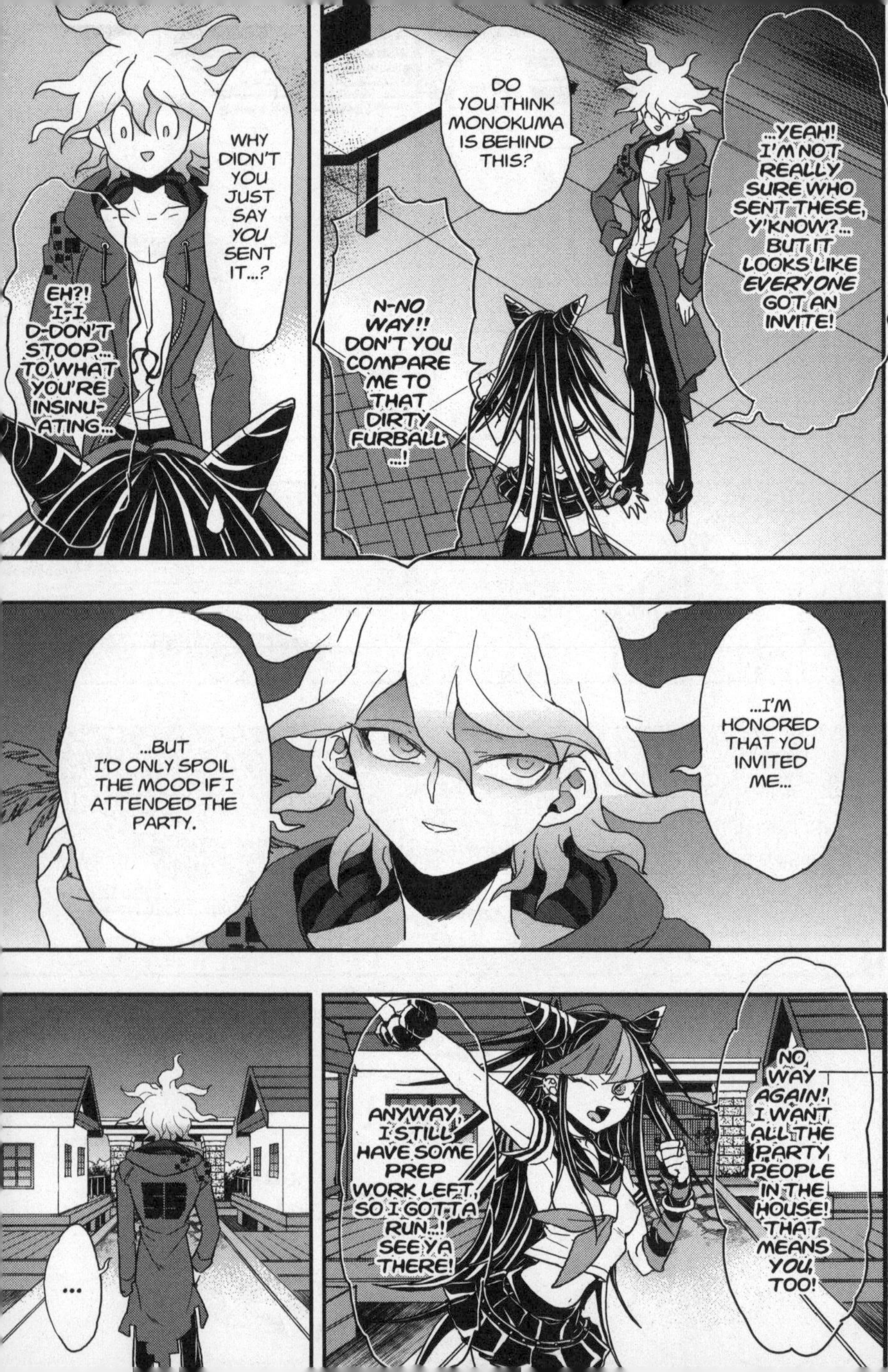
...YEAH! I'M NOT REALLY SURE WHO SENT THESE, Y'KNOW?... BUT IT LOOKS LIKE *EVERYONE* GOT AN INVITE!
DO YOU THINK MONOKUMA IS BEHIND THIS?
N-NO *WAY*!! DON'T YOU COMPARE ME TO THAT DIRTY FURBALL ...!
WHY DIDN'T YOU JUST SAY *YOU* SENT IT...?
EH?! I-I D-DON'T STOOP... TO WHAT YOU'RE INSINUATING...
...I'M HONORED THAT YOU INVITED ME...
...BUT I'D ONLY SPOIL THE MOOD IF I ATTENDED THE PARTY.
NO WAY AGAIN! I WANT ALL THE PARTY PEOPLE IN THE HOUSE! THAT MEANS *YOU*, TOO!
ANYWAY, I STILL HAVE SOME PREP WORK LEFT, SO I GOTTA RUN...! SEE YA THERE!
...

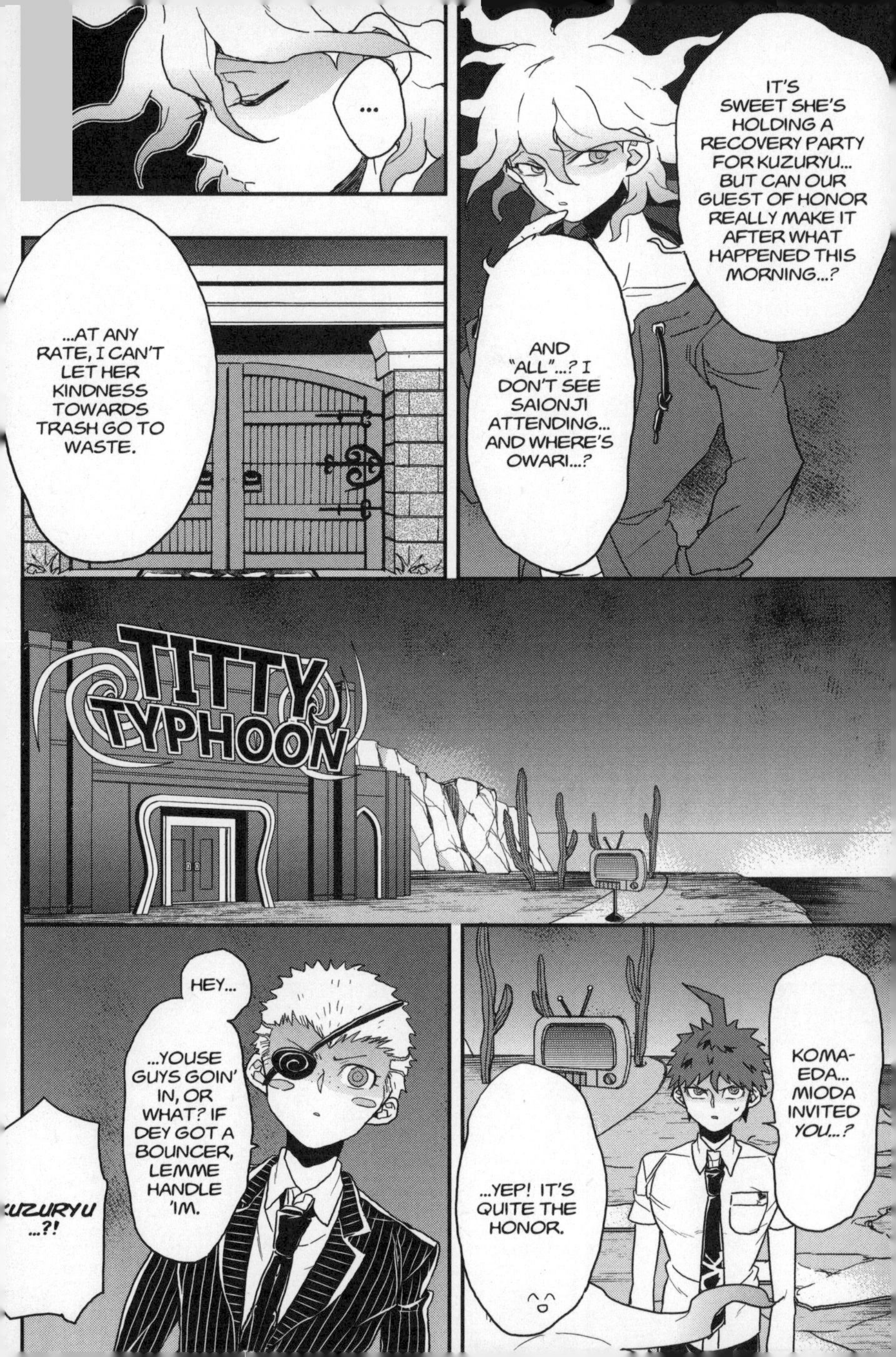

IT'S SWEET SHE'S HOLDING A RECOVERY PARTY FOR KUZURYU... BUT CAN OUR GUEST OF HONOR REALLY MAKE IT AFTER WHAT HAPPENED THIS MORNING...?
AND "ALL"...? I DON'T SEE SAIONJI ATTENDING... AND WHERE'S OWARI...?
...
...AT ANY RATE, I CAN'T LET HER KINDNESS TOWARDS TRASH GO TO WASTE.
TITTY TYPHOON
KOMA-EDA... MIODA INVITED YOU...?
...YEP! IT'S QUITE THE HONOR.
HEY...
...YOUSE GUYS GOIN' IN, OR WHAT? IF DEY GOT A BOUNCER, LEMME HANDLE 'IM.
KUZURYU ...?!

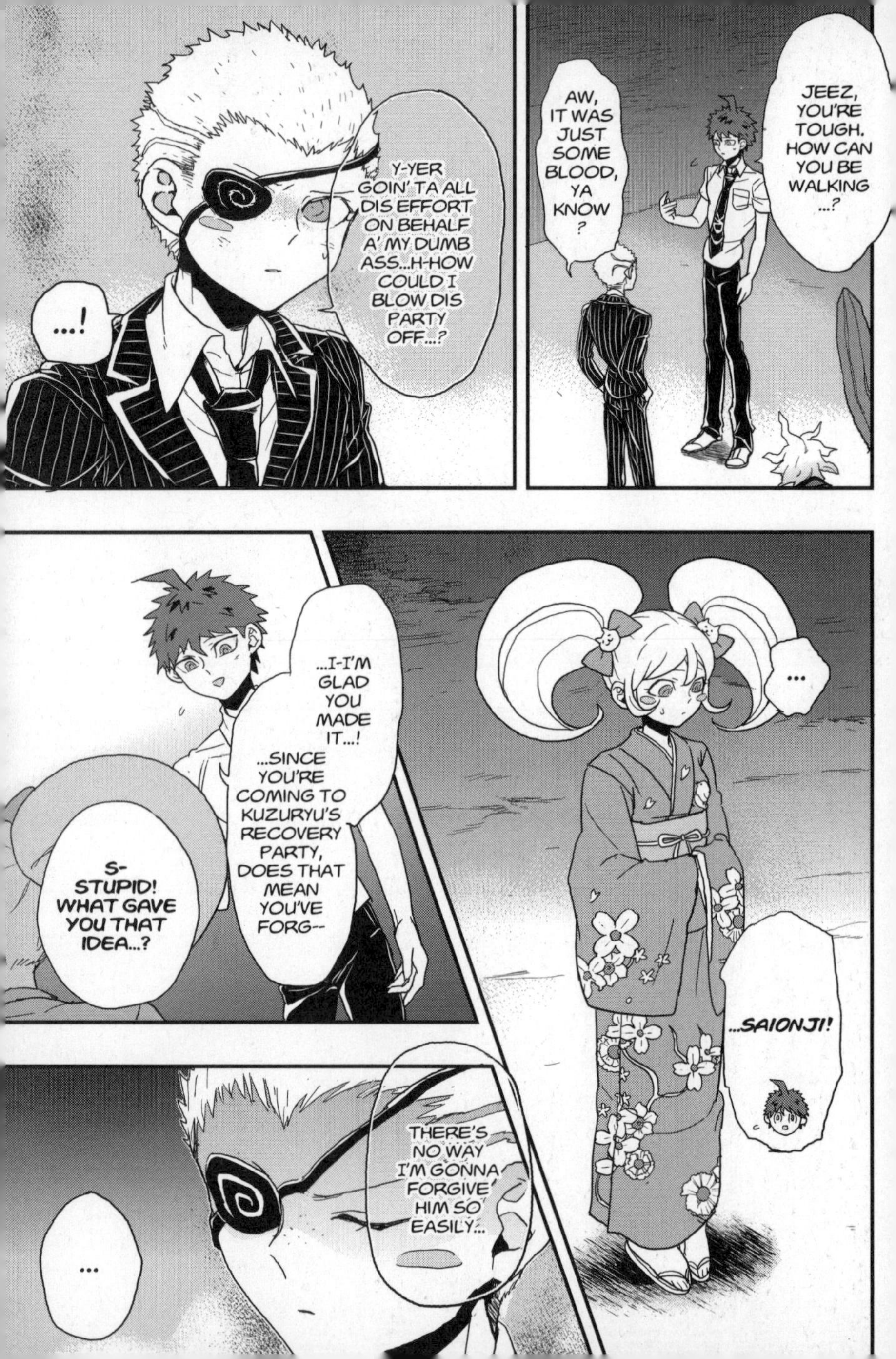
JEEZ, YOU'RE TOUGH. HOW CAN YOU BE WALKING ...?
AW, IT WAS JUST SOME BLOOD, YA KNOW?
Y-YER GOIN' TA ALL DIS EFFORT ON BEHALF A' MY DUMB ASS...H-HOW COULD I BLOW DIS PARTY OFF...?
...!
...
...SAIONJI!
...I-I'M GLAD YOU MADE IT...!
...SINCE YOU'RE COMING TO KUZURYU'S RECOVERY PARTY, DOES THAT MEAN YOU'VE FORG--
S-STUPID! WHAT GAVE YOU THAT IDEA...?
THERE'S NO WAY I'M GONNA FORGIVE HIM SO EASILY...
...

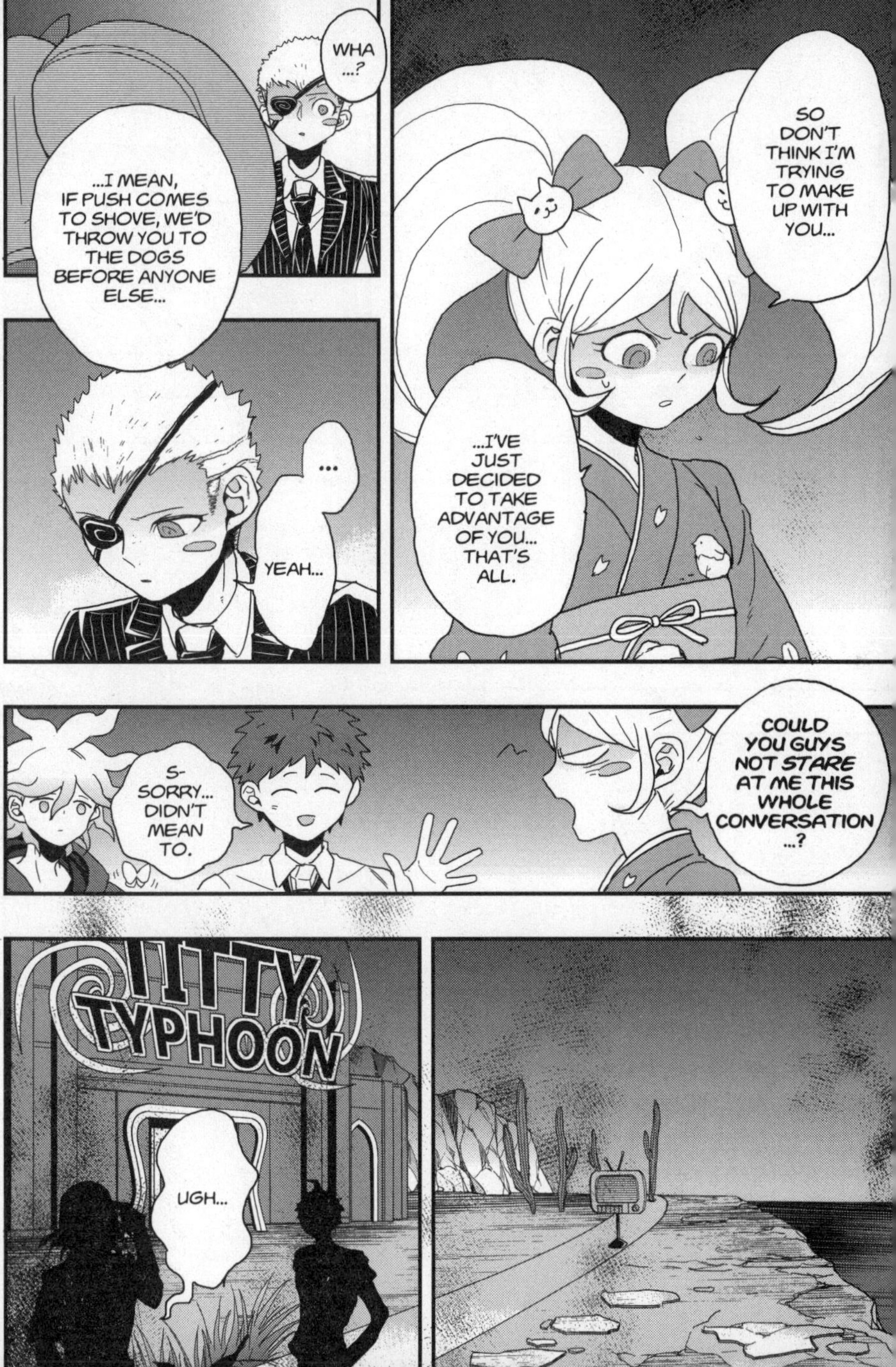
SO DON'T THINK I'M TRYING TO MAKE UP WITH YOU...
...I'VE JUST DECIDED TO TAKE ADVANTAGE OF YOU... THAT'S ALL.
WHA ...?
...I MEAN, IF PUSH COMES TO SHOVE, WE'D THROW YOU TO THE DOGS BEFORE ANYONE ELSE...
...
YEAH...
COULD YOU GUYS NOT *STARE* AT ME THIS WHOLE CONVERSATION ...?
S-SORRY... DIDN'T MEAN TO.
ITTY TYPHOON
UGH...

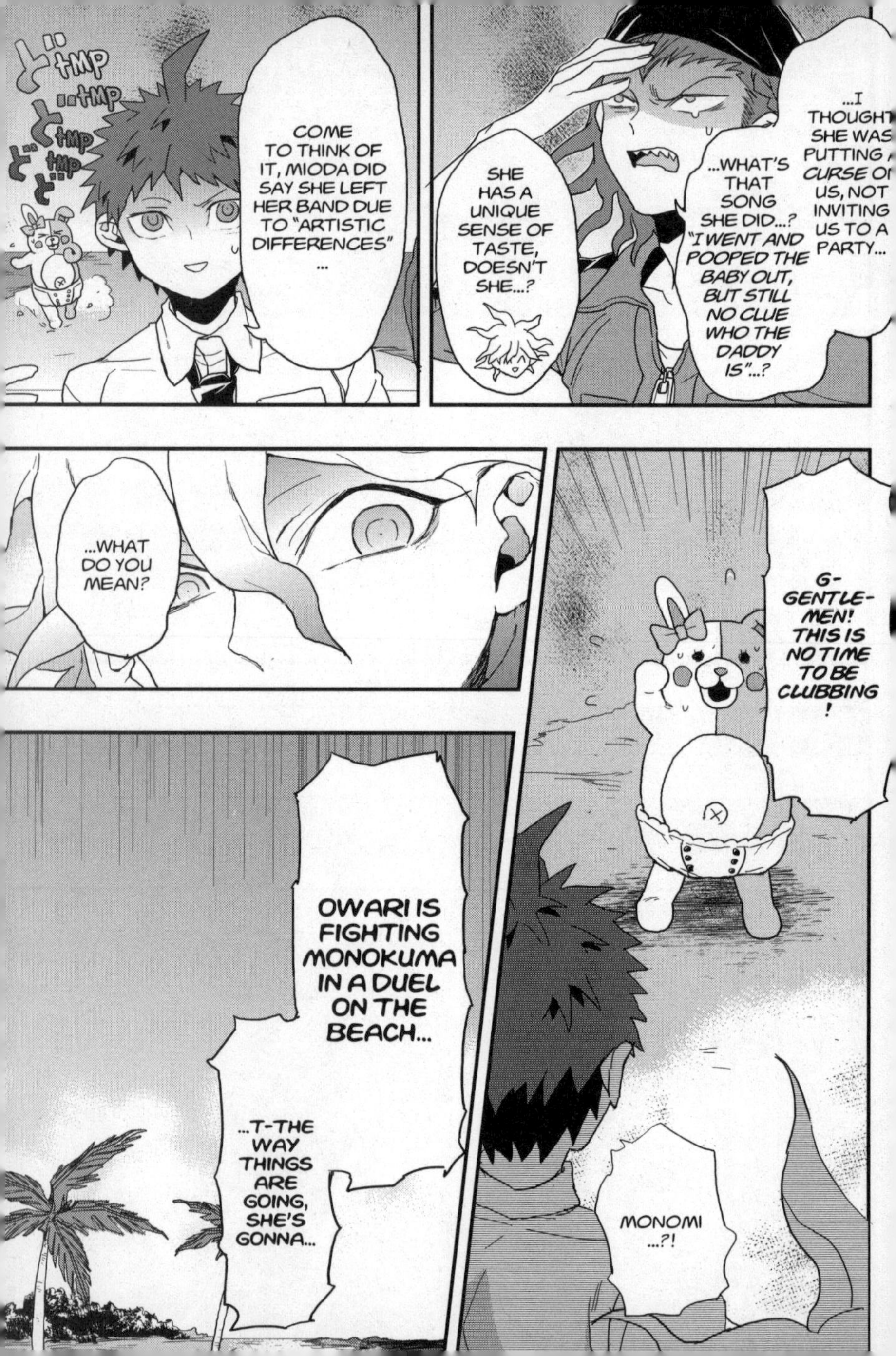
...I THOUGHT SHE WAS PUTTING CURSE O US, NOT INVITING US TO A PARTY...
...WHAT'S THAT SONG SHE DID...? "I WENT AND POOPED THE BABY OUT, BUT STILL NO CLUE WHO THE DADDY IS"...?
SHE HAS A UNIQUE SENSE OF TASTE, DOESN'T SHE...?
COME TO THINK OF IT, MIODA DID SAY SHE LEFT HER BAND DUE TO "ARTISTIC DIFFERENCES"...
tmp ..tmp tmp tmp
G-GENTLEMEN! THIS IS NO TIME TO BE CLUBBING!
...WHAT DO YOU MEAN?
MONOMI...?!
OWARI IS FIGHTING MONOKUMA IN A DUEL ON THE BEACH...
...T-THE WAY THINGS ARE GOING, SHE'S GONNA...

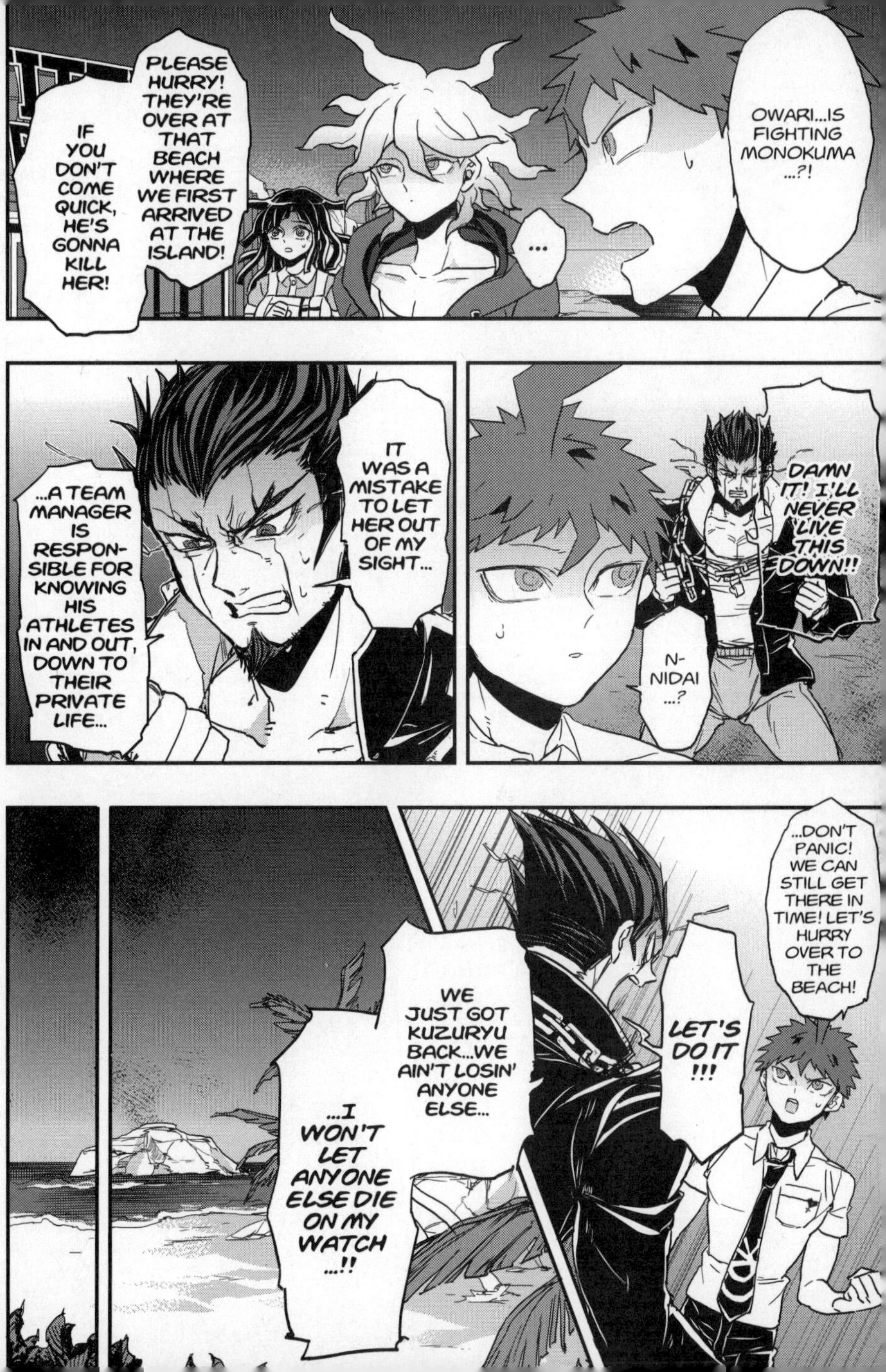
OWARI...IS FIGHTING MONOKUMA...?!
...
PLEASE HURRY! THEY'RE OVER AT THAT BEACH WHERE WE FIRST ARRIVED AT THE ISLAND!
IF YOU DON'T COME QUICK, HE'S GONNA KILL HER!
DAMN IT! I'LL NEVER LIVE THIS DOWN!!
N-NIDAI...?
IT WAS A MISTAKE TO LET HER OUT OF MY SIGHT...
...A TEAM MANAGER IS RESPONSIBLE FOR KNOWING HIS ATHLETES IN AND OUT, DOWN TO THEIR PRIVATE LIFE...
...DON'T PANIC! WE CAN STILL GET THERE IN TIME! LET'S HURRY OVER TO THE BEACH!
LET'S DO IT!!!
WE JUST GOT KUZURYU BACK...WE AIN'T LOSIN' ANYONE ELSE...
...I WON'T LET ANYONE ELSE DIE ON MY WATCH...!!

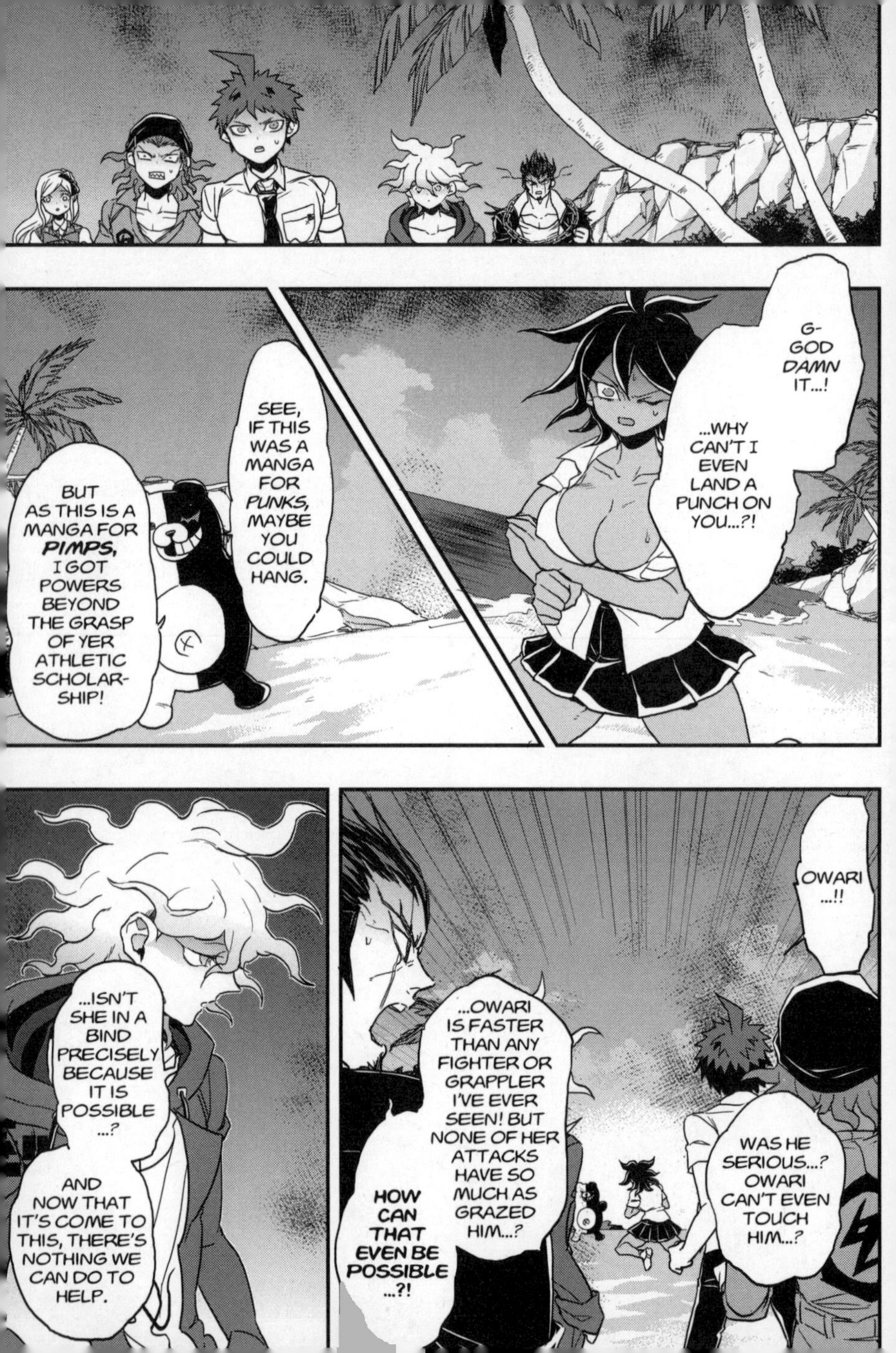
G-GOD DAMN IT...!
...WHY CAN'T I EVEN LAND A PUNCH ON YOU...?!
SEE, IF THIS WAS A MANGA FOR PUNKS, MAYBE YOU COULD HANG.
BUT AS THIS IS A MANGA FOR PIMPS, I GOT POWERS BEYOND THE GRASP OF YER ATHLETIC SCHOLAR-SHIP!
OWARI...!!
WAS HE SERIOUS...? OWARI CAN'T EVEN TOUCH HIM...?
...OWARI IS FASTER THAN ANY FIGHTER OR GRAPPLER I'VE EVER SEEN! BUT NONE OF HER ATTACKS HAVE SO MUCH AS GRAZED HIM...?
HOW CAN THAT EVEN BE POSSIBLE...?!
...ISN'T SHE IN A BIND PRECISELY BECAUSE IT IS POSSIBLE...?
AND NOW THAT IT'S COME TO THIS, THERE'S NOTHING WE CAN DO TO HELP.

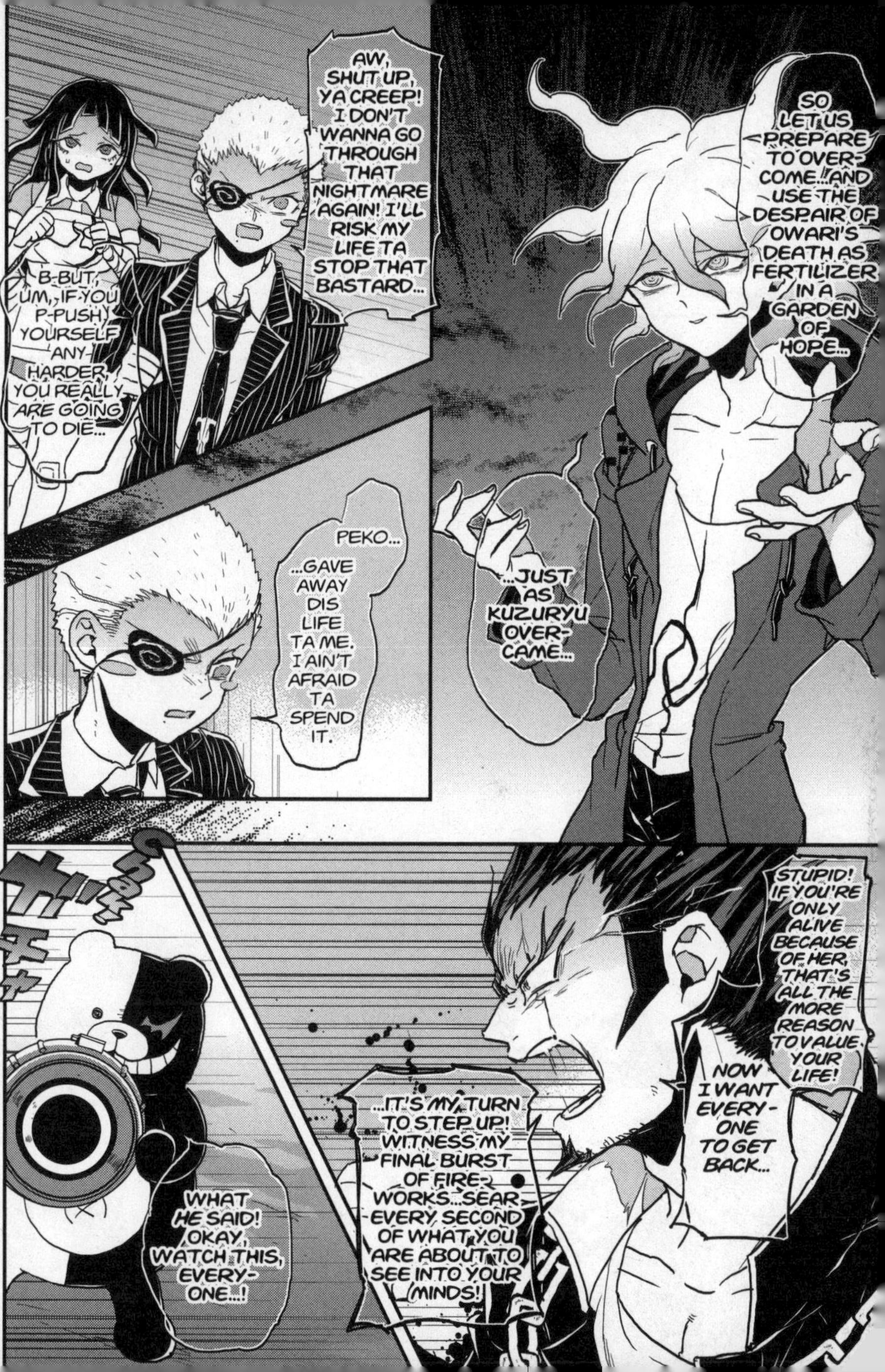
SO LET US PREPARE TO OVERCOME... AND USE THE DESPAIR OF OWARI'S DEATH AS FERTILIZER IN A GARDEN OF HOPE...
...JUST AS KUZURYU OVERCAME...
AW, SHUT UP, YA CREEP! I DON'T WANNA GO THROUGH THAT NIGHTMARE AGAIN! I'LL RISK MY LIFE TA STOP THAT BASTARD...
B-BUT, UM, IF YOU P-PUSH YOURSELF ANY HARDER, YOU REALLY ARE GOING TO DIE...
PEKO...
...GAVE AWAY DIS LIFE TA ME. I AIN'T AFRAID TA SPEND IT.
STUPID! IF YOU'RE ONLY ALIVE BECAUSE OF HER, THAT'S ALL THE MORE REASON TO VALUE YOUR LIFE!
NOW I WANT EVERY-ONE TO GET BACK...
...IT'S MY TURN TO STEP UP! WITNESS MY FINAL BURST OF FIRE-WORKS... SEAR EVERY SECOND OF WHAT YOU ARE ABOUT TO SEE INTO YOUR MINDS!
WHAT HE SAID! OKAY, WATCH THIS, EVERY-ONE...!

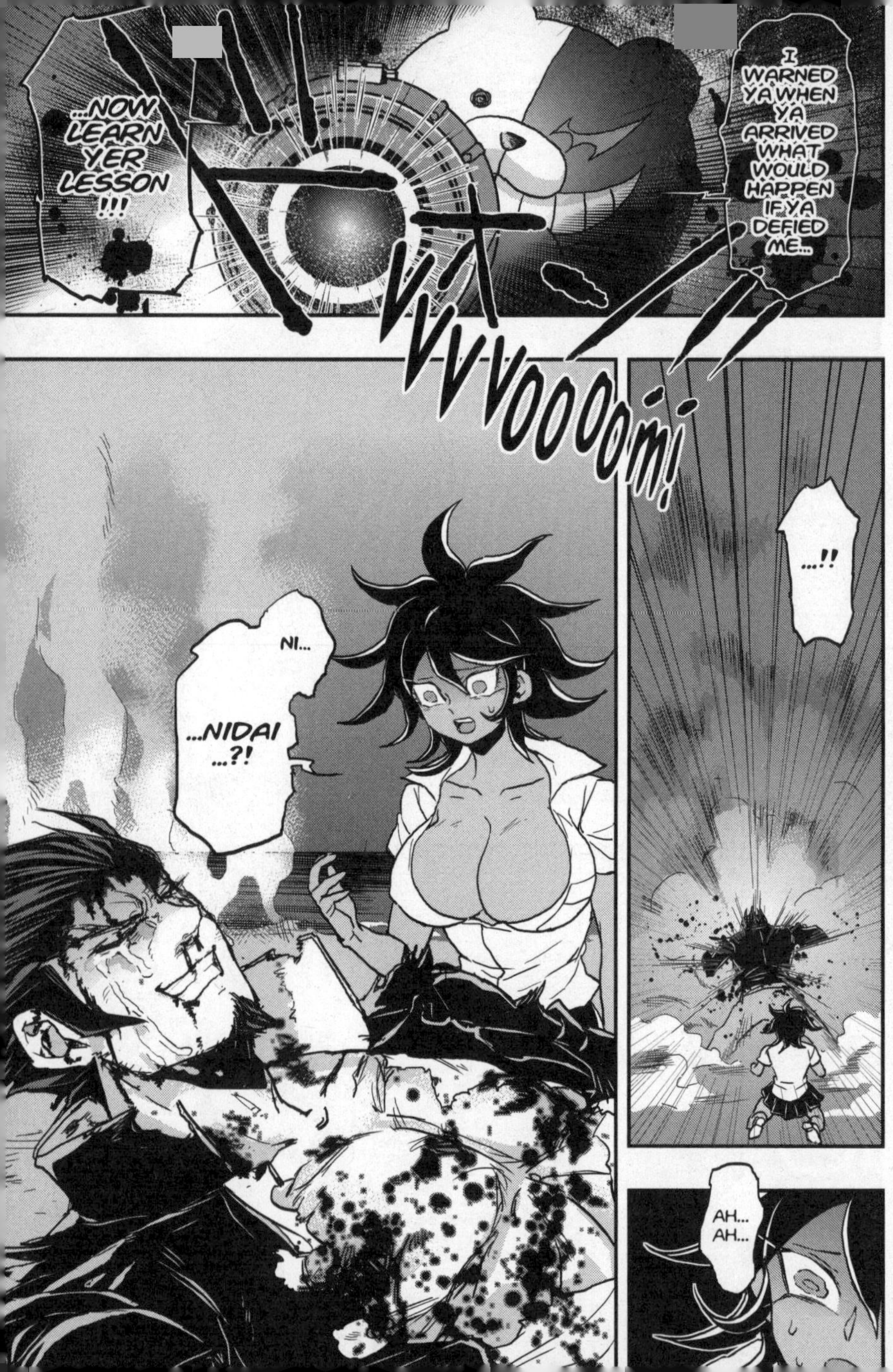
I WARNED YA WHEN YA ARRIVED WHAT WOULD HAPPEN IF YA DEFIED ME...
...NOW LEARN YER LESSON!!!
VVVVOOOOM!
...!!
AH... AH...
NI...
...NIDAI...?!

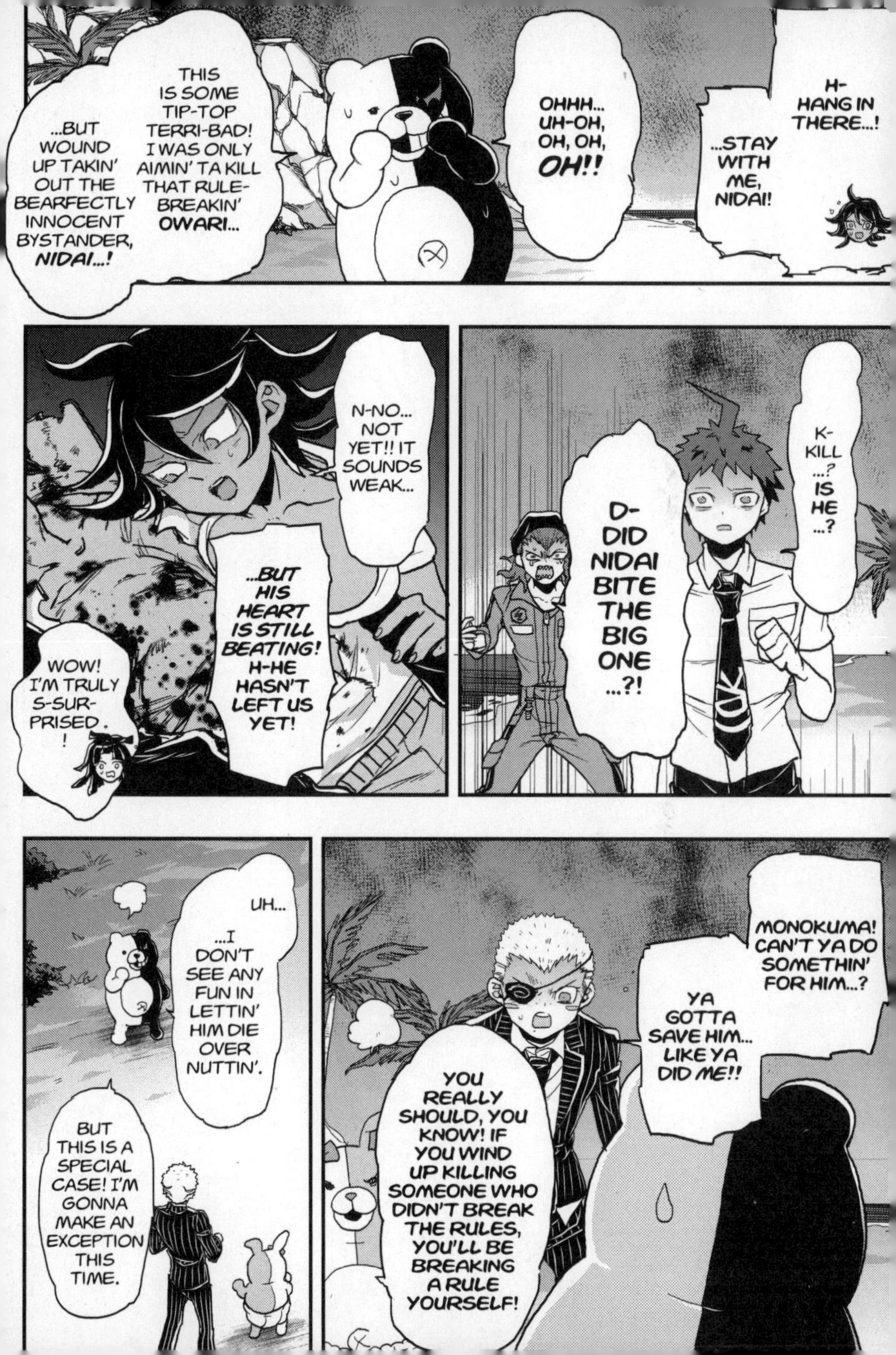

H-HANG IN THERE...!
...STAY WITH ME, NIDAI!
OHHH... UH-OH, OH, OH, OH!!
THIS IS SOME TIP-TOP TERRI-BAD! I WAS ONLY AIMIN' TA KILL THAT RULE-BREAKIN' OWARI...
...BUT WOUND UP TAKIN' OUT THE BEARFECTLY INNOCENT BYSTANDER, NIDAI...!
K-KILL...? IS HE...?
D-DID NIDAI BITE THE BIG ONE...?!
N-NO... NOT YET!! IT SOUNDS WEAK...
...BUT HIS HEART IS STILL BEATING! H-HE HASN'T LEFT US YET!
WOW! I'M TRULY S-SURPRISED.!
MONOKUMA! CAN'T YA DO SOMETHIN' FOR HIM...?
YA GOTTA SAVE HIM... LIKE YA DID ME!!
YOU REALLY SHOULD, YOU KNOW! IF YOU WIND UP KILLING SOMEONE WHO DIDN'T BREAK THE RULES, YOU'LL BE BREAKING A RULE YOURSELF!
UH...
...I DON'T SEE ANY FUN IN LETTIN' HIM DIE OVER NUTTIN'.
BUT THIS IS A SPECIAL CASE! I'M GONNA MAKE AN EXCEPTION THIS TIME.

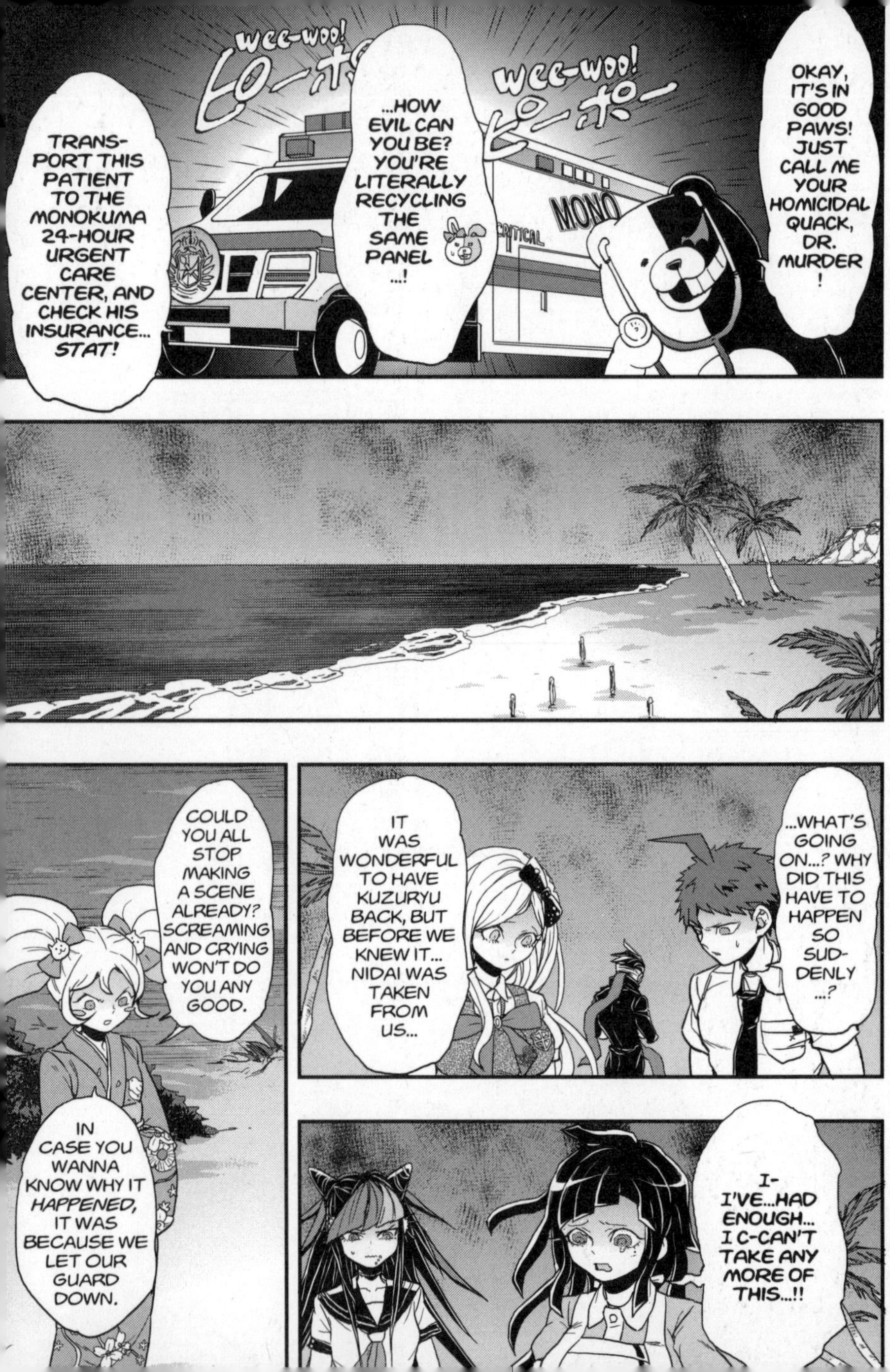
OKAY, IT'S IN GOOD PAWS! JUST CALL ME YOUR HOMICIDAL QUACK, DR. MURDER!
wee-woo!
ピーポー
...HOW EVIL CAN YOU BE? YOU'RE LITERALLY RECYCLING THE SAME PANEL ...!
wee-woo!
MONO
CRITICAL
TRANSPORT THIS PATIENT TO THE MONOKUMA 24-HOUR URGENT CARE CENTER, AND CHECK HIS INSURANCE... STAT!
...WHAT'S GOING ON...? WHY DID THIS HAVE TO HAPPEN SO SUDDENLY ...?
IT WAS WONDERFUL TO HAVE KUZURYU BACK, BUT BEFORE WE KNEW IT... NIDAI WAS TAKEN FROM US...
I- I'VE...HAD ENOUGH... I C-CAN'T TAKE ANY MORE OF THIS...!!
COULD YOU ALL STOP MAKING A SCENE ALREADY? SCREAMING AND CRYING WON'T DO YOU ANY GOOD.
IN CASE YOU WANNA KNOW WHY IT HAPPENED, IT WAS BECAUSE WE LET OUR GUARD DOWN.

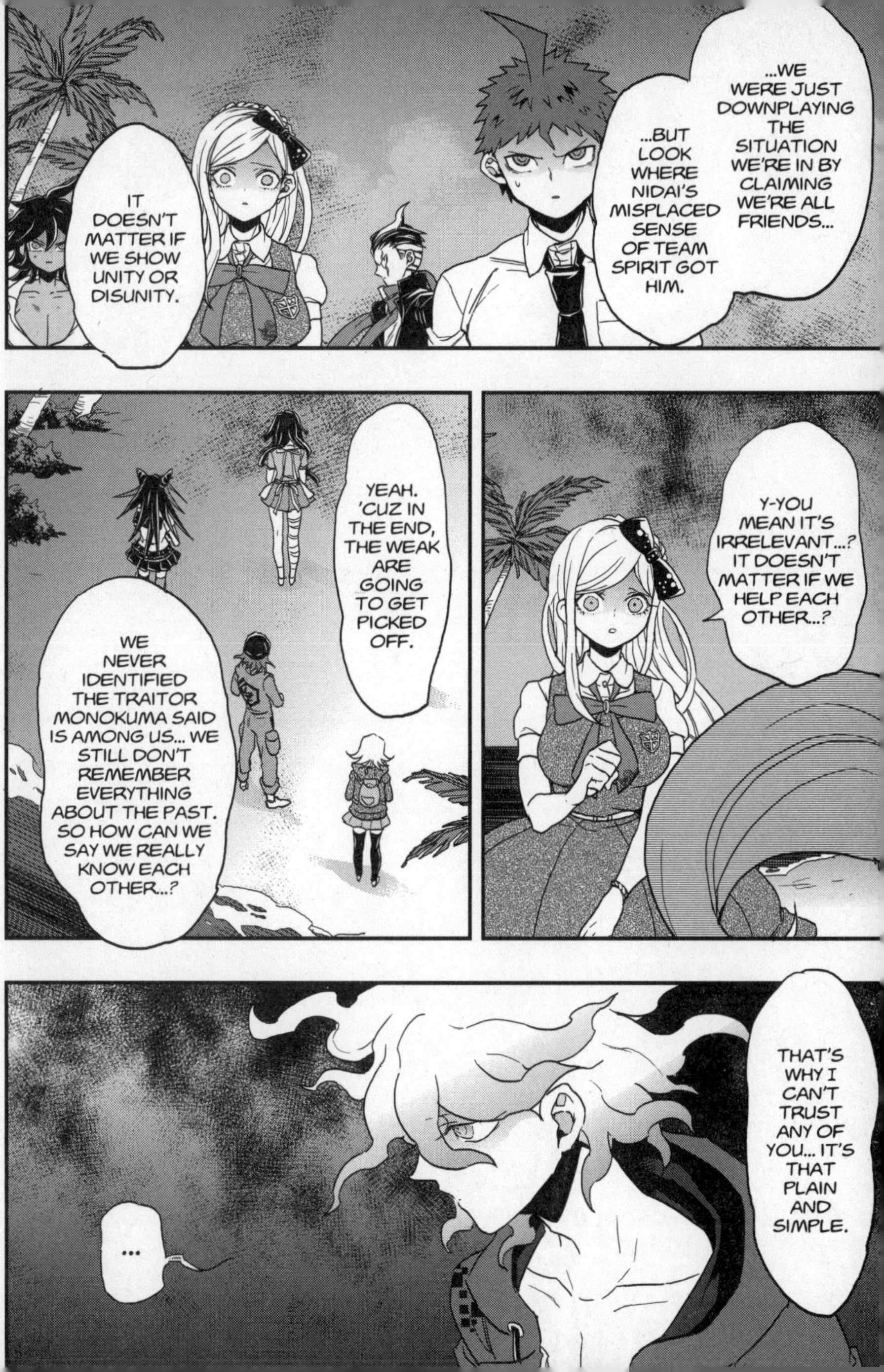
...WE WERE JUST DOWNPLAYING THE SITUATION WE'RE IN BY CLAIMING WE'RE ALL FRIENDS...
...BUT LOOK WHERE NIDAI'S MISPLACED SENSE OF TEAM SPIRIT GOT HIM.
IT DOESN'T MATTER IF WE SHOW UNITY OR DISUNITY.
Y-YOU MEAN IT'S IRRELEVANT...? IT DOESN'T MATTER IF WE HELP EACH OTHER...?
YEAH. 'CUZ IN THE END, THE WEAK ARE GOING TO GET PICKED OFF.
WE NEVER IDENTIFIED THE TRAITOR MONOKUMA SAID IS AMONG US... WE STILL DON'T REMEMBER EVERYTHING ABOUT THE PAST. SO HOW CAN WE SAY WE REALLY KNOW EACH OTHER...?
THAT'S WHY I CAN'T TRUST ANY OF YOU... IT'S THAT PLAIN AND SIMPLE.
...

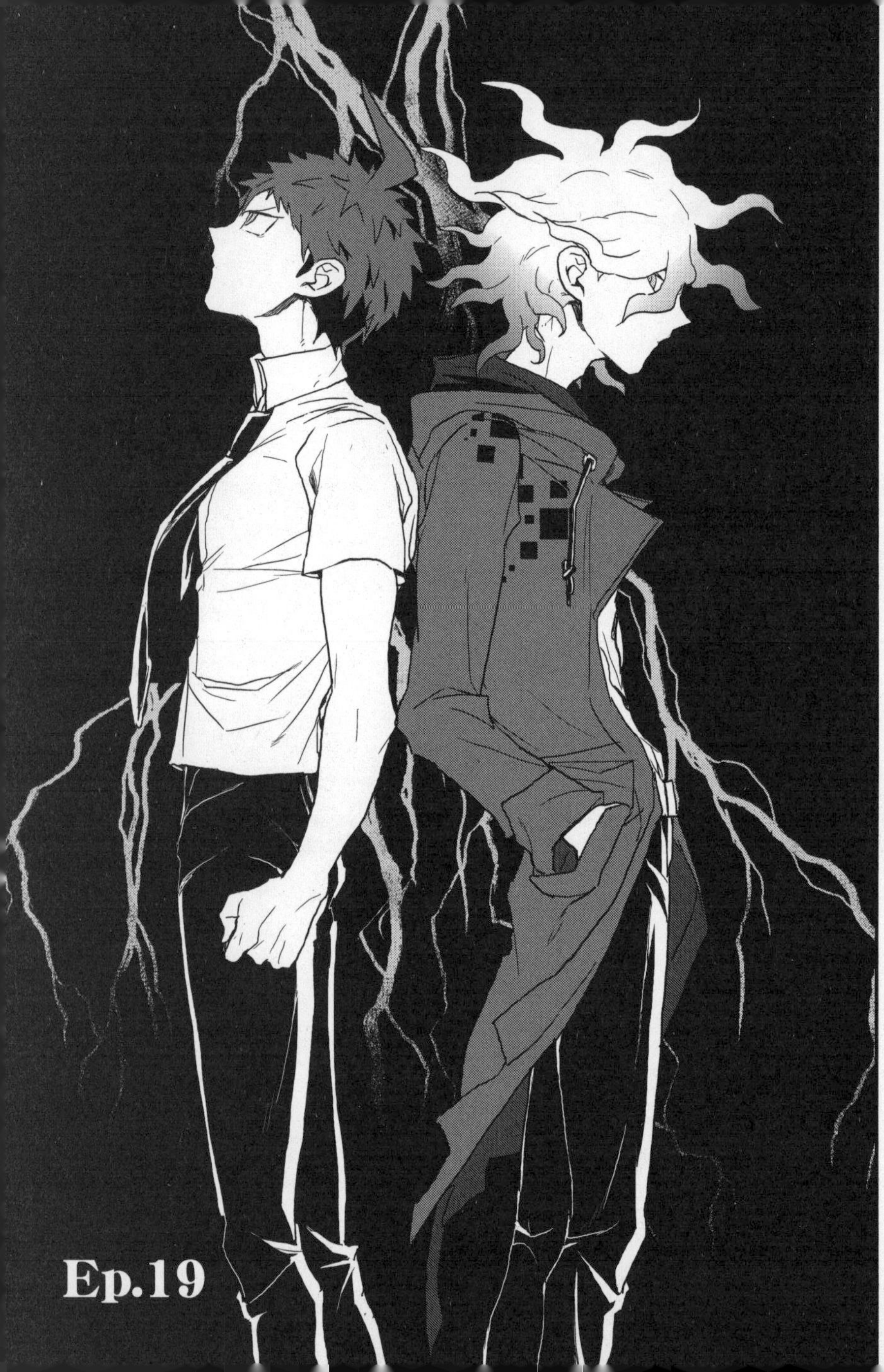
Ep.19

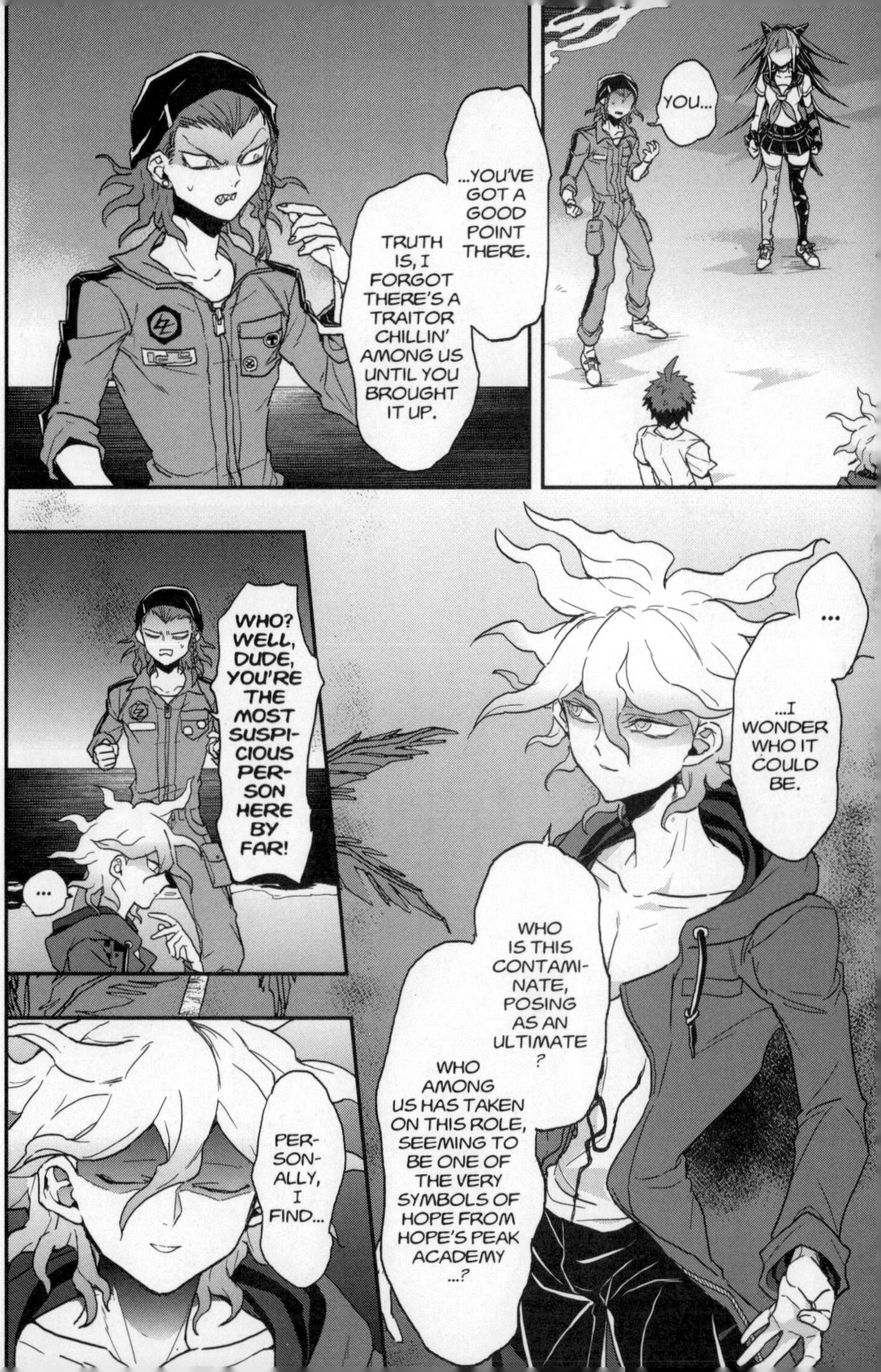
YOU...
...YOU'VE GOT A GOOD POINT THERE.
TRUTH IS, I FORGOT THERE'S A TRAITOR CHILLIN' AMONG US UNTIL YOU BROUGHT IT UP.
...
...I WONDER WHO IT COULD BE.
WHO IS THIS CONTAMINATE, POSING AS AN ULTIMATE?
WHO AMONG US HAS TAKEN ON THIS ROLE, SEEMING TO BE ONE OF THE VERY SYMBOLS OF HOPE FROM HOPE'S PEAK ACADEMY...?
WHO? WELL, DUDE, YOU'RE THE MOST SUSPICIOUS PERSON HERE BY FAR!
...
PERSONALLY, I FIND...

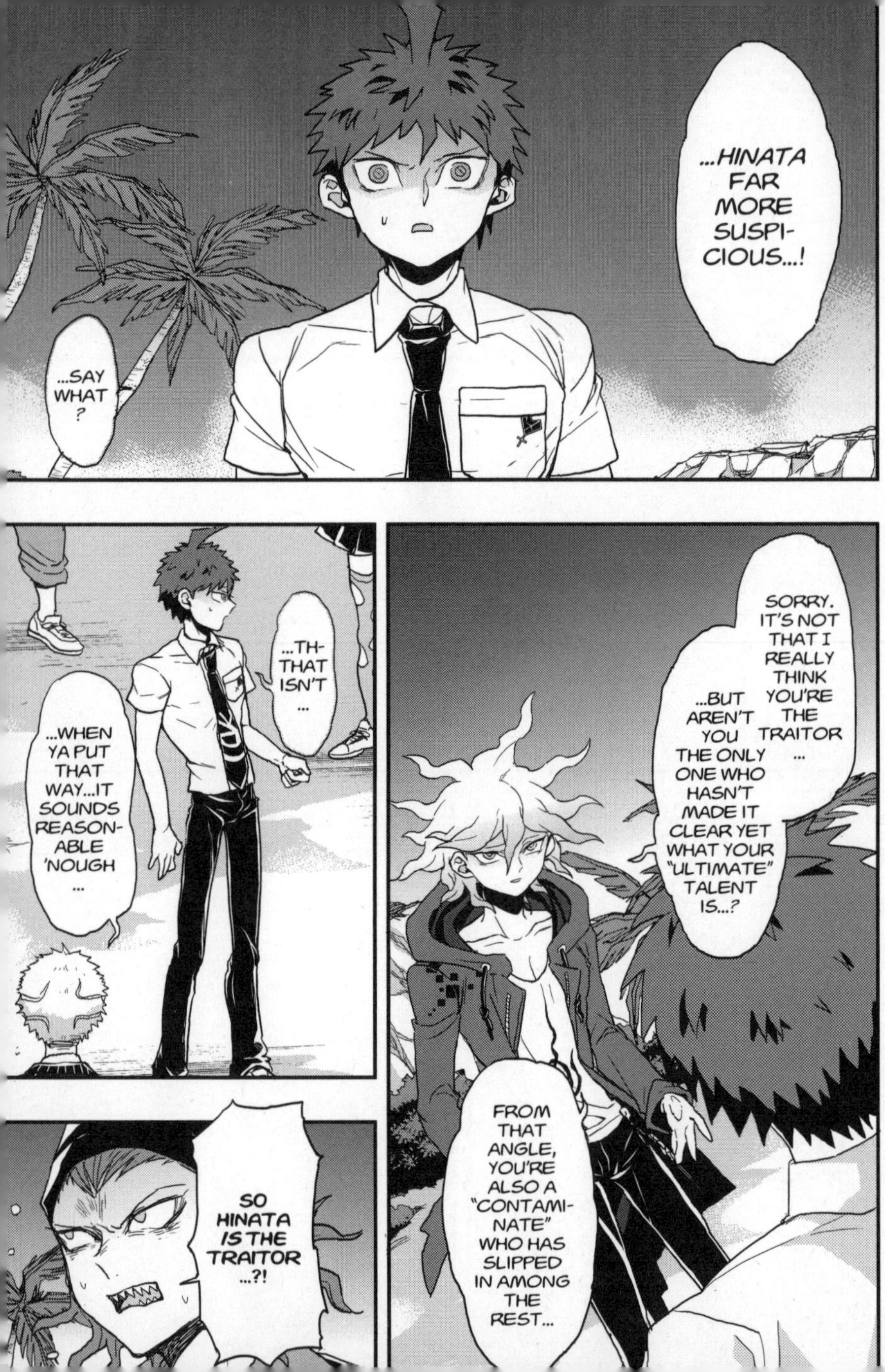
...HINATA FAR MORE SUSPICIOUS...!
...SAY WHAT?
SORRY. IT'S NOT THAT I REALLY THINK YOU'RE THE TRAITOR...
...BUT AREN'T YOU THE ONLY ONE WHO HASN'T MADE IT CLEAR YET WHAT YOUR "ULTIMATE" TALENT IS...?
FROM THAT ANGLE, YOU'RE ALSO A "CONTAMINATE" WHO HAS SLIPPED IN AMONG THE REST...
...TH-THAT ISN'T...
...WHEN YA PUT THAT WAY...IT SOUNDS REASONABLE 'NOUGH...
SO HINATA *IS* THE TRAITOR...?!

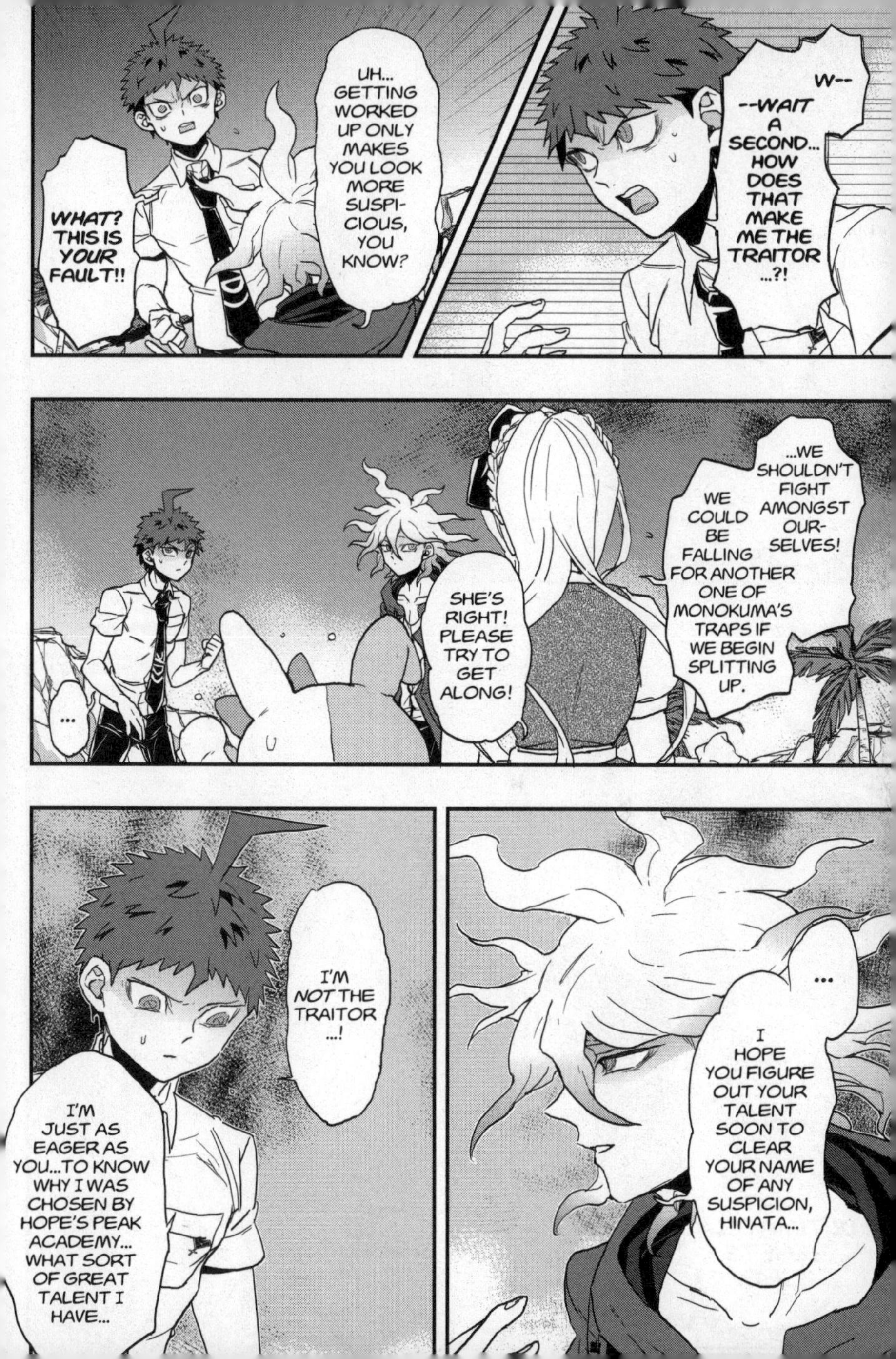
W--
--WAIT A SECOND... HOW DOES THAT MAKE ME THE TRAITOR ...?!
UH... GETTING WORKED UP ONLY MAKES YOU LOOK MORE SUSPICIOUS, YOU KNOW?
WHAT? THIS IS YOUR FAULT!!
...WE SHOULDN'T FIGHT AMONGST OURSELVES!
WE COULD BE FALLING FOR ANOTHER ONE OF MONOKUMA'S TRAPS IF WE BEGIN SPLITTING UP.
SHE'S RIGHT! PLEASE TRY TO GET ALONG!
...
...
I HOPE YOU FIGURE OUT YOUR TALENT SOON TO CLEAR YOUR NAME OF ANY SUSPICION, HINATA...
I'M NOT THE TRAITOR ...!
I'M JUST AS EAGER AS YOU...TO KNOW WHY I WAS CHOSEN BY HOPE'S PEAK ACADEMY... WHAT SORT OF GREAT TALENT I HAVE...

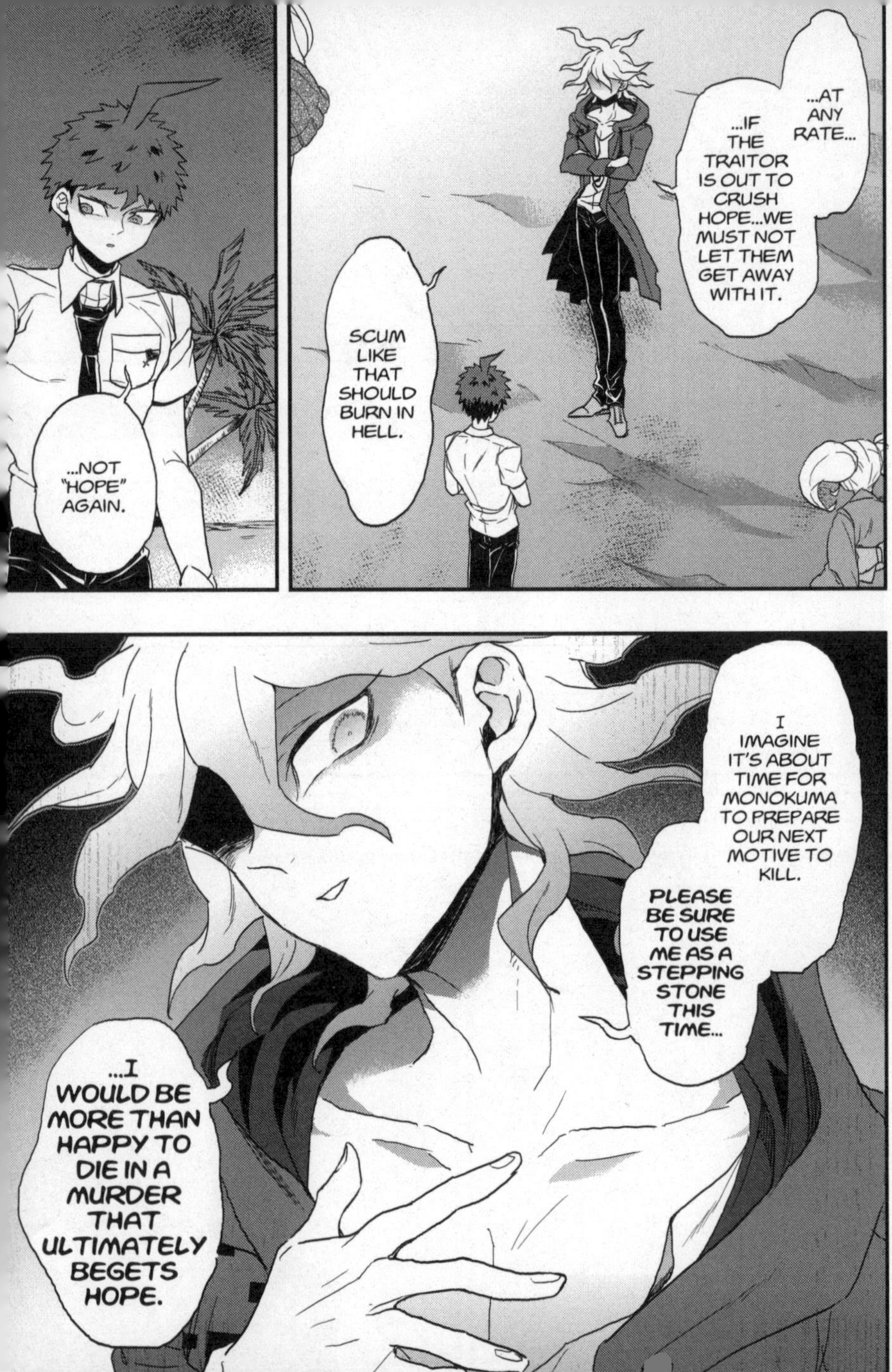
...AT ANY RATE...
...IF THE TRAITOR IS OUT TO CRUSH HOPE...WE MUST NOT LET THEM GET AWAY WITH IT.
SCUM LIKE THAT SHOULD BURN IN HELL.
...NOT "HOPE" AGAIN.
I IMAGINE IT'S ABOUT TIME FOR MONOKUMA TO PREPARE OUR NEXT MOTIVE TO KILL.
PLEASE BE SURE TO USE ME AS A STEPPING STONE THIS TIME...
...I WOULD BE MORE THAN HAPPY TO DIE IN A MURDER THAT ULTIMATELY BEGETS HOPE.

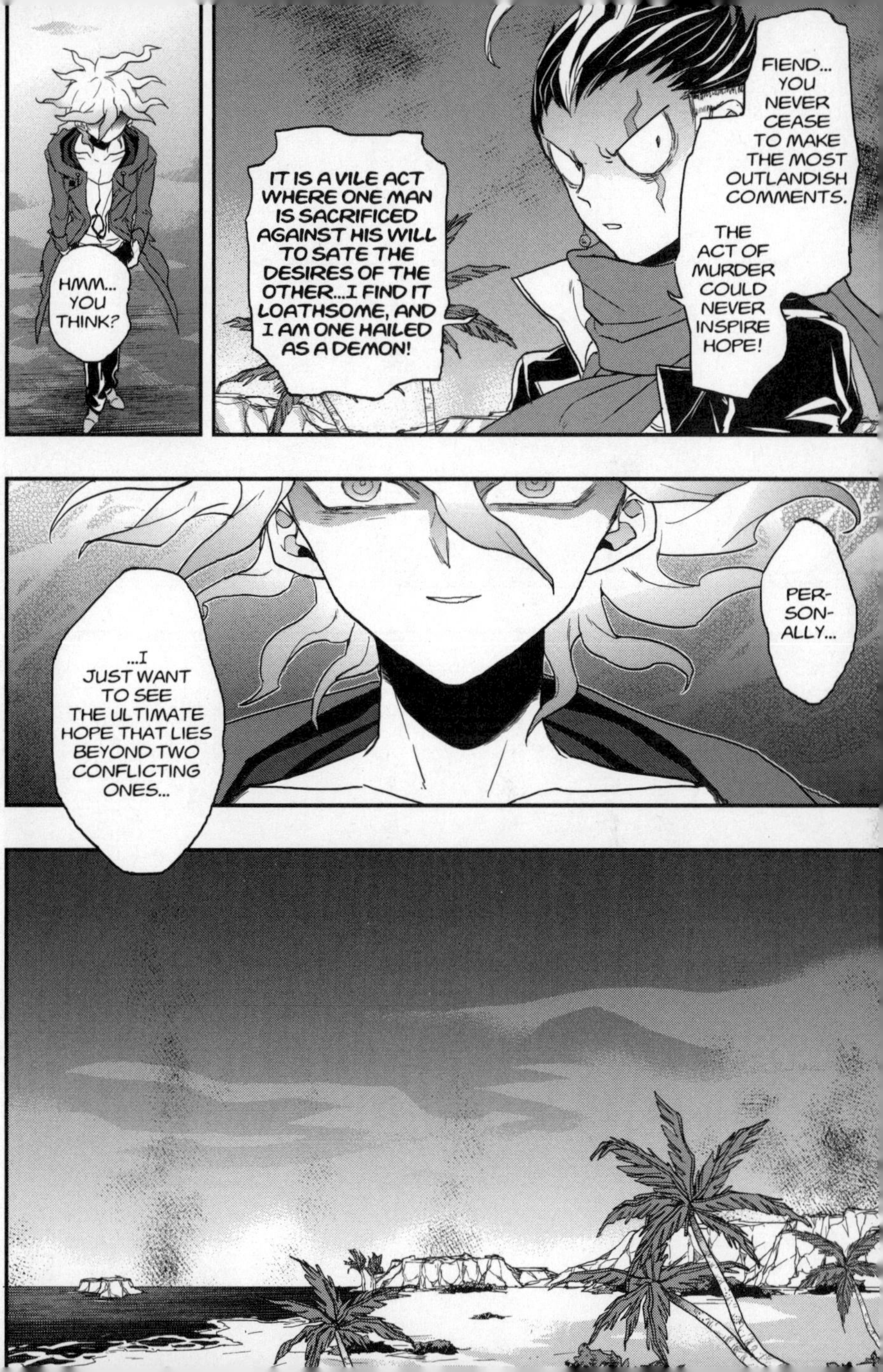
FIEND... YOU NEVER CEASE TO MAKE THE MOST OUTLANDISH COMMENTS.
THE ACT OF MURDER COULD NEVER INSPIRE HOPE!
IT IS A VILE ACT WHERE ONE MAN IS SACRIFICED AGAINST HIS WILL TO SATE THE DESIRES OF THE OTHER...I FIND IT LOATHSOME, AND I AM ONE HAILED AS A DEMON!
HMM... YOU THINK?
PER-SON-ALLY...
...I JUST WANT TO SEE THE ULTIMATE HOPE THAT LIES BEYOND TWO CONFLICTING ONES...

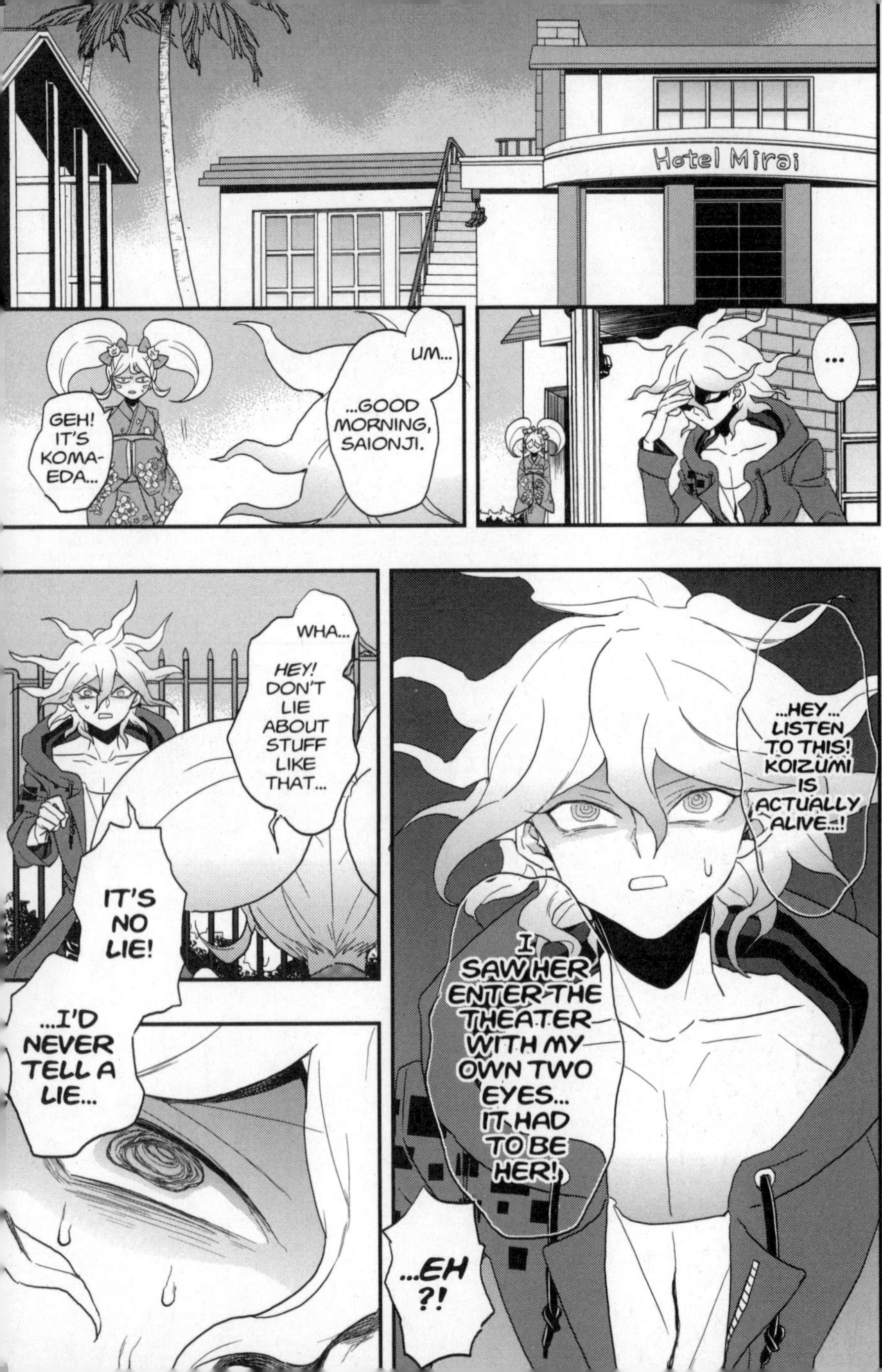
Hotel Mirai
...
UM...
...GOOD MORNING, SAIONJI.
GEH! IT'S KOMA-EDA...
...HEY... LISTEN TO THIS! KOIZUMI IS ACTUALLY ALIVE...!
I SAW HER ENTER THE THEATER WITH MY OWN TWO EYES... IT HAD TO BE HER!
...EH ?!
WHA...
HEY! DON'T LIE ABOUT STUFF LIKE THAT...
IT'S NO LIE!
...I'D NEVER TELL A LIE...

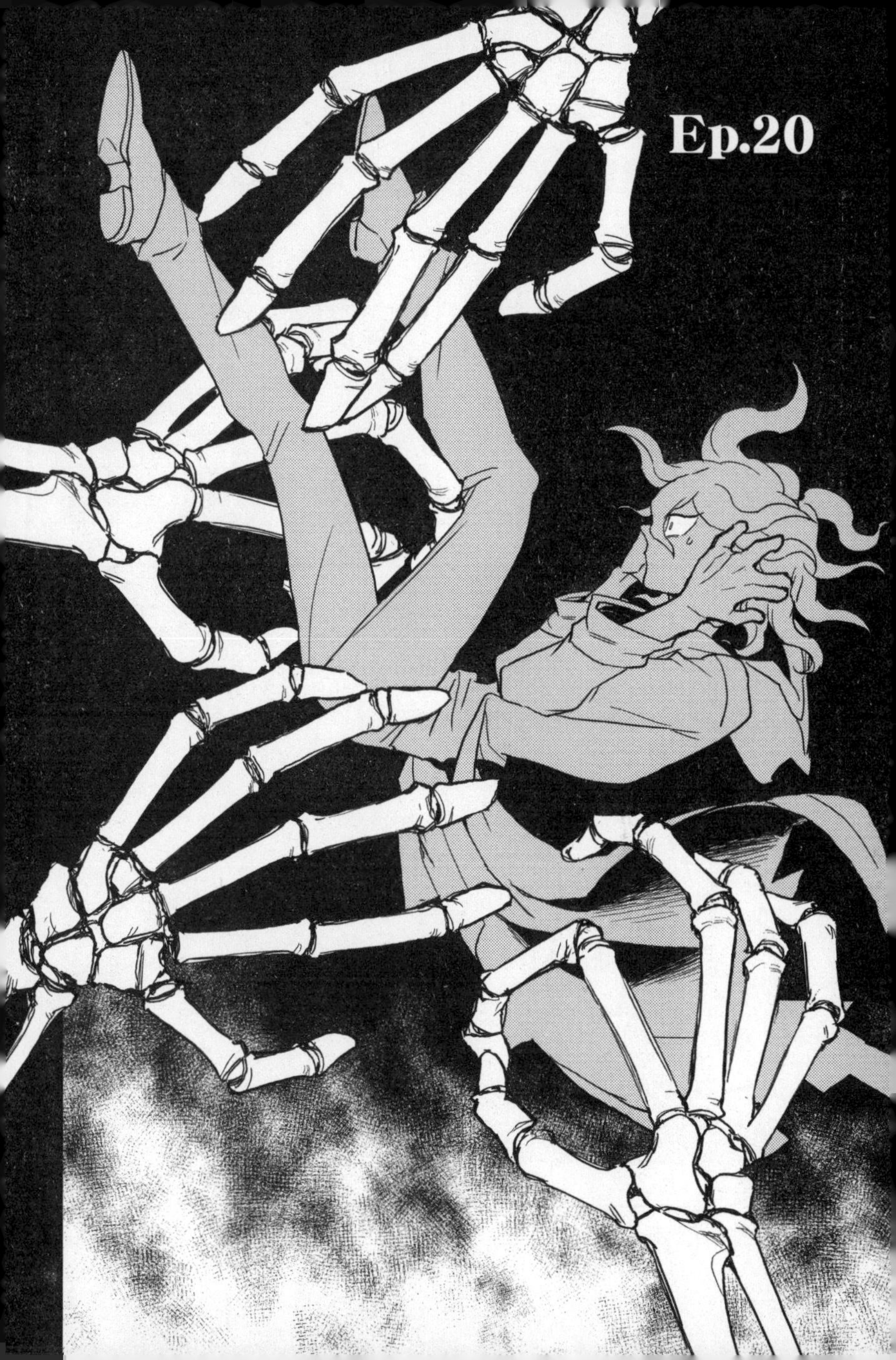
Ep.20

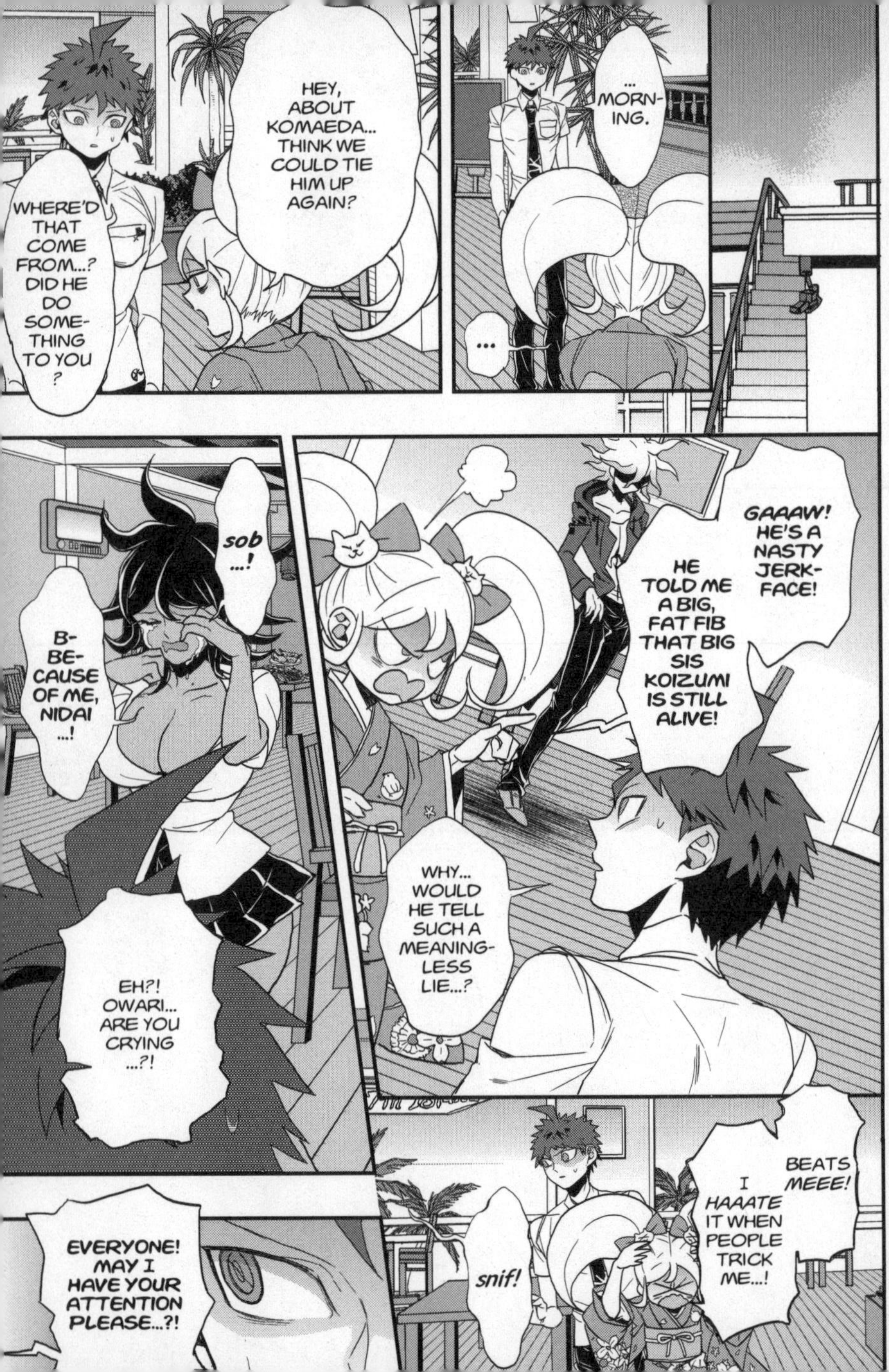
... MORNING.
...
HEY, ABOUT KOMAEDA... THINK WE COULD TIE HIM UP AGAIN?
WHERE'D THAT COME FROM...? DID HE DO SOMETHING TO YOU?
GAAAW! HE'S A NASTY JERK-FACE!
HE TOLD ME A BIG, FAT FIB THAT BIG SIS KOIZUMI IS STILL ALIVE!
WHY... WOULD HE TELL SUCH A MEANINGLESS LIE...?
sob ...!
B-BE-CAUSE OF ME, NIDAI ...!
EH?! OWARI... ARE YOU CRYING ...?!
BEATS MEEE!
I HAAATE IT WHEN PEOPLE TRICK ME...!
snif!
EVERYONE! MAY I HAVE YOUR ATTENTION PLEASE...?!

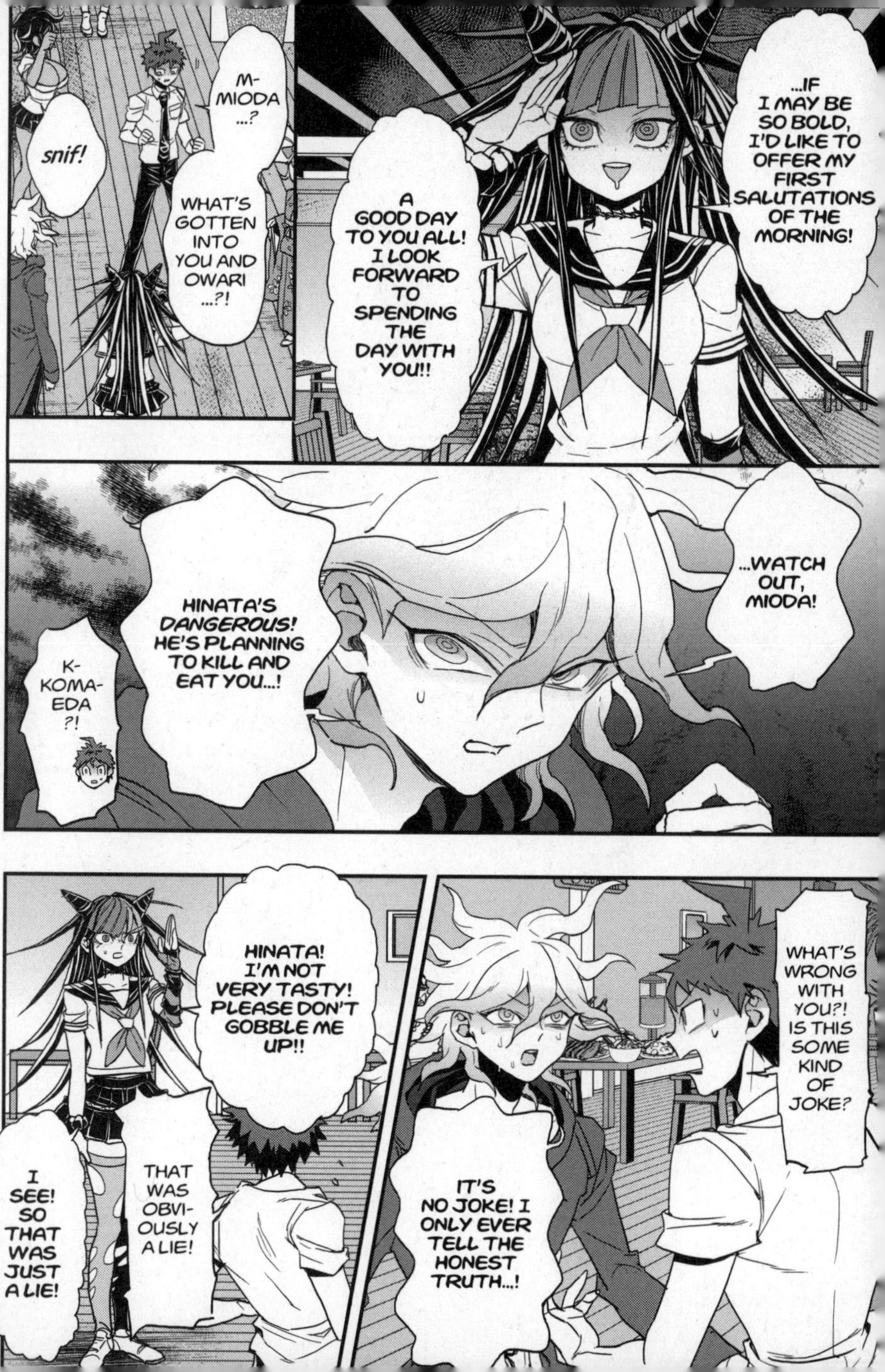
...IF I MAY BE SO BOLD, I'D LIKE TO OFFER MY FIRST SALUTATIONS OF THE MORNING!
A GOOD DAY TO YOU ALL! I LOOK FORWARD TO SPENDING THE DAY WITH YOU!!
M-MIODA ...?
WHAT'S GOTTEN INTO YOU AND OWARI ...?!
snif!
...WATCH OUT, MIODA!
HINATA'S DANGEROUS! HE'S PLANNING TO KILL AND EAT YOU...!
K-KOMA-EDA ?!
WHAT'S WRONG WITH YOU?! IS THIS SOME KIND OF JOKE?
IT'S NO JOKE! I ONLY EVER TELL THE HONEST TRUTH...!
HINATA! I'M NOT VERY TASTY! PLEASE DON'T GOBBLE ME UP!!
THAT WAS OBVI-OUSLY A LIE!
I SEE! SO THAT WAS JUST A LIE!

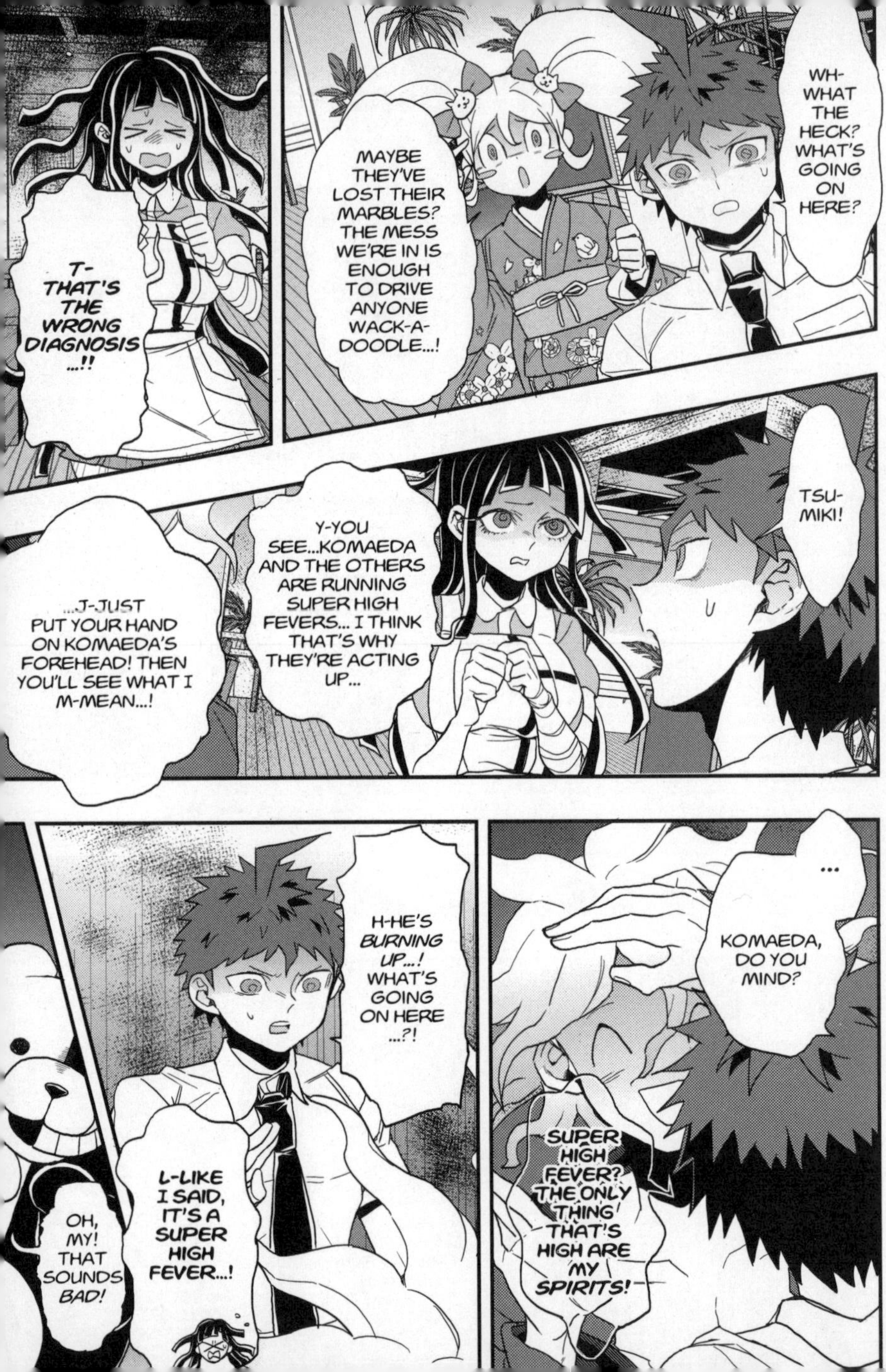
WH-WHAT THE HECK? WHAT'S GOING ON HERE?
MAYBE THEY'VE LOST THEIR MARBLES? THE MESS WE'RE IN IS ENOUGH TO DRIVE ANYONE WACK-A-DOODLE...!
T-THAT'S THE WRONG DIAGNOSIS ...!!
TSU-MIKI!
Y-YOU SEE...KOMAEDA AND THE OTHERS ARE RUNNING SUPER HIGH FEVERS... I THINK THAT'S WHY THEY'RE ACTING UP...
...J-JUST PUT YOUR HAND ON KOMAEDA'S FOREHEAD! THEN YOU'LL SEE WHAT I M-MEAN...!
...
KOMAEDA, DO YOU MIND?
SUPER HIGH FEVER? THE ONLY THING THAT'S HIGH ARE MY SPIRITS!
H-HE'S BURNING UP...! WHAT'S GOING ON HERE ...?!
L-LIKE I SAID, IT'S A SUPER HIGH FEVER...!
OH, MY! THAT SOUNDS BAD!

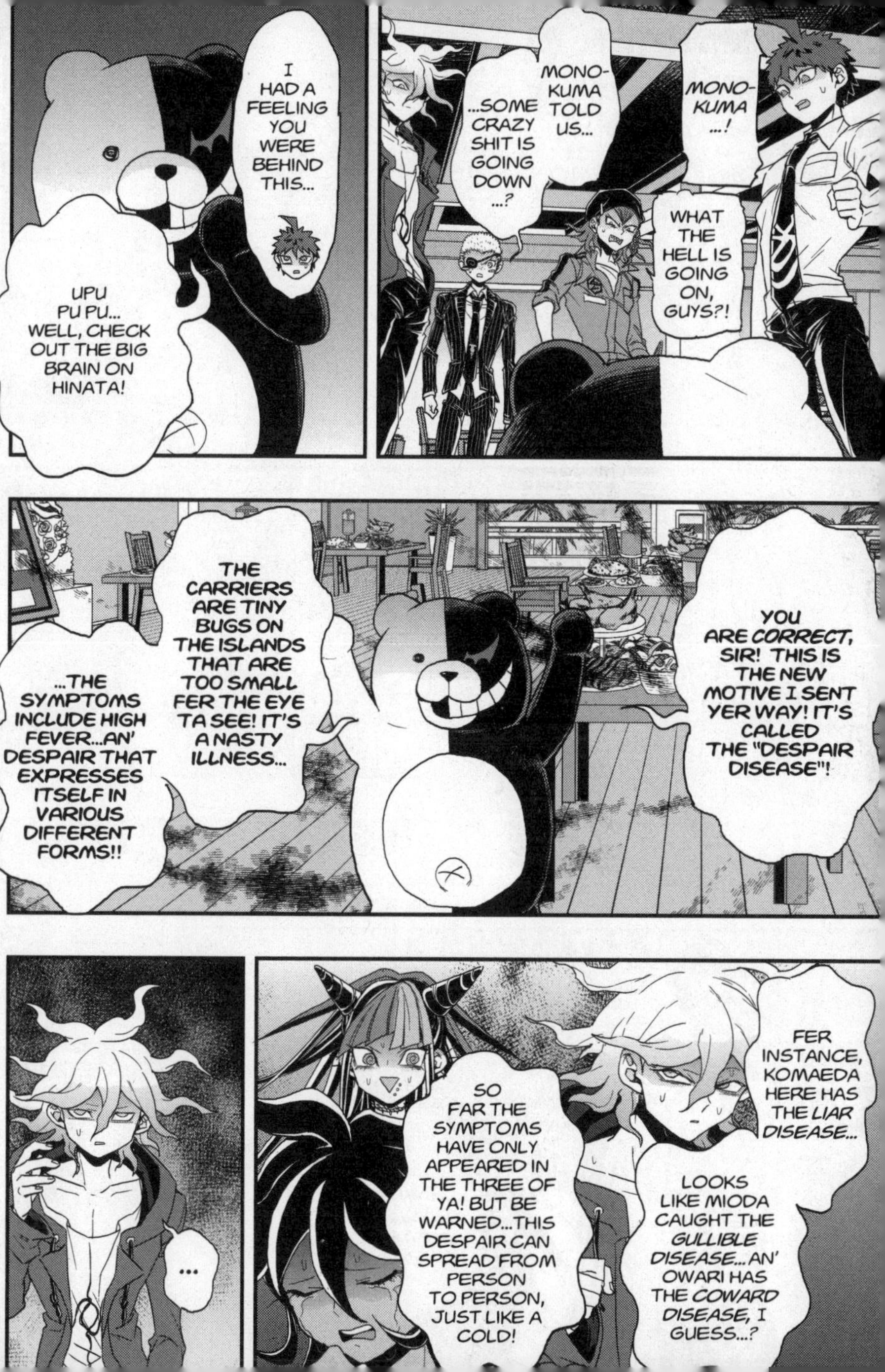
MONO-KUMA ...!
WHAT THE HELL IS GOING ON, GUYS?!
MONO-KUMA TOLD US...
...SOME CRAZY SHIT IS GOING DOWN ...?
I HAD A FEELING YOU WERE BEHIND THIS...
UPU PU PU... WELL, CHECK OUT THE BIG BRAIN ON HINATA!
YOU ARE *CORRECT*, SIR! THIS IS THE NEW MOTIVE I SENT YER WAY! IT'S CALLED THE "DESPAIR DISEASE"!
THE CARRIERS ARE TINY BUGS ON THE ISLANDS THAT ARE TOO SMALL FER THE EYE TA SEE! IT'S A NASTY ILLNESS...
...THE SYMPTOMS INCLUDE HIGH FEVER...AN' DESPAIR THAT EXPRESSES ITSELF IN VARIOUS DIFFERENT FORMS!!
FER INSTANCE, KOMAEDA HERE HAS THE *LIAR DISEASE*...
LOOKS LIKE MIODA CAUGHT THE *GULLIBLE DISEASE*...AN' OWARI HAS THE *COWARD DISEASE*, I GUESS...?
SO FAR THE SYMPTOMS HAVE ONLY APPEARED IN THE THREE OF YA! BUT BE WARNED...THIS DESPAIR CAN SPREAD FROM PERSON TO PERSON, JUST LIKE A COLD!
...

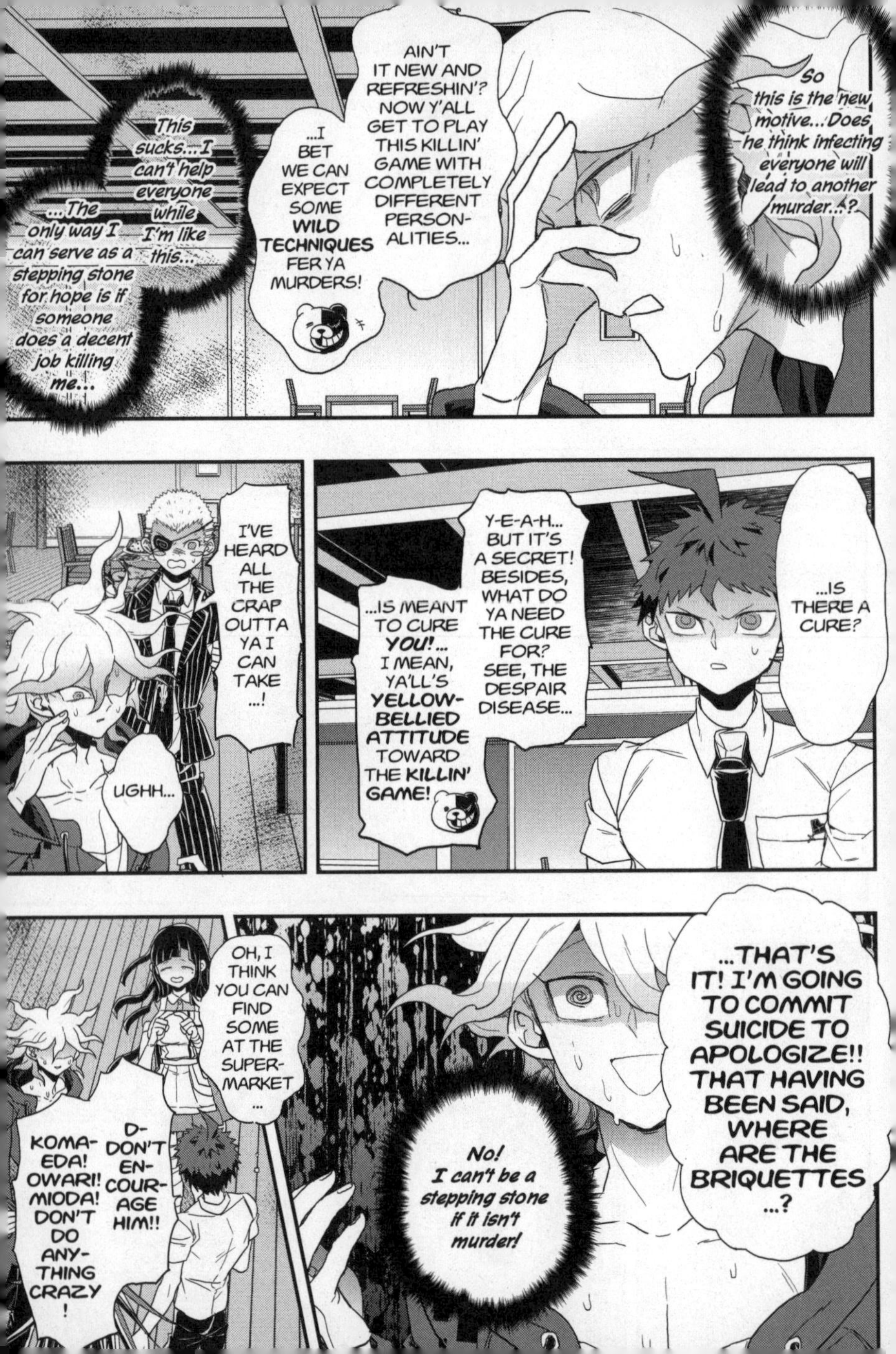
So this is the new motive... Does he think infecting everyone will lead to another murder...?
AIN'T IT NEW AND REFRESHIN'? NOW Y'ALL GET TO PLAY THIS KILLIN' GAME WITH COMPLETELY DIFFERENT PERSON-ALITIES...
...I BET WE CAN EXPECT SOME WILD TECHNIQUES FER YA MURDERS!
This sucks... I can't help everyone while I'm like this...
...The only way I can serve as a stepping stone for hope is if someone does a decent job killing me...
...IS THERE A CURE?
Y-E-A-H... BUT IT'S A SECRET! BESIDES, WHAT DO YA NEED THE CURE FOR? SEE, THE DESPAIR DISEASE...
...IS MEANT TO CURE YOU!... I MEAN, YA'LL'S YELLOW-BELLIED ATTITUDE TOWARD THE KILLIN' GAME!
I'VE HEARD ALL THE CRAP OUTTA YA I CAN TAKE ...!
UGHH...
...THAT'S IT! I'M GOING TO COMMIT SUICIDE TO APOLOGIZE!! THAT HAVING BEEN SAID, WHERE ARE THE BRIQUETTES ...?
No! I can't be a stepping stone if it isn't murder!
OH, I THINK YOU CAN FIND SOME AT THE SUPER-MARKET ...
D-DON'T EN-COUR-AGE HIM!!
KOMA-EDA! OWARI!! MIODA! DON'T DO ANY-THING CRAZY !

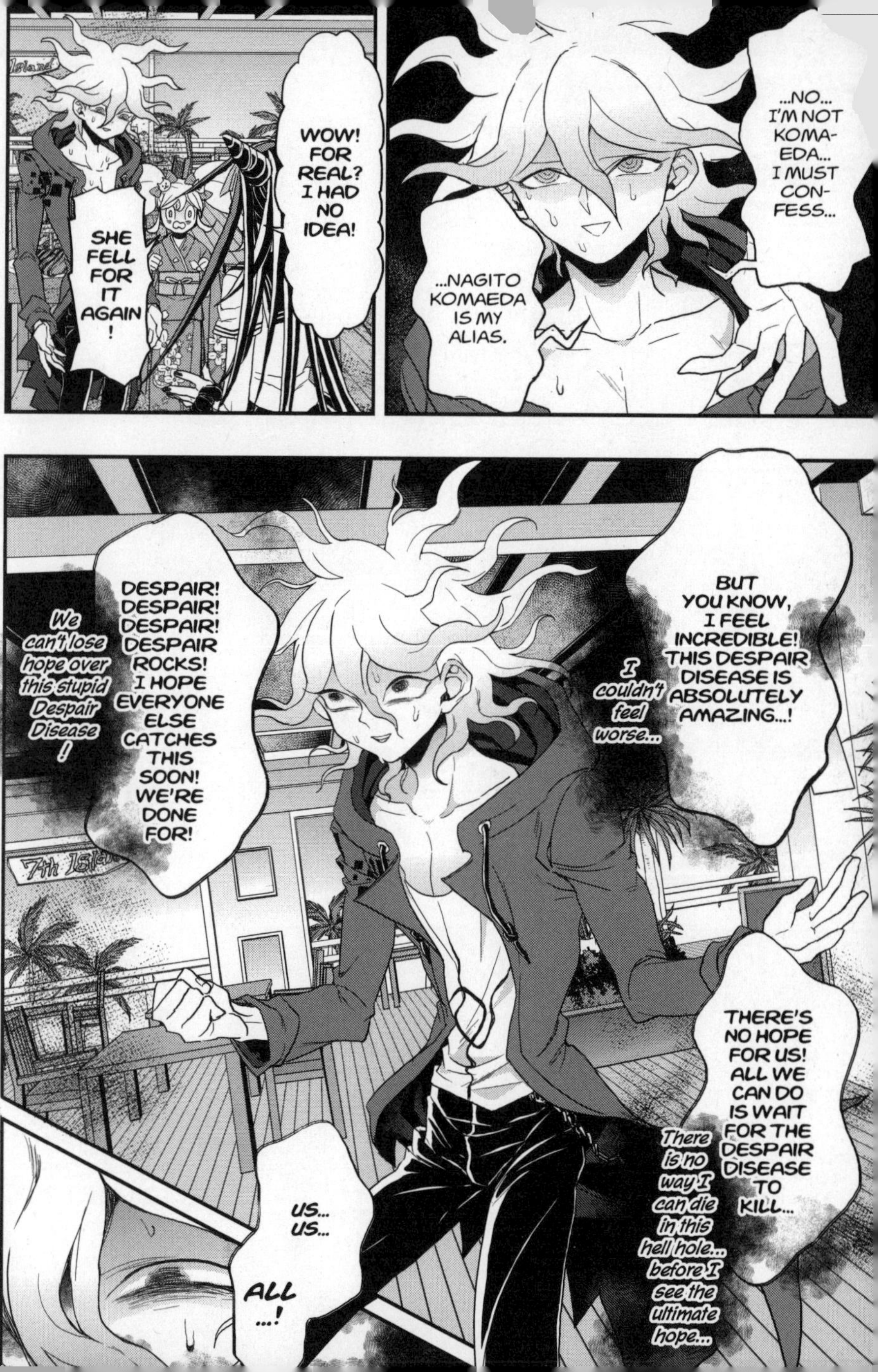
...NO... I'M NOT KOMAEDA... I MUST CONFESS...
...NAGITO KOMAEDA IS MY ALIAS.
WOW! FOR REAL? I HAD NO IDEA!
SHE FELL FOR IT AGAIN!
BUT YOU KNOW, I FEEL INCREDIBLE! THIS DESPAIR DISEASE IS ABSOLUTELY AMAZING...!
I couldn't feel worse...
DESPAIR! DESPAIR! DESPAIR! DESPAIR ROCKS! I HOPE EVERYONE ELSE CATCHES THIS SOON! WE'RE DONE FOR!
We can't lose hope over this stupid Despair Disease!
THERE'S NO HOPE FOR US! ALL WE CAN DO IS WAIT FOR THE DESPAIR DISEASE TO KILL...
There is no way I can die in this hell hole... before I see the ultimate hope...
US... US...
ALL...!

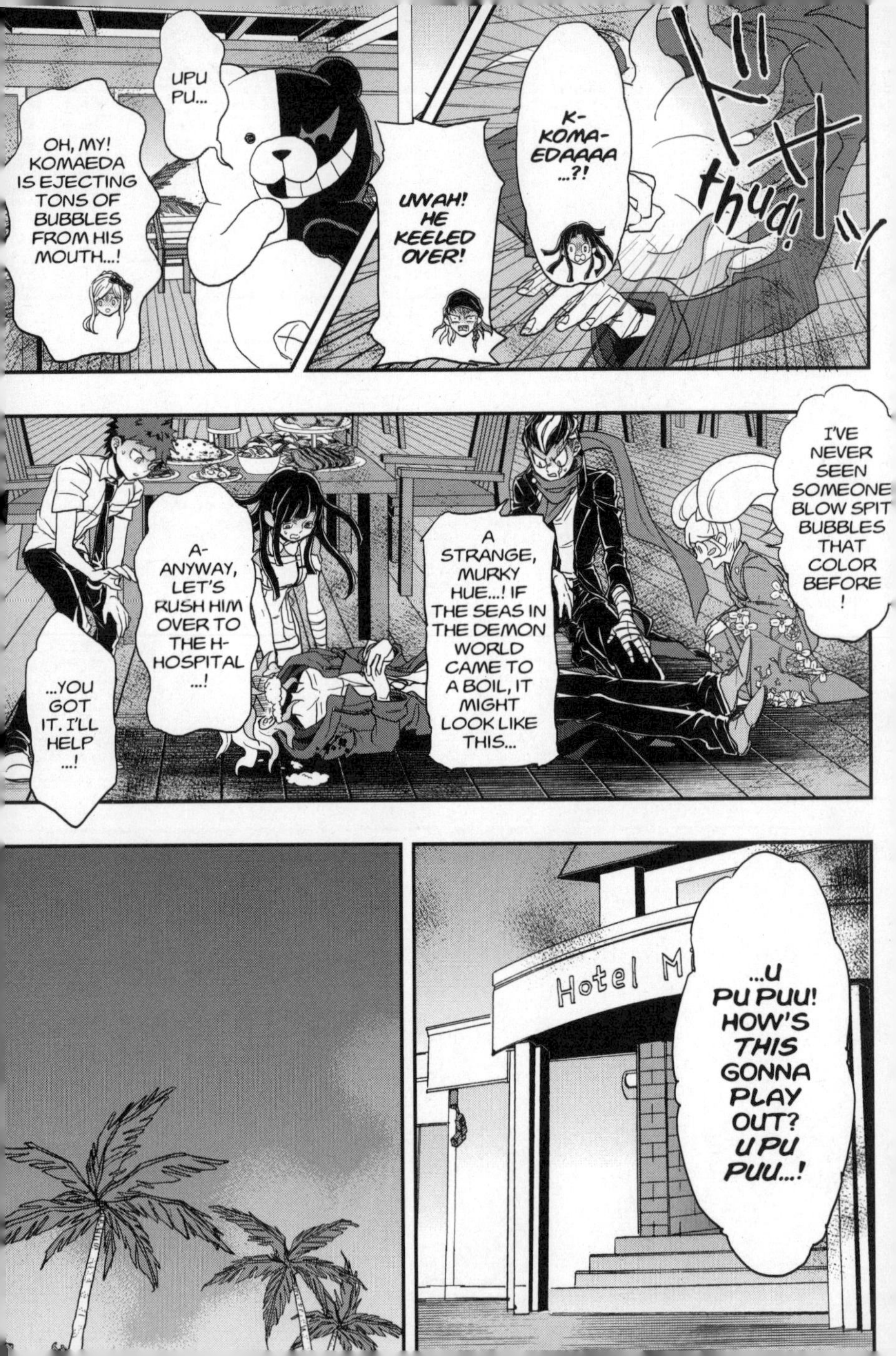
thud!
K-KOMA-EDAAAA...?!
UWAH! HE KEELED OVER!
UPU PU...
OH, MY! KOMAEDA IS EJECTING TONS OF BUBBLES FROM HIS MOUTH...!
I'VE NEVER SEEN SOMEONE BLOW SPIT BUBBLES THAT COLOR BEFORE!
A STRANGE, MURKY HUE...! IF THE SEAS IN THE DEMON WORLD CAME TO A BOIL, IT MIGHT LOOK LIKE THIS...
A-ANYWAY, LET'S RUSH HIM OVER TO THE H-HOSPITAL...!
...YOU GOT IT. I'LL HELP...!
...U PU PUU! HOW'S THIS GONNA PLAY OUT? U PU PUU...!
Hotel Mi

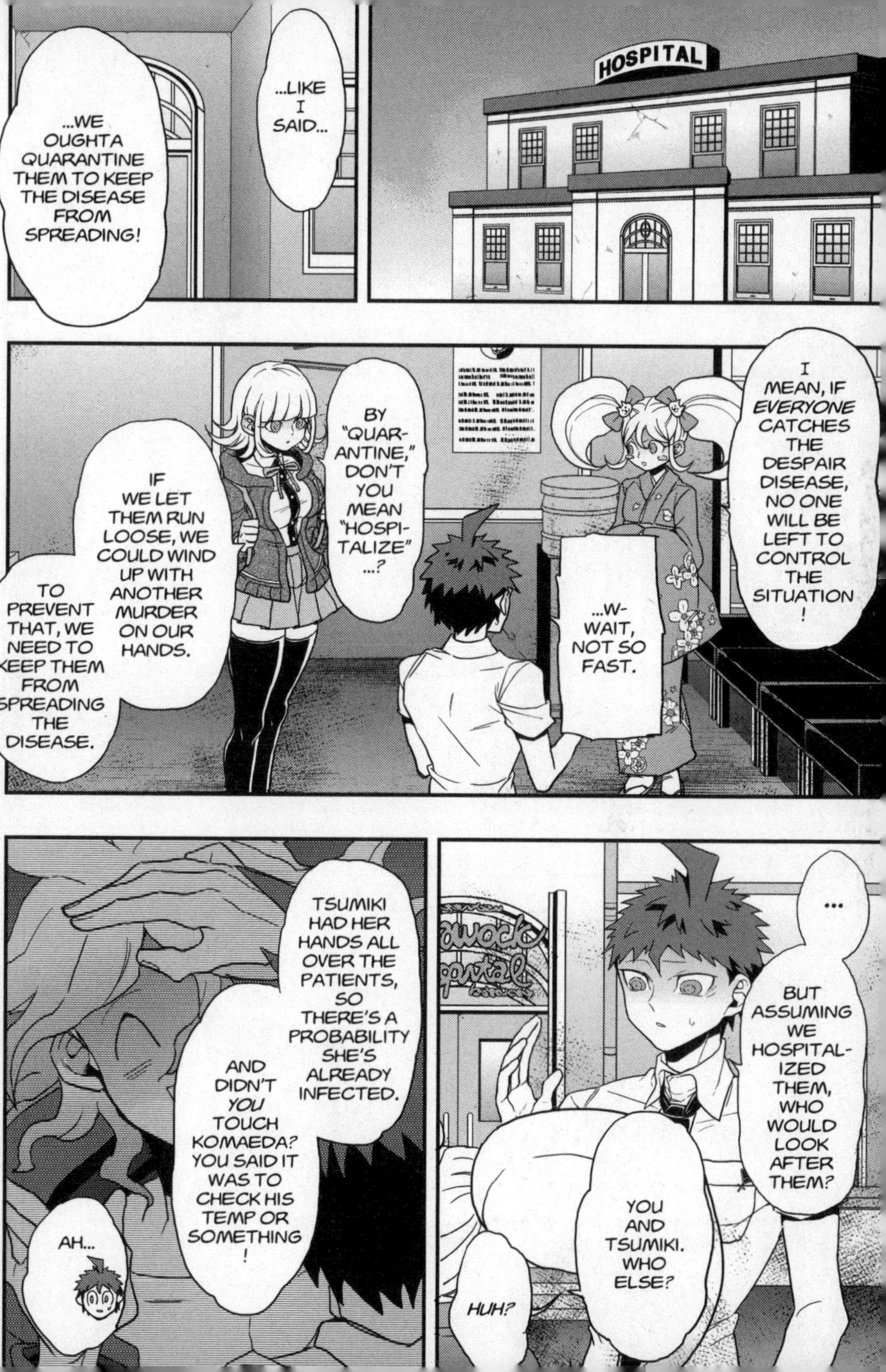
HOSPITAL
...LIKE I SAID...
...WE OUGHTA QUARANTINE THEM TO KEEP THE DISEASE FROM SPREADING!
I MEAN, IF *EVERYONE* CATCHES THE DESPAIR DISEASE, NO ONE WILL BE LEFT TO CONTROL THE SITUATION!
...W-WAIT, NOT SO FAST.
BY "QUARANTINE," DON'T YOU MEAN "HOSPITALIZE"...?
IF WE LET THEM RUN LOOSE, WE COULD WIND UP WITH ANOTHER MURDER ON OUR HANDS.
TO PREVENT THAT, WE NEED TO KEEP THEM FROM SPREADING THE DISEASE.
...
BUT ASSUMING WE HOSPITALIZED THEM, WHO WOULD LOOK AFTER THEM?
YOU AND TSUMIKI. WHO ELSE?
HUH?
TSUMIKI HAD HER HANDS ALL OVER THE PATIENTS, SO THERE'S A PROBABILITY SHE'S ALREADY INFECTED.
AND DIDN'T *YOU* TOUCH KOMAEDA? YOU SAID IT WAS TO CHECK HIS TEMP OR SOMETHING!
AH...

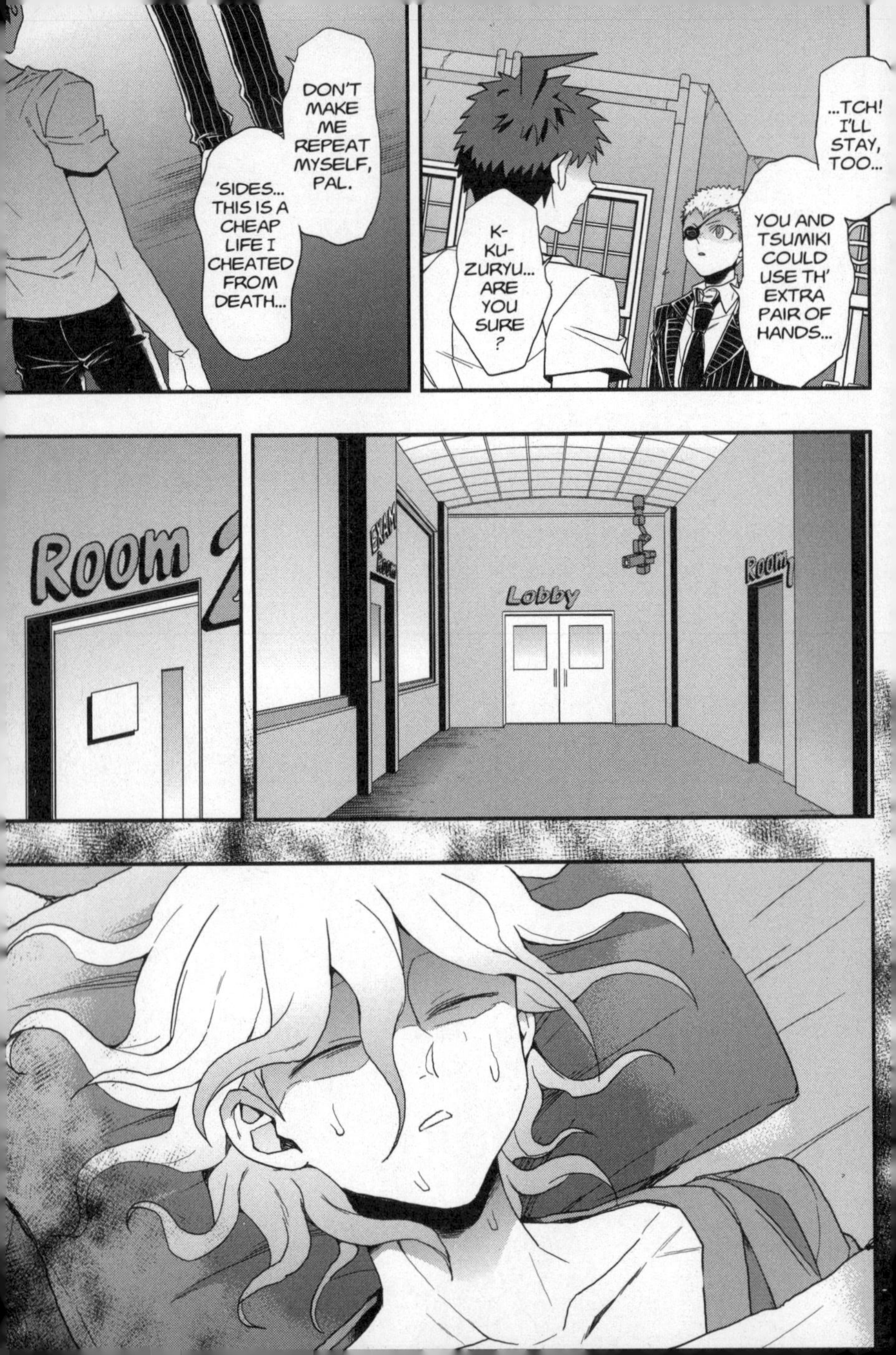
...TCH! I'LL STAY, TOO...
YOU AND TSUMIKI COULD USE TH' EXTRA PAIR OF HANDS...
K-KU-ZURYU... ARE YOU SURE?
DON'T MAKE ME REPEAT MYSELF, PAL.
'SIDES... THIS IS A CHEAP LIFE I CHEATED FROM DEATH...
Room
Lobby
ROOM

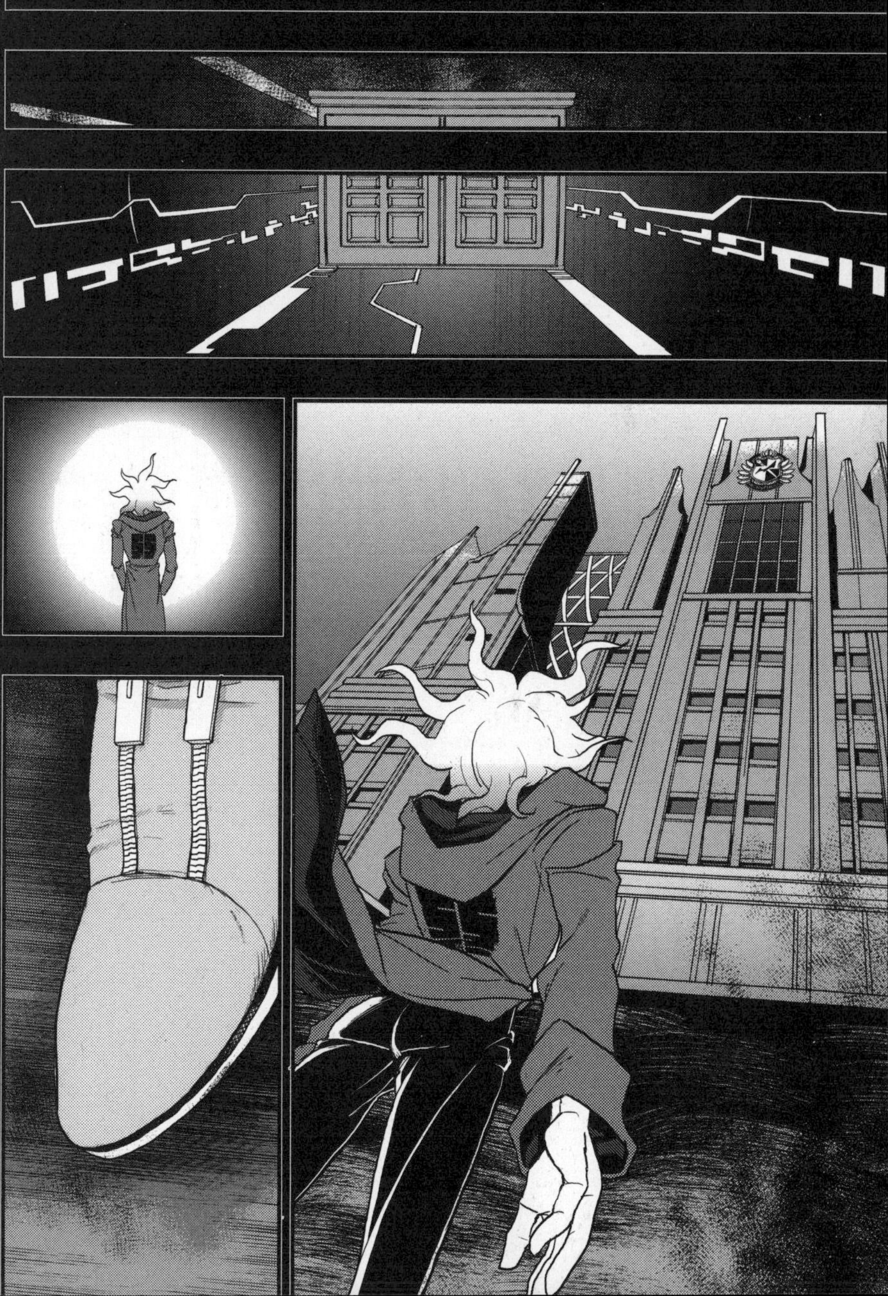

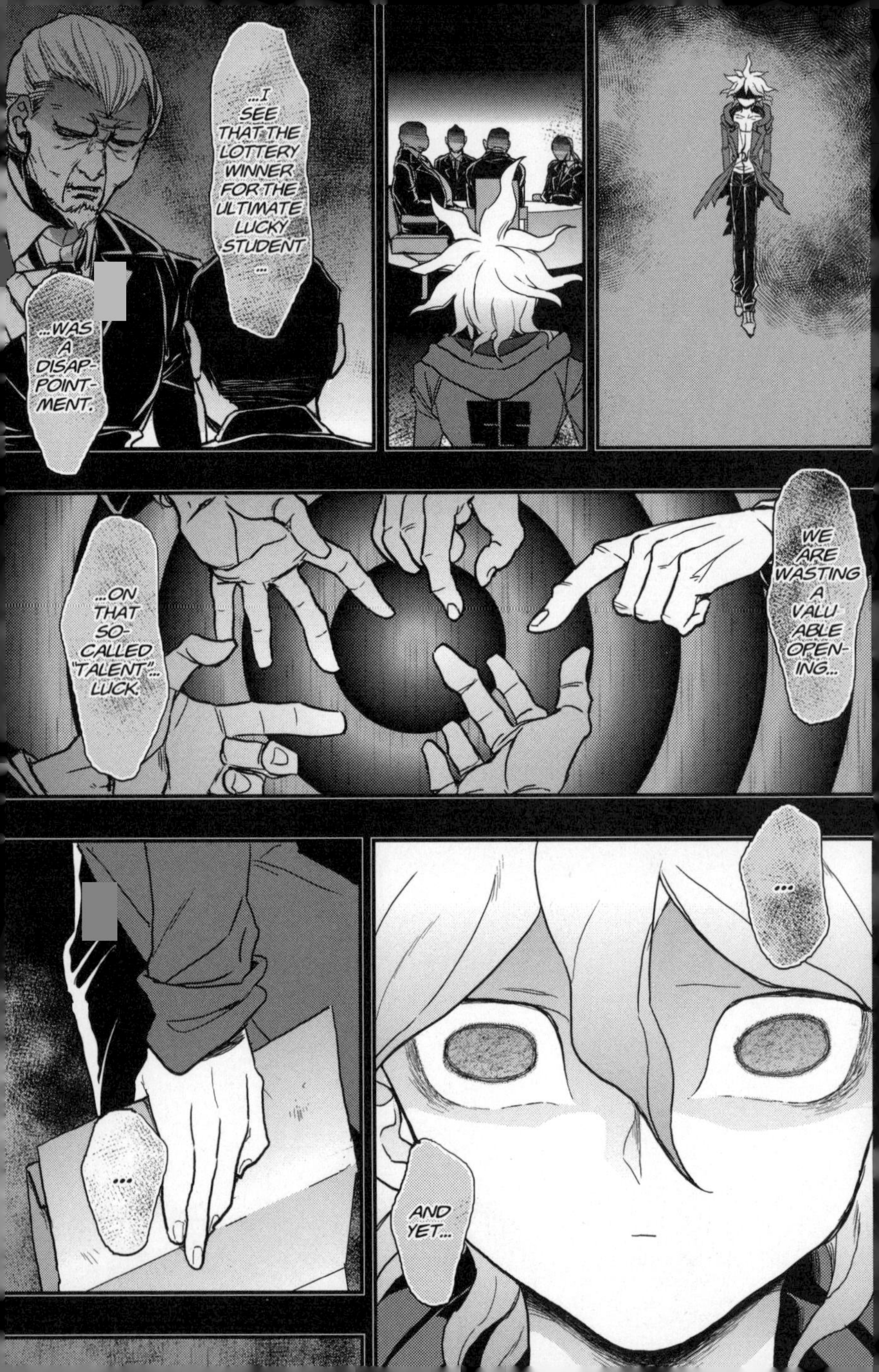
...I SEE THAT THE LOTTERY WINNER FOR THE ULTIMATE LUCKY STUDENT...
...WAS A DISAPPOINTMENT.
WE ARE WASTING A VALUABLE OPENING...
...ON THAT SO-CALLED "TALENT"... LUCK.
...
AND YET...
...

Ep.21

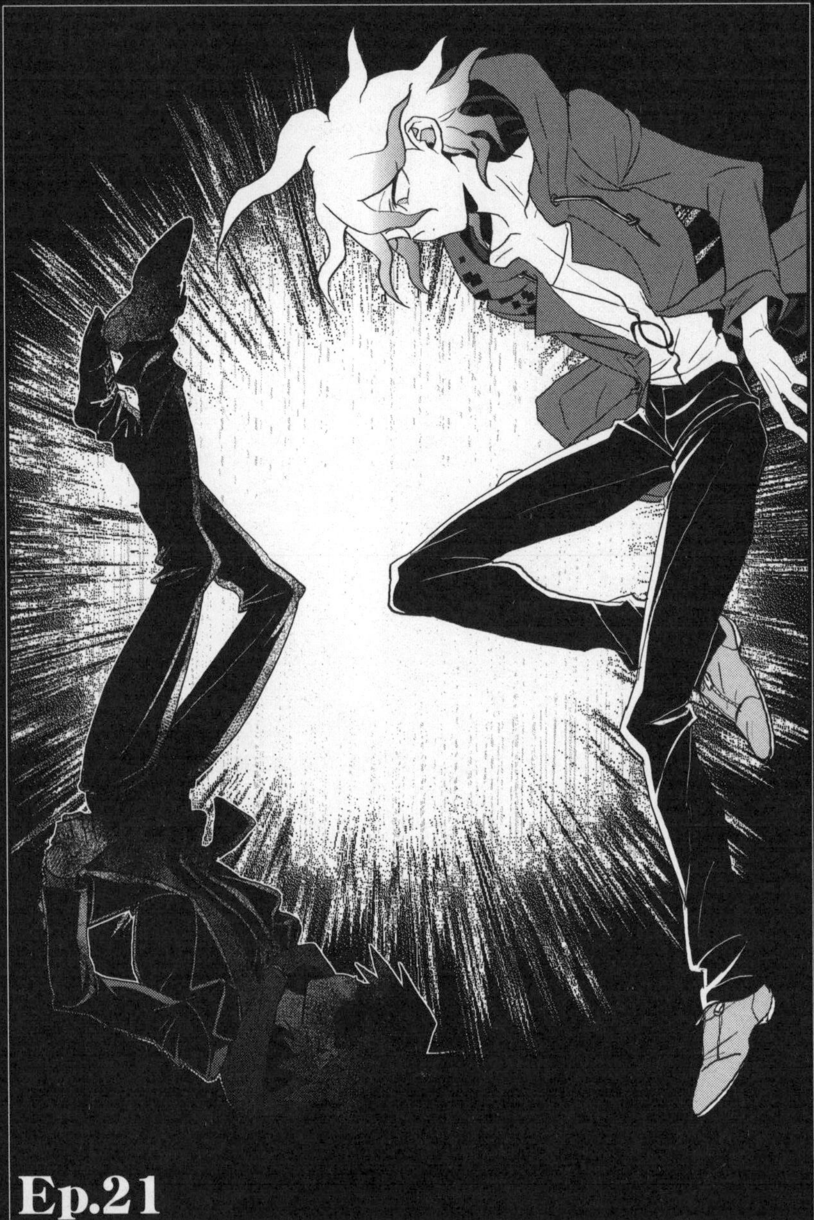

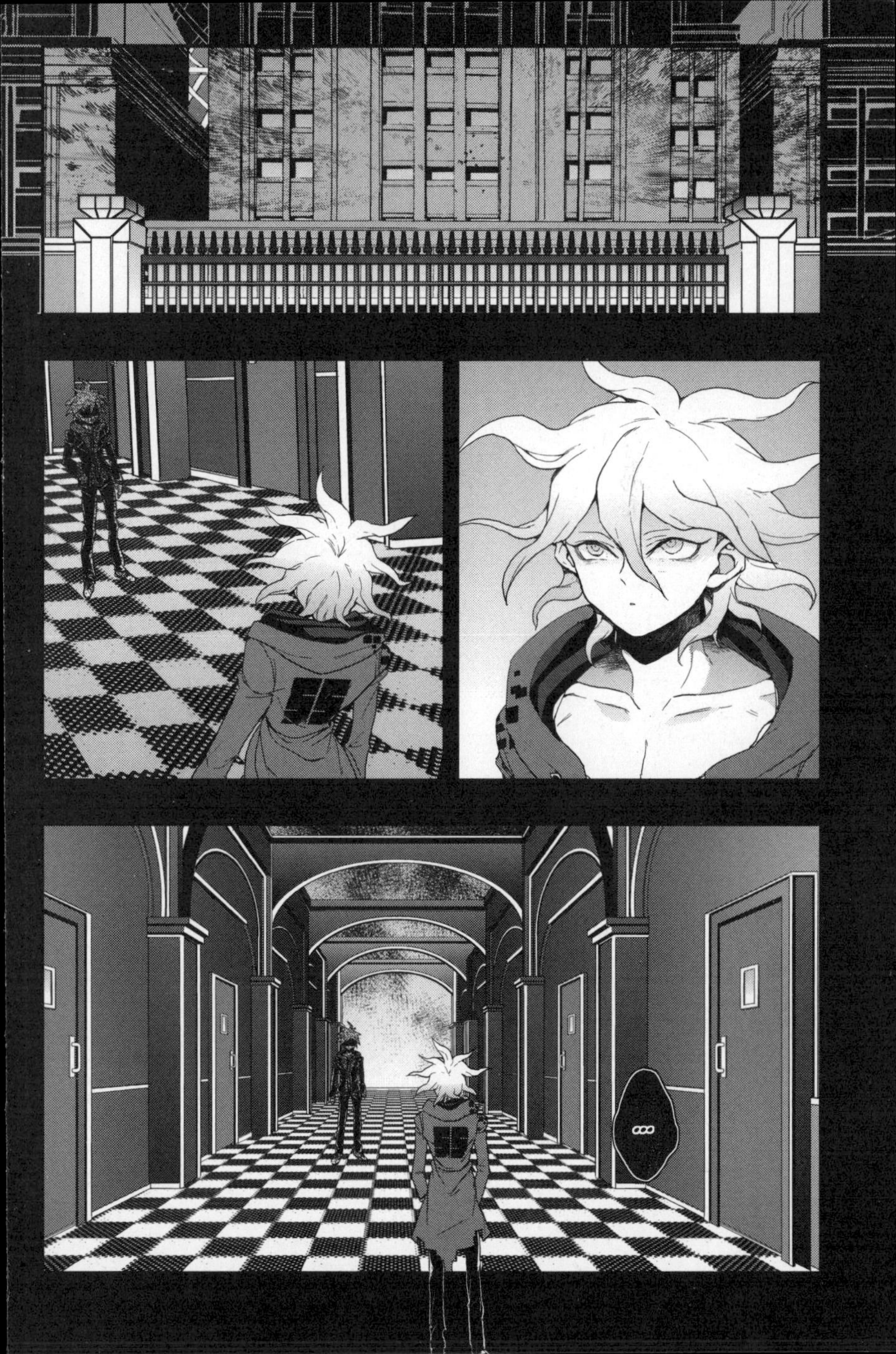
...

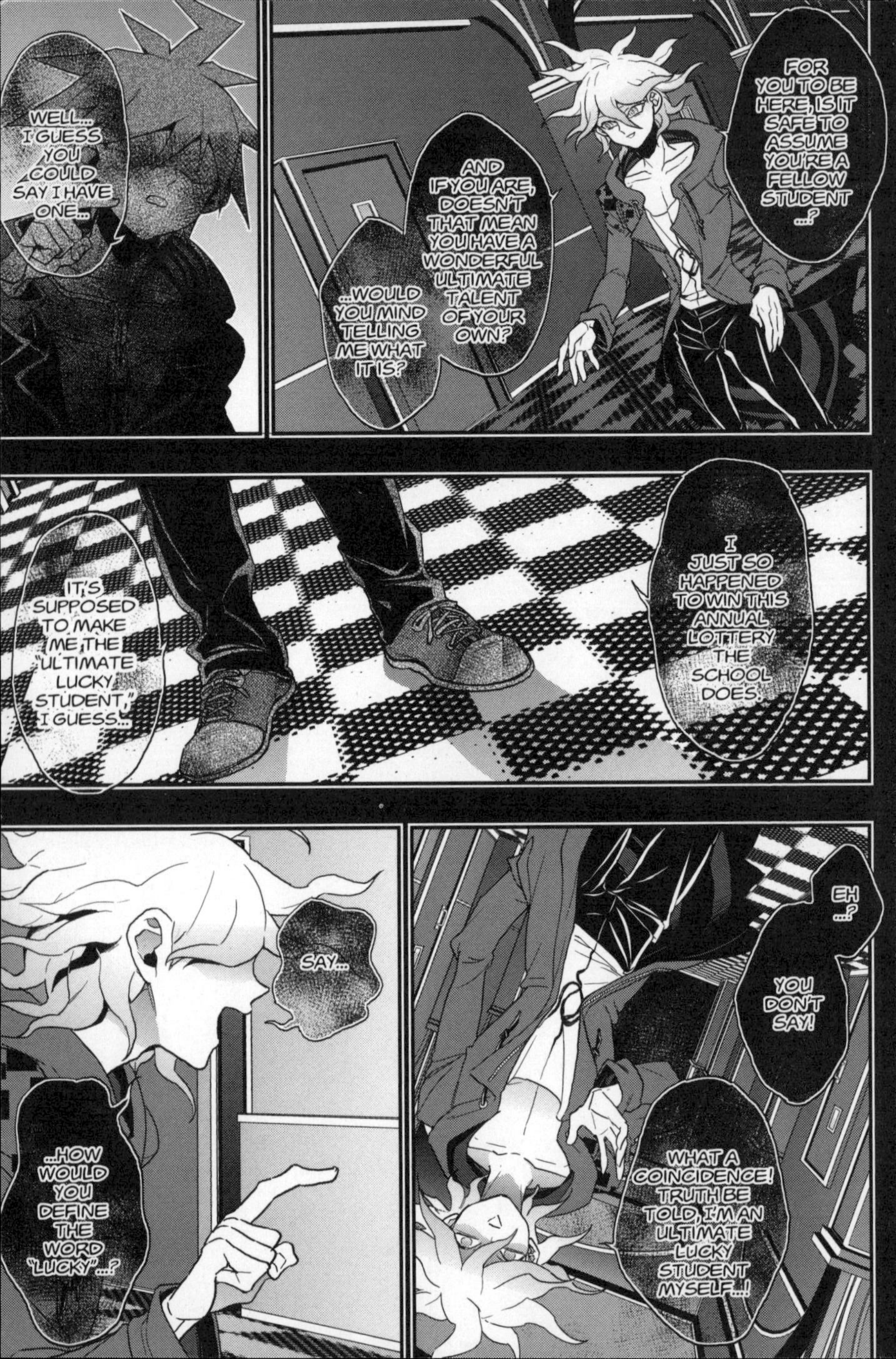
FOR YOU TO BE HERE, IS IT SAFE TO ASSUME YOU'RE A FELLOW STUDENT ...?
AND IF YOU ARE, DOESN'T THAT MEAN YOU HAVE A WONDERFUL ULTIMATE TALENT OF YOUR OWN?
...WOULD YOU MIND TELLING ME WHAT IT IS?
WELL... I GUESS YOU COULD SAY I HAVE ONE...
I JUST SO HAPPENED TO WIN THIS ANNUAL LOTTERY THE SCHOOL DOES.
IT'S SUPPOSED TO MAKE ME THE "ULTIMATE LUCKY STUDENT," I GUESS...
EH ...?
YOU DON'T SAY!
WHAT A COINCIDENCE! TRUTH BE TOLD, I'M AN ULTIMATE LUCKY STUDENT MYSELF...!
SAY...
...HOW WOULD YOU DEFINE THE WORD "LUCKY"...?

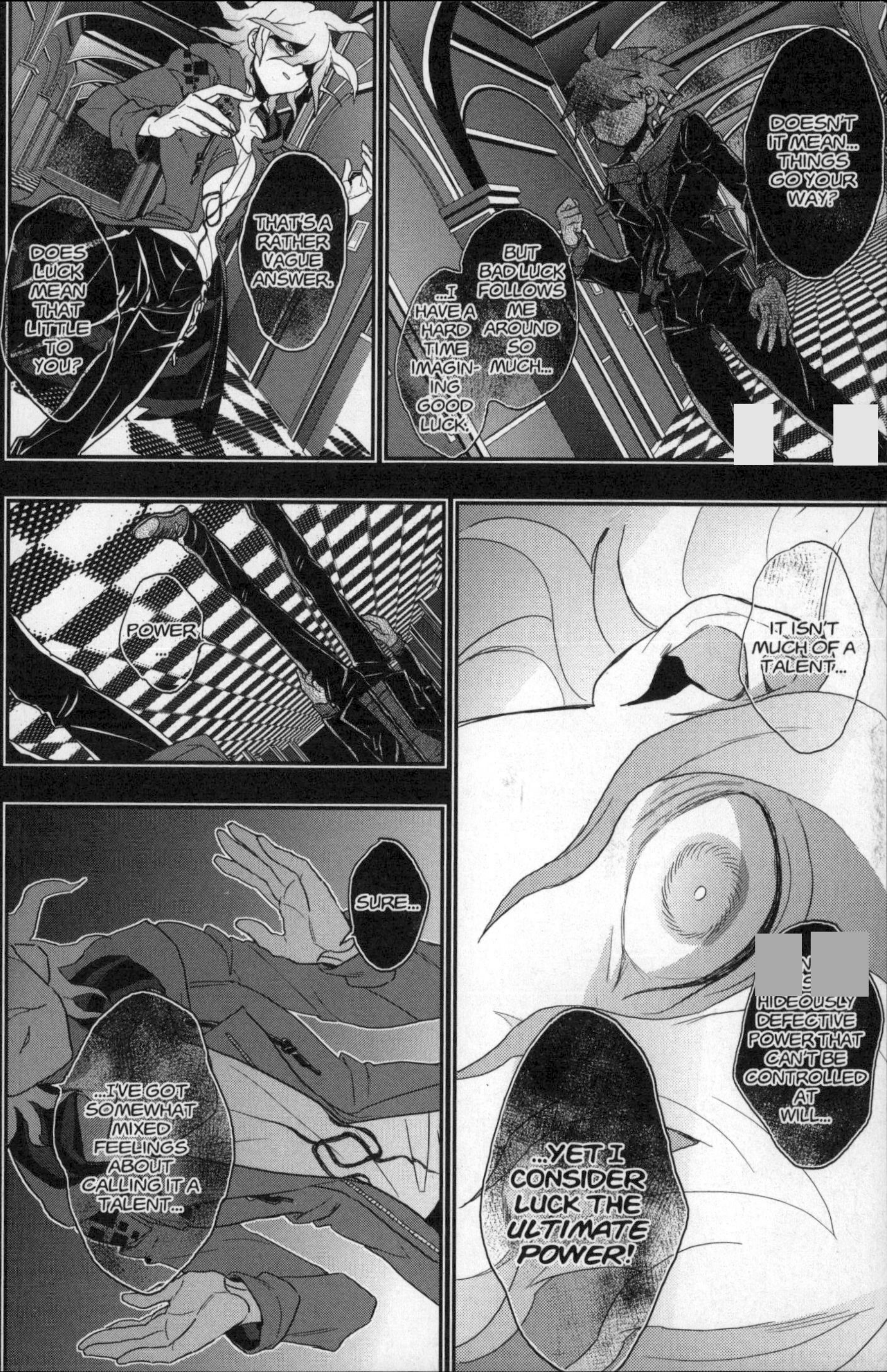
DOESN'T IT MEAN... THINGS GO YOUR WAY?
BUT BAD LUCK FOLLOWS ME AROUND SO MUCH...
...I HAVE A HARD TIME IMAGINING GOOD LUCK.
THAT'S A RATHER VAGUE ANSWER.
DOES LUCK MEAN THAT LITTLE TO YOU?
IT ISN'T MUCH OF A TALENT...
HIDEOUSLY DEFECTIVE POWER THAT CAN'T BE CONTROLLED AT WILL...
...YET I CONSIDER LUCK THE ULTIMATE POWER!
POWER...
SURE...
...I'VE GOT SOMEWHAT MIXED FEELINGS ABOUT CALLING IT A TALENT...

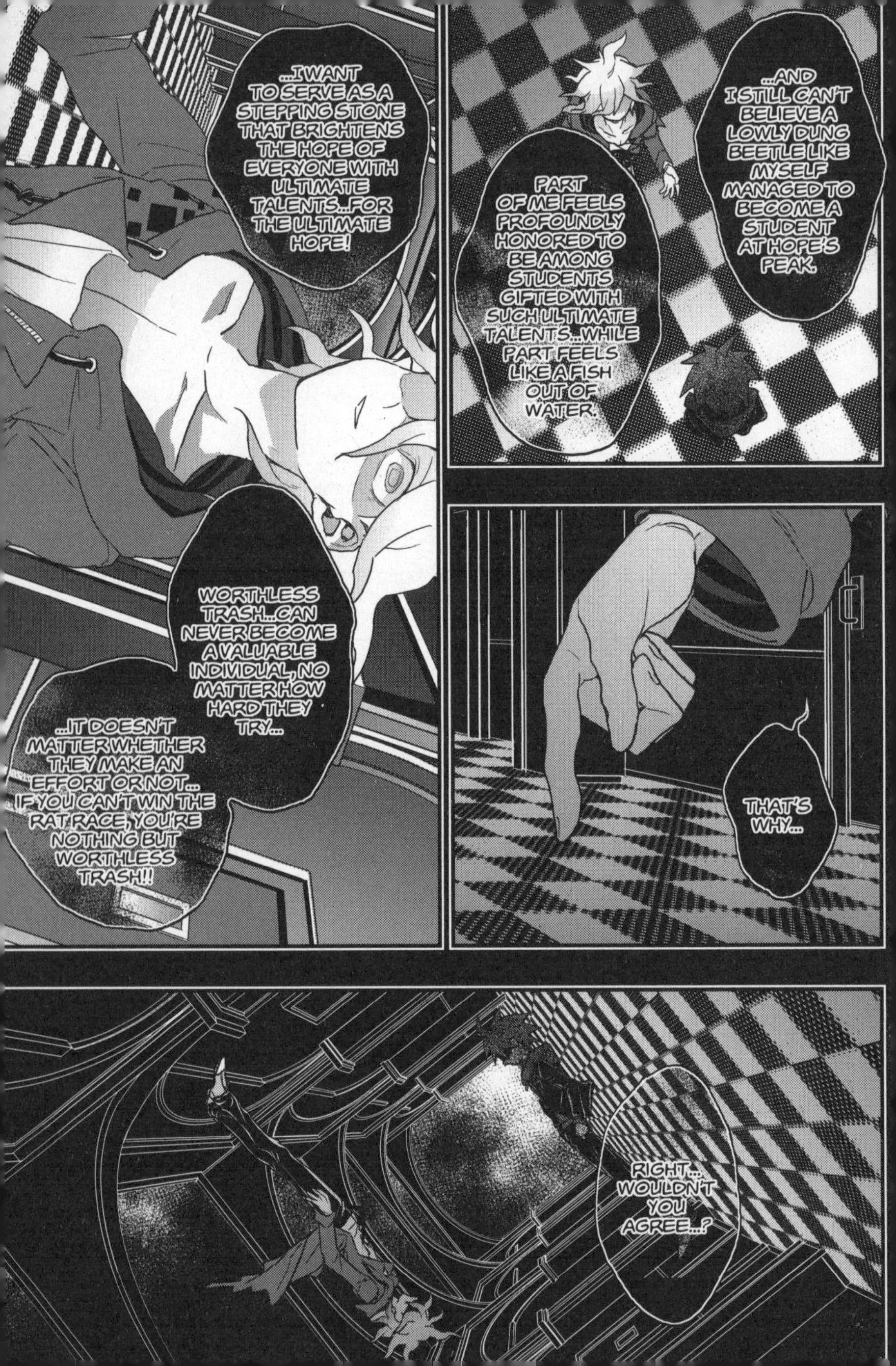
...AND I STILL CAN'T BELIEVE A LOWLY DUNG BEETLE LIKE MYSELF MANAGED TO BECOME A STUDENT AT HOPE'S PEAK.
PART OF ME FEELS PROFOUNDLY HONORED TO BE AMONG STUDENTS GIFTED WITH SUCH ULTIMATE TALENTS...WHILE PART FEELS LIKE A FISH OUT OF WATER.
THAT'S WHY...
...I WANT TO SERVE AS A STEPPING STONE THAT BRIGHTENS THE HOPE OF EVERYONE WITH ULTIMATE TALENTS...FOR THE ULTIMATE HOPE!
WORTHLESS TRASH...CAN NEVER BECOME A VALUABLE INDIVIDUAL, NO MATTER HOW HARD THEY TRY...
...IT DOESN'T MATTER WHETHER THEY MAKE AN EFFORT OR NOT... IF YOU CAN'T WIN THE RAT RACE, YOU'RE NOTHING BUT WORTHLESS TRASH!!
RIGHT... WOULDN'T YOU AGREE...?

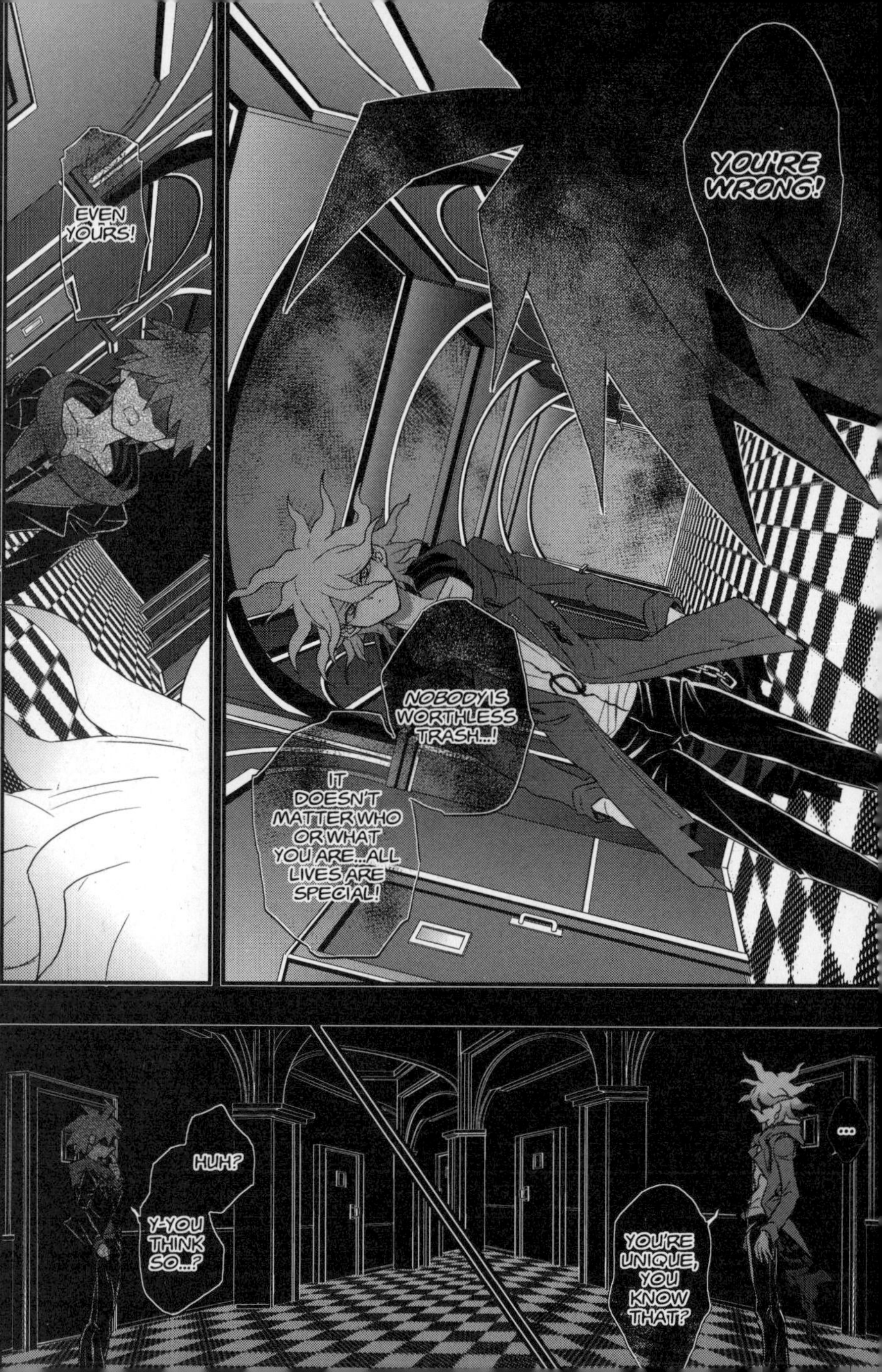
YOU'RE WRONG!
NOBODY IS WORTHLESS TRASH...!
IT DOESN'T MATTER WHO OR WHAT YOU ARE...ALL LIVES ARE SPECIAL!
EVEN YOURS!
...
YOU'RE UNIQUE, YOU KNOW THAT?
HUH?
Y-YOU THINK SO...?

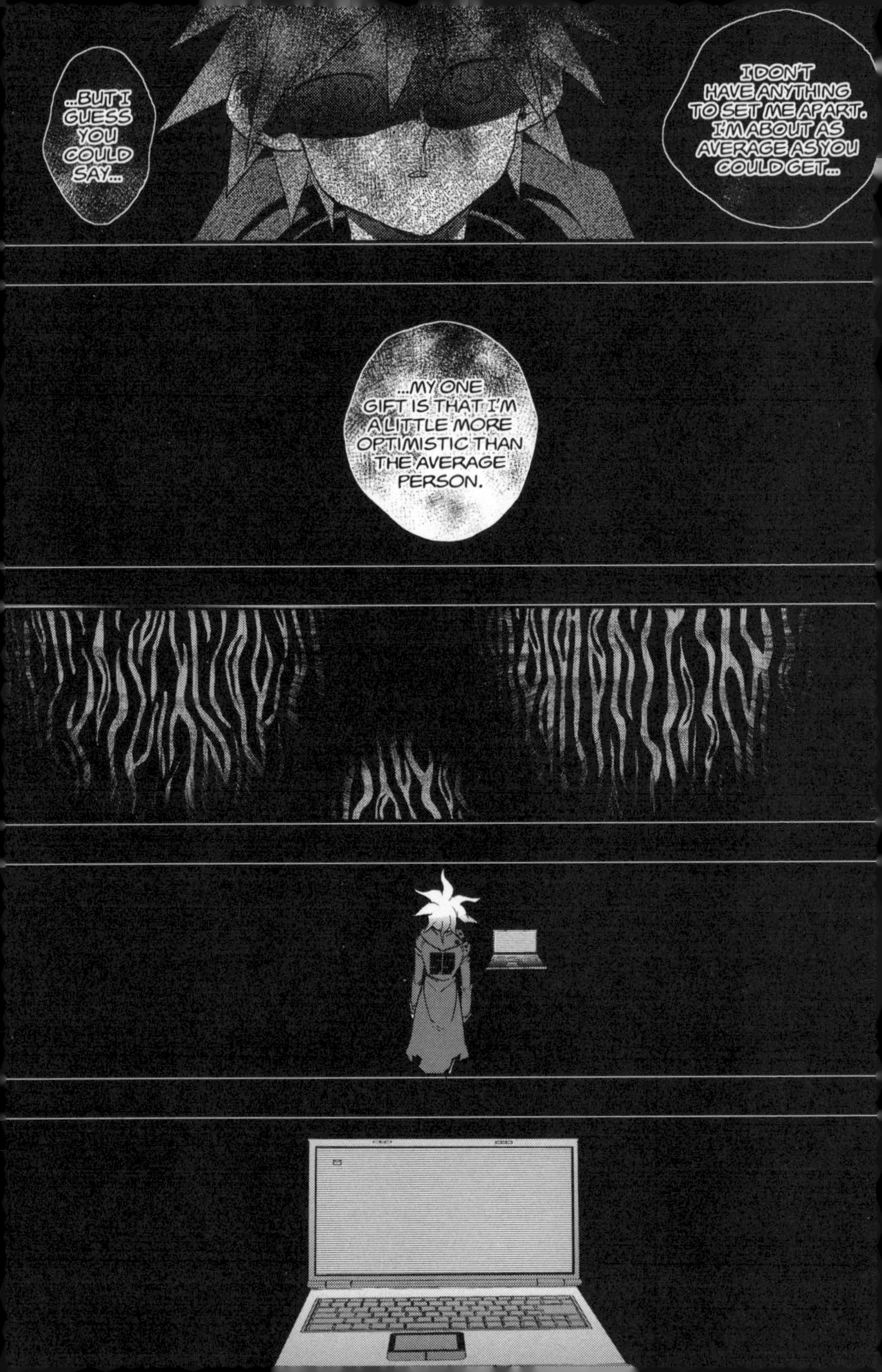
I DON'T HAVE ANYTHING TO SET ME APART. I'M ABOUT AS AVERAGE AS YOU COULD GET...
...BUT I GUESS YOU COULD SAY...
...MY ONE GIFT IS THAT I'M A LITTLE MORE OPTIMISTIC THAN THE AVERAGE PERSON.

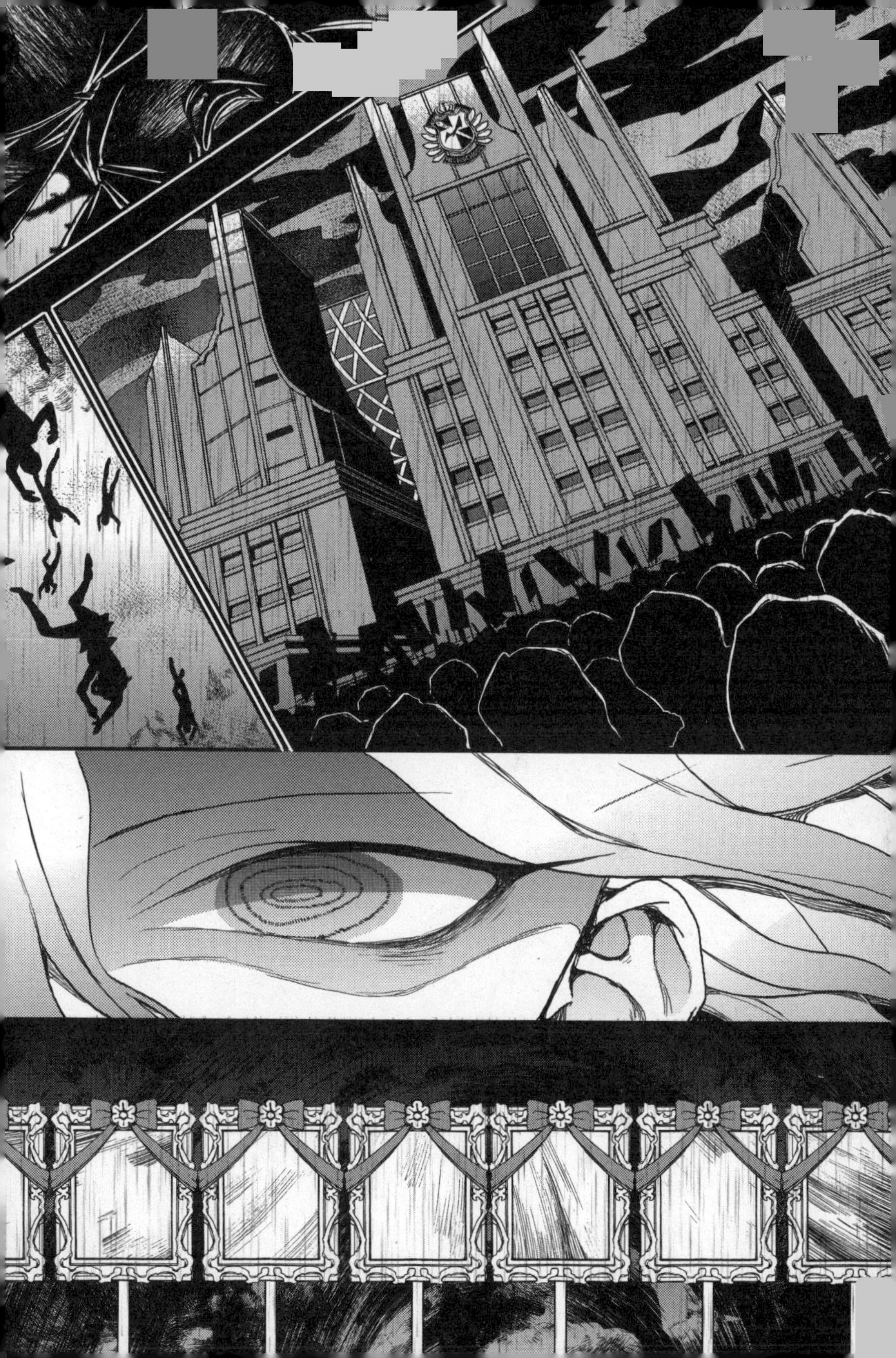

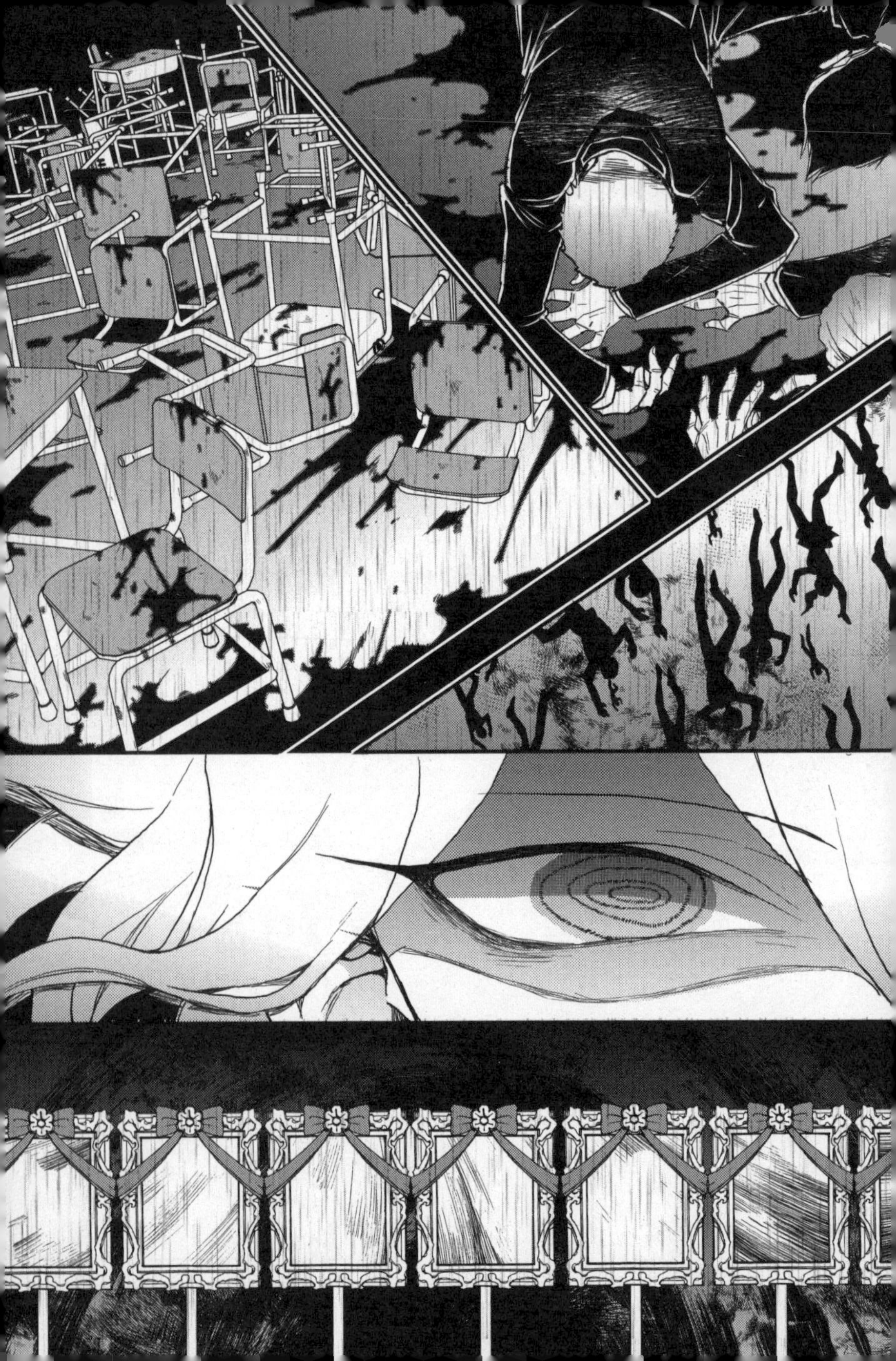

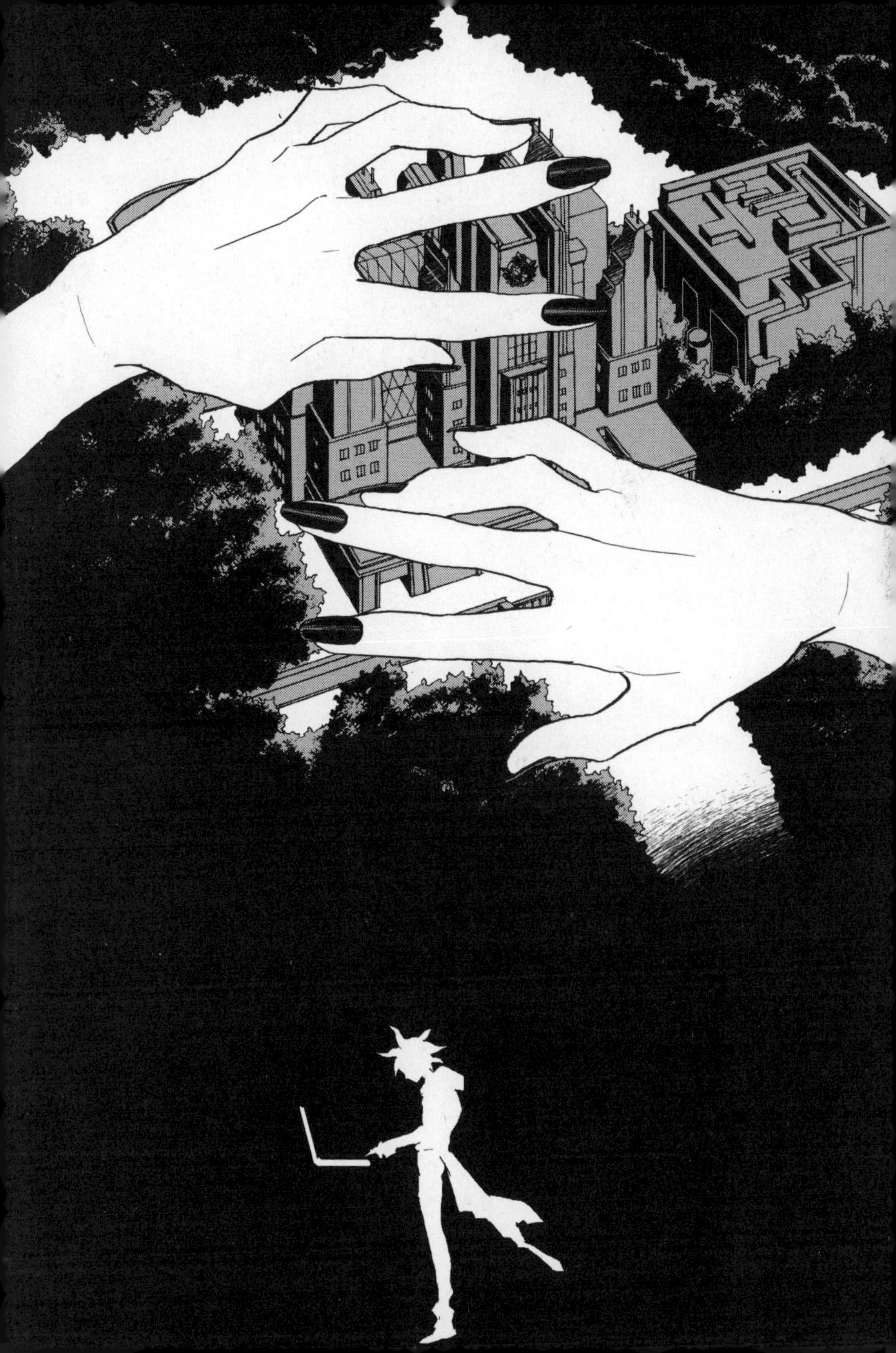

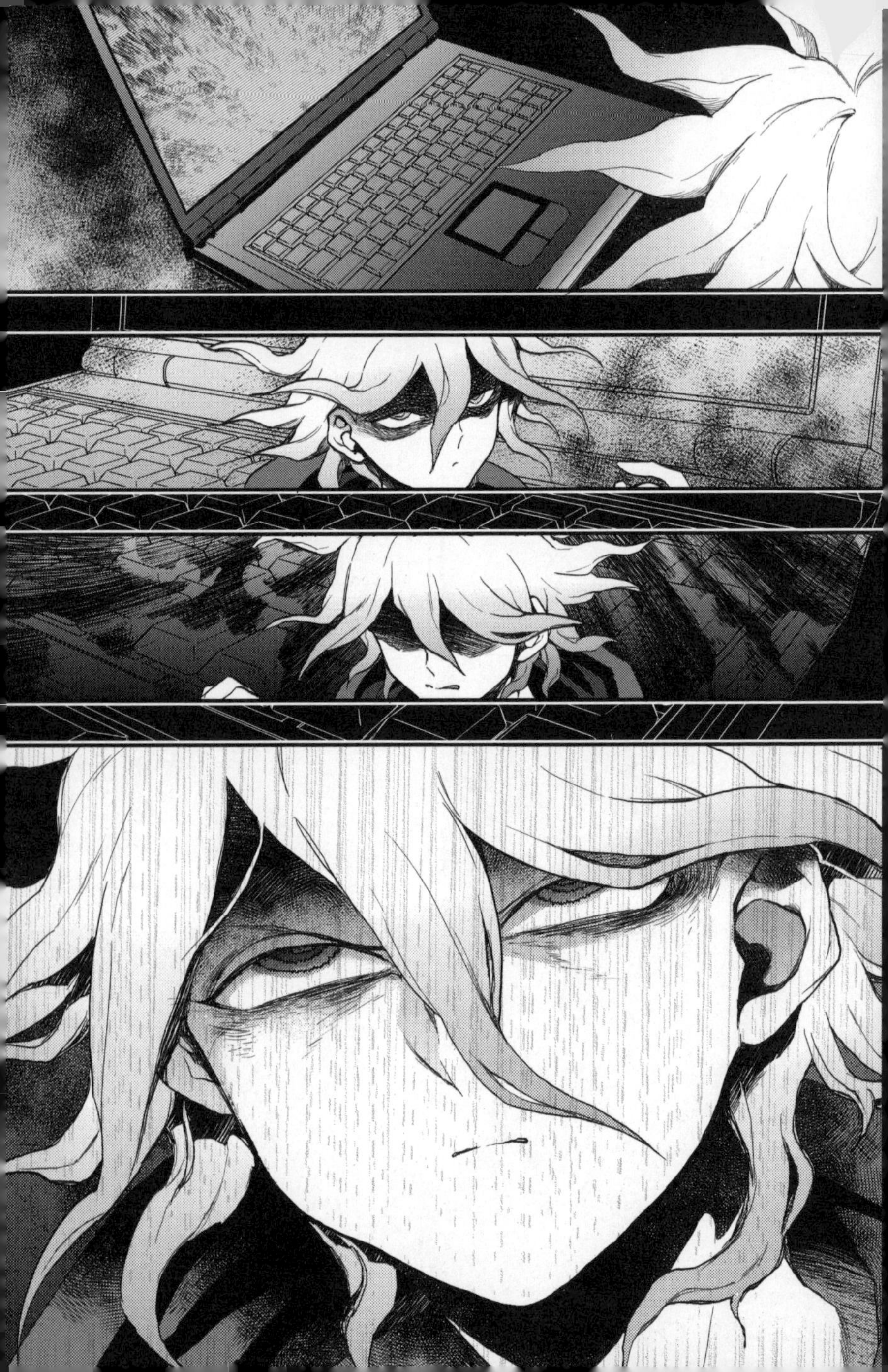

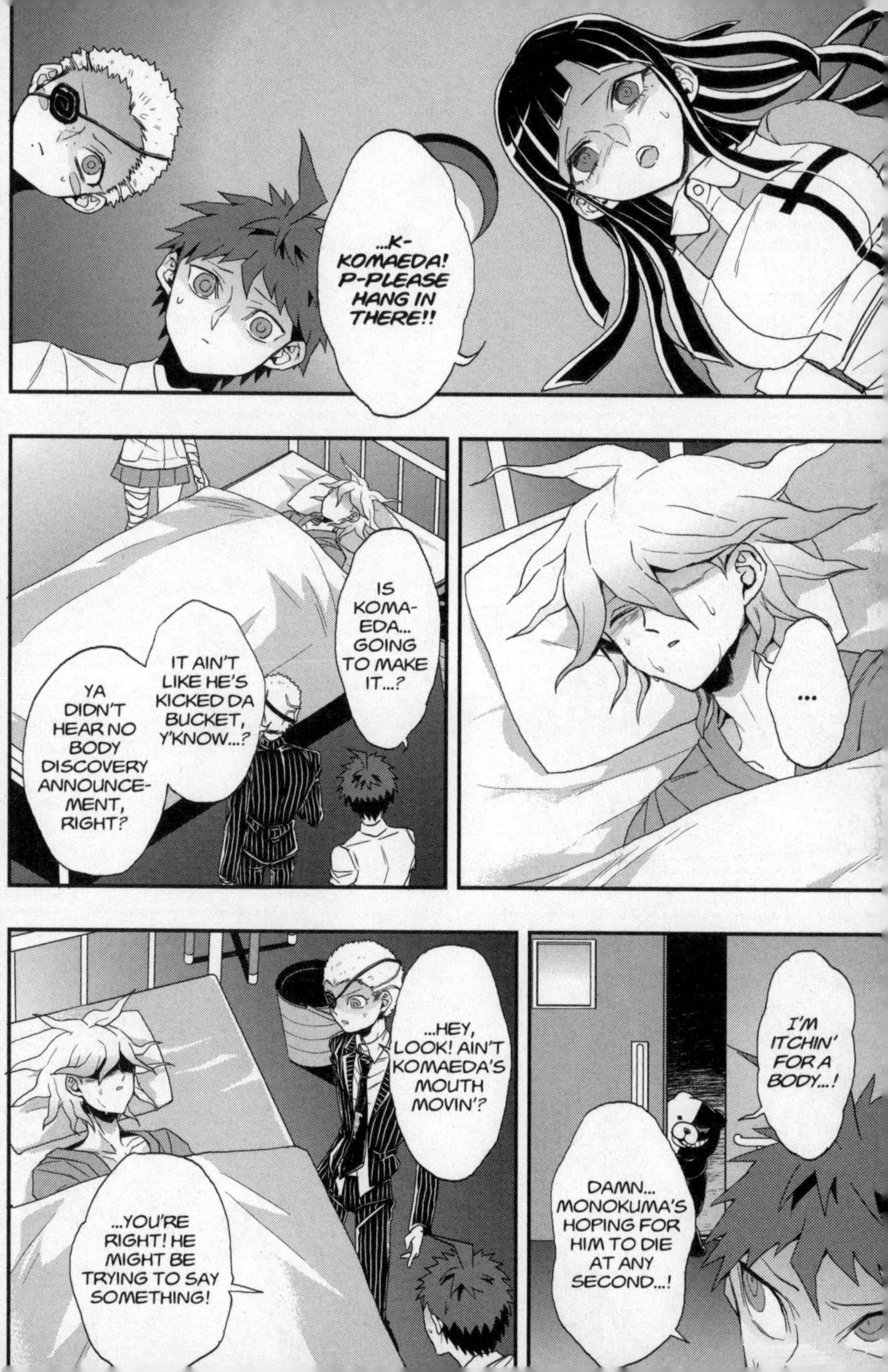
...K-KOMAEDA! P-PLEASE HANG IN THERE!!
...
IS KOMA-EDA... GOING TO MAKE IT...?
IT AIN'T LIKE HE'S KICKED DA BUCKET, Y'KNOW...?
YA DIDN'T HEAR NO BODY DISCOVERY ANNOUNCE-MENT, RIGHT?
I'M ITCHIN' FOR A BODY...!
DAMN... MONOKUMA'S HOPING FOR HIM TO DIE AT ANY SECOND...!
...HEY, LOOK! AIN'T KOMAEDA'S MOUTH MOVIN'?
...YOU'RE RIGHT! HE MIGHT BE TRYING TO SAY SOMETHING!

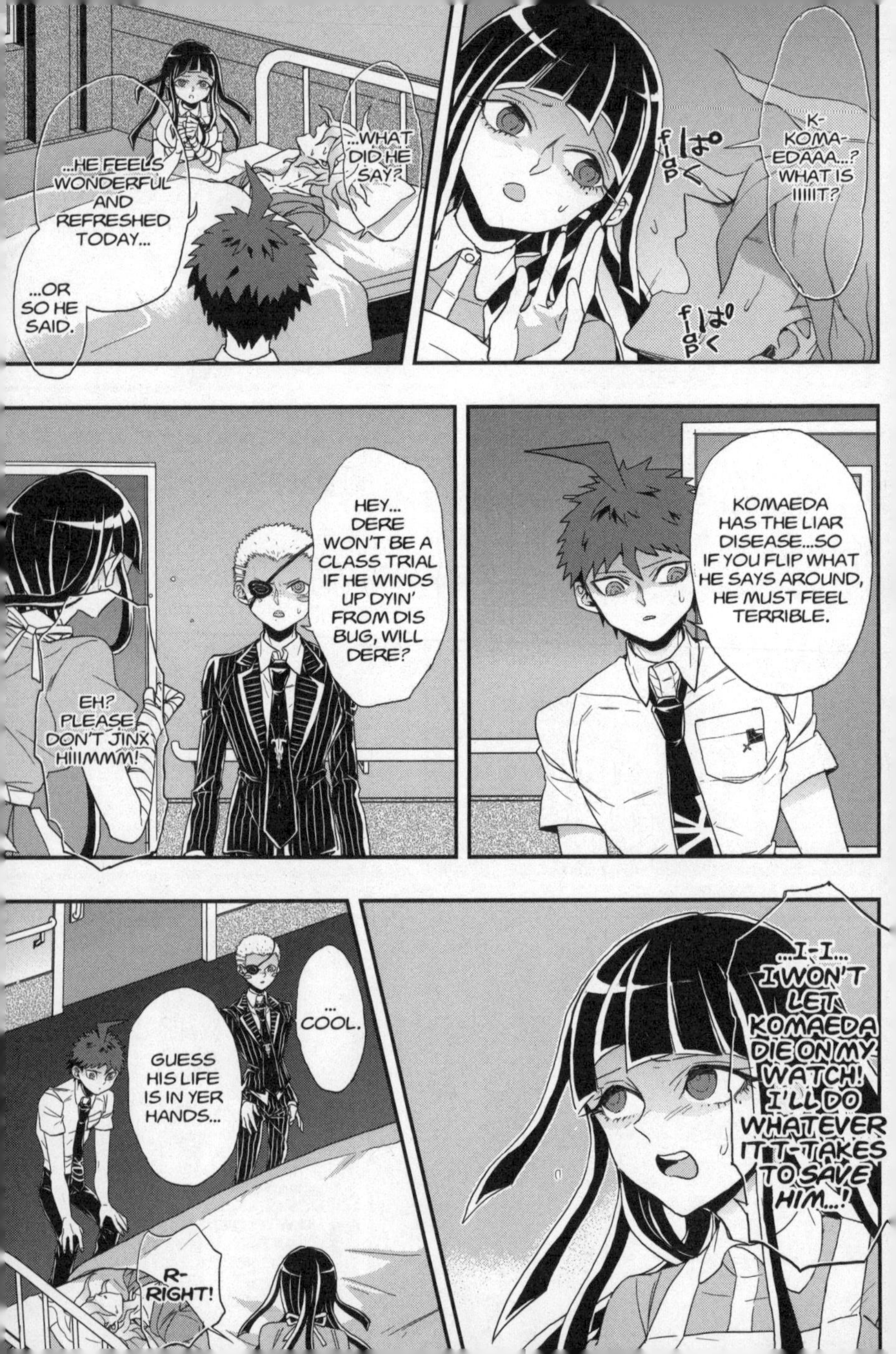
K-KOMA-EDAAA...? WHAT IS IIIIIT?
flap ぱく
flap ぱく
...WHAT DID HE SAY?
...HE FEELS WONDERFUL AND REFRESHED TODAY...
...OR SO HE SAID.
KOMAEDA HAS THE LIAR DISEASE...SO IF YOU FLIP WHAT HE SAYS AROUND, HE MUST FEEL TERRIBLE.
HEY... DERE WON'T BE A CLASS TRIAL IF HE WINDS UP DYIN' FROM DIS BUG, WILL DERE?
EH? PLEASE DON'T JINX HIIIMMM!
...I-I... I WON'T LET KOMAEDA DIE ON MY WATCH! I'LL DO WHATEVER IT T-TAKES TO SAVE HIM...!
... COOL.
GUESS HIS LIFE IS IN YER HANDS...
R-RIGHT!

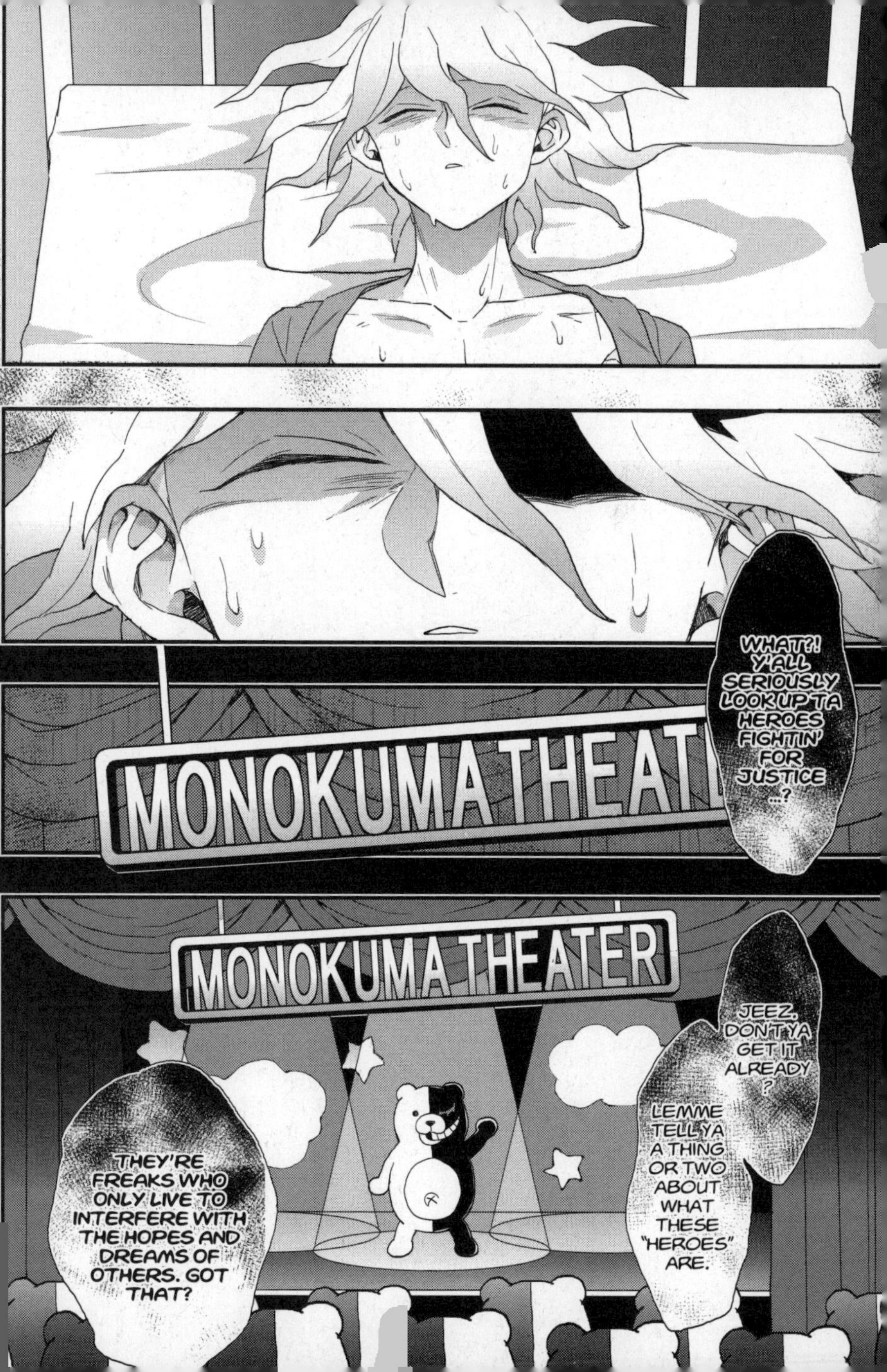
WHAT?! Y'ALL SERIOUSLY LOOK UP TA HEROES FIGHTIN' FOR JUSTICE ...?
MONOKUMA THEAT
MONOKUMA THEATER
JEEZ, DON'T YA GET IT ALREADY?
LEMME TELL YA A THING OR TWO ABOUT WHAT THESE "HEROES" ARE.
THEY'RE FREAKS WHO ONLY LIVE TO INTERFERE WITH THE HOPES AND DREAMS OF OTHERS. GOT THAT?

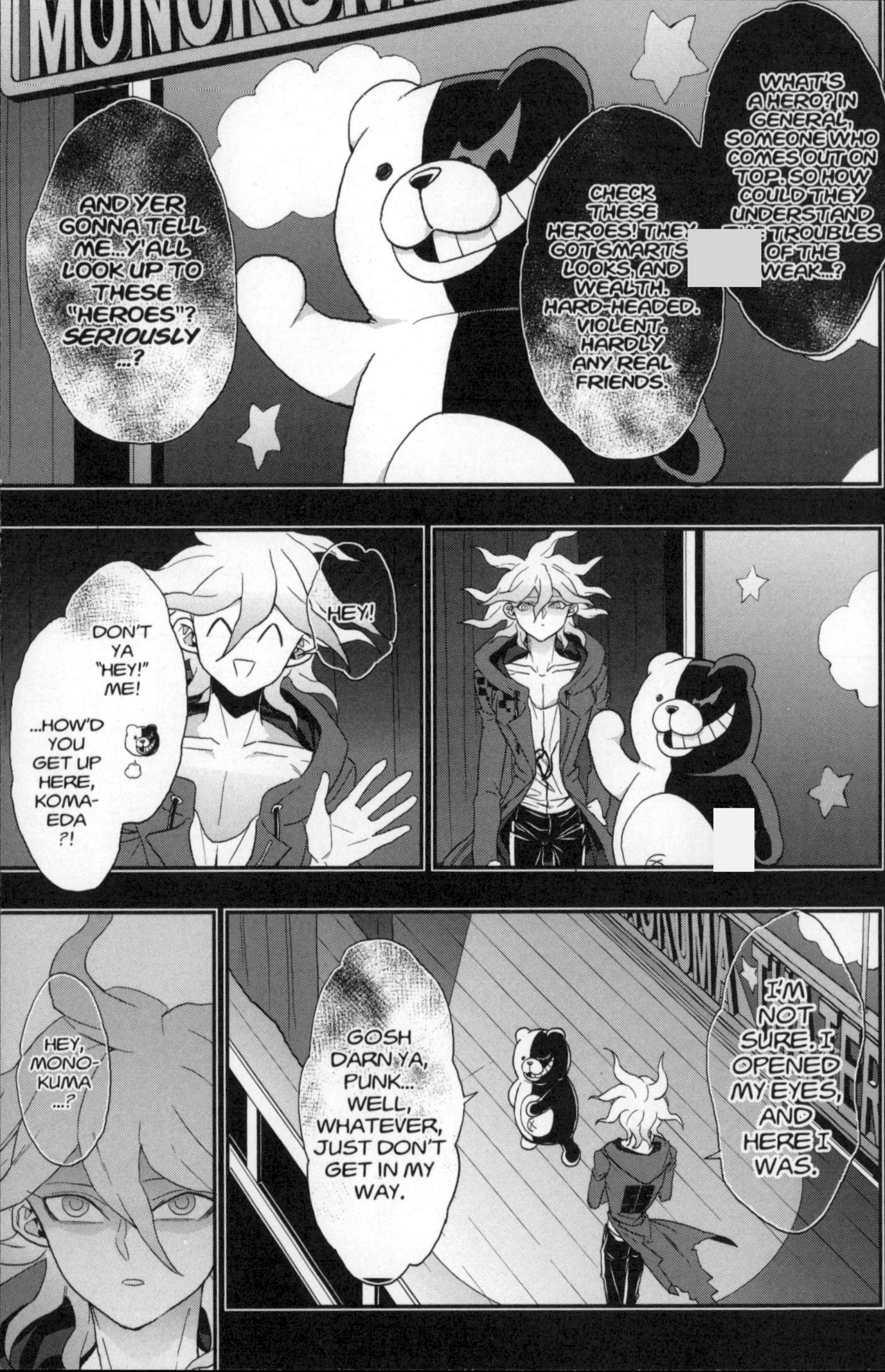
WHAT'S A HERO? IN GENERAL, SOMEONE WHO COMES OUT ON TOP. SO HOW COULD THEY UNDERSTAND THE TROUBLES OF THE WEAK...?
CHECK THESE HEROES! THEY GOT SMARTS, LOOKS, AND WEALTH. HARD-HEADED. VIOLENT. HARDLY ANY REAL FRIENDS.
AND YER GONNA TELL ME... Y'ALL LOOK UP TO THESE "HEROES"? *SERIOUSLY*...?
HEY!
DON'T YA "HEY!" ME!
...HOW'D YOU GET UP HERE, KOMAEDA?!
I'M NOT SURE. I OPENED MY EYES, AND HERE I WAS.
GOSH DARN YA, PUNK... WELL, WHATEVER, JUST DON'T GET IN MY WAY.
HEY, MONOKUMA...?

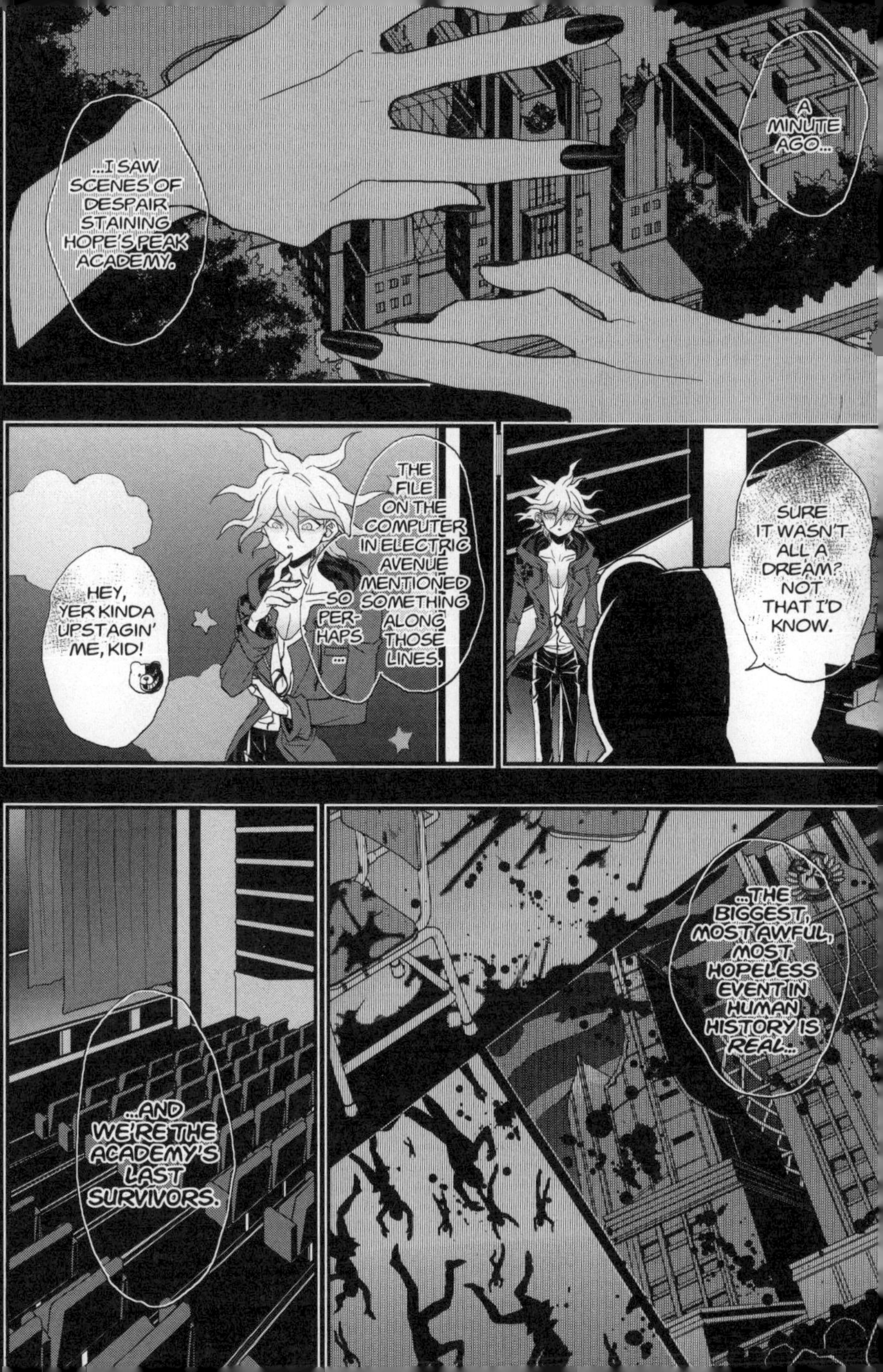
A MINUTE AGO...
...I SAW SCENES OF DESPAIR STAINING HOPE'S PEAK ACADEMY.
SURE IT WASN'T ALL A DREAM? NOT THAT I'D KNOW.
THE FILE ON THE COMPUTER IN ELECTRIC AVENUE MENTIONED SOMETHING ALONG THOSE LINES.
SO PER-HAPS...
HEY, YER KINDA UPSTAGIN' ME, KID!
...THE BIGGEST, MOST AWFUL, MOST HOPELESS EVENT IN HUMAN HISTORY IS REAL...
...AND WE'RE THE ACADEMY'S LAST SURVIVORS.

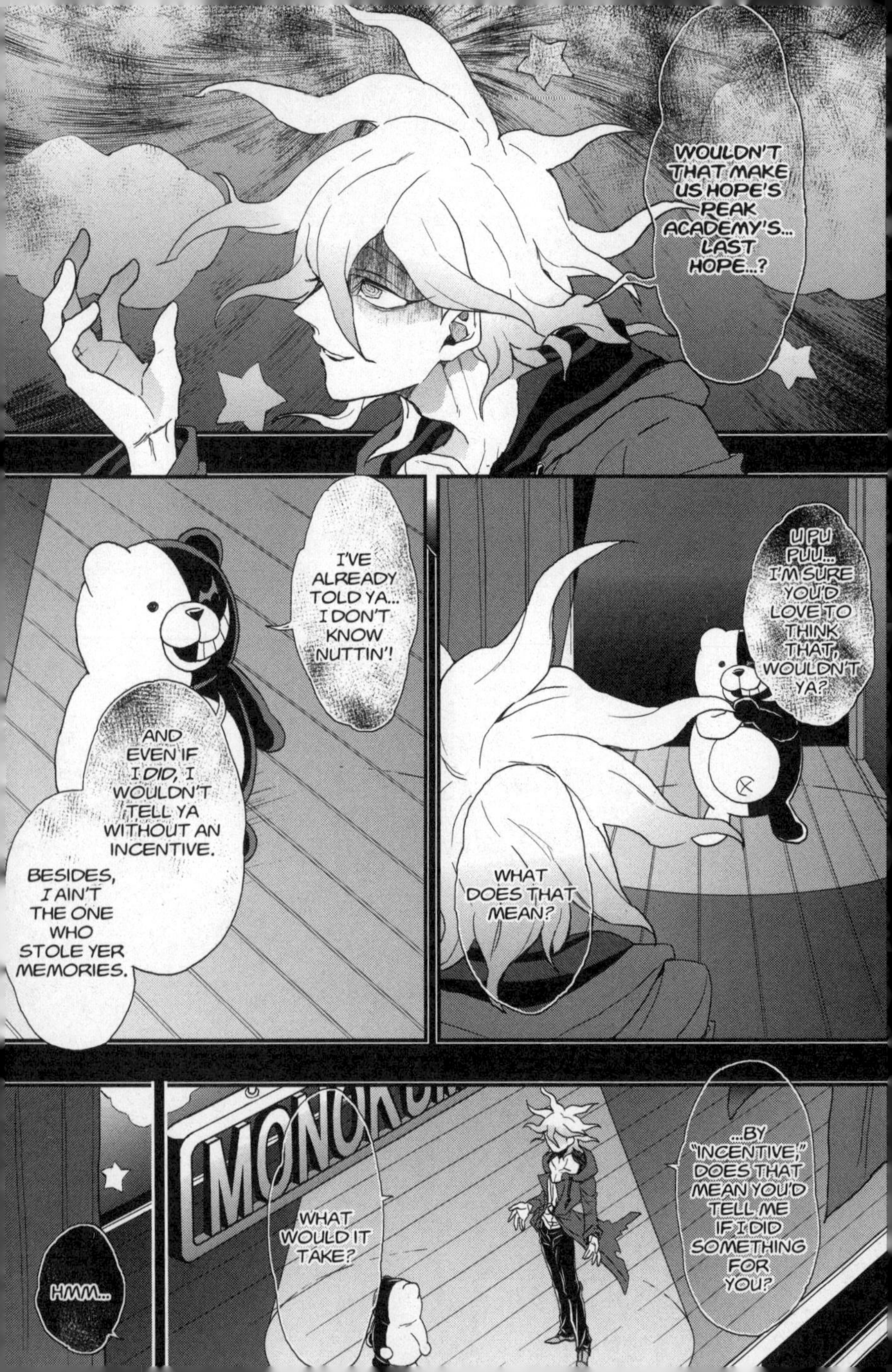
WOULDN'T THAT MAKE US HOPE'S PEAK ACADEMY'S... LAST HOPE...?
UPU PUU... I'M SURE YOU'D LOVE TO THINK THAT, WOULDN'T YA?
WHAT DOES THAT MEAN?
I'VE ALREADY TOLD YA... I DON'T KNOW NUTTIN'!
AND EVEN IF I *DID*, I WOULDN'T TELL YA WITHOUT AN INCENTIVE.
BESIDES, I AIN'T THE ONE WHO STOLE YER MEMORIES.
...BY "INCENTIVE," DOES THAT MEAN YOU'D TELL ME IF I DID SOMETHING FOR YOU?
WHAT WOULD IT TAKE?
HMM...

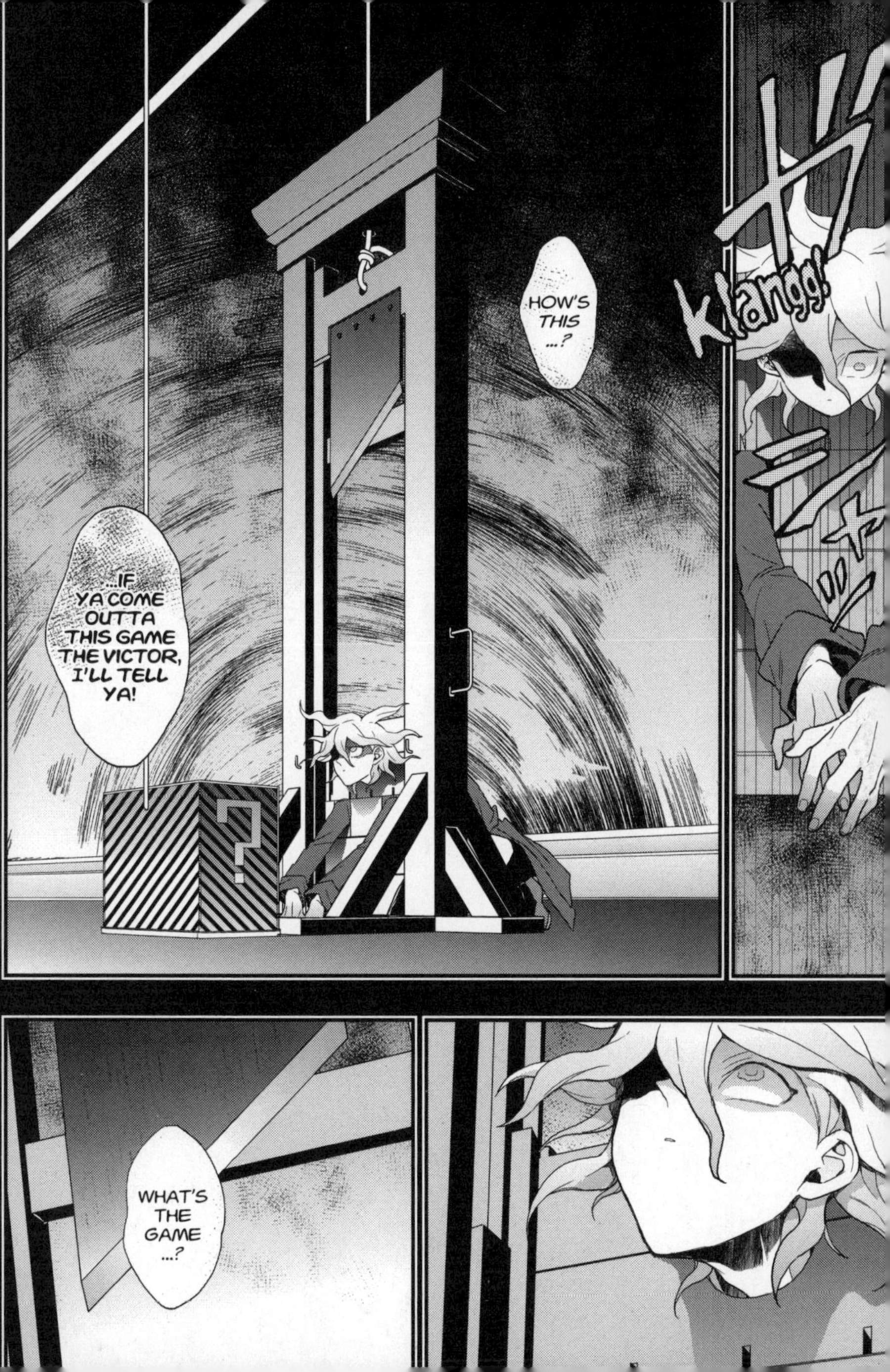
Klangg!
HOW'S THIS ...?
...IF YA COME OUTTA THIS GAME THE VICTOR, I'LL TELL YA!
WHAT'S THE GAME ...?

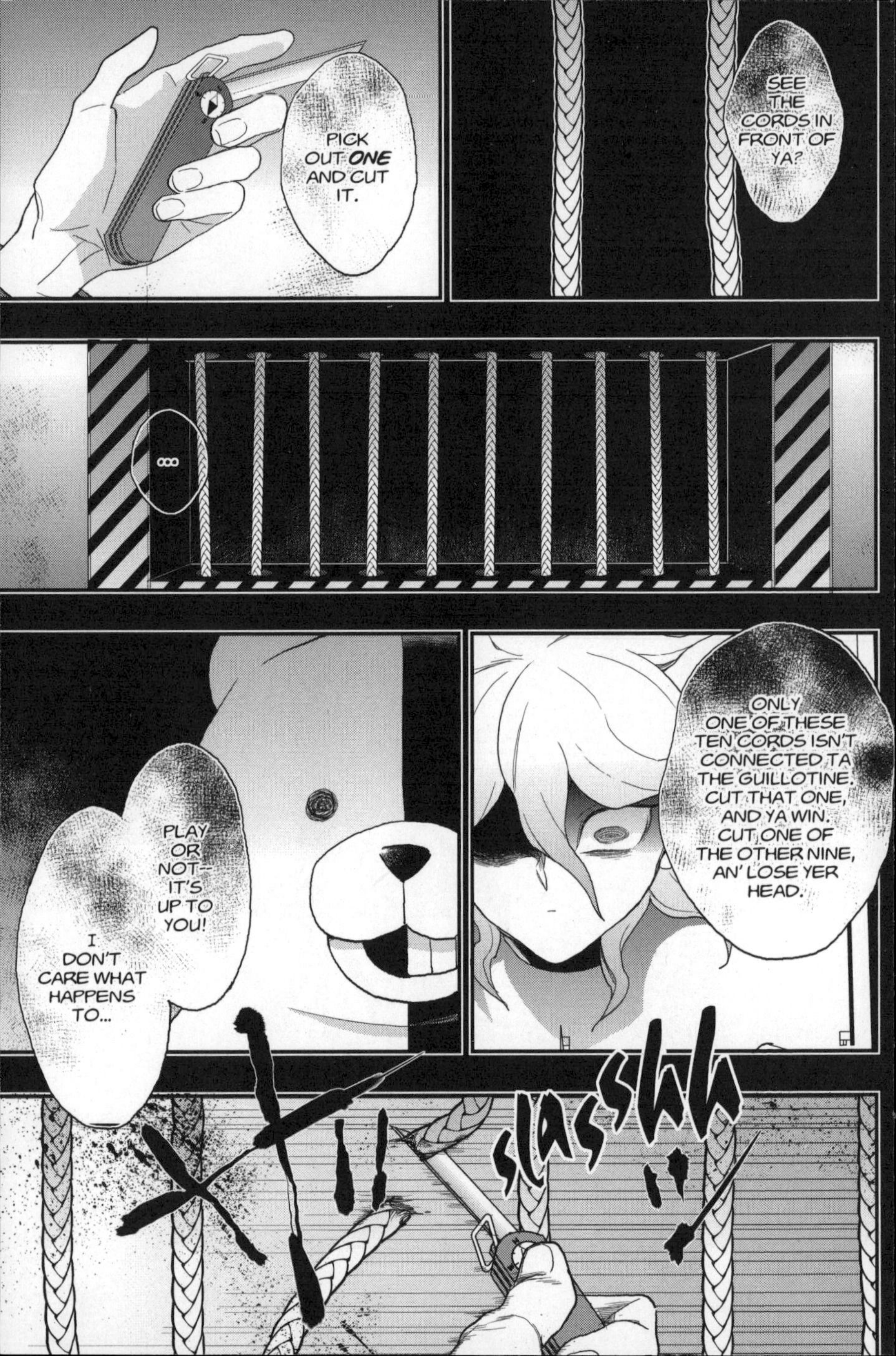
SEE THE CORDS IN FRONT OF YA?
PICK OUT **ONE** AND CUT IT.
...
ONLY ONE OF THESE TEN CORDS ISN'T CONNECTED TA THE GUILLOTINE. CUT THAT ONE, AND YA WIN. CUT ONE OF THE OTHER NINE, AN' LOSE YER HEAD.
PLAY OR NOT-- IT'S UP TO YOU!
I DON'T CARE WHAT HAPPENS TO...
slasshh
!!

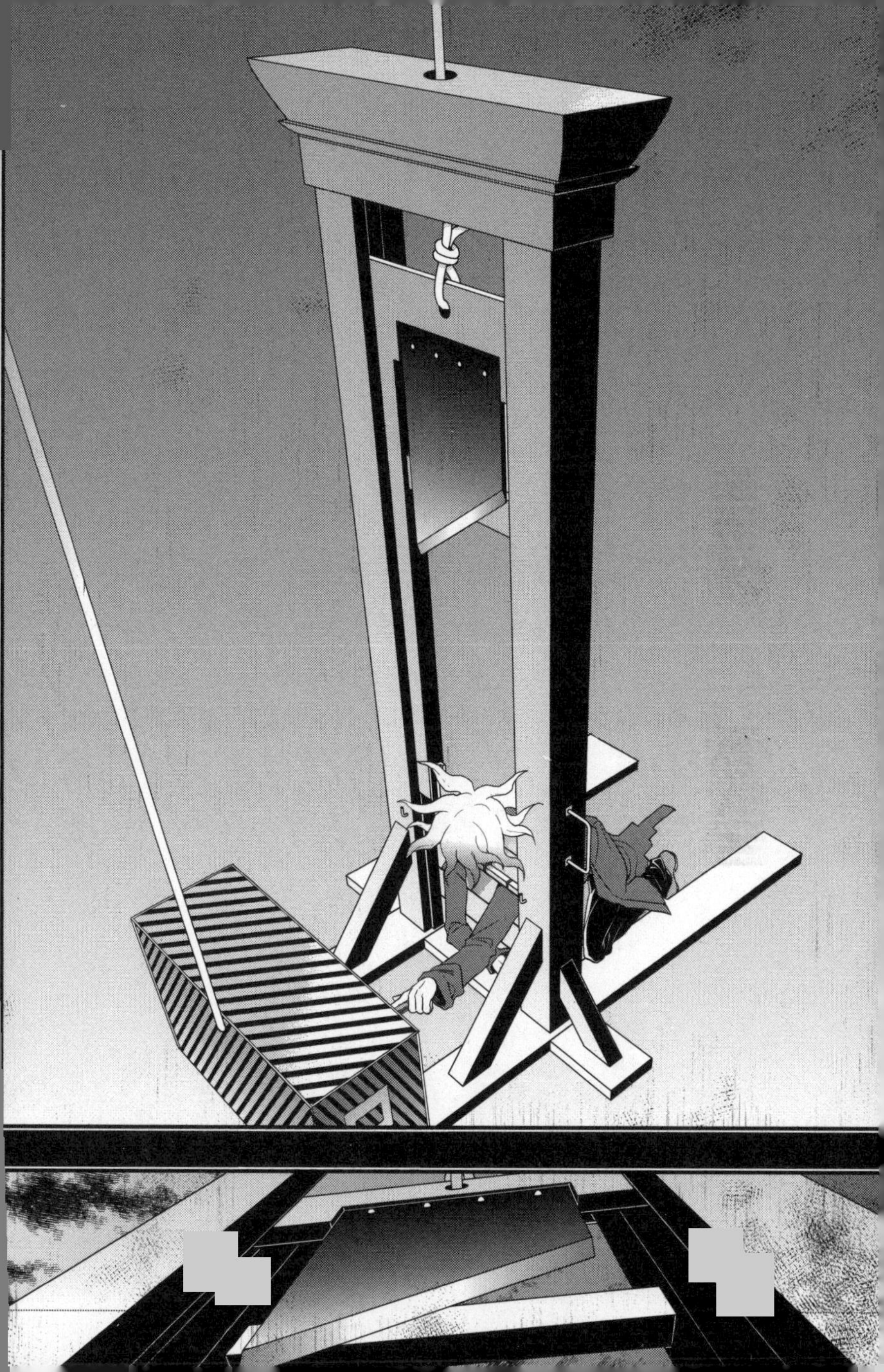

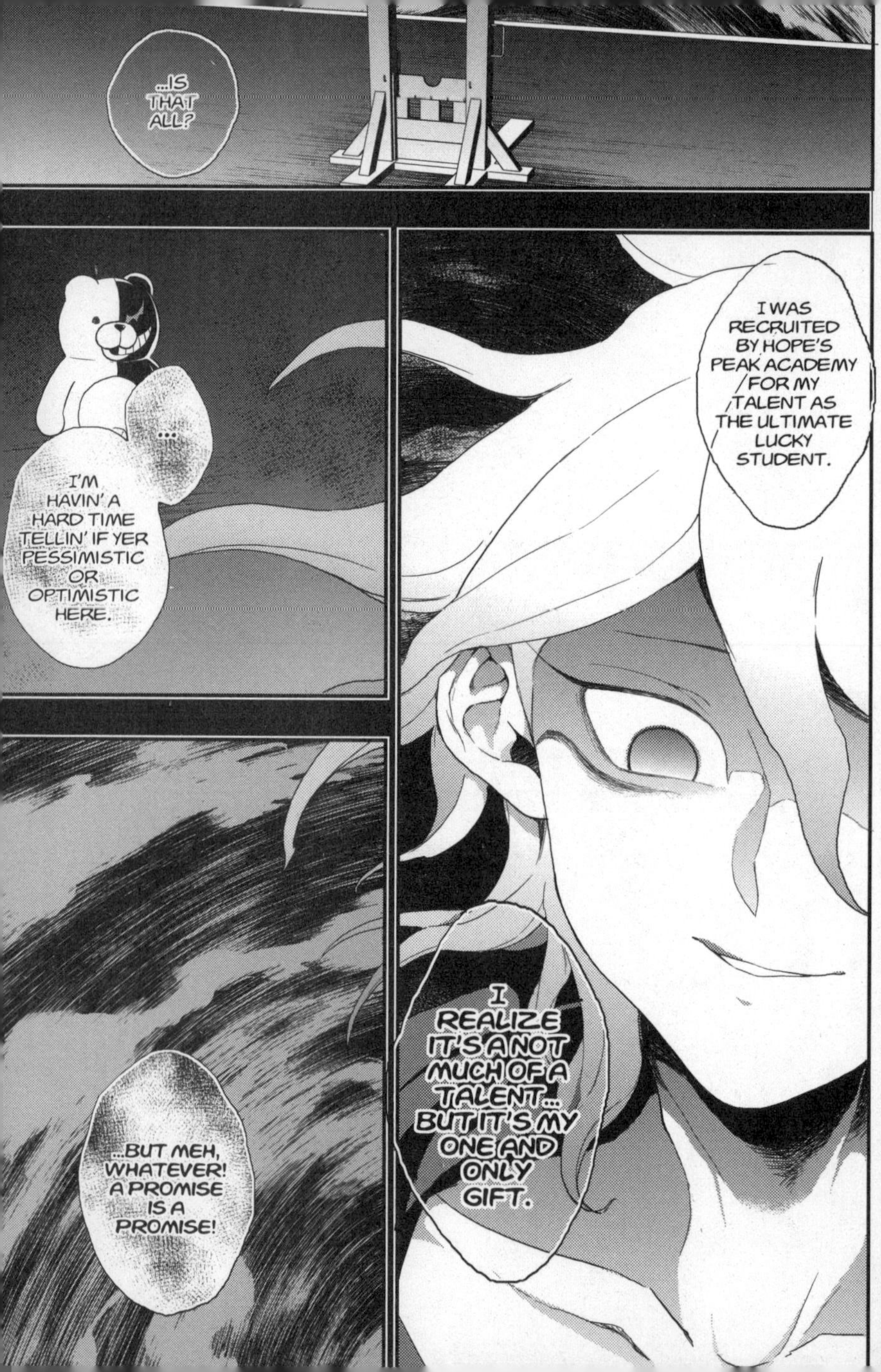
...IS THAT ALL?
I WAS RECRUITED BY HOPE'S PEAK ACADEMY FOR MY TALENT AS THE ULTIMATE LUCKY STUDENT.
I REALIZE IT'S A NOT MUCH OF A TALENT... BUT IT'S MY ONE AND ONLY GIFT.
...
I'M HAVIN' A HARD TIME TELLIN' IF YER PESSIMISTIC OR OPTIMISTIC HERE.
...BUT MEH, WHATEVER! A PROMISE IS A PROMISE!

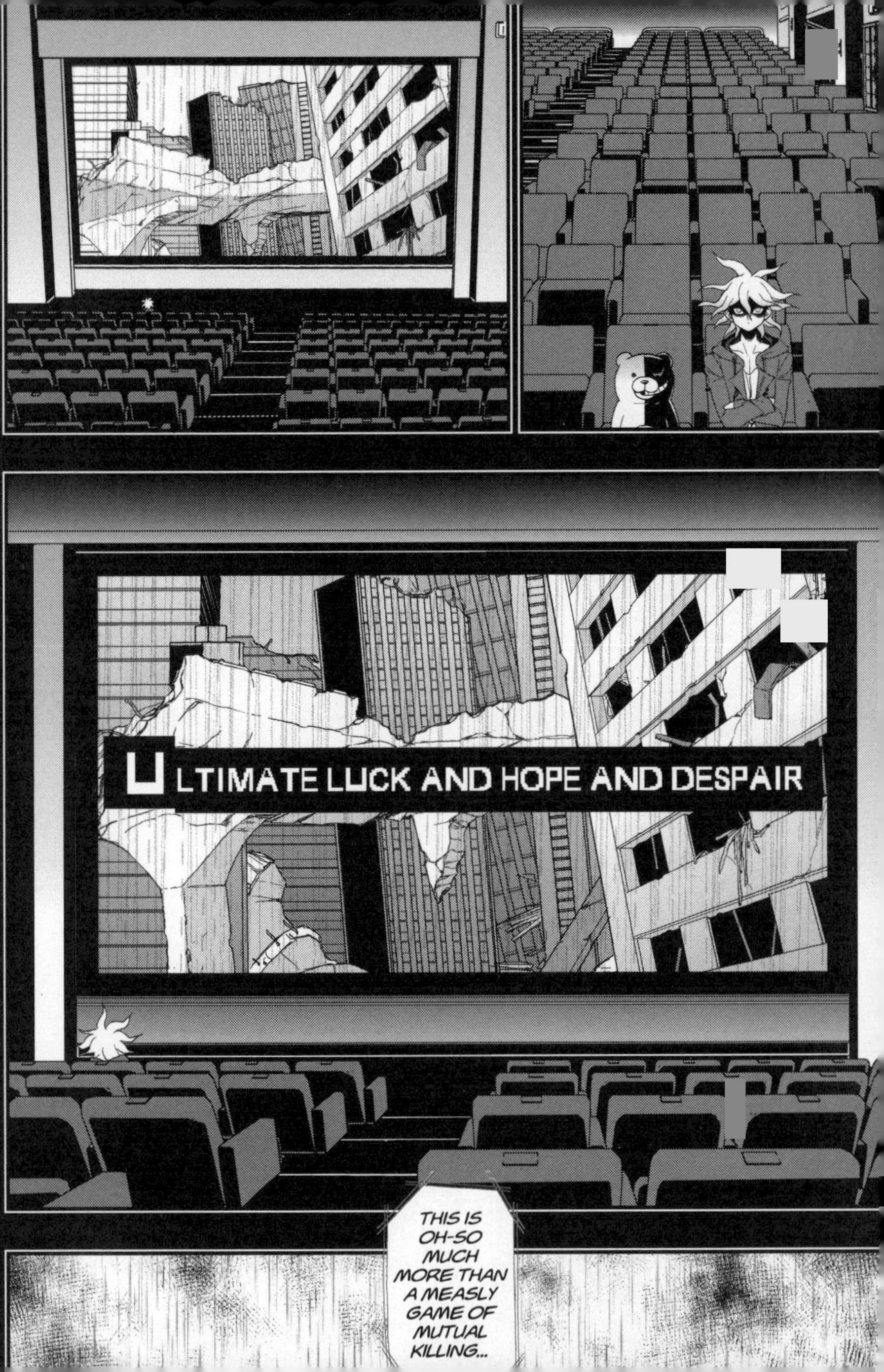

ULTIMATE LUCK AND HOPE AND DESPAIR
THIS IS OH-SO MUCH MORE THAN A MEASLY GAME OF MUTUAL KILLING...

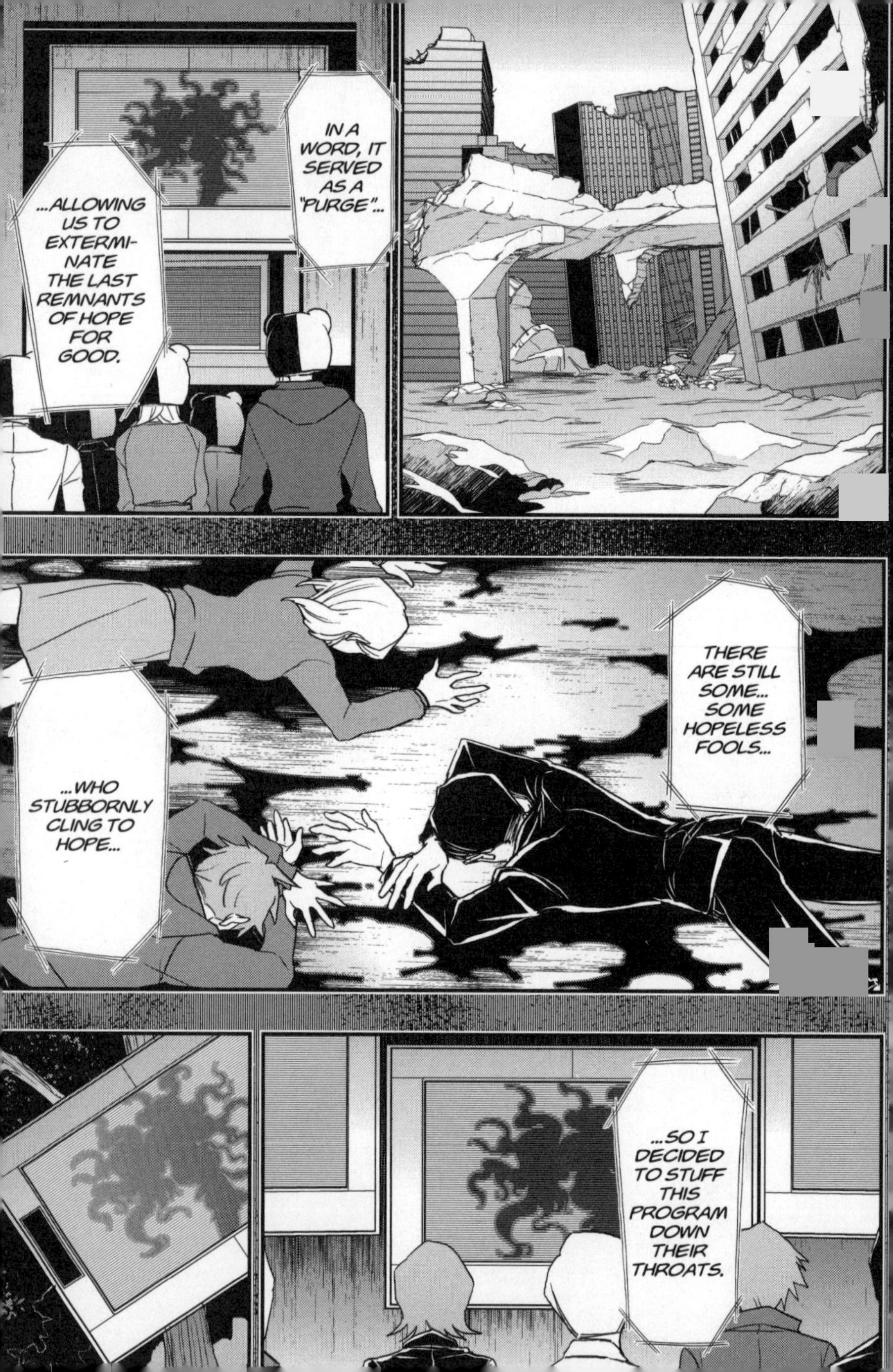
IN A WORD, IT SERVED AS A "PURGE"...
...ALLOWING US TO EXTERMINATE THE LAST REMNANTS OF HOPE FOR GOOD.
THERE ARE STILL SOME... SOME HOPELESS FOOLS...
...WHO STUBBORNLY CLING TO HOPE...
...SO I DECIDED TO STUFF THIS PROGRAM DOWN THEIR THROATS.

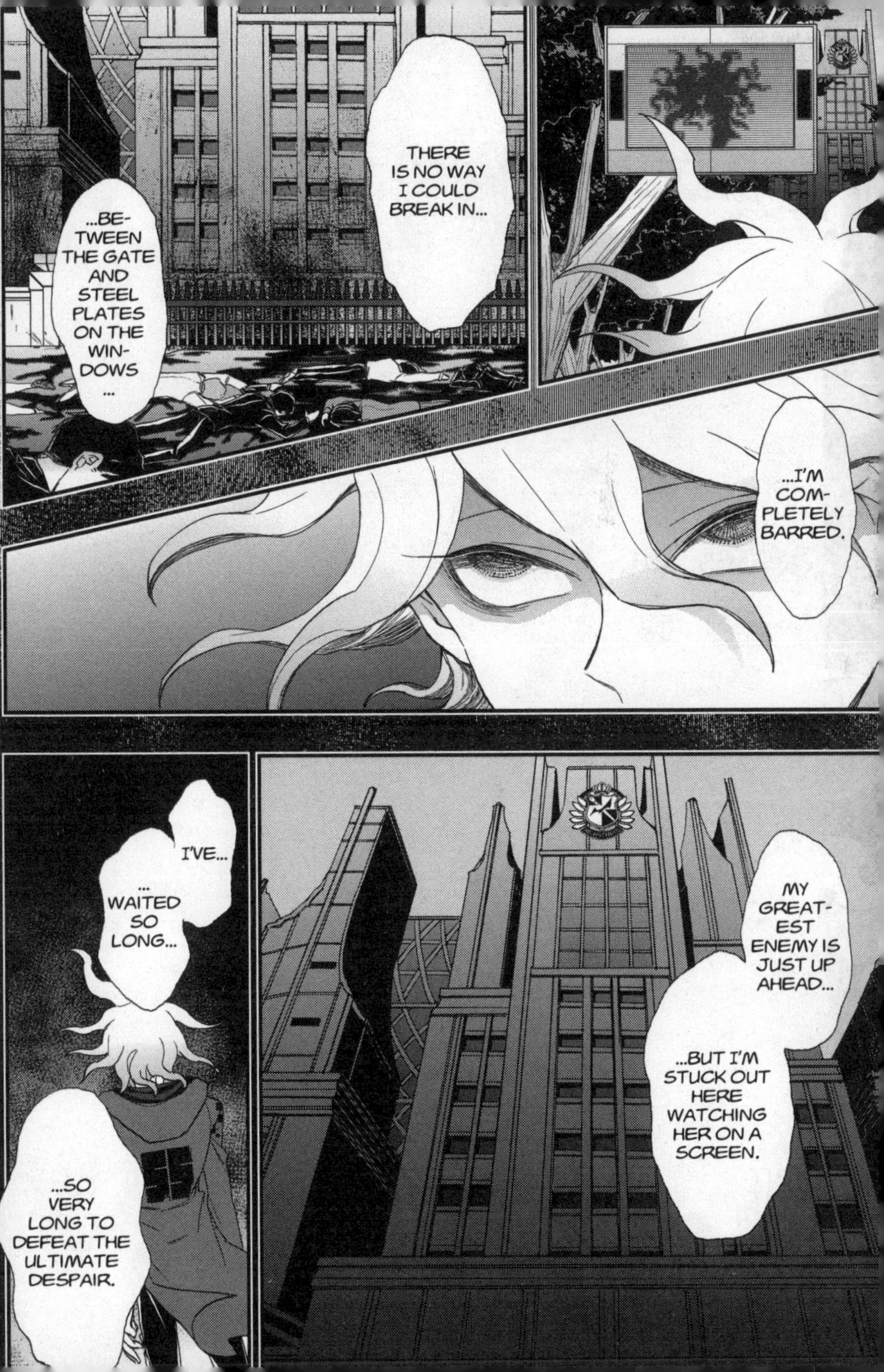
THERE IS NO WAY I COULD BREAK IN...
...BETWEEN THE GATE AND STEEL PLATES ON THE WINDOWS...
...I'M COMPLETELY BARRED.
MY GREATEST ENEMY IS JUST UP AHEAD...
...BUT I'M STUCK OUT HERE WATCHING HER ON A SCREEN.
I'VE...
...WAITED SO LONG...
...SO VERY LONG TO DEFEAT THE ULTIMATE DESPAIR.

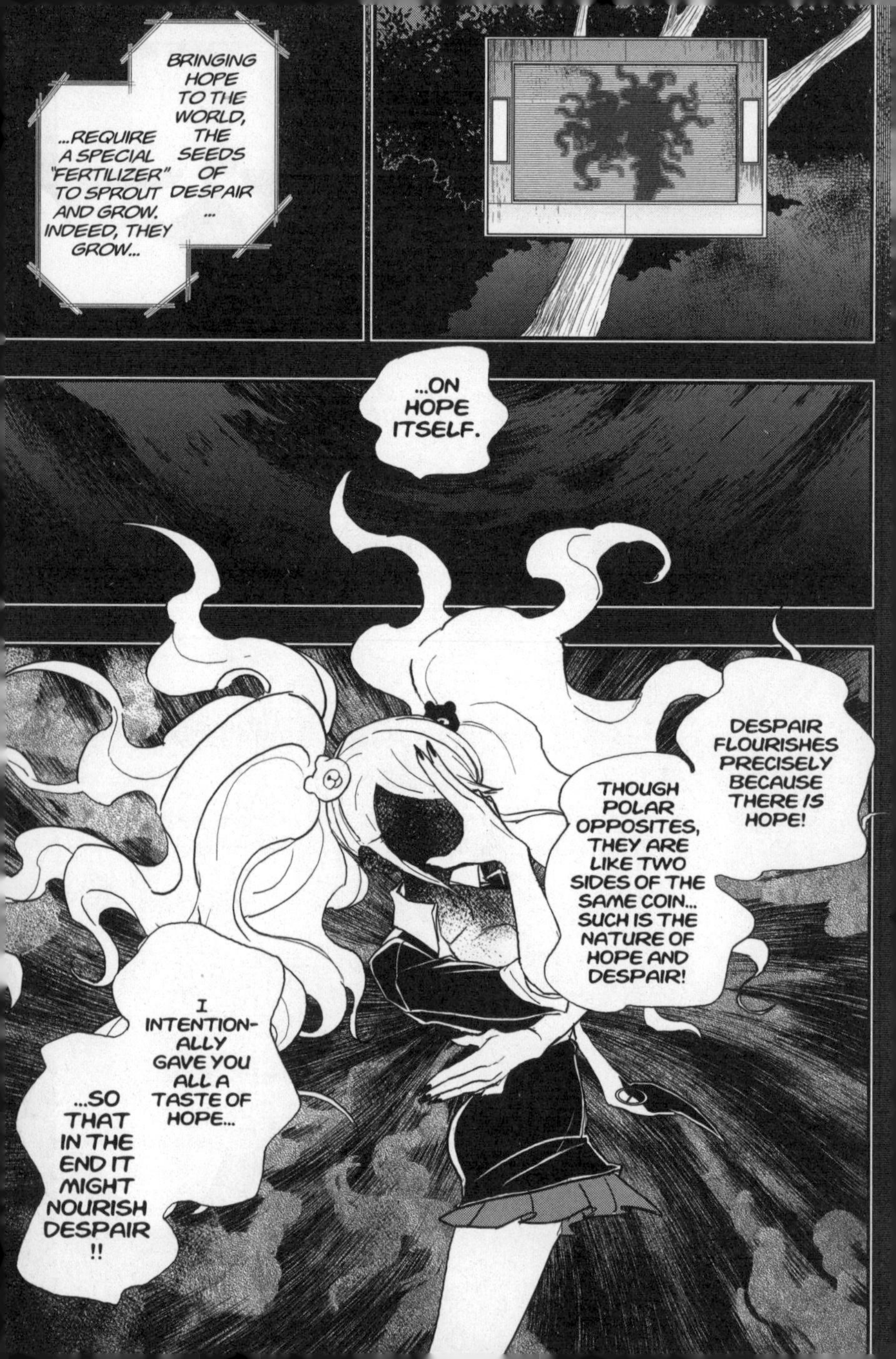
BRINGING HOPE TO THE WORLD, THE SEEDS OF DESPAIR ...
...REQUIRE A SPECIAL "FERTILIZER" TO SPROUT AND GROW. INDEED, THEY GROW...
...ON HOPE ITSELF.
DESPAIR FLOURISHES PRECISELY BECAUSE THERE IS HOPE!
THOUGH POLAR OPPOSITES, THEY ARE LIKE TWO SIDES OF THE SAME COIN... SUCH IS THE NATURE OF HOPE AND DESPAIR!
I INTENTIONALLY GAVE YOU ALL A TASTE OF HOPE...
...SO THAT IN THE END IT MIGHT NOURISH DESPAIR!!

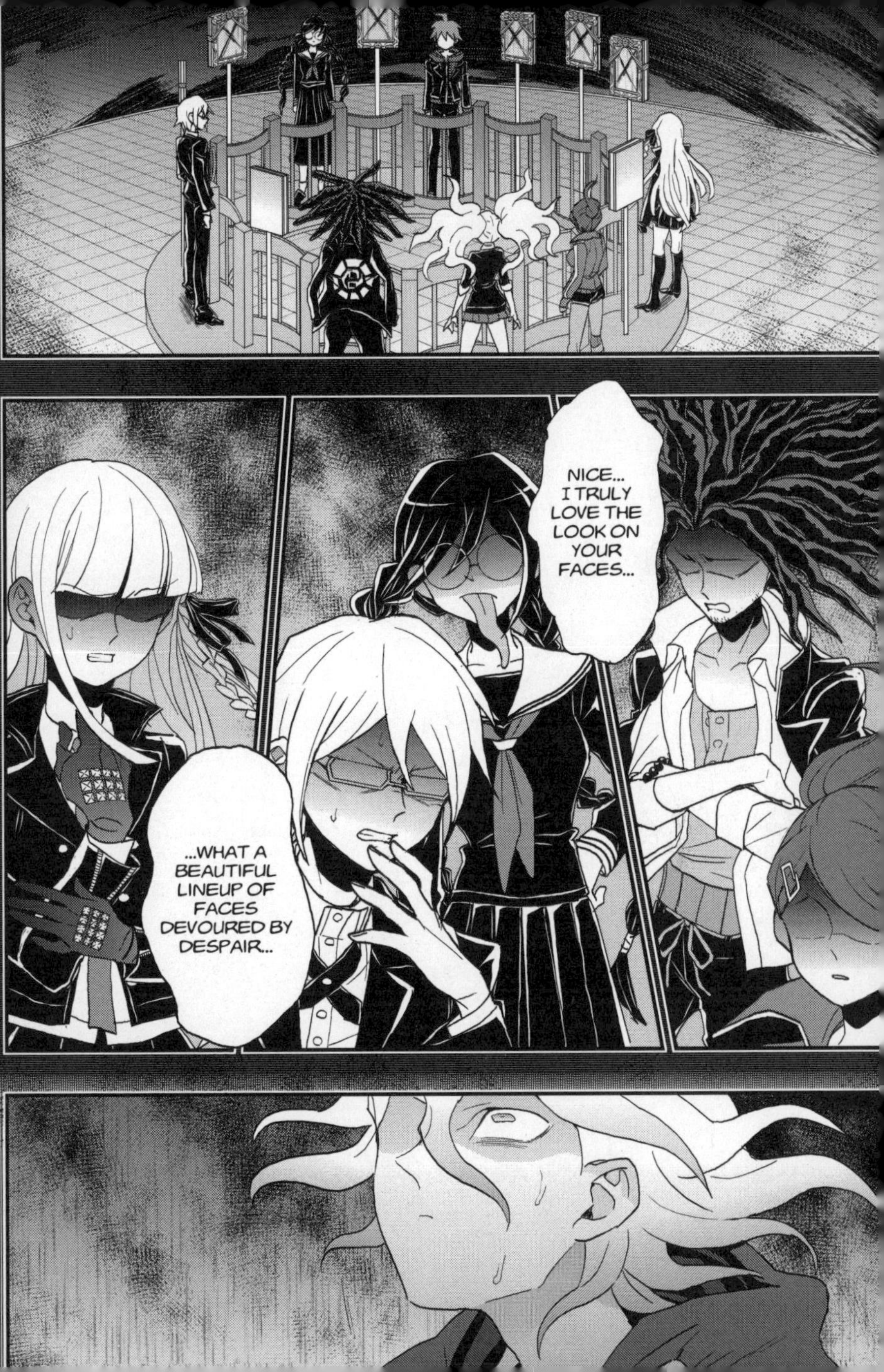
NICE... I TRULY LOVE THE LOOK ON YOUR FACES...
...WHAT A BEAUTIFUL LINEUP OF FACES DEVOURED BY DESPAIR...

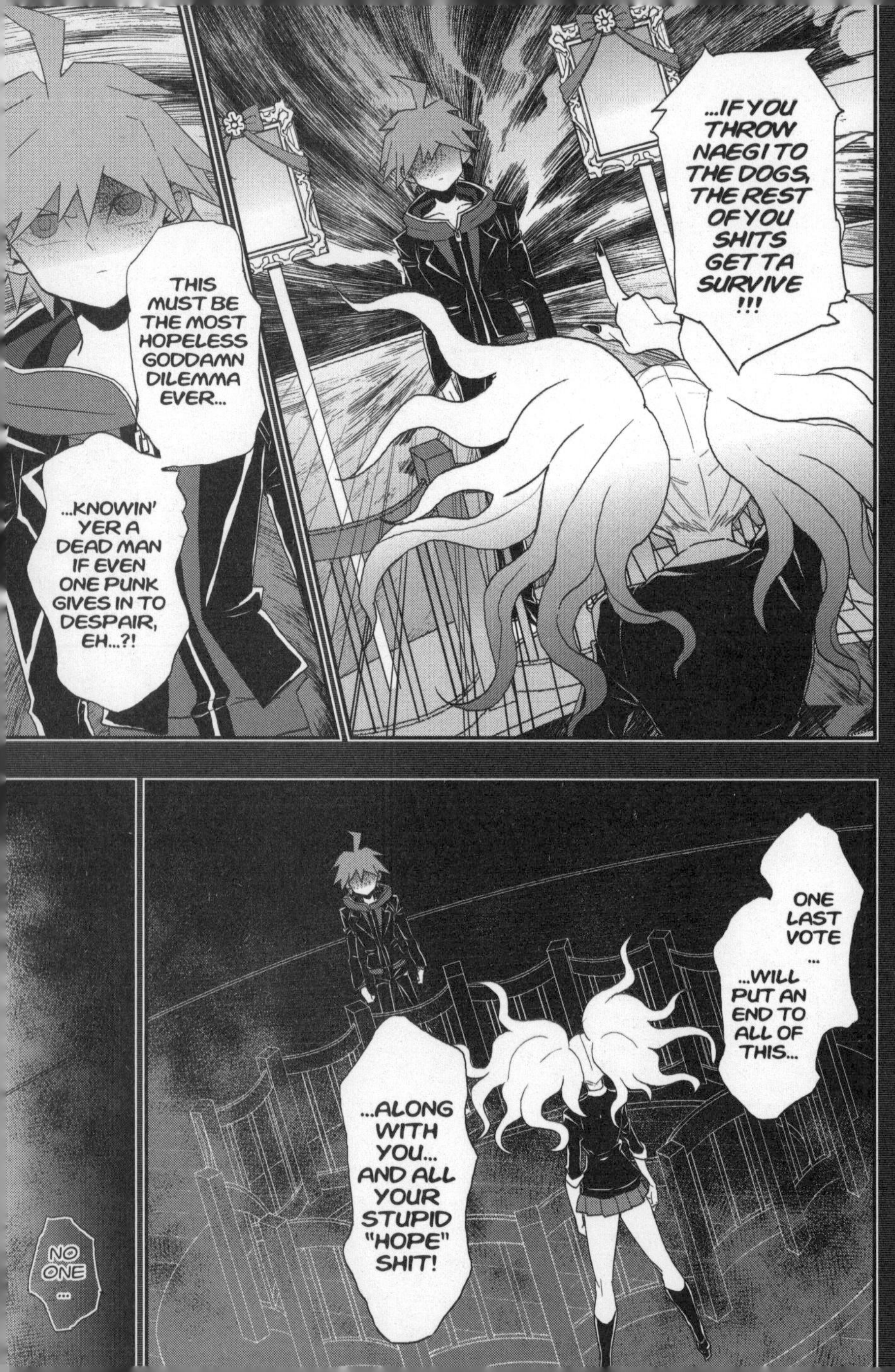
...IF YOU THROW NAEGI TO THE DOGS, THE REST OF YOU SHITS GET TA SURVIVE!!!
THIS MUST BE THE MOST HOPELESS GODDAMN DILEMMA EVER...
...KNOWIN' YER A DEAD MAN IF EVEN ONE PUNK GIVES IN TO DESPAIR, EH...?!
ONE LAST VOTE ... ...WILL PUT AN END TO ALL OF THIS...
...ALONG WITH YOU... AND ALL YOUR STUPID "HOPE" SHIT!
NO ONE ...

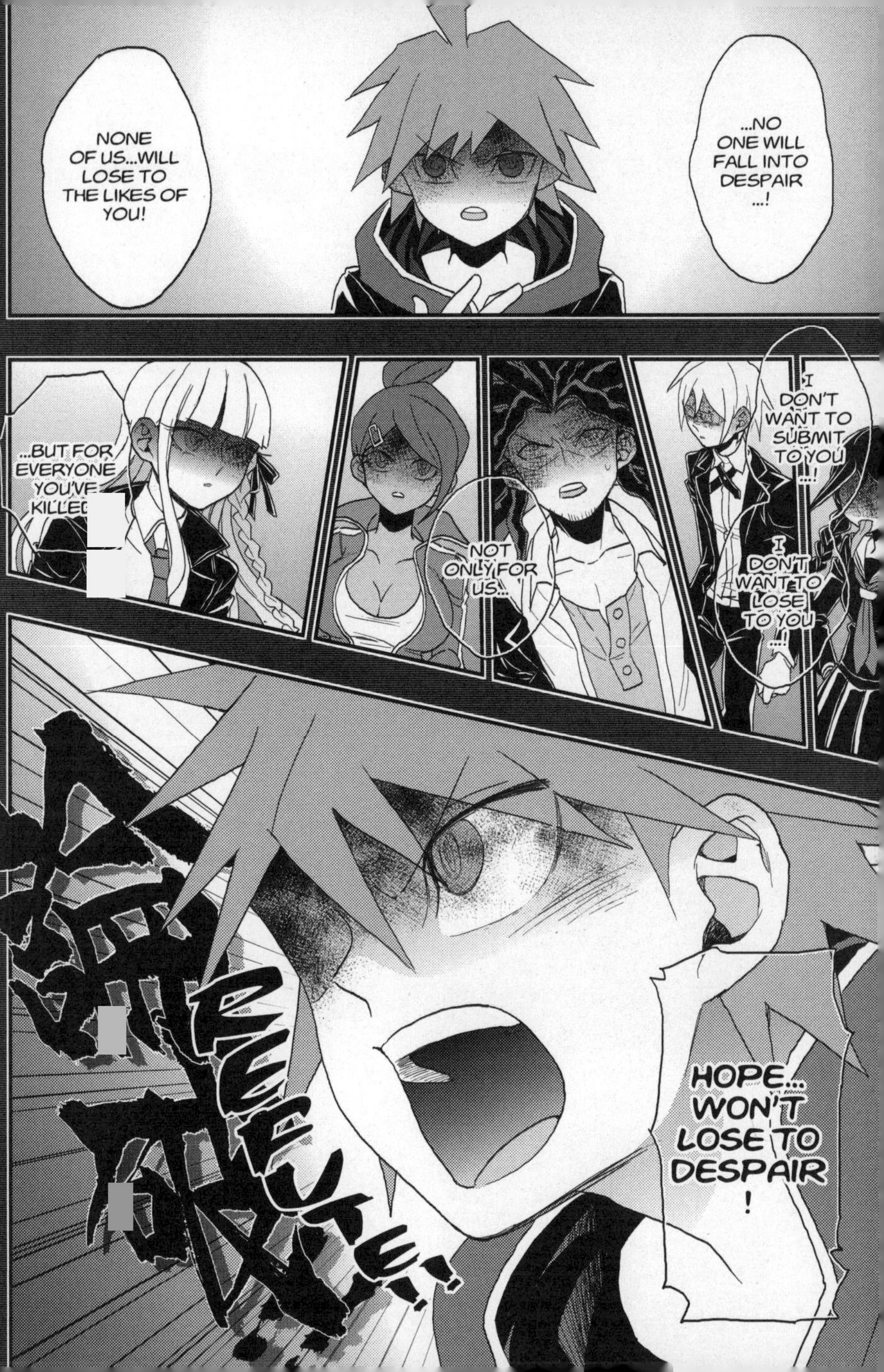
...NO ONE WILL FALL INTO DESPAIR ...!
NONE OF US...WILL LOSE TO THE LIKES OF YOU!
I DON'T WANT TO SUBMIT TO YOU ...!
I DON'T WANT TO LOSE TO YOU ....
NOT ONLY FOR US...
...BUT FOR EVERYONE YOU'VE KILLE
HOPE... WON'T LOSE TO DESPAIR !

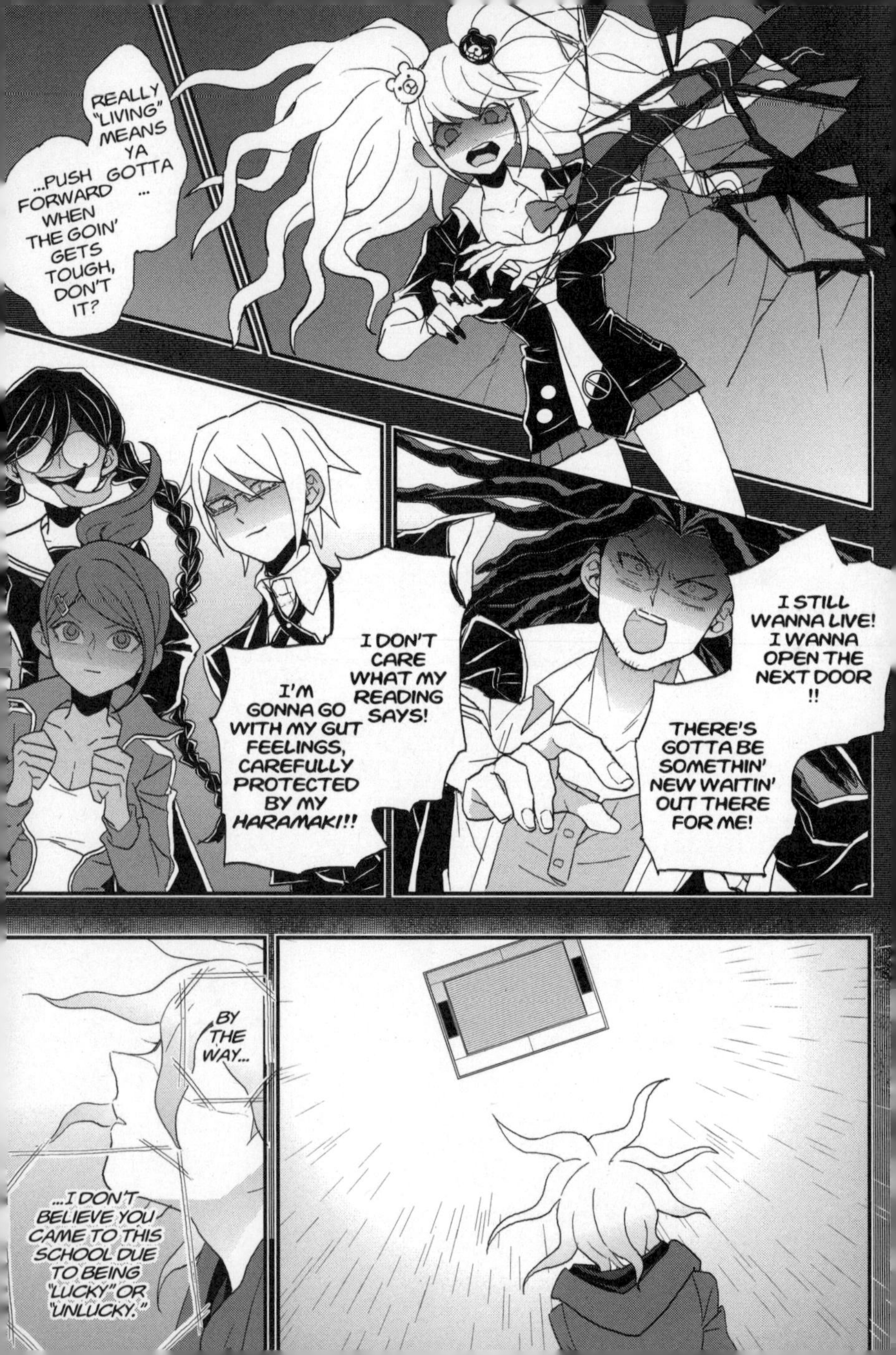
REALLY "LIVING" MEANS YA GOTTA ... ...PUSH FORWARD WHEN THE GOIN' GETS TOUGH, DON'T IT?
I STILL WANNA LIVE! I WANNA OPEN THE NEXT DOOR!!
THERE'S GOTTA BE SOMETHIN' NEW WAITIN' OUT THERE FOR ME!
I DON'T CARE WHAT MY READING SAYS!
I'M GONNA GO WITH MY GUT FEELINGS, CAREFULLY PROTECTED BY MY HARAMAKI!!
BY THE WAY...
...I DON'T BELIEVE YOU CAME TO THIS SCHOOL DUE TO BEING "LUCKY" OR "UNLUCKY."

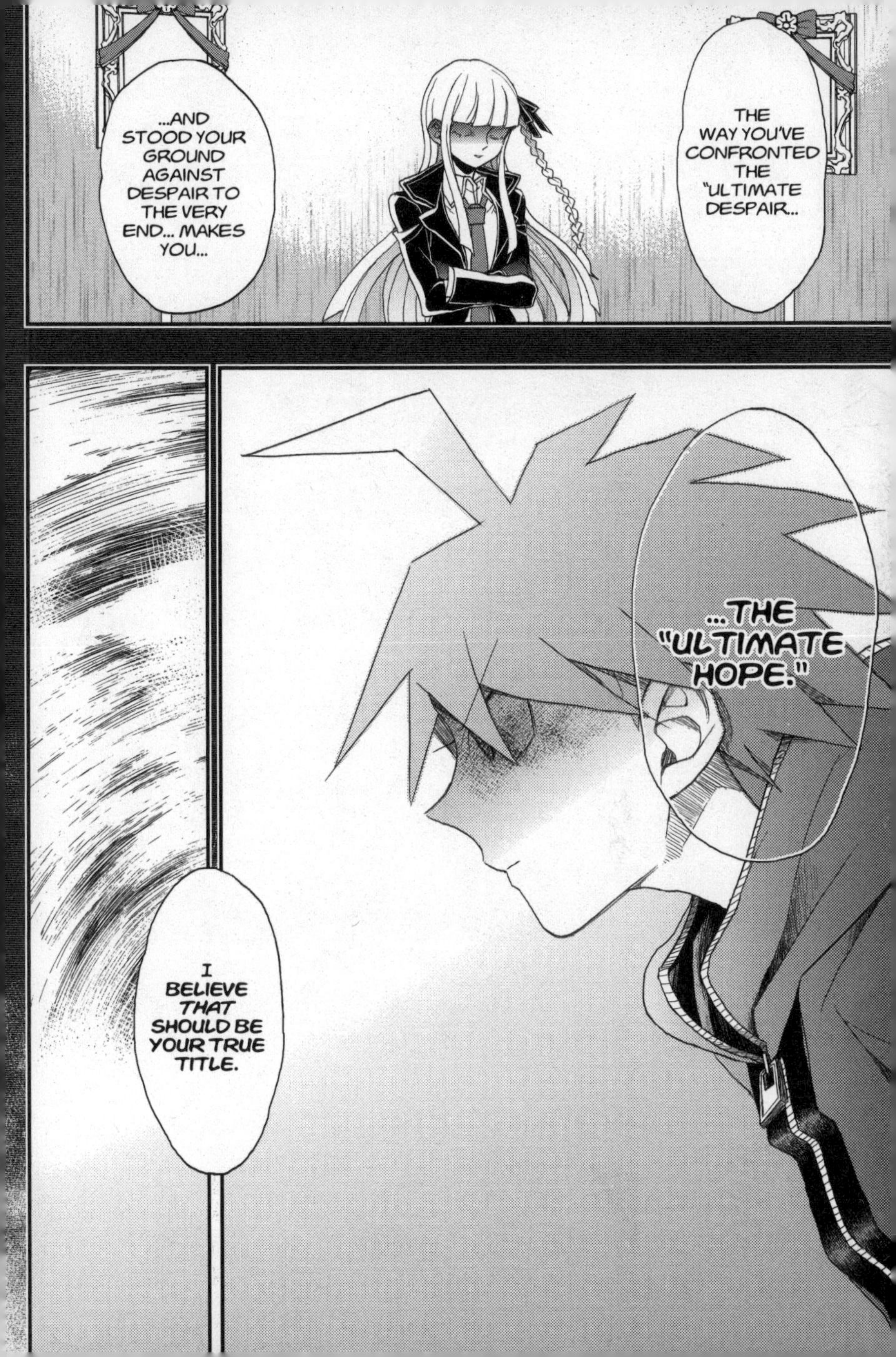
THE WAY YOU'VE CONFRONTED THE "ULTIMATE DESPAIR...
...AND STOOD YOUR GROUND AGAINST DESPAIR TO THE VERY END... MAKES YOU...
...THE "ULTIMATE HOPE."
I BELIEVE *THAT* SHOULD BE YOUR TRUE TITLE.

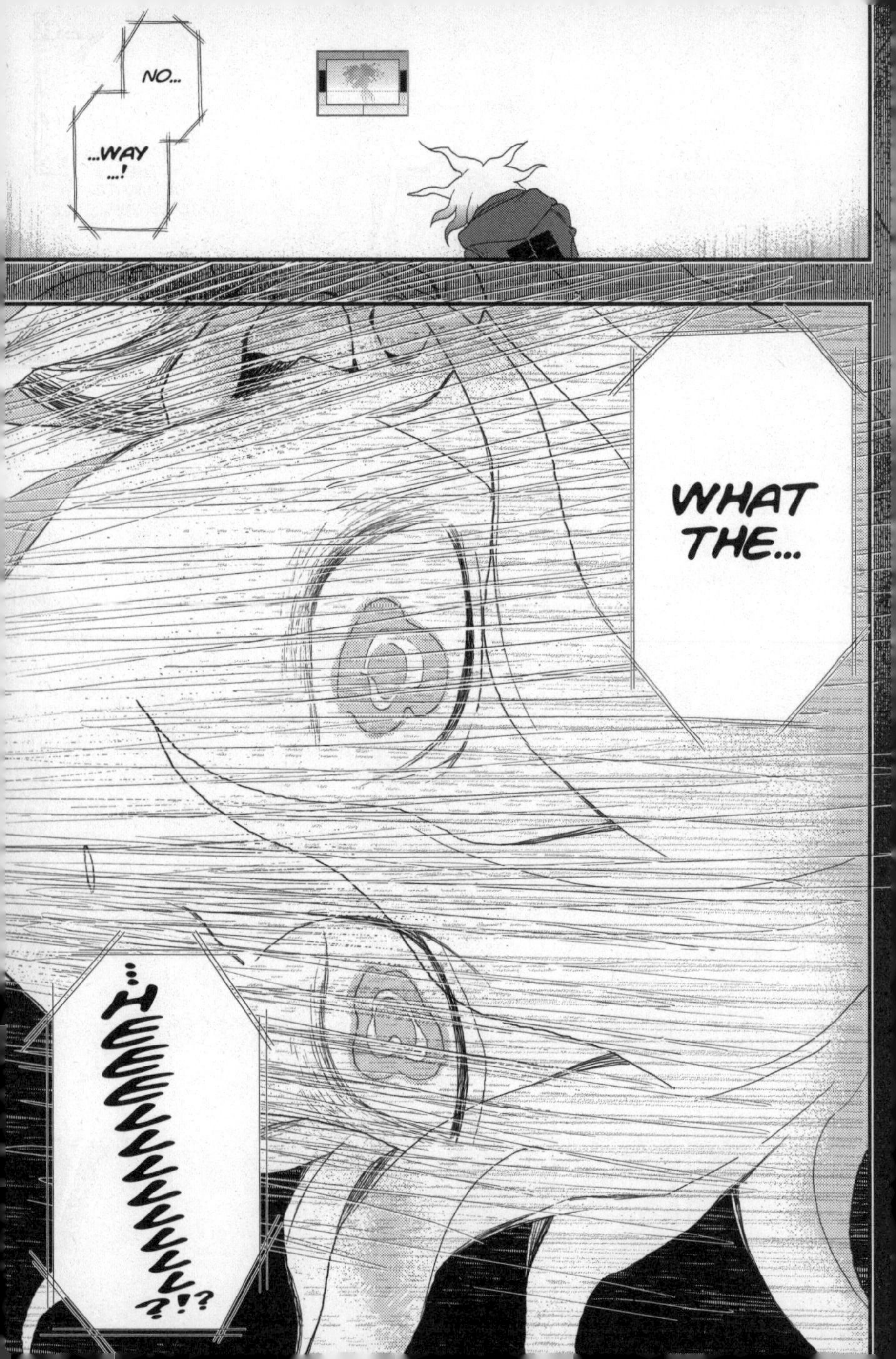
NO...
...WAY ...!
WHAT THE...
...HEEEUUUUUUUUU?!?

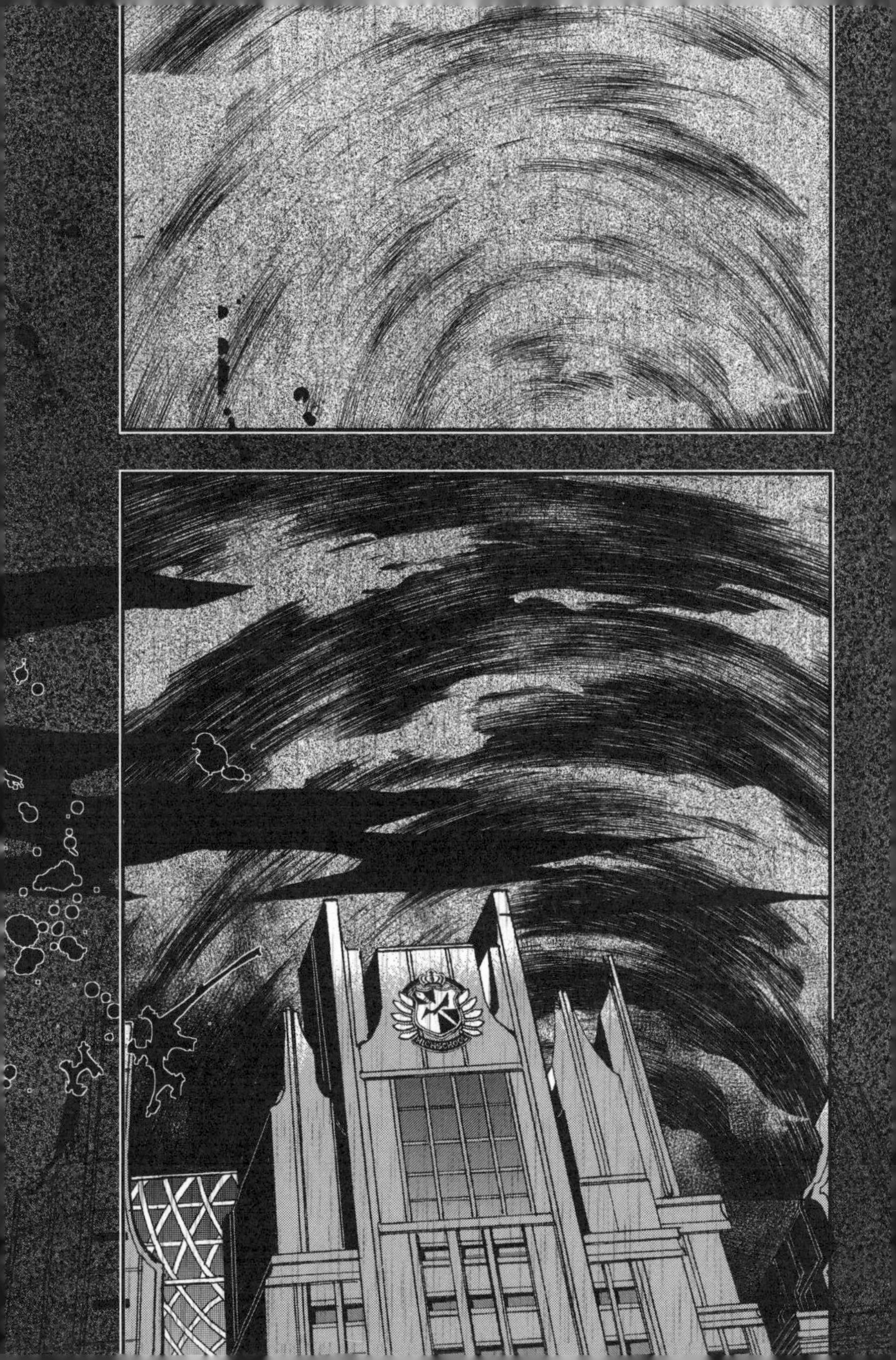

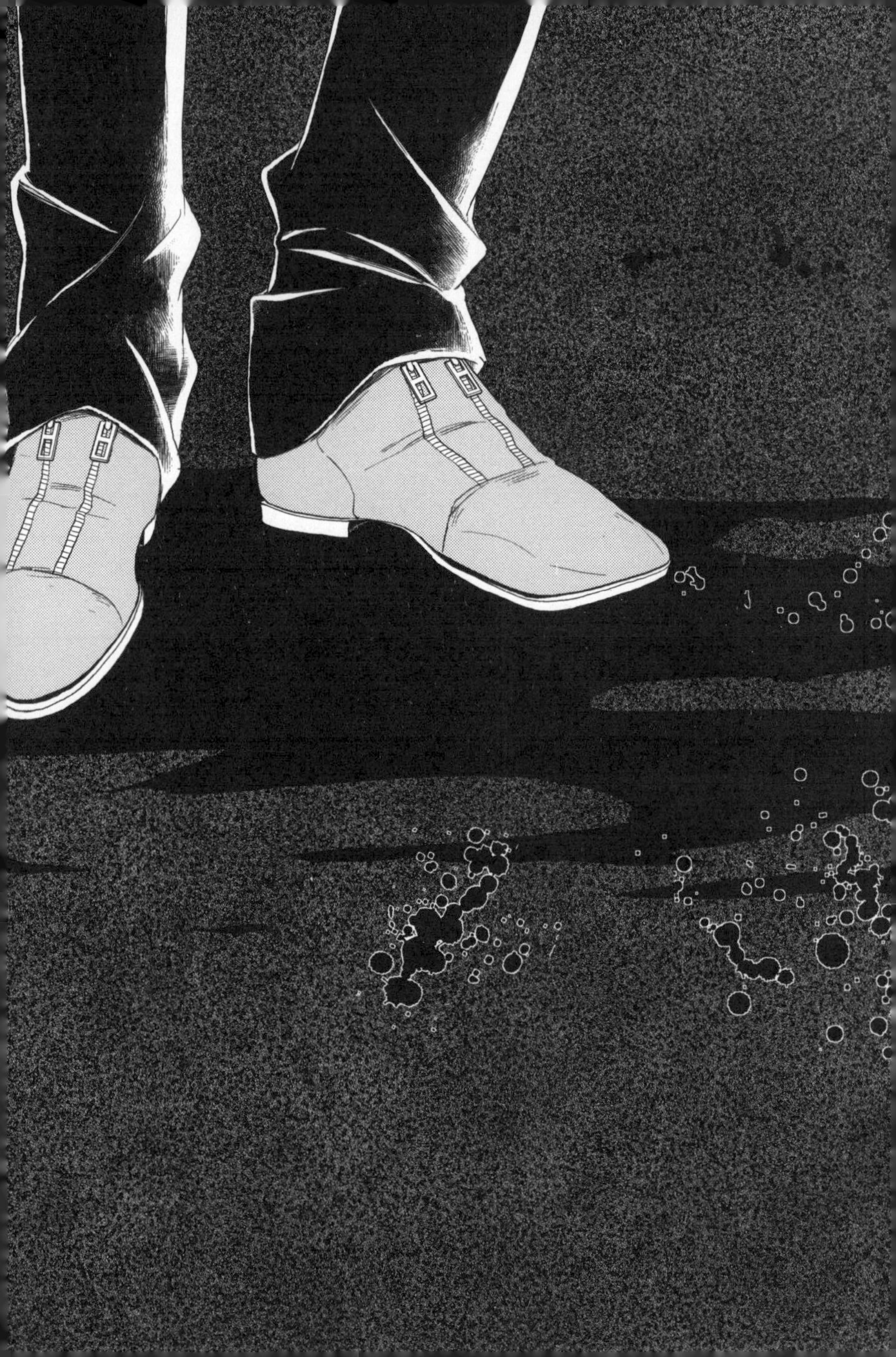

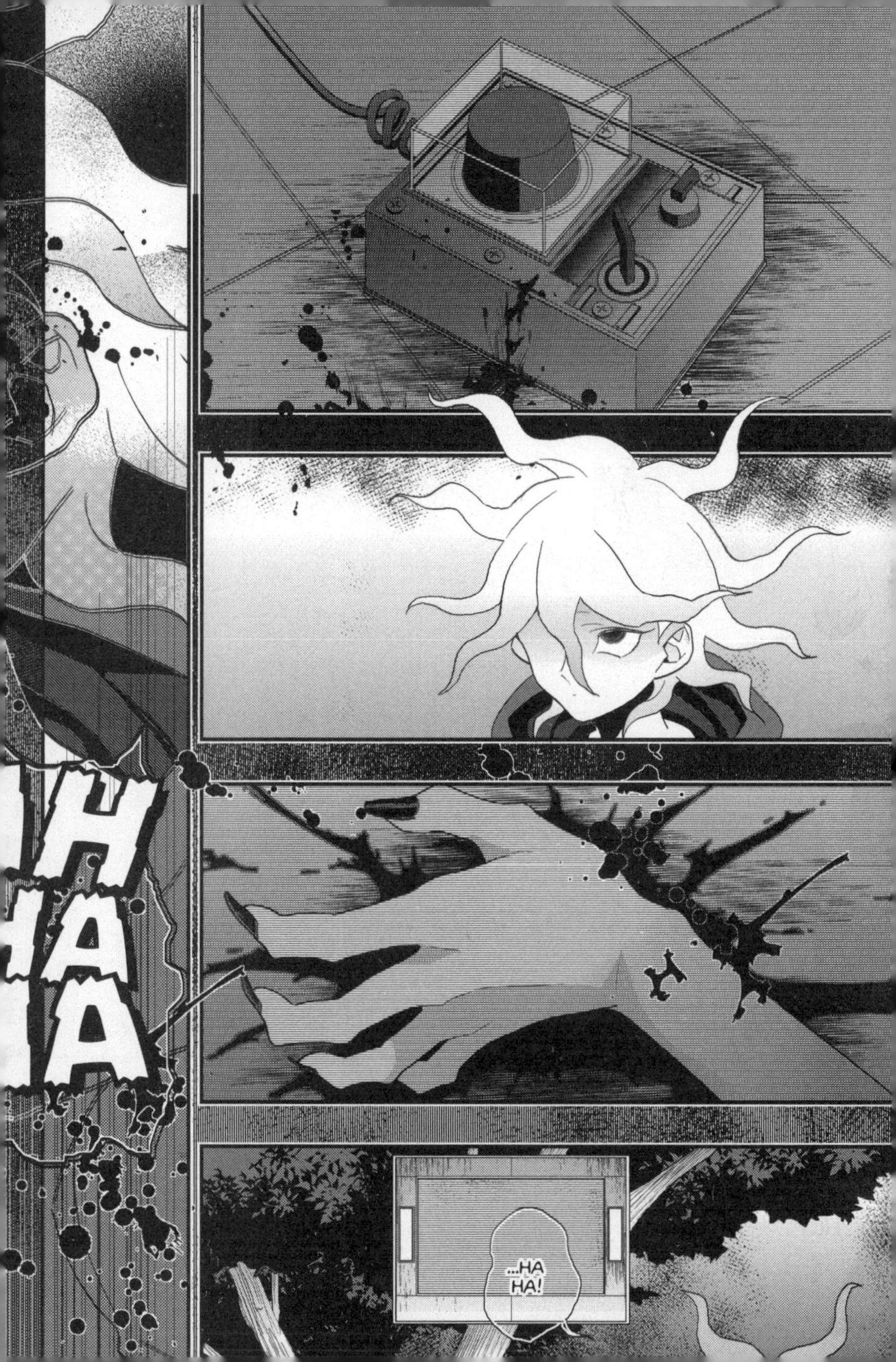
...HA HA!
HAA

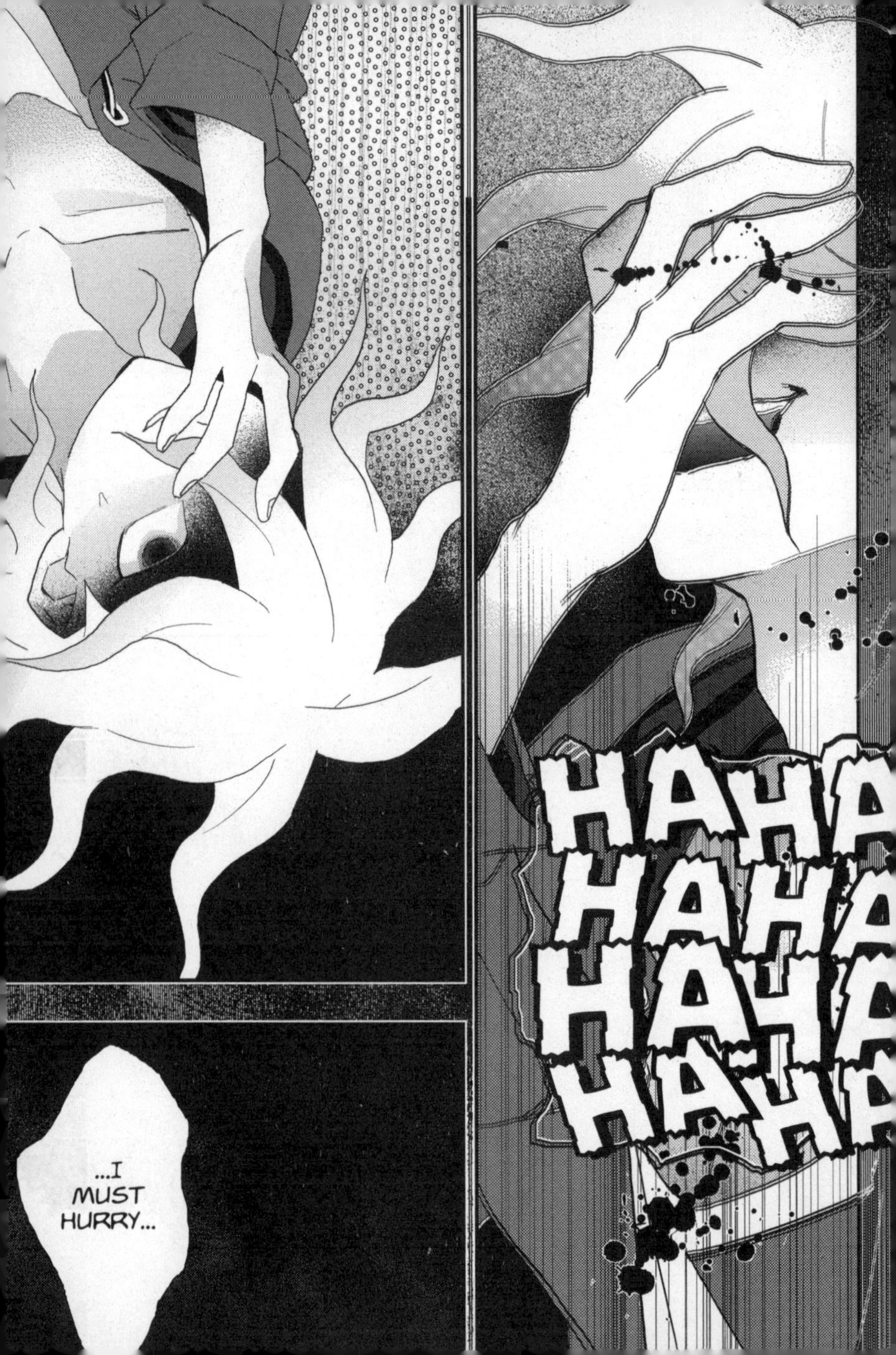
HAHA HAHA HAHA HAHA
...I MUST HURRY...

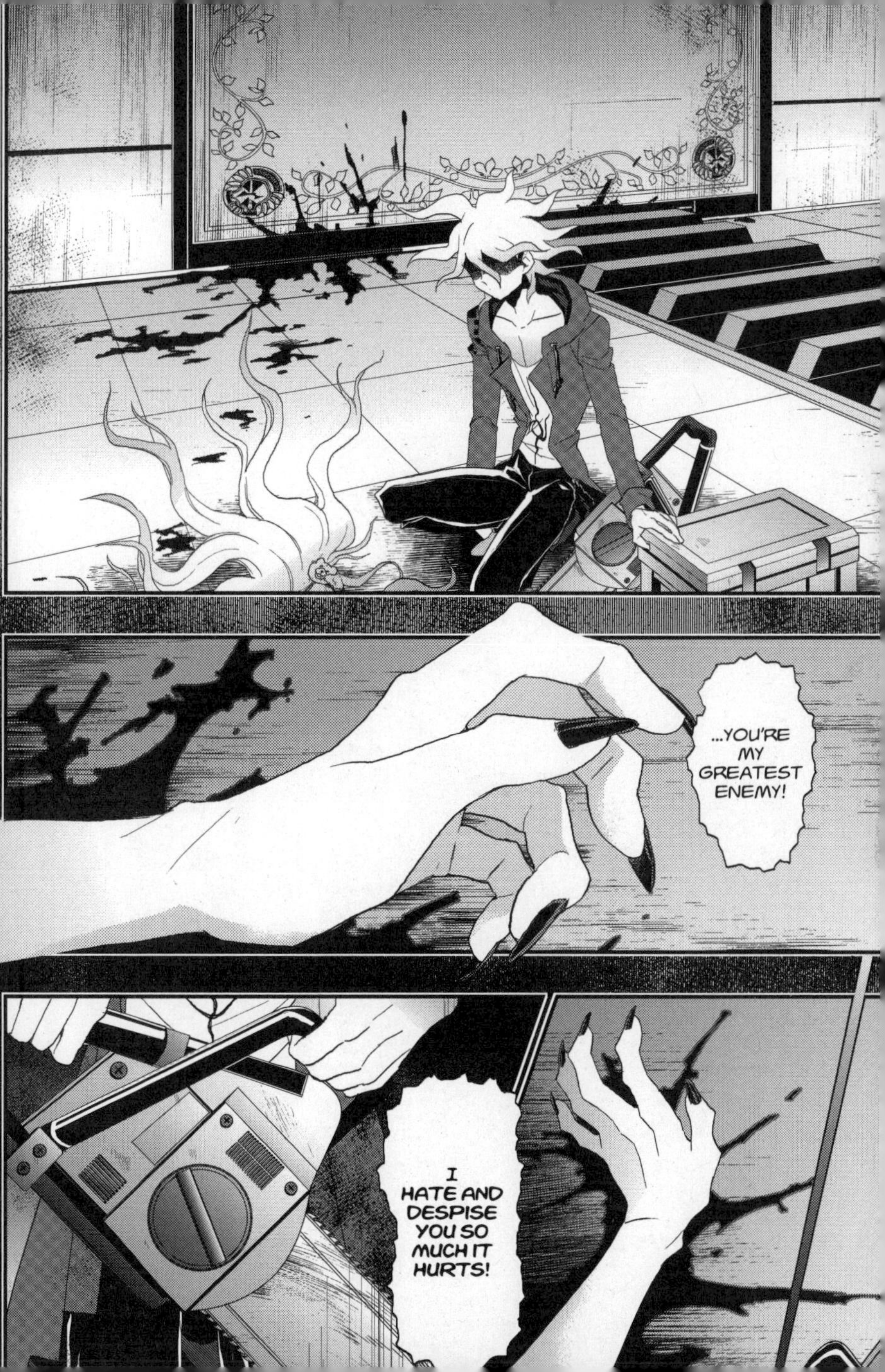
...YOU'RE MY GREATEST ENEMY!
I HATE AND DESPISE YOU SO MUCH IT HURTS!

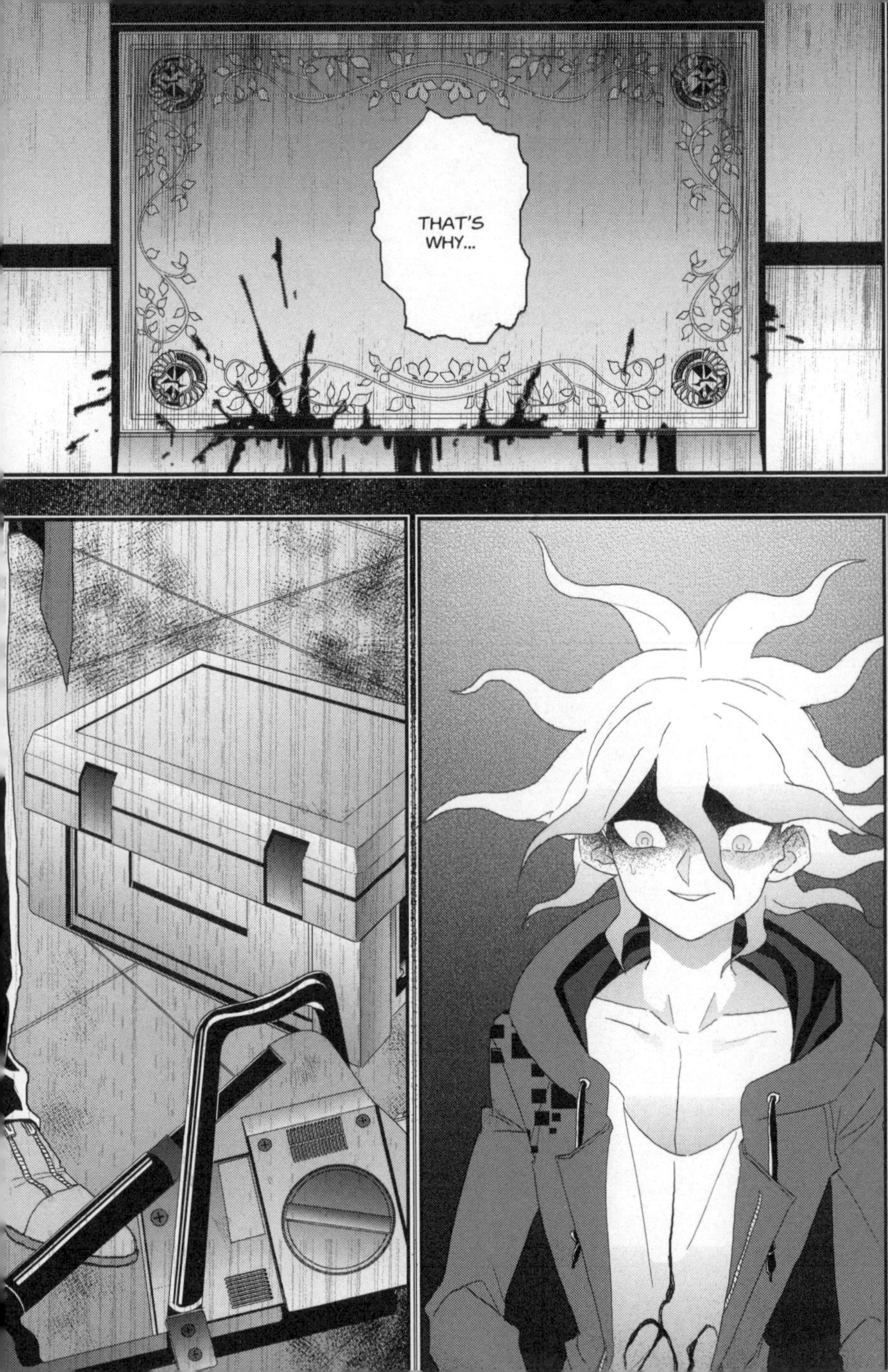
THAT'S WHY...

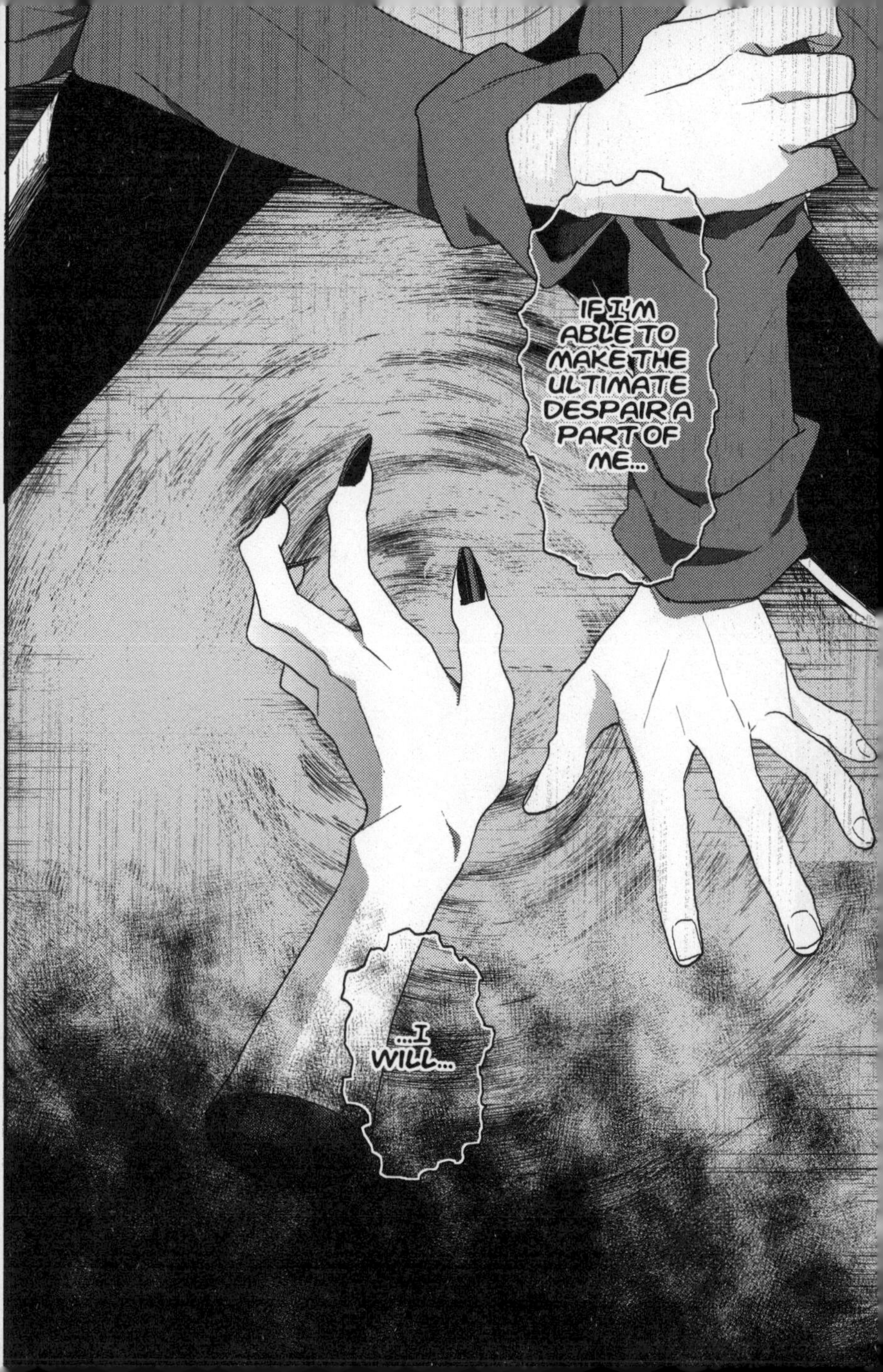
IF I'M ABLE TO MAKE THE ULTIMATE DESPAIR A PART OF ME...
...I WILL...

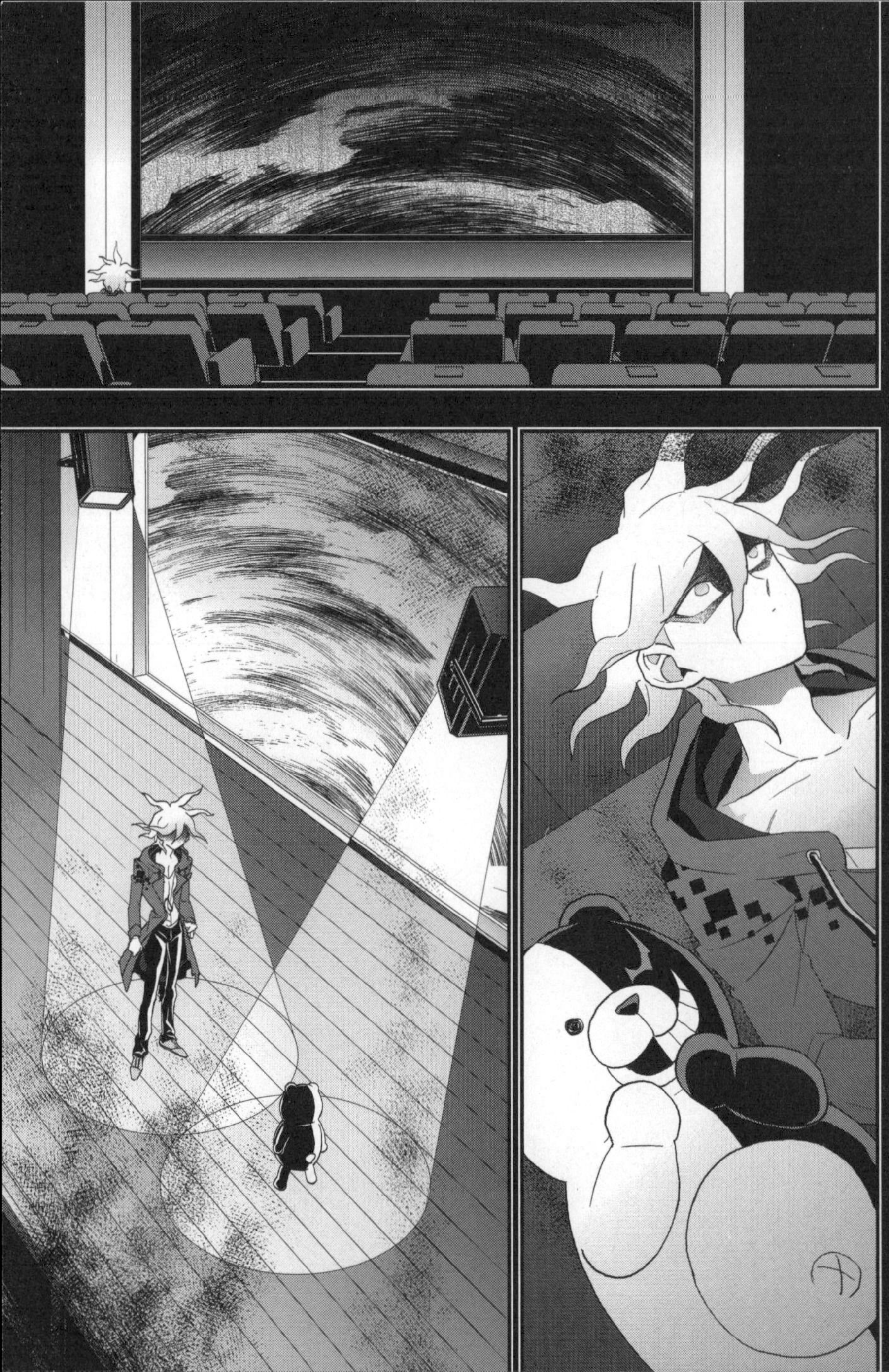

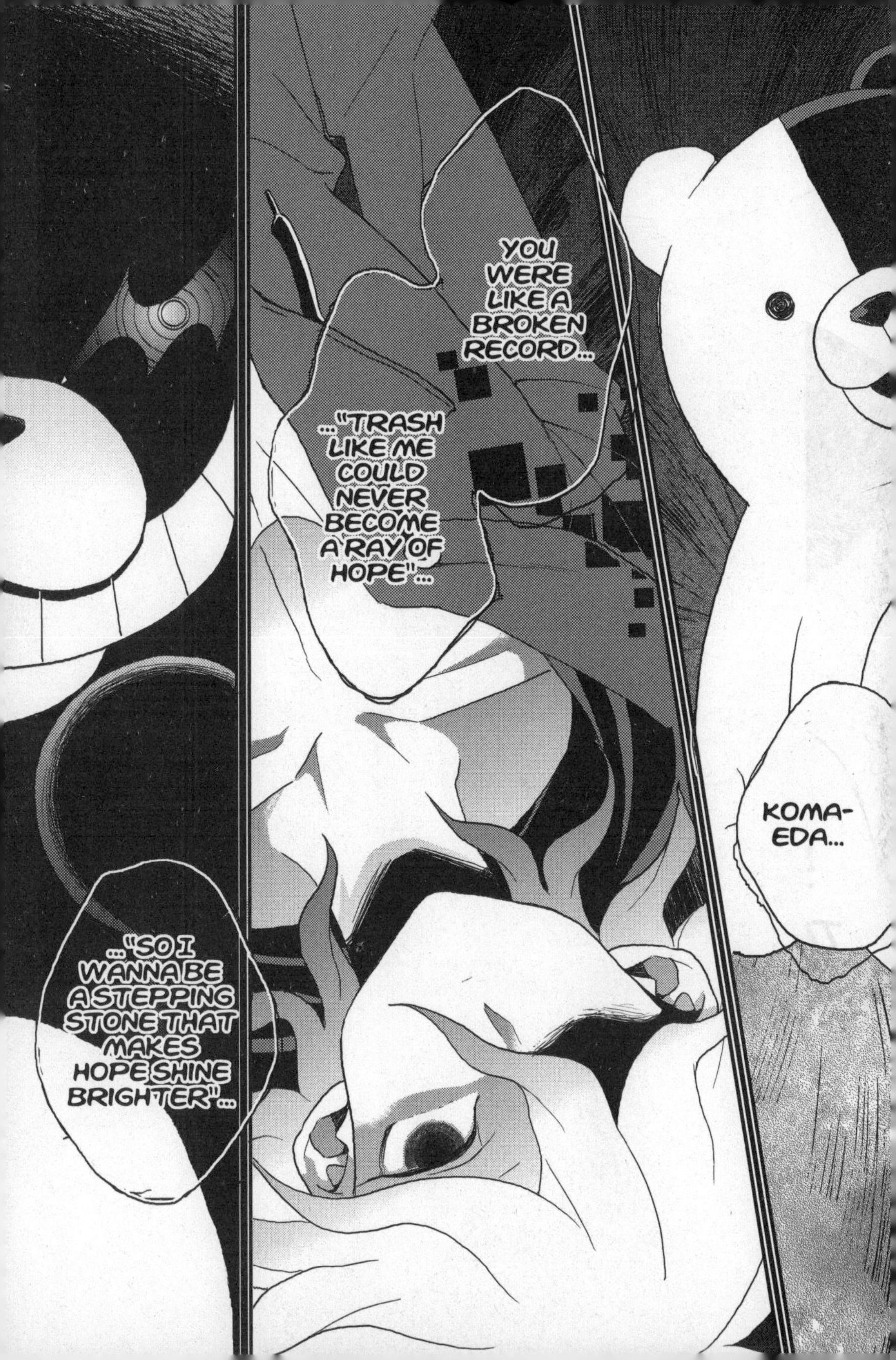
KOMA-EDA...
YOU WERE LIKE A BROKEN RECORD...
..."TRASH LIKE ME COULD NEVER BECOME A RAY OF HOPE"...
..."SO I WANNA BE A STEPPING STONE THAT MAKES HOPE SHINE BRIGHTER"...

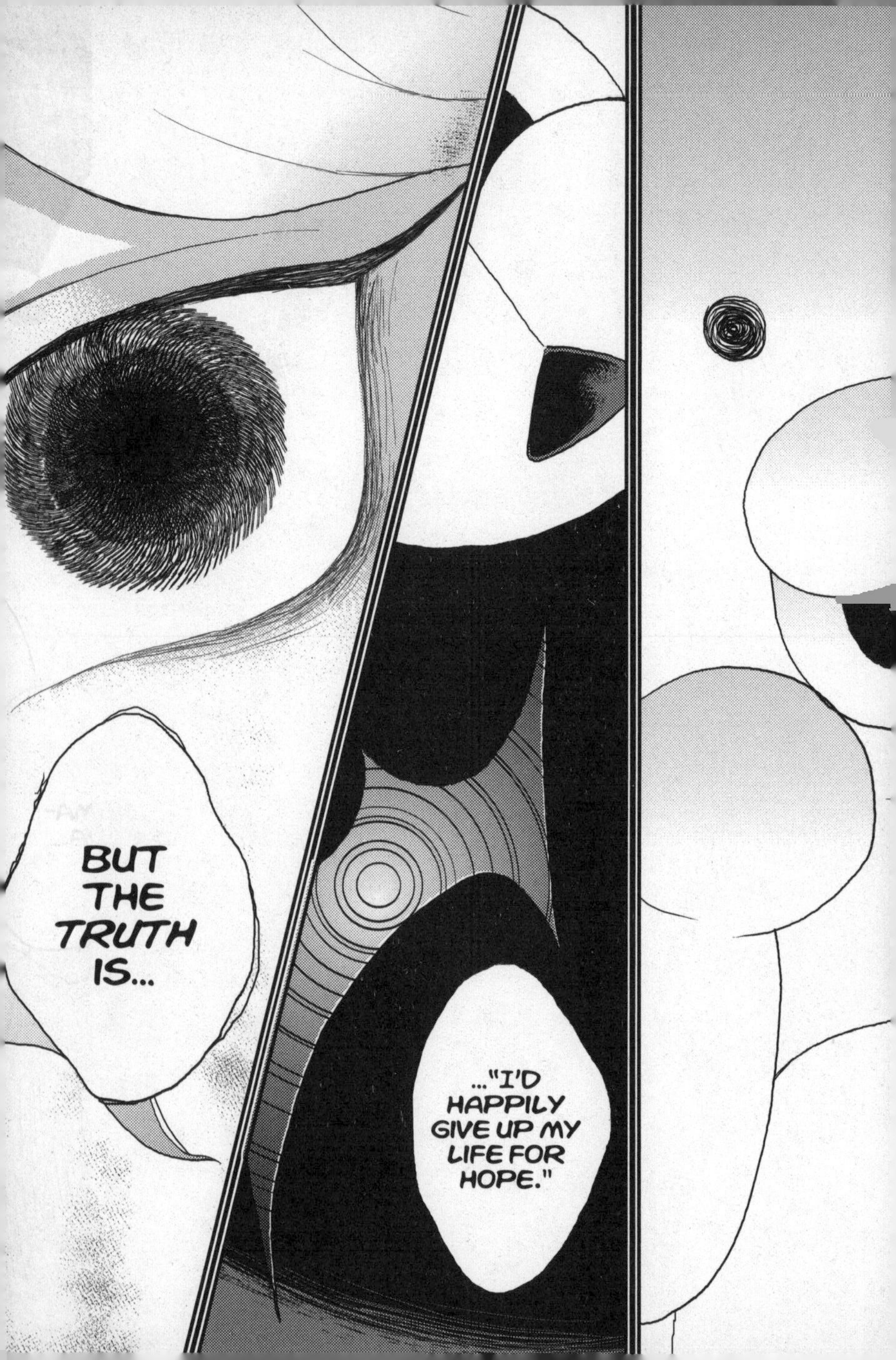
BUT THE TRUTH IS...
..."I'D HAPPILY GIVE UP MY LIFE FOR HOPE."

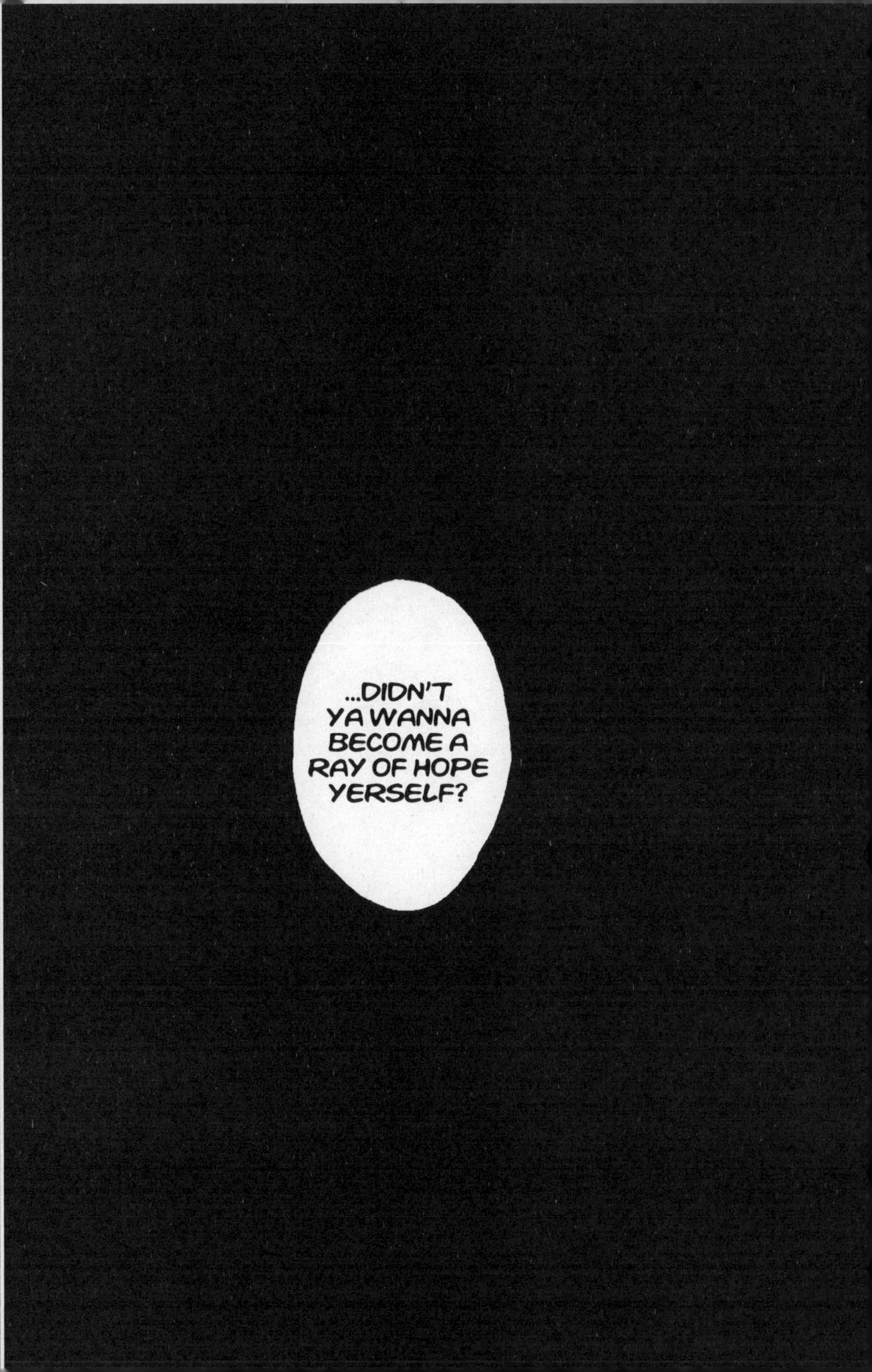
...DIDN'T YA WANNA BECOME A RAY OF HOPE YERSELF?

Ep.22

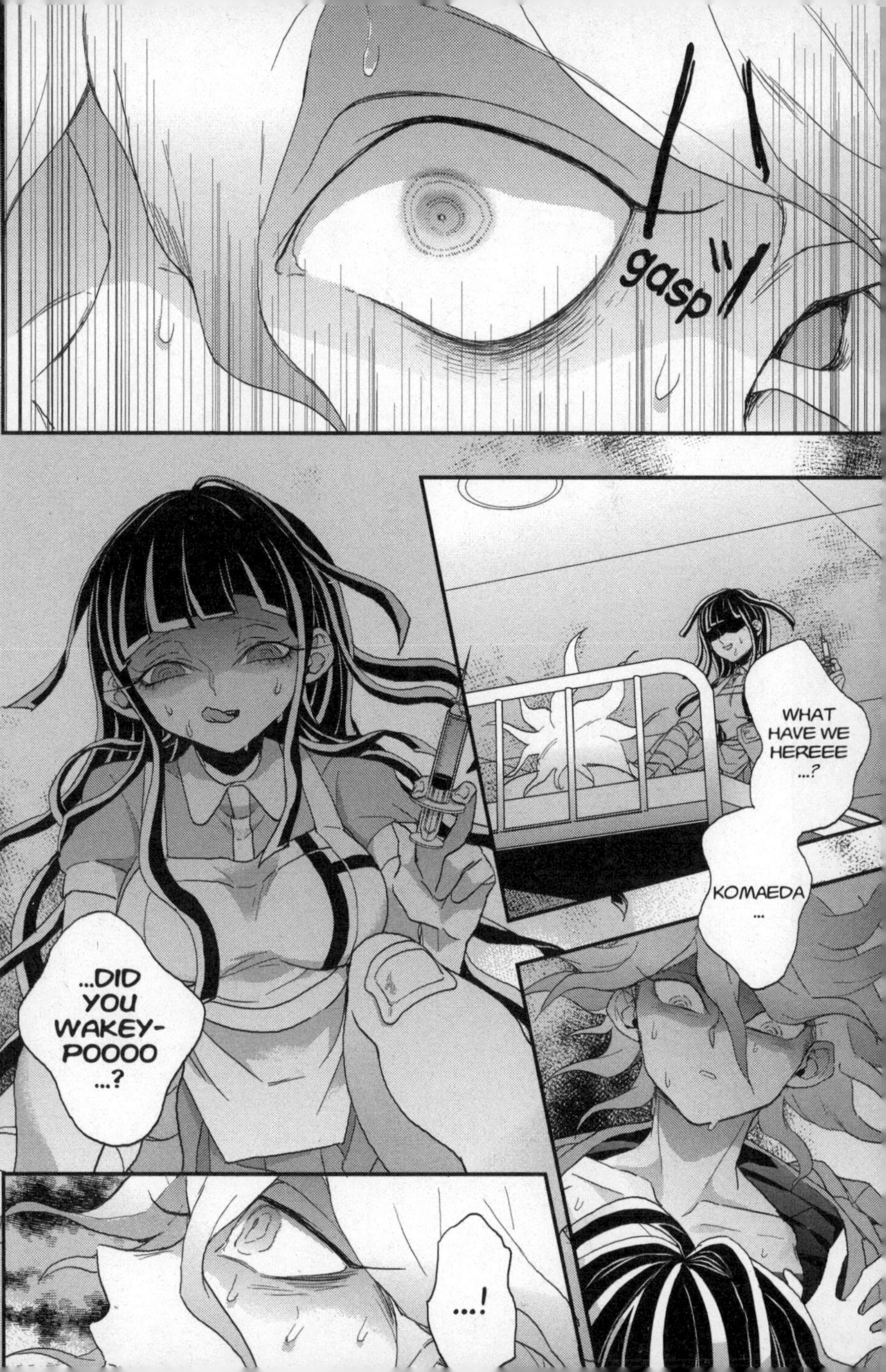
gasp
WHAT HAVE WE HEREEE ...?
KOMAEDA ...
...DID YOU WAKEY-POOOO ...?
...!

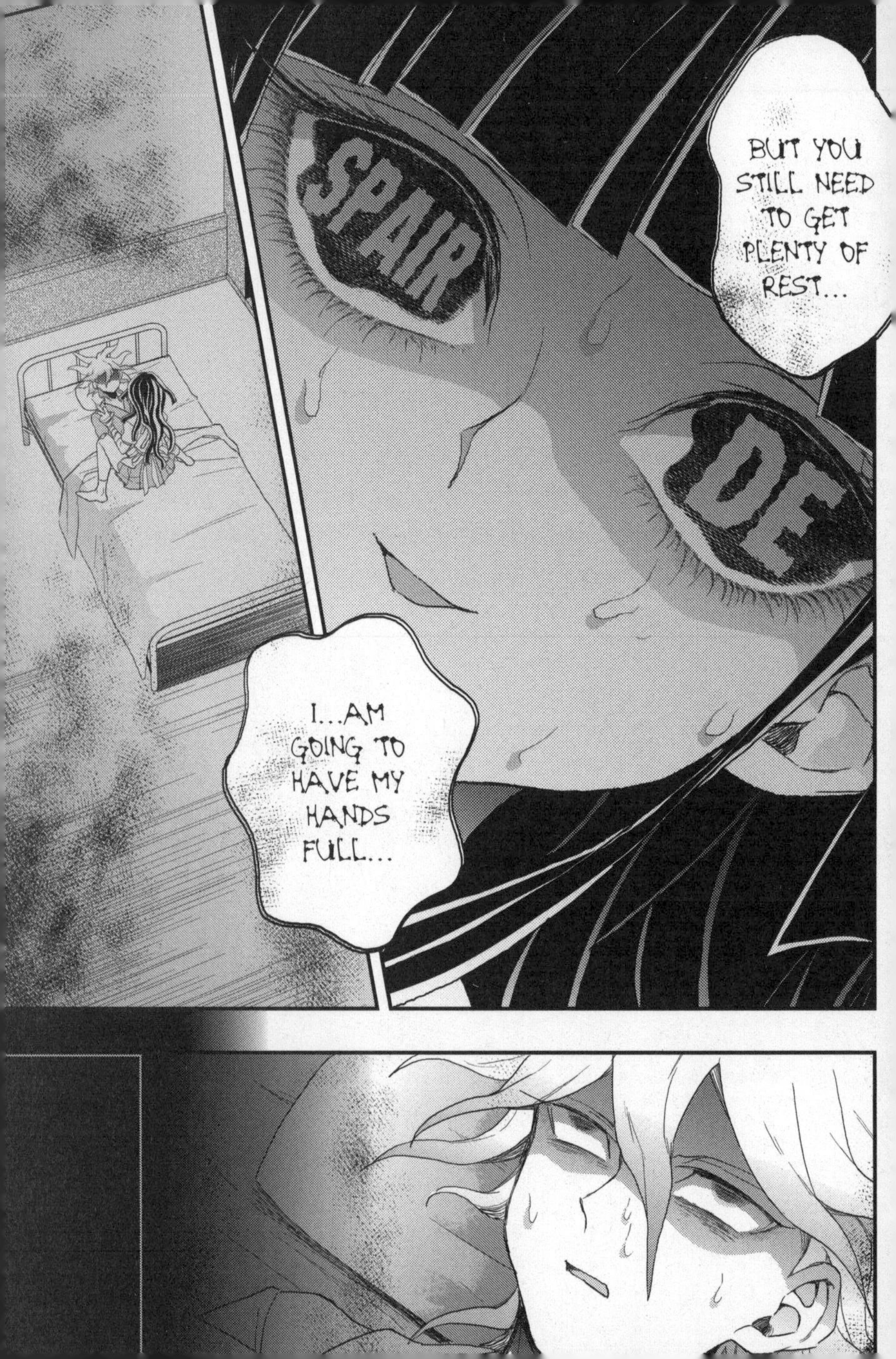
BUT YOU STILL NEED TO GET PLENTY OF REST...
DE
SPAIR
I...AM GOING TO HAVE MY HANDS FULL...

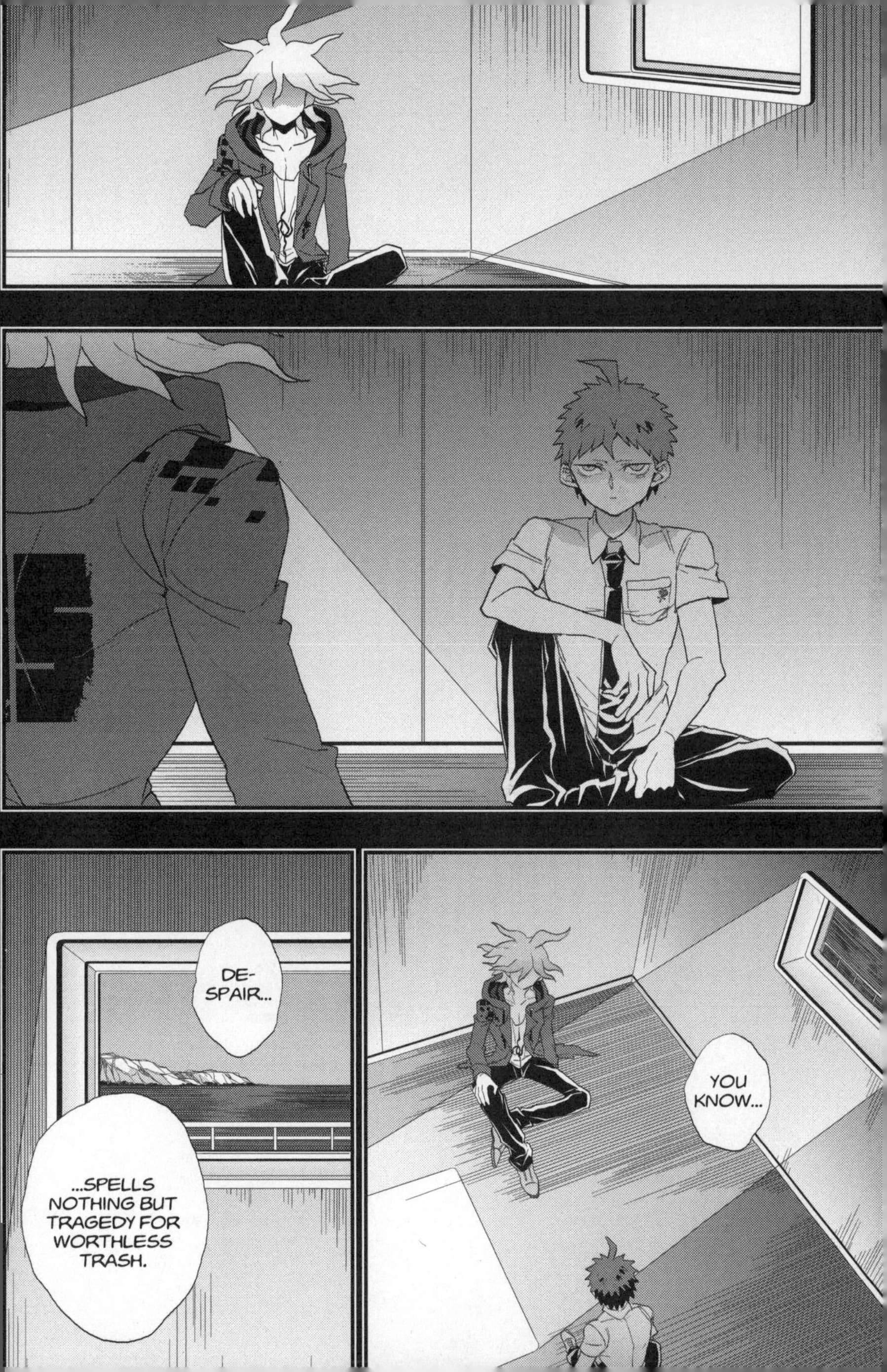
YOU KNOW...
DE-SPAIR...
...SPELLS NOTHING BUT TRAGEDY FOR WORTHLESS TRASH.

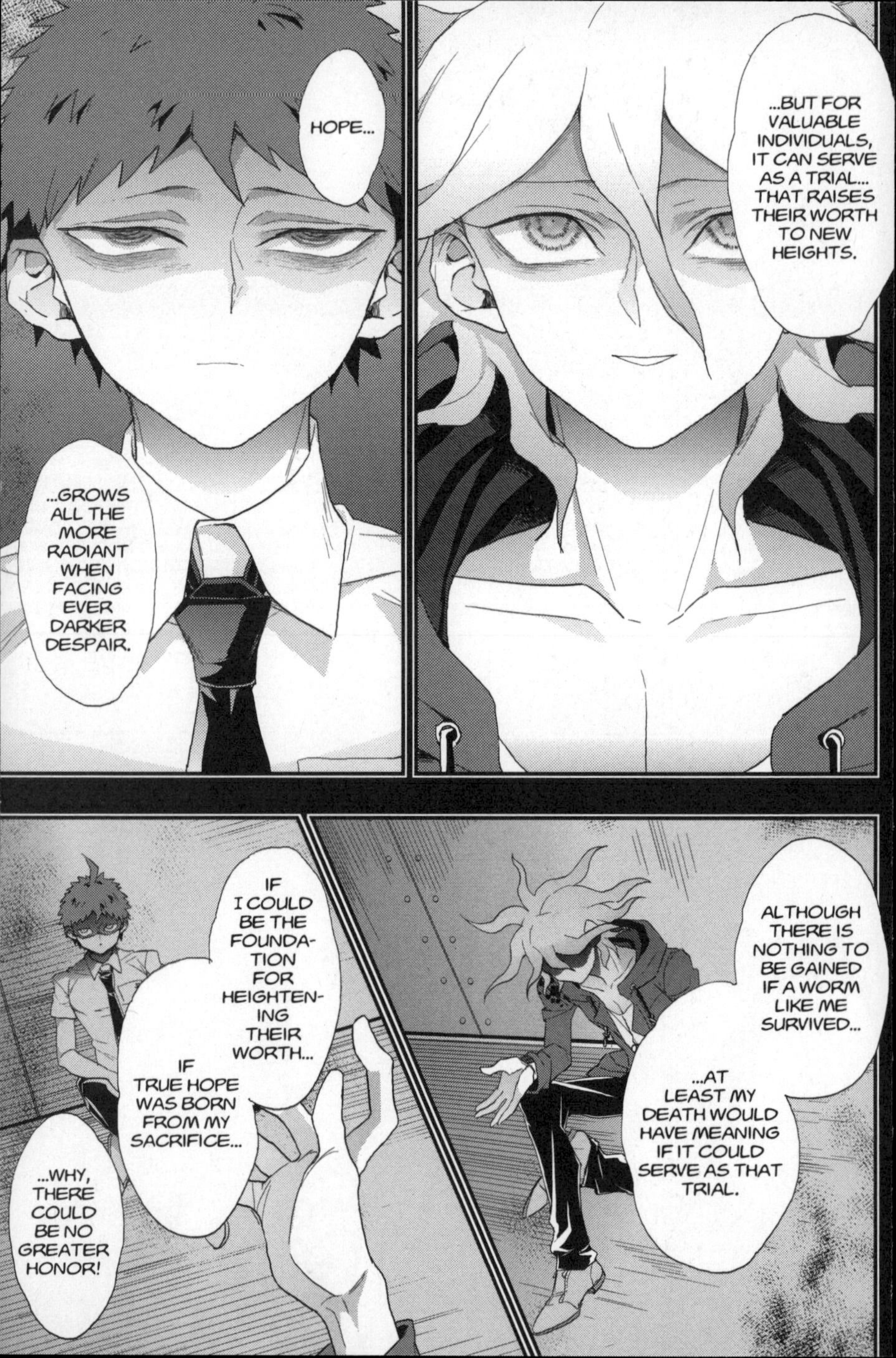
...BUT FOR VALUABLE INDIVIDUALS, IT CAN SERVE AS A TRIAL... THAT RAISES THEIR WORTH TO NEW HEIGHTS.
HOPE...
...GROWS ALL THE MORE RADIANT WHEN FACING EVER DARKER DESPAIR.
ALTHOUGH THERE IS NOTHING TO BE GAINED IF A WORM LIKE ME SURVIVED...
...AT LEAST MY DEATH WOULD HAVE MEANING IF IT COULD SERVE AS THAT TRIAL.
IF I COULD BE THE FOUNDATION FOR HEIGHTENING THEIR WORTH...
IF TRUE HOPE WAS BORN FROM MY SACRIFICE...
...WHY, THERE COULD BE NO GREATER HONOR!

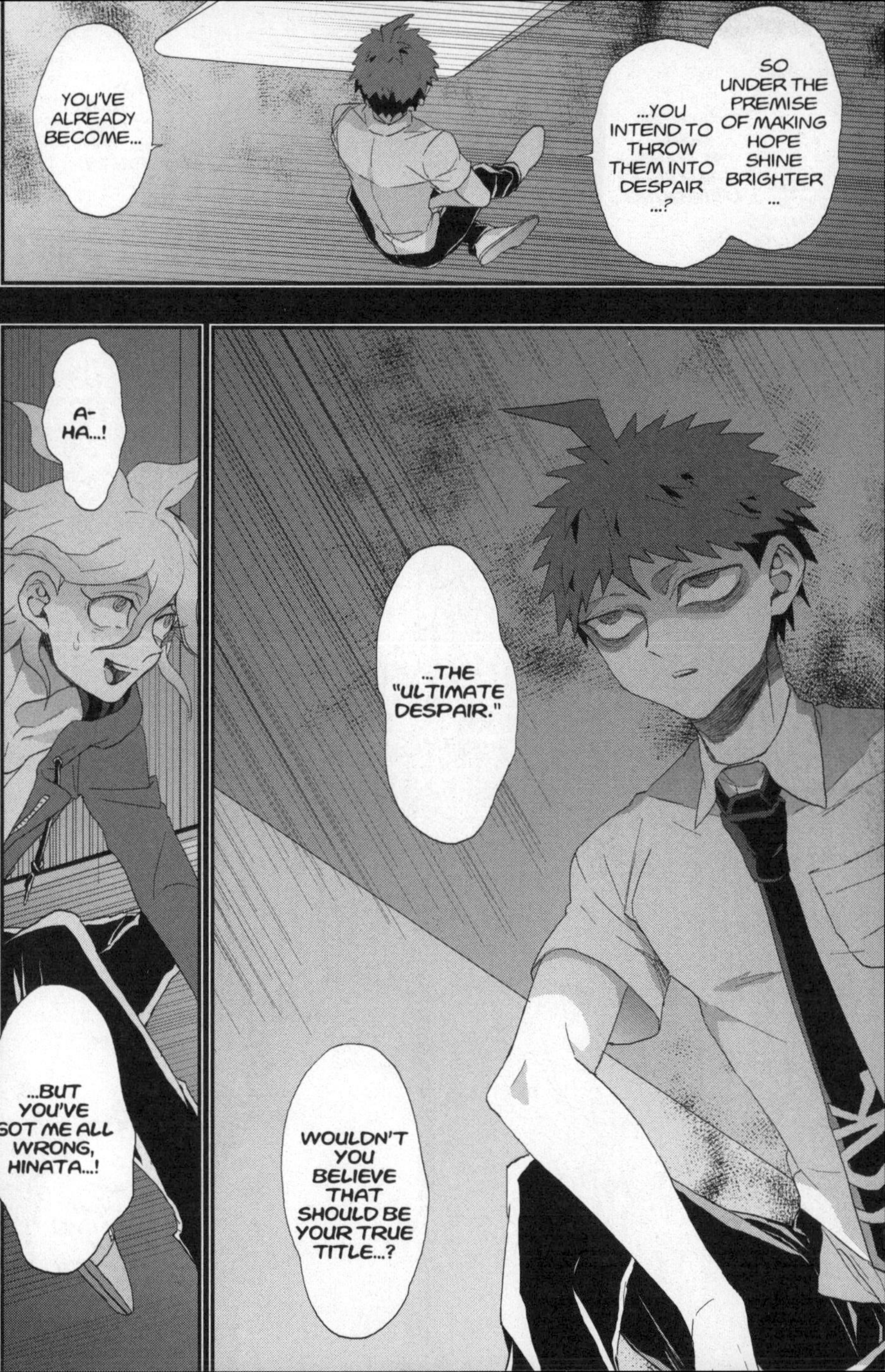
SO UNDER THE PREMISE OF MAKING HOPE SHINE BRIGHTER ...
...YOU INTEND TO THROW THEM INTO DESPAIR ...?
YOU'VE ALREADY BECOME...
...THE "ULTIMATE DESPAIR."
WOULDN'T YOU BELIEVE THAT SHOULD BE YOUR TRUE TITLE...?
A-HA...!
...BUT YOU'VE GOT ME ALL WRONG, HINATA...!

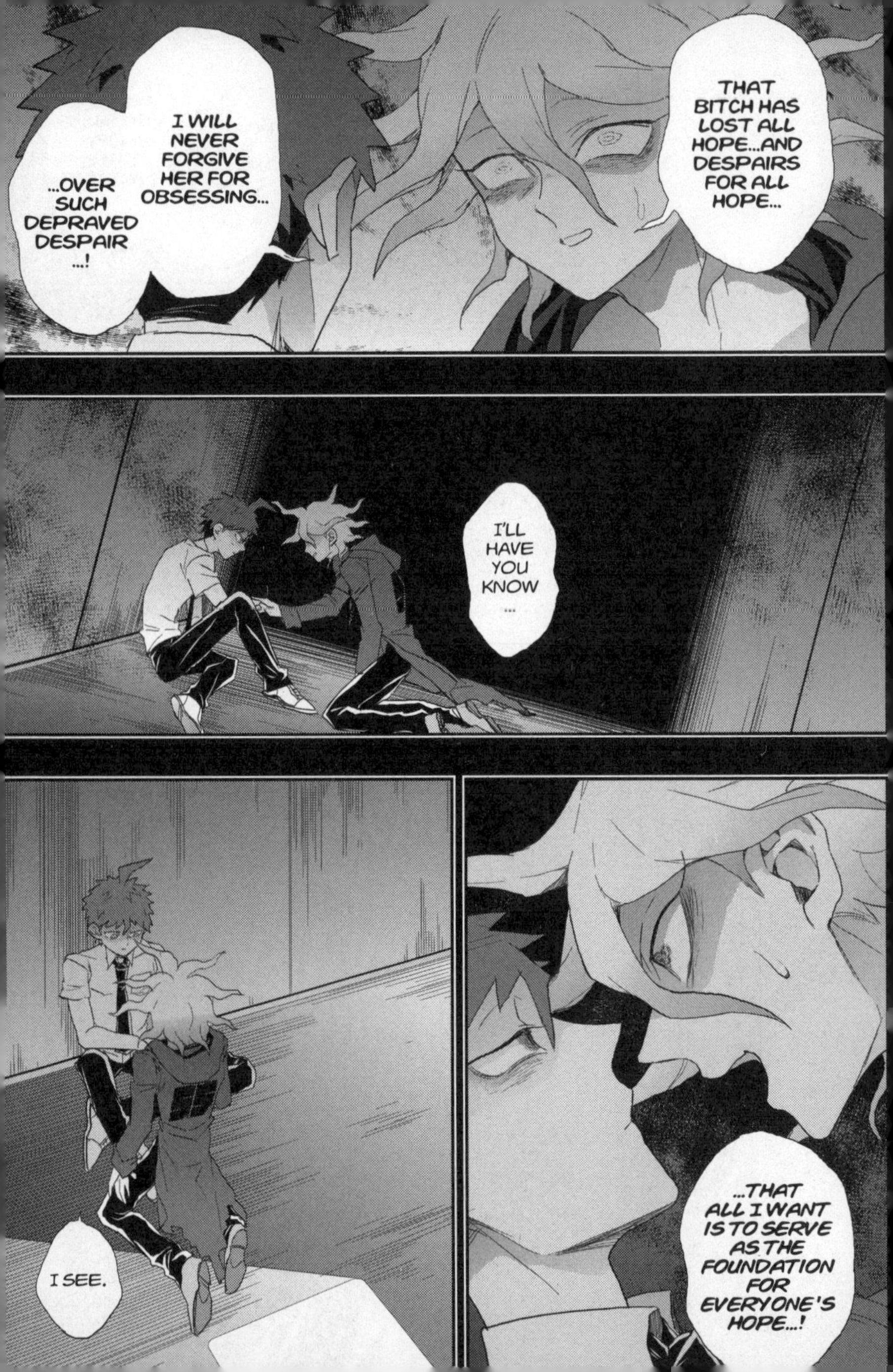
THAT BITCH HAS LOST ALL HOPE...AND DESPAIRS FOR ALL HOPE...
I WILL NEVER FORGIVE HER FOR OBSESSING...
...OVER SUCH DEPRAVED DESPAIR ...!
I'LL HAVE YOU KNOW ...
...THAT ALL I WANT IS TO SERVE AS THE FOUNDATION FOR EVERYONE'S HOPE...!
I SEE.

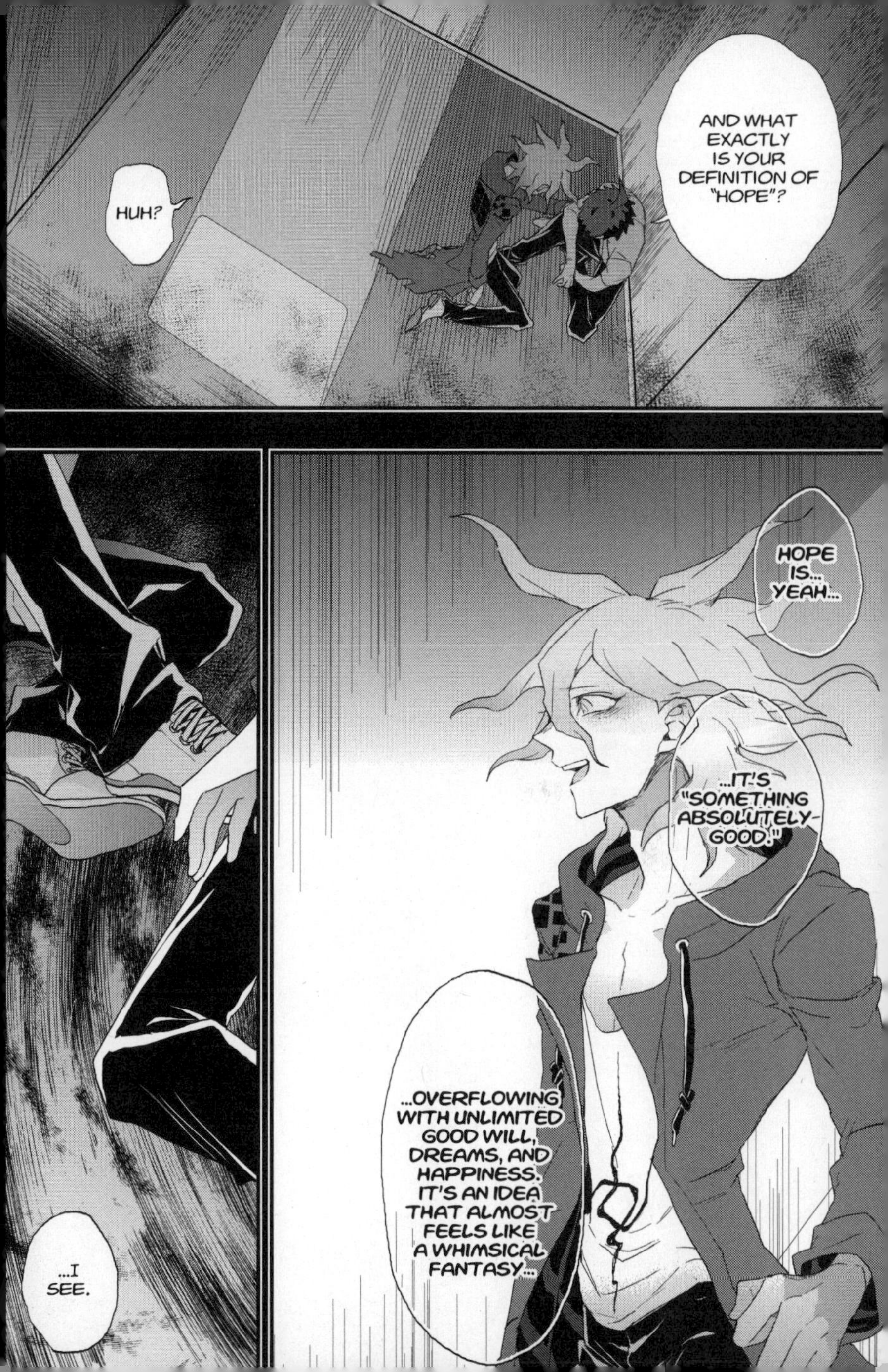
AND WHAT EXACTLY IS YOUR DEFINITION OF "HOPE"?
HUH?
HOPE IS... YEAH...
...IT'S "SOMETHING ABSOLUTELY-GOOD."
...OVERFLOWING WITH UNLIMITED GOOD WILL, DREAMS, AND HAPPINESS. IT'S AN IDEA THAT ALMOST FEELS LIKE A WHIMSICAL FANTASY...
...I SEE.

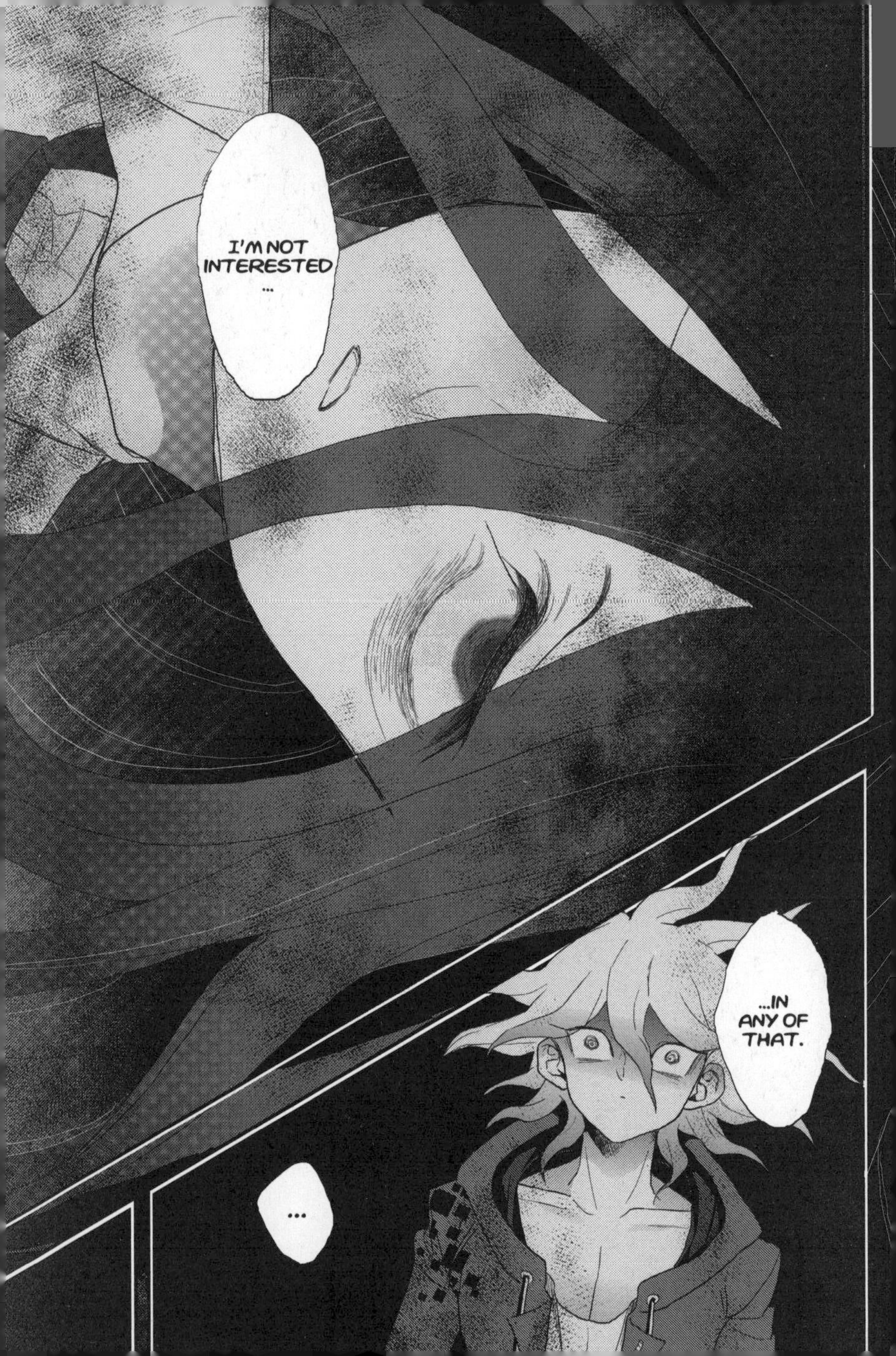
I'M NOT INTERESTED ...
...IN ANY OF THAT.
...

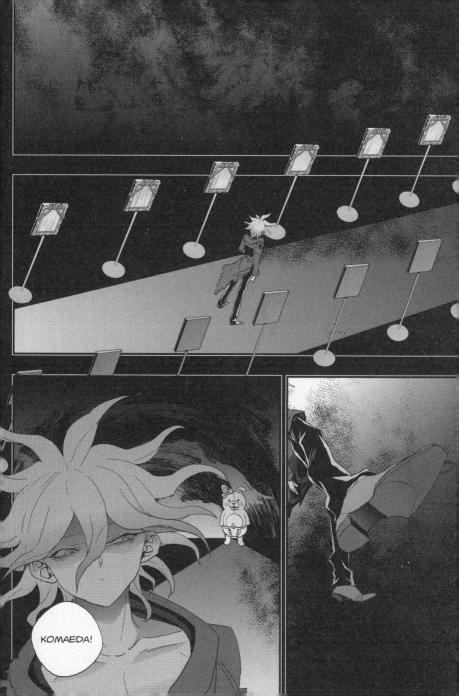

KOMAEDA!

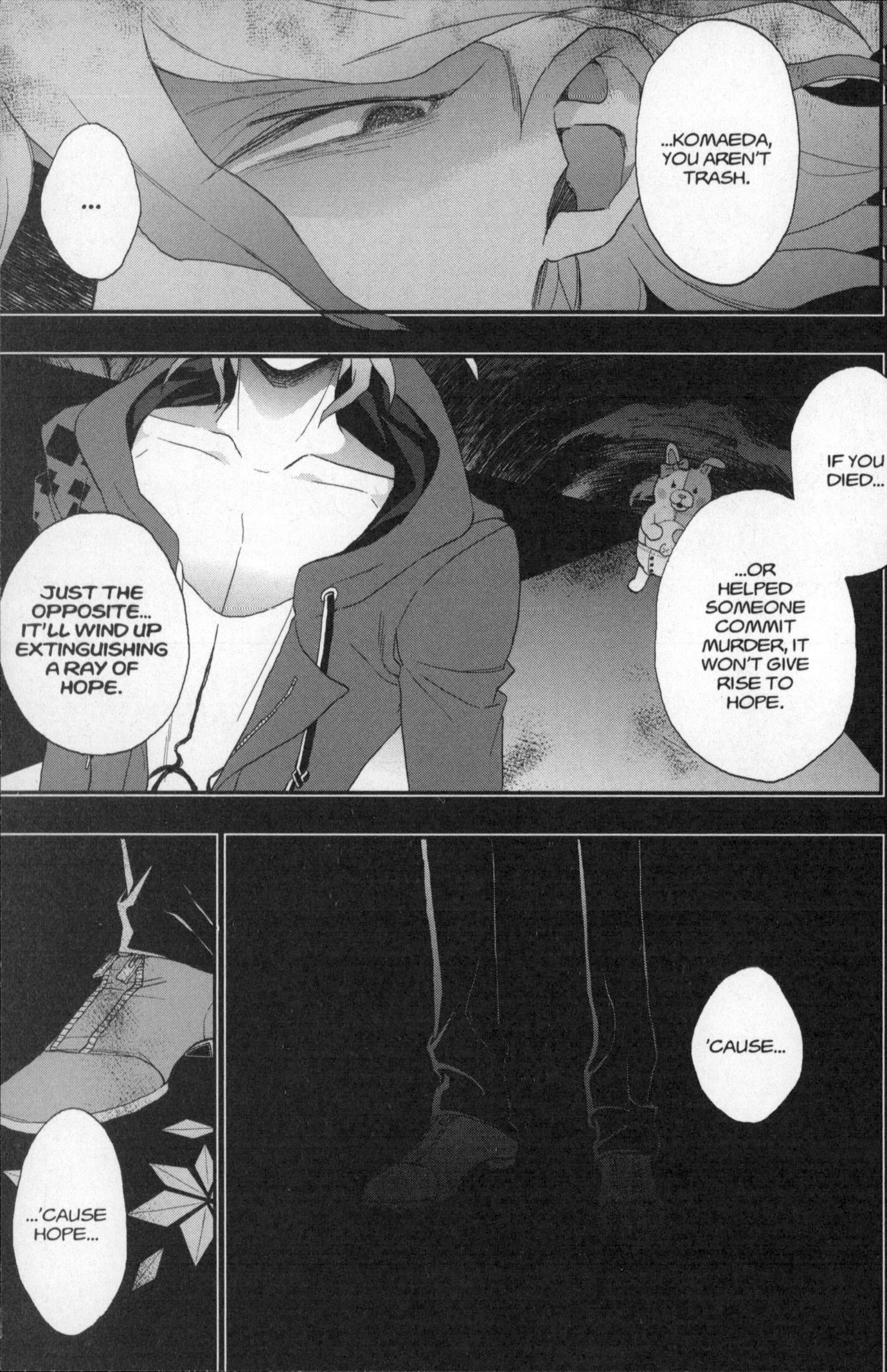
...KOMAEDA, YOU AREN'T TRASH.
...
IF YOU DIED...
...OR HELPED SOMEONE COMMIT MURDER, IT WON'T GIVE RISE TO HOPE.
JUST THE OPPOSITE... IT'LL WIND UP EXTINGUISHING A RAY OF HOPE.
'CAUSE...
...'CAUSE HOPE...

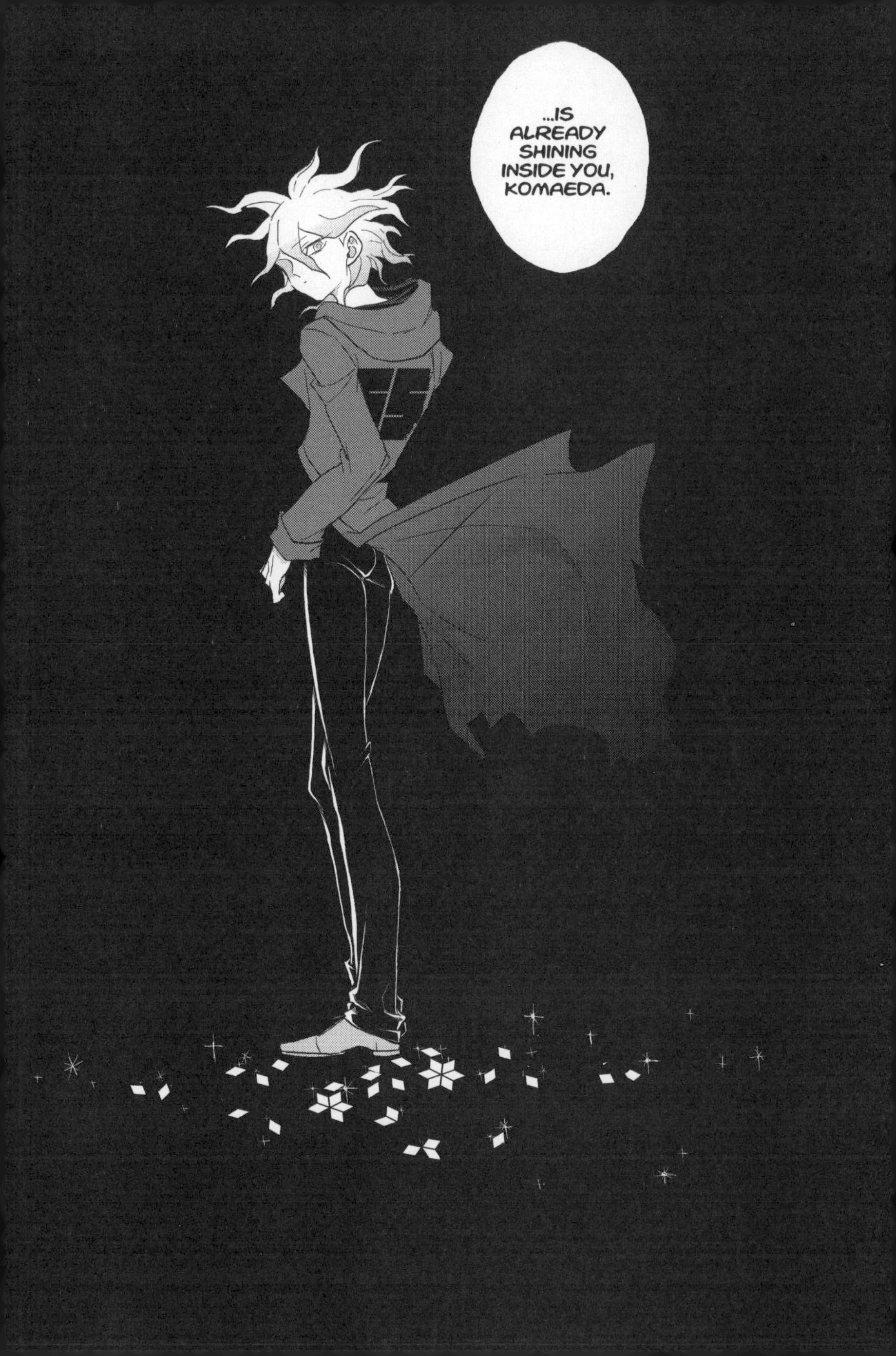
...IS ALREADY SHINING INSIDE YOU, KOMAEDA.

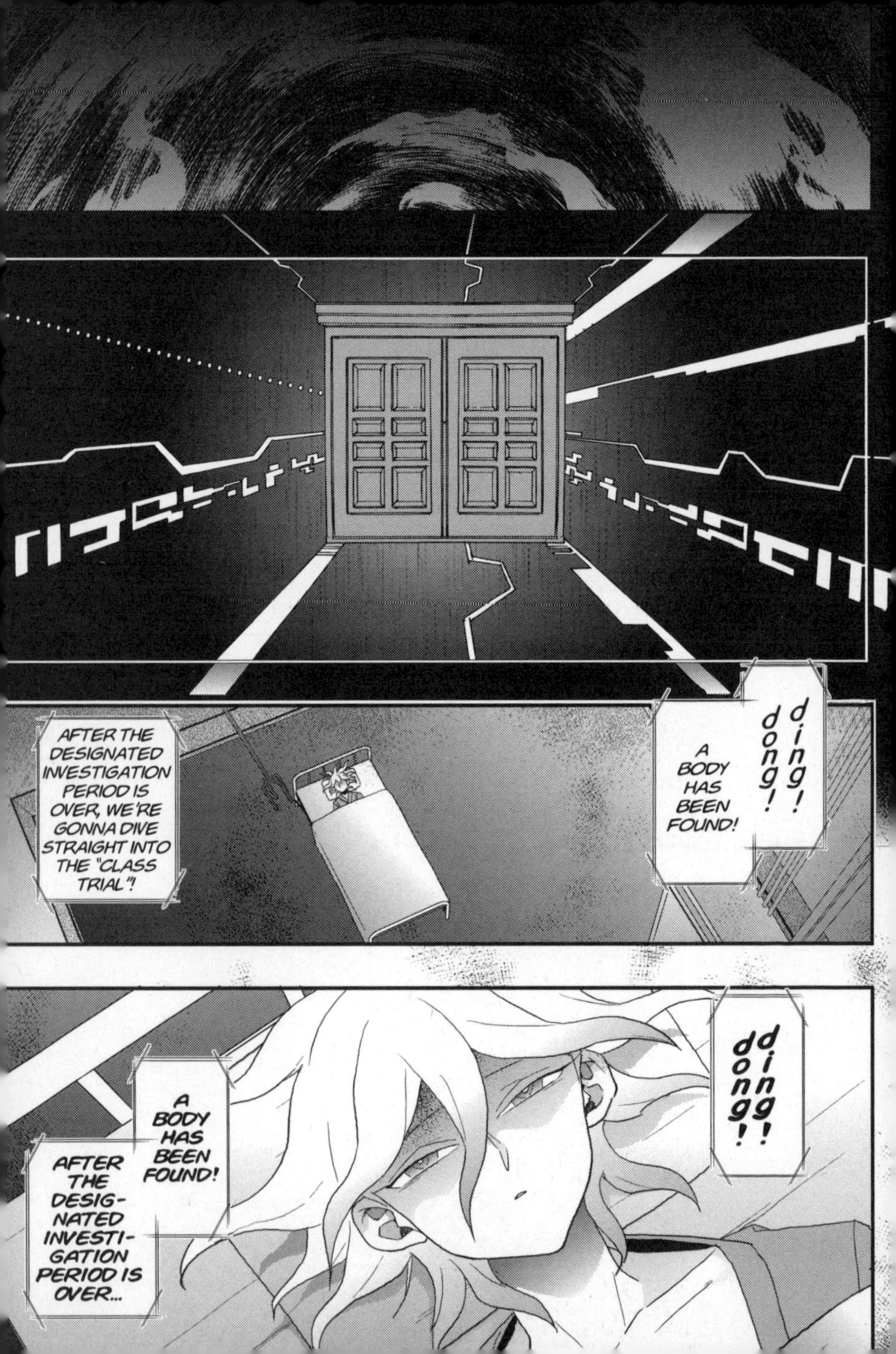

ding! dong!
A BODY HAS BEEN FOUND!
AFTER THE DESIGNATED INVESTIGATION PERIOD IS OVER, WE'RE GONNA DIVE STRAIGHT INTO THE "CLASS TRIAL"!
ding! dong!
A BODY HAS BEEN FOUND!
AFTER THE DESIGNATED INVESTIGATION PERIOD IS OVER...

Danganronpa 2
ULTIMATE LUCK AND HOPE AND DESPAIR

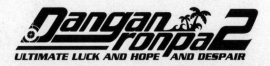

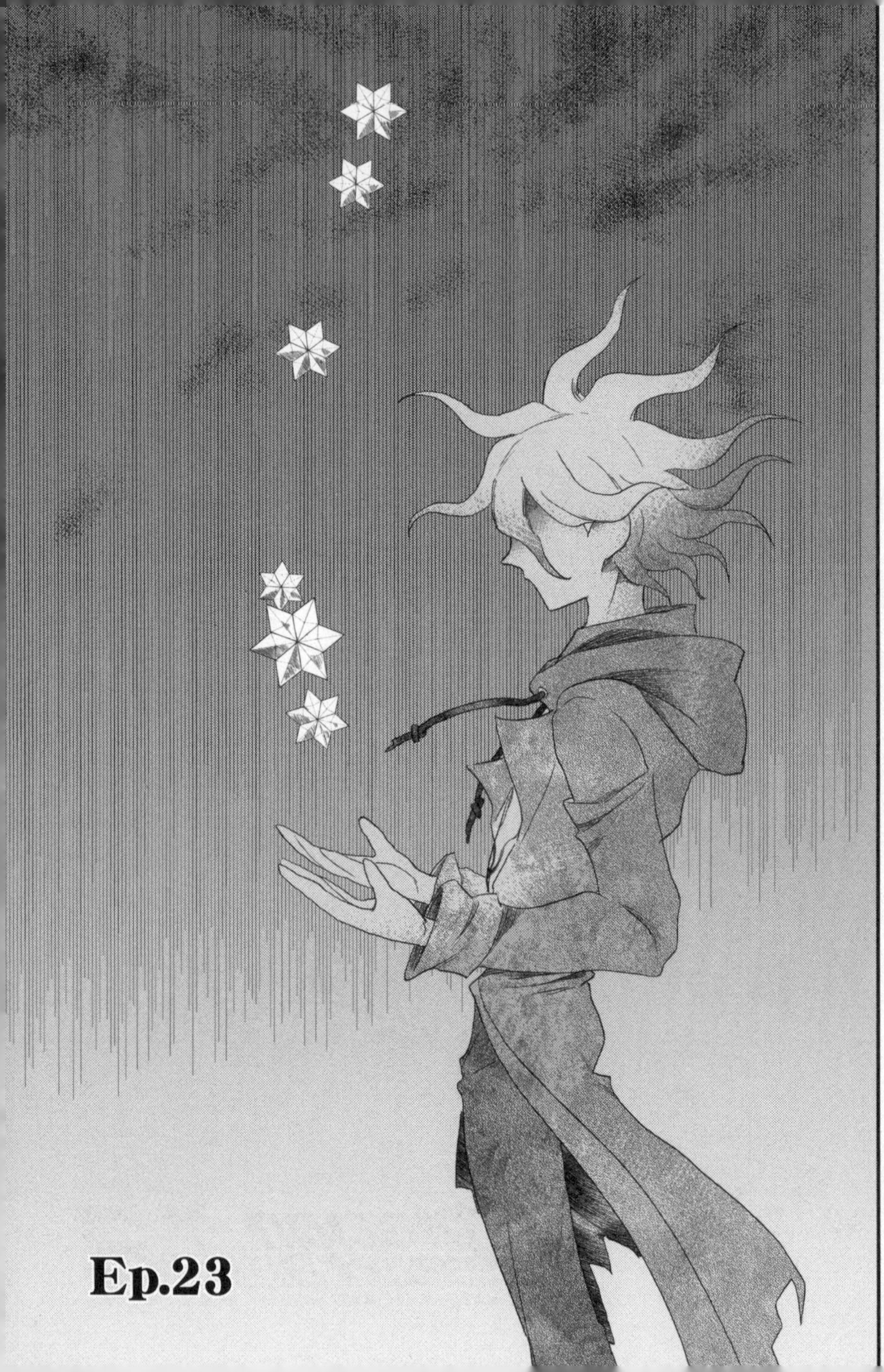
Ep.23

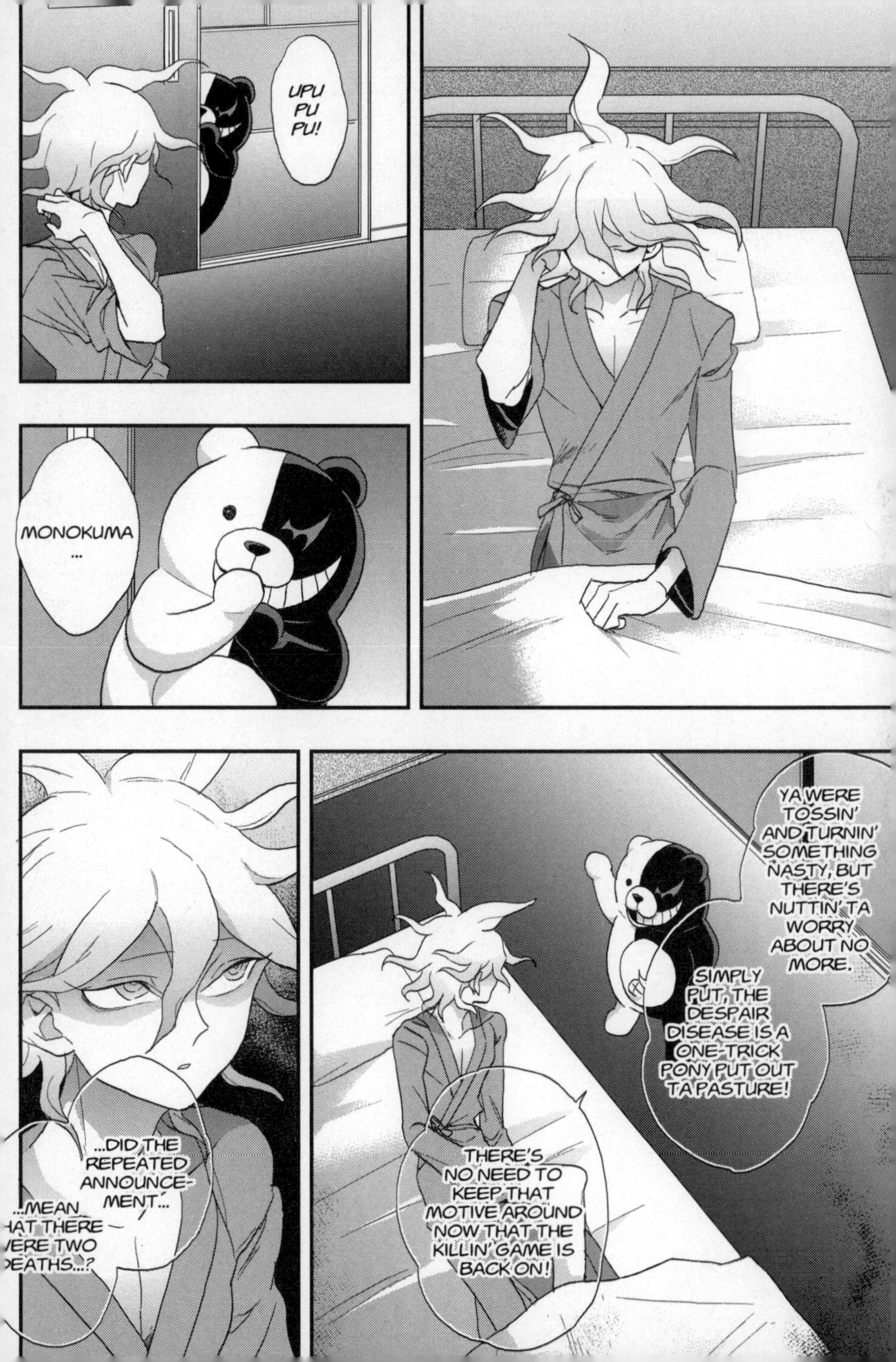
UPU PU PU!
MONOKUMA ...
YA WERE TOSSIN' AND TURNIN' SOMETHING NASTY, BUT THERE'S NUTTIN' TA WORRY ABOUT NO MORE.
SIMPLY PUT, THE DESPAIR DISEASE IS A ONE-TRICK PONY PUT OUT TA PASTURE!
THERE'S NO NEED TO KEEP THAT MOTIVE AROUND NOW THAT THE KILLIN' GAME IS BACK ON!
...DID THE REPEATED ANNOUNCEMENT...
...MEAN HAT THERE ERE TWO EATHS...?

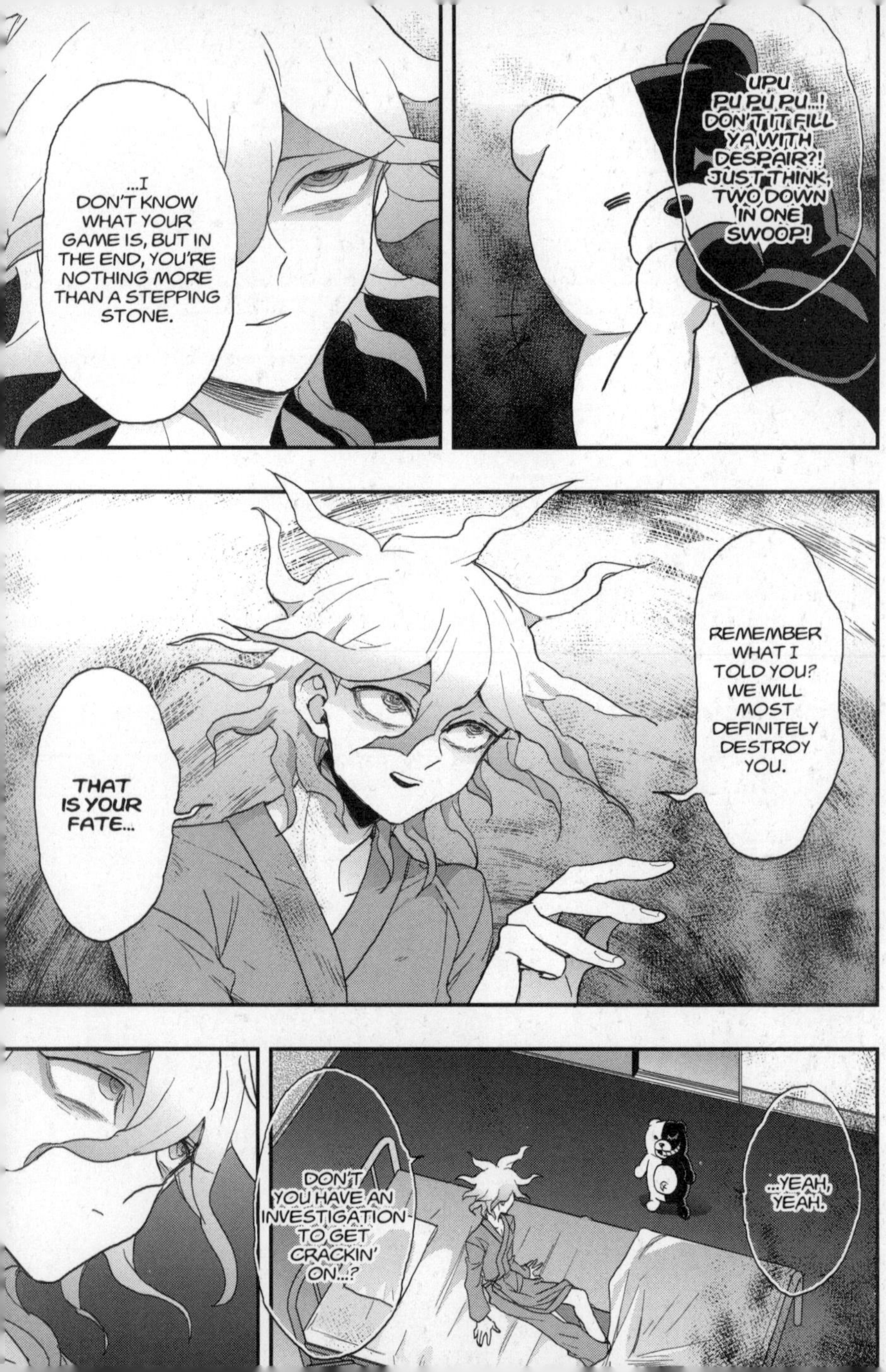
UPU PU PU PU...! DON'T IT FILL YA WITH DESPAIR?! JUST THINK, TWO DOWN IN ONE SWOOP!
...I DON'T KNOW WHAT YOUR GAME IS, BUT IN THE END, YOU'RE NOTHING MORE THAN A STEPPING STONE.
REMEMBER WHAT I TOLD YOU? WE WILL MOST DEFINITELY DESTROY YOU.
THAT IS YOUR FATE...
...YEAH, YEAH.
DON'T YOU HAVE AN INVESTIGATION TO GET CRACKIN' ON...?

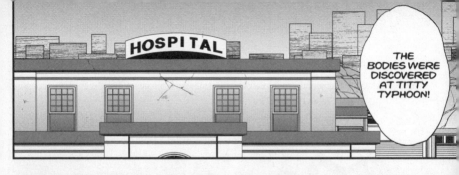

HOSPITAL

THE BODIES WERE DISCOVERED AT TITTY TYPHOON!

TITTY TYPHOON

STAFF ONLY

DAMN...!

TWO MORE OF US GONE...

...HOW LONG MUST THIS NIGHTMARE CONTINUE...?

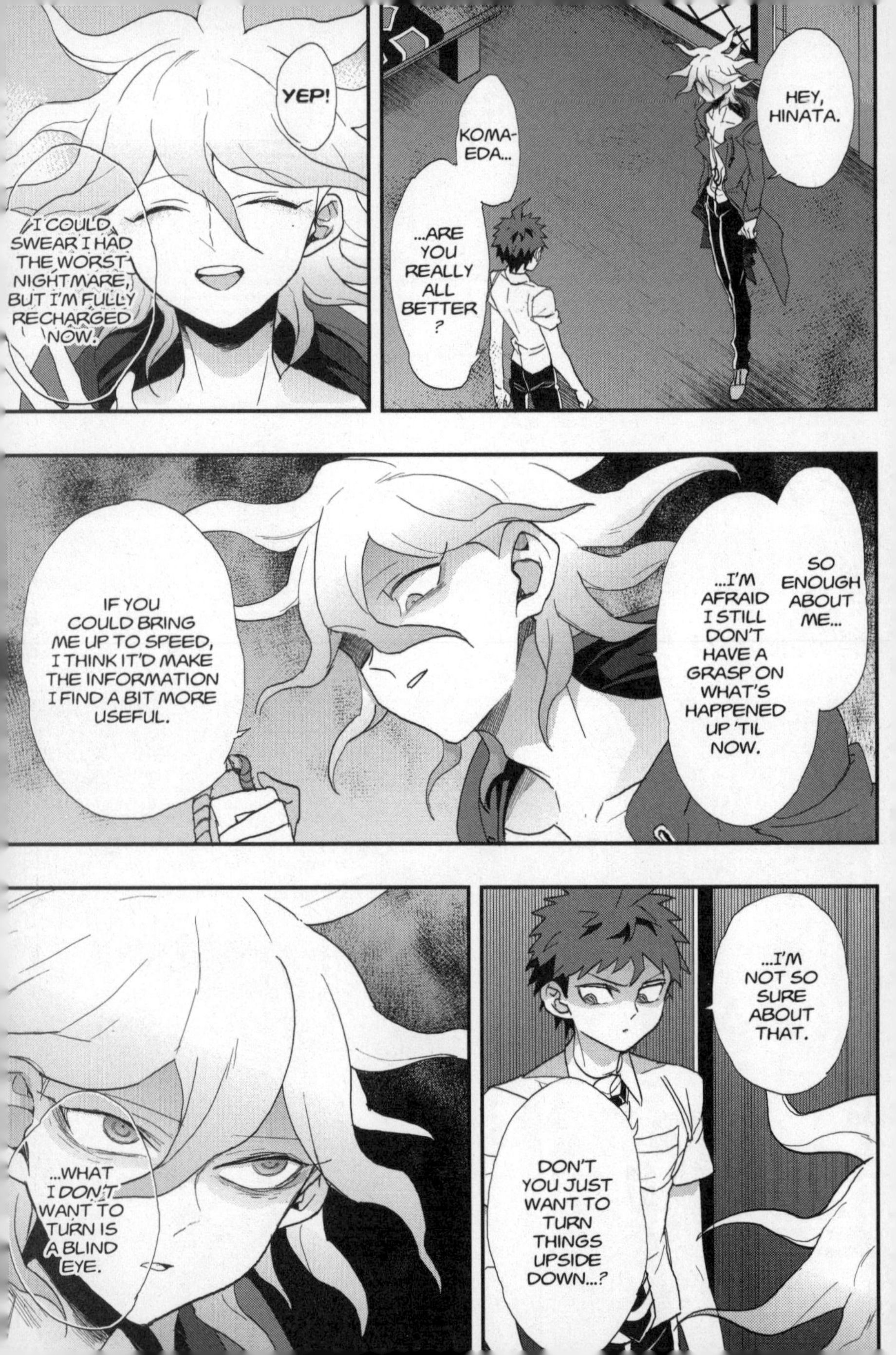
HEY, HINATA.
KOMA-EDA...
...ARE YOU REALLY ALL BETTER?
YEP!
I COULD SWEAR I HAD THE WORST NIGHTMARE, BUT I'M FULLY RECHARGED NOW.
SO ENOUGH ABOUT ME...
...I'M AFRAID I STILL DON'T HAVE A GRASP ON WHAT'S HAPPENED UP 'TIL NOW.
IF YOU COULD BRING ME UP TO SPEED, I THINK IT'D MAKE THE INFORMATION I FIND A BIT MORE USEFUL.
...I'M NOT SO SURE ABOUT THAT.
DON'T YOU JUST WANT TO TURN THINGS UPSIDE DOWN...?
...WHAT I *DON'T* WANT TO TURN IS A BLIND EYE.

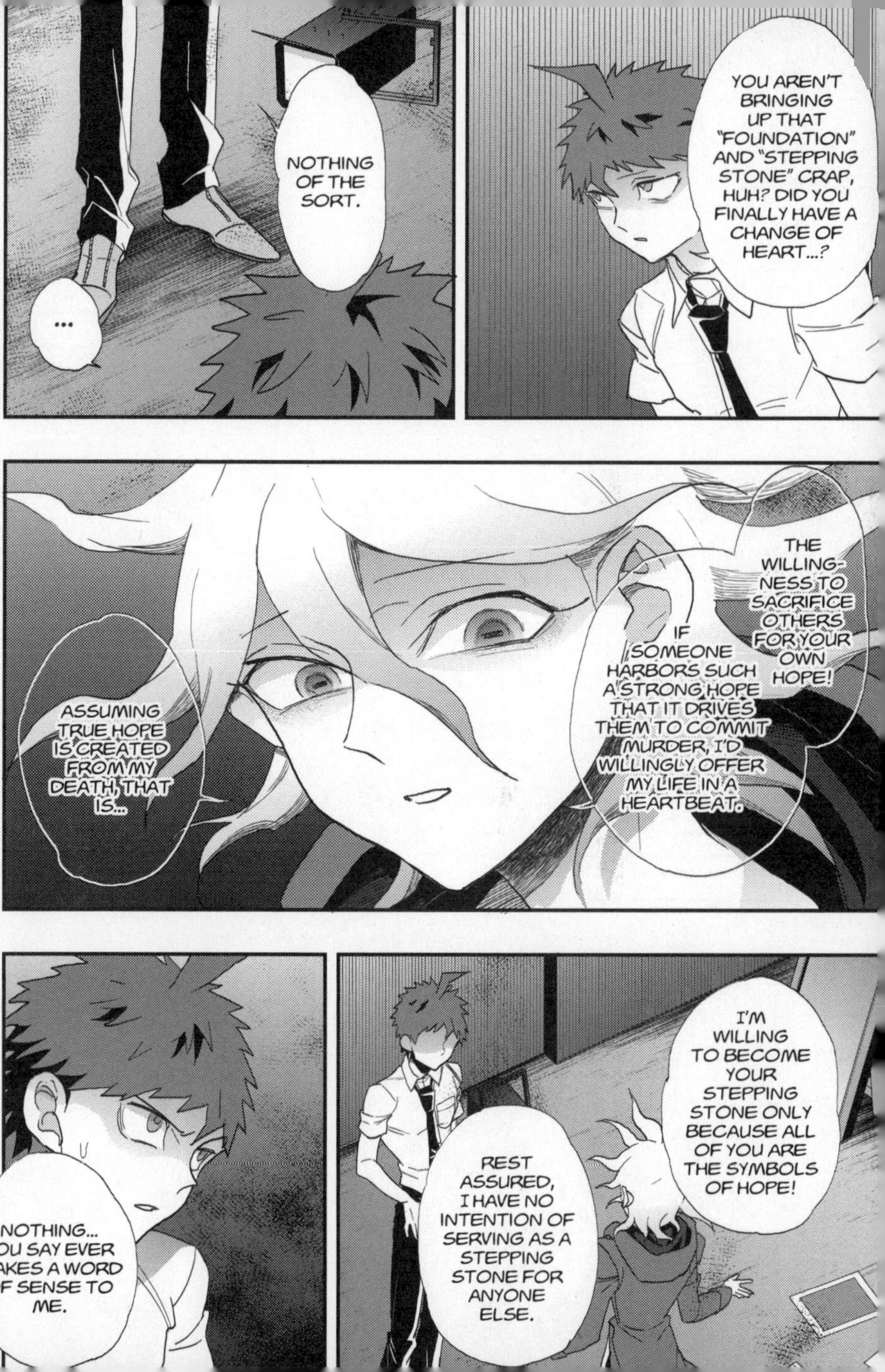
YOU AREN'T BRINGING UP THAT "FOUNDATION" AND "STEPPING STONE" CRAP, HUH? DID YOU FINALLY HAVE A CHANGE OF HEART...?
NOTHING OF THE SORT.
...
THE WILLING-NESS TO SACRIFICE OTHERS FOR YOUR OWN HOPE!
IF SOMEONE HARBORS SUCH A STRONG HOPE THAT IT DRIVES THEM TO COMMIT MURDER, I'D WILLINGLY OFFER MY LIFE IN A HEARTBEAT.
ASSUMING TRUE HOPE IS CREATED FROM MY DEATH, THAT IS...
I'M WILLING TO BECOME YOUR STEPPING STONE ONLY BECAUSE ALL OF YOU ARE THE SYMBOLS OF HOPE!
REST ASSURED, I HAVE NO INTENTION OF SERVING AS A STEPPING STONE FOR ANYONE ELSE.
NOTHING... YOU SAY EVER MAKES A WORD OF SENSE TO ME.

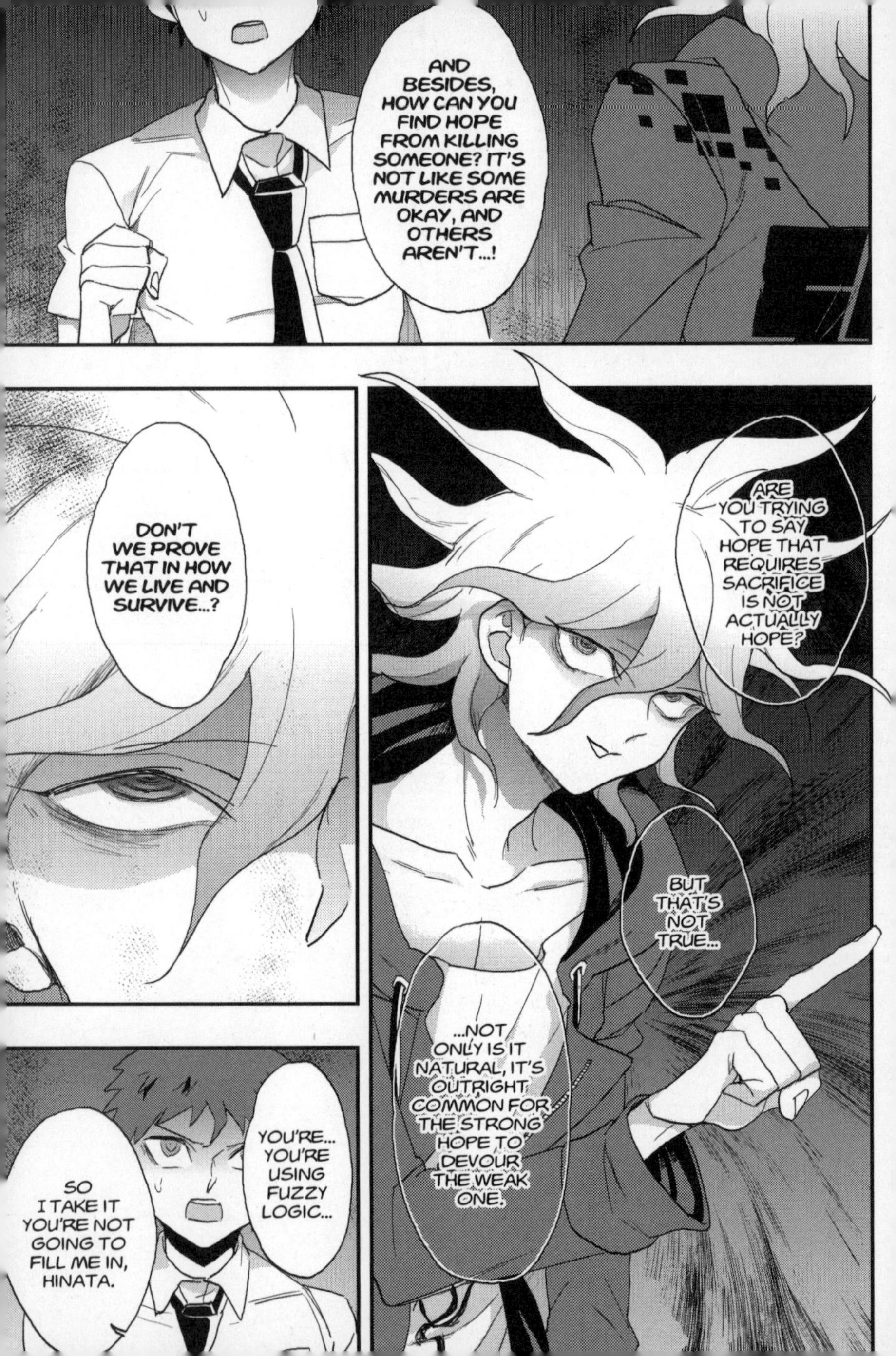
AND BESIDES, HOW CAN YOU FIND HOPE FROM KILLING SOMEONE? IT'S NOT LIKE SOME MURDERS ARE OKAY, AND OTHERS AREN'T...!
ARE YOU TRYING TO SAY HOPE THAT REQUIRES SACRIFICE IS NOT ACTUALLY HOPE?
BUT THAT'S NOT TRUE...
...NOT ONLY IS IT NATURAL, IT'S OUTRIGHT COMMON FOR THE STRONG HOPE TO DEVOUR THE WEAK ONE.
DON'T WE PROVE THAT IN HOW WE LIVE AND SURVIVE...?
YOU'RE... YOU'RE USING FUZZY LOGIC...
SO I TAKE IT YOU'RE NOT GOING TO FILL ME IN, HINATA.

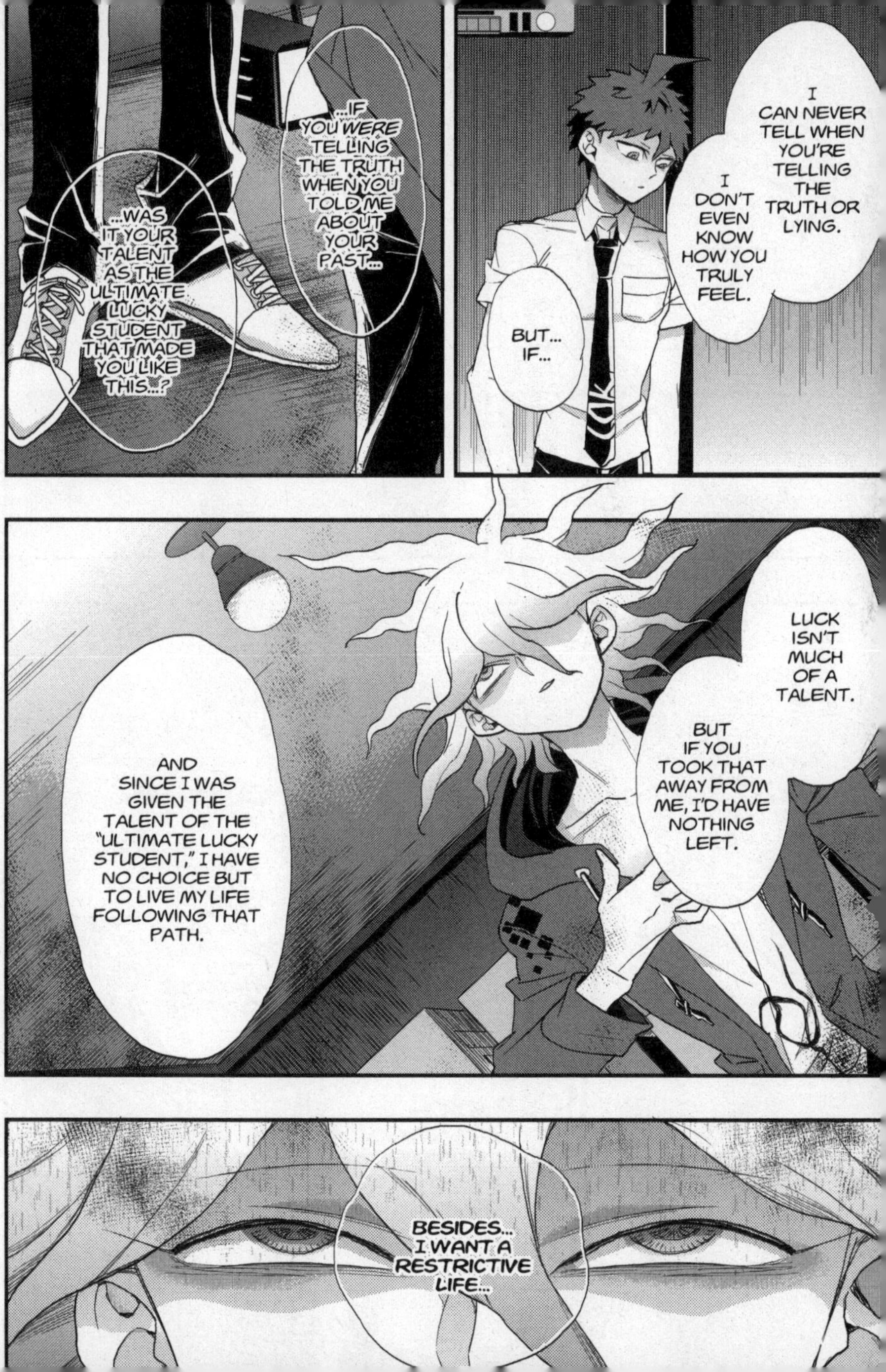
I CAN NEVER TELL WHEN YOU'RE TELLING THE TRUTH OR LYING.
I DON'T EVEN KNOW HOW YOU TRULY FEEL.
BUT... IF...
...IF YOU WERE TELLING THE TRUTH WHEN YOU TOLD ME ABOUT YOUR PAST...
...WAS IT YOUR TALENT AS THE ULTIMATE LUCKY STUDENT THAT MADE YOU LIKE THIS...?
LUCK ISN'T MUCH OF A TALENT.
BUT IF YOU TOOK THAT AWAY FROM ME, I'D HAVE NOTHING LEFT.
AND SINCE I WAS GIVEN THE TALENT OF THE "ULTIMATE LUCKY STUDENT," I HAVE NO CHOICE BUT TO LIVE MY LIFE FOLLOWING THAT PATH.
BESIDES... I WANT A RESTRICTIVE LIFE...

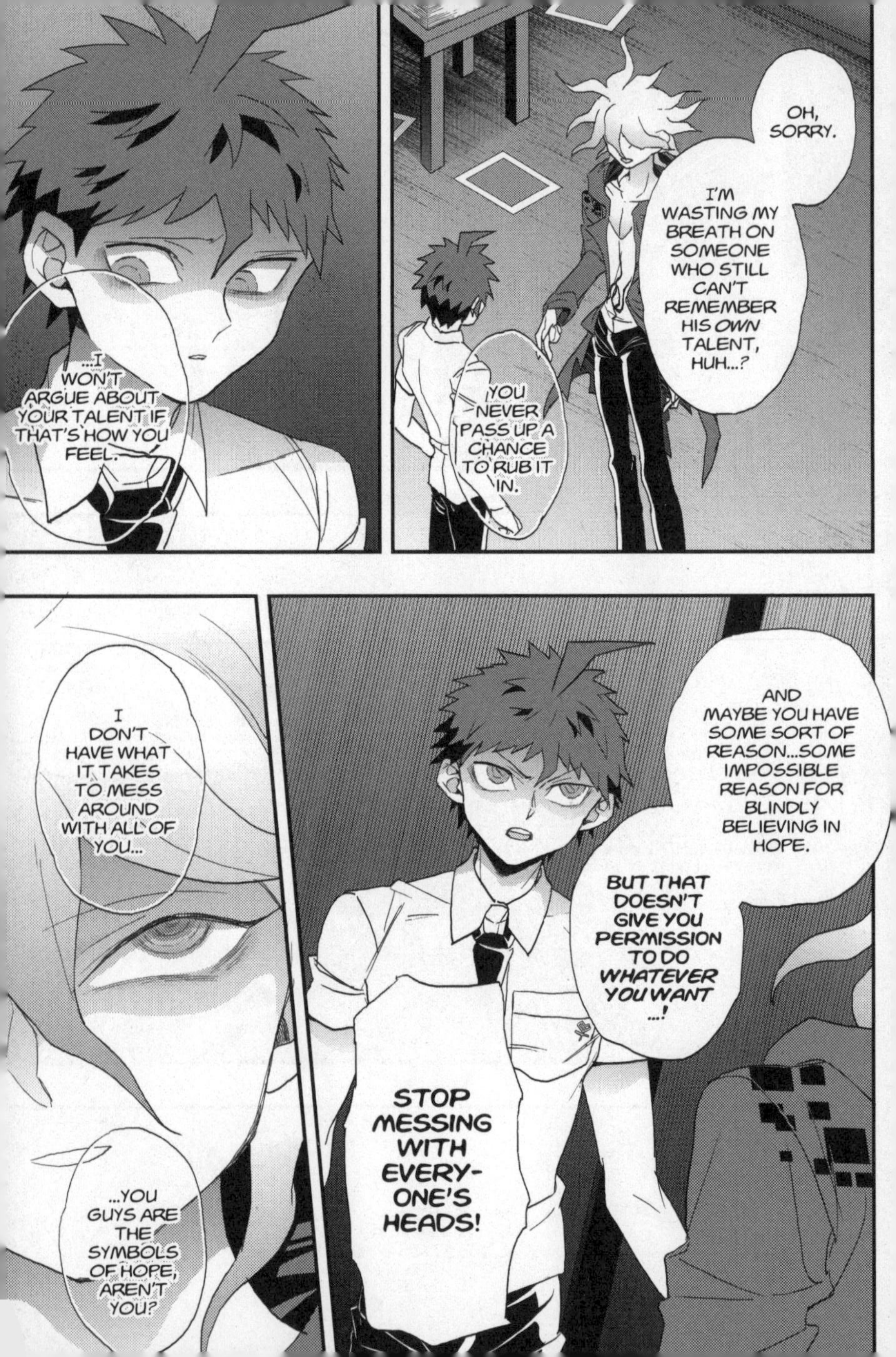
OH, SORRY.
I'M WASTING MY BREATH ON SOMEONE WHO STILL CAN'T REMEMBER HIS *OWN* TALENT, HUH...?
YOU NEVER PASS UP A CHANCE TO RUB IT IN.
...I WON'T ARGUE ABOUT YOUR TALENT IF THAT'S HOW YOU FEEL.
AND MAYBE YOU HAVE SOME SORT OF REASON...SOME IMPOSSIBLE REASON FOR BLINDLY BELIEVING IN HOPE.
BUT THAT DOESN'T GIVE YOU PERMISSION TO DO *WHATEVER YOU WANT*...!
STOP MESSING WITH EVERY-ONE'S HEADS!
I DON'T HAVE WHAT IT TAKES TO MESS AROUND WITH ALL OF YOU...
...YOU GUYS ARE THE SYMBOLS OF HOPE, AREN'T YOU?

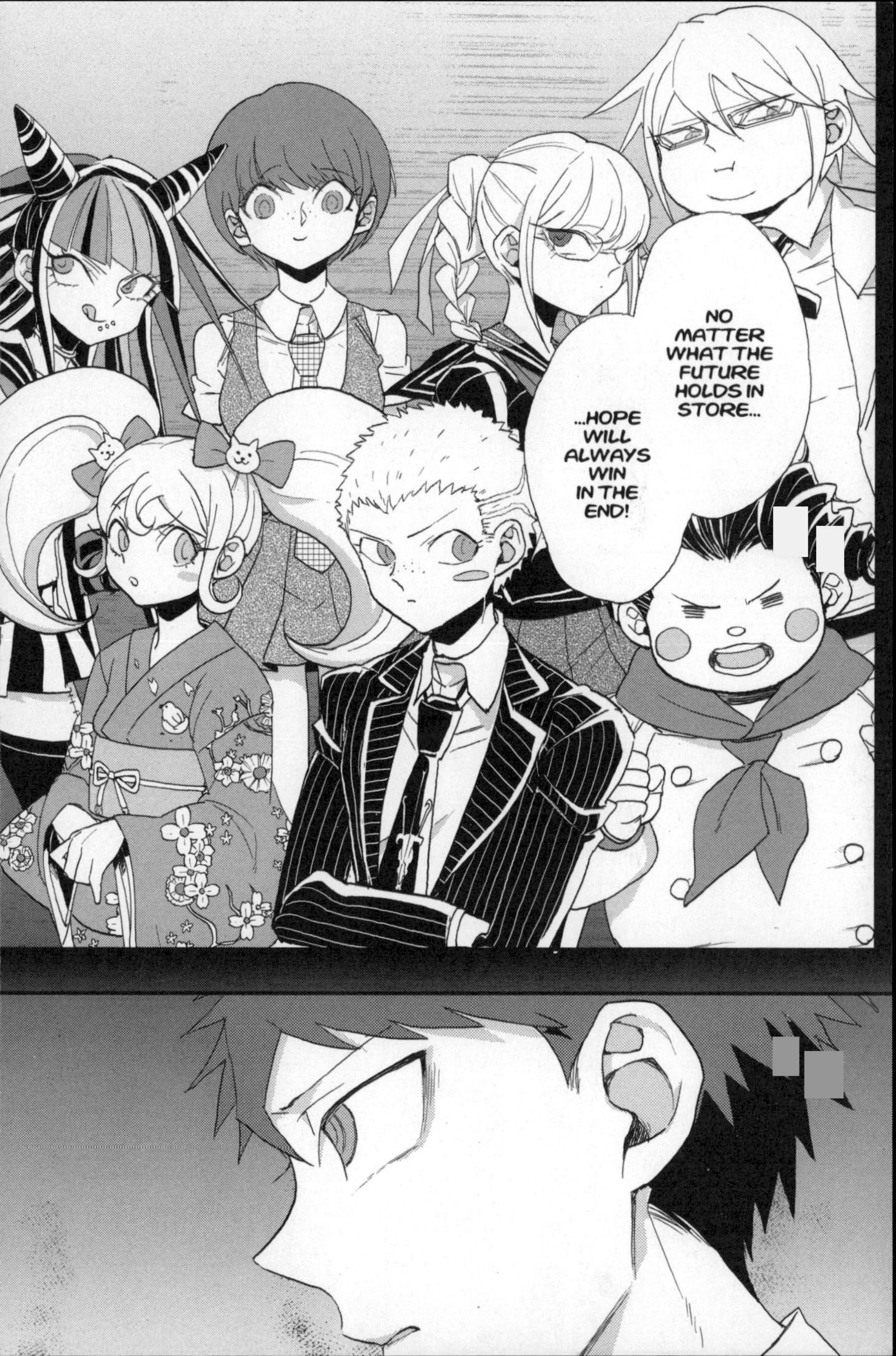
NO MATTER WHAT THE FUTURE HOLDS IN STORE...
...HOPE WILL ALWAYS WIN IN THE END!

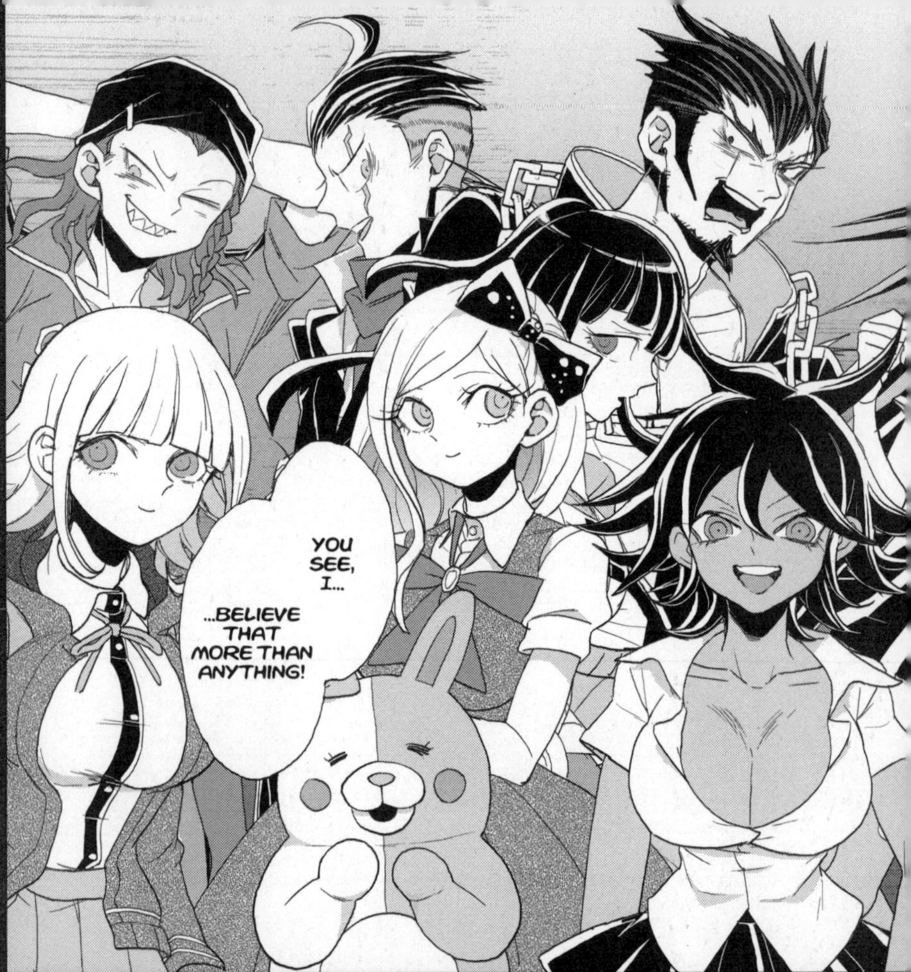
YOU SEE, I...
...BELIEVE THAT MORE THAN ANYTHING!

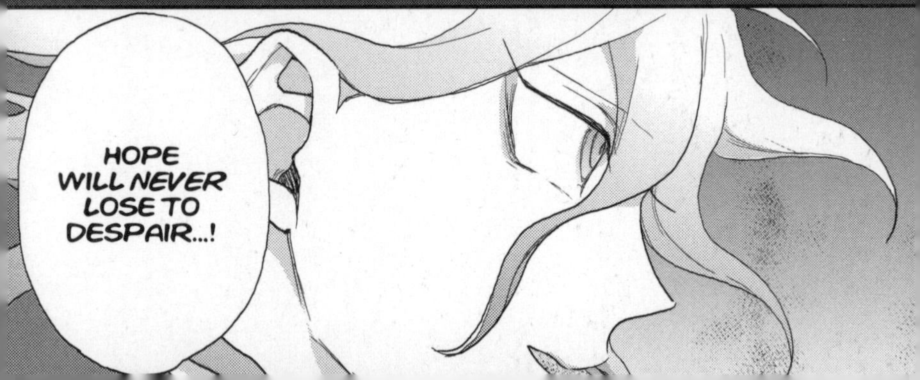
HOPE WILL NEVER LOSE TO DESPAIR...!

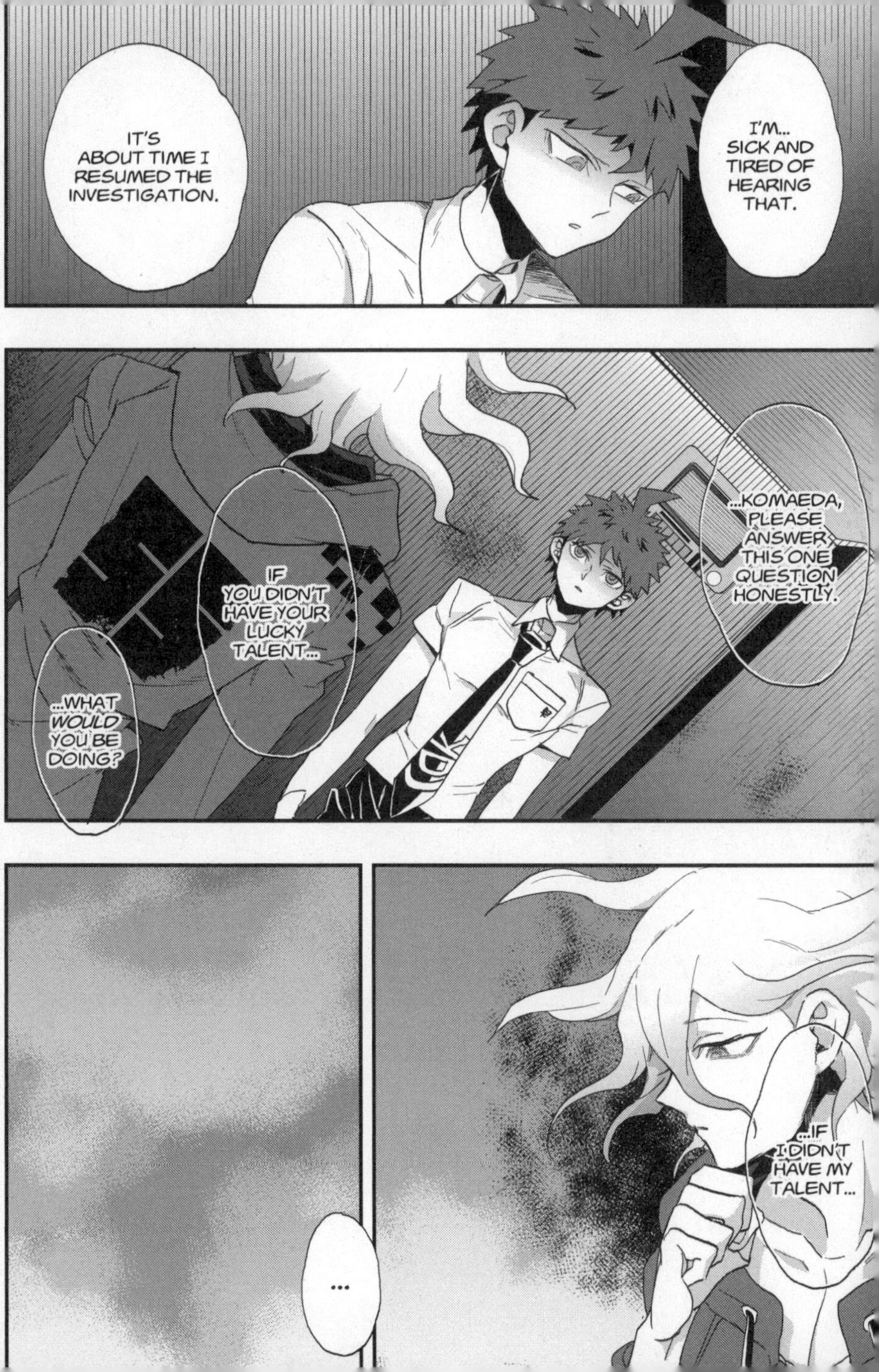
I'M... SICK AND TIRED OF HEARING THAT.
IT'S ABOUT TIME I RESUMED THE INVESTIGATION.
...KOMAEDA, PLEASE ANSWER THIS ONE QUESTION HONESTLY.
IF YOU DIDN'T HAVE YOUR LUCKY TALENT...
...WHAT WOULD YOU BE DOING?
...IF I DIDN'T HAVE MY TALENT...
...

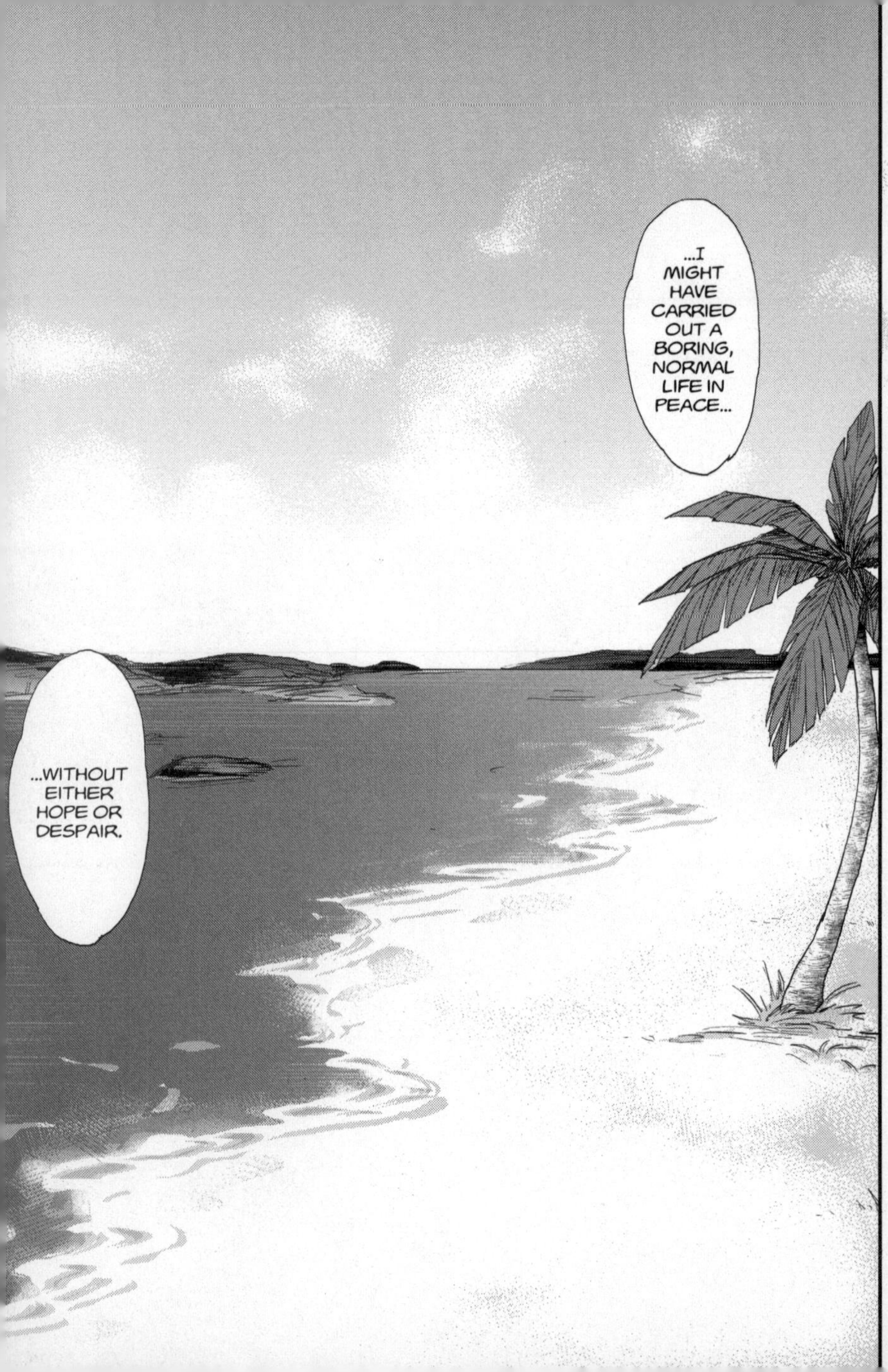
...I MIGHT HAVE CARRIED OUT A BORING, NORMAL LIFE IN PEACE...
...WITHOUT EITHER HOPE OR DESPAIR.

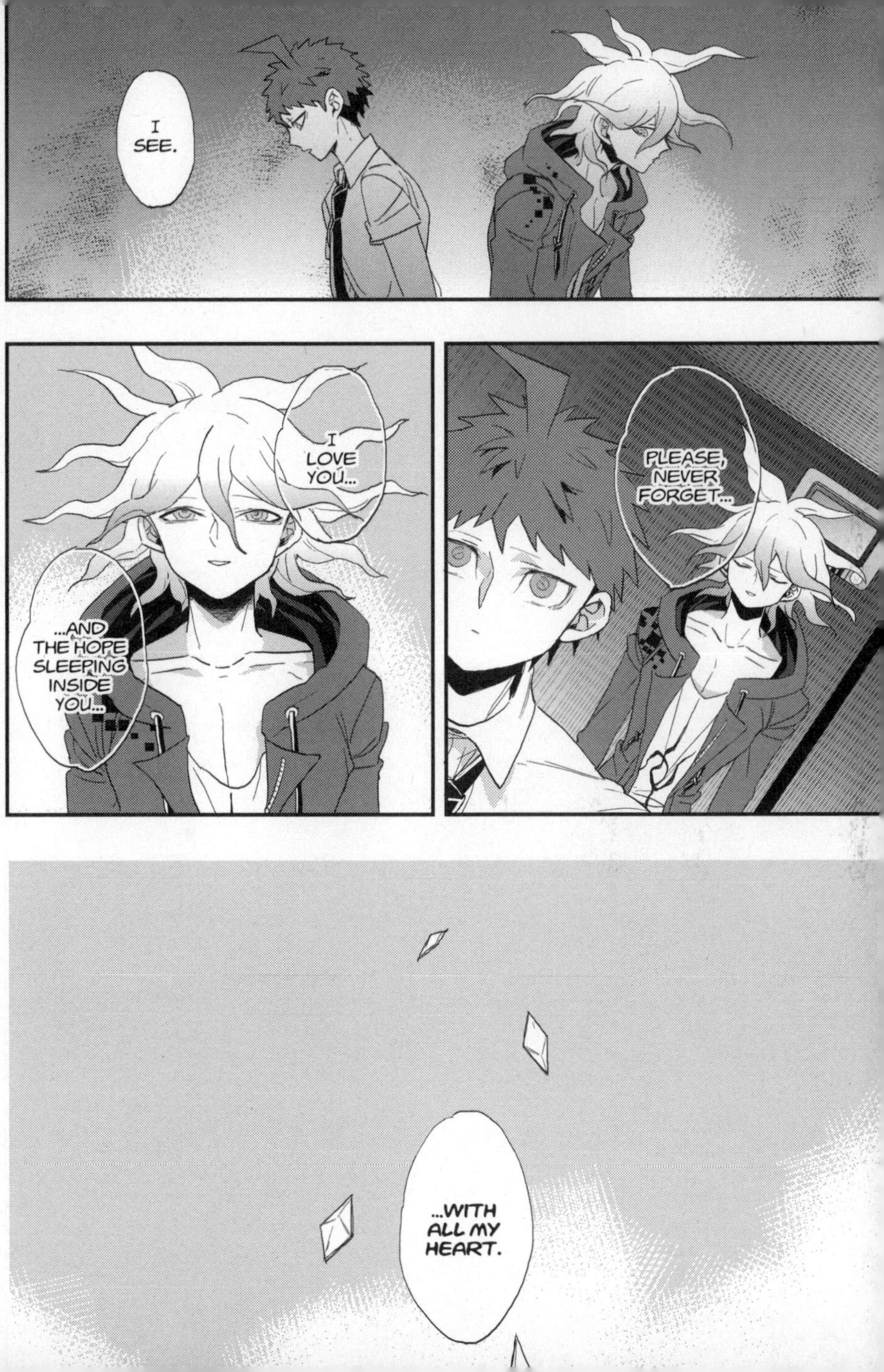
I SEE.
PLEASE, NEVER FORGET...
I LOVE YOU...
...AND THE HOPE SLEEPING INSIDE YOU...
...WITH ALL MY HEART.

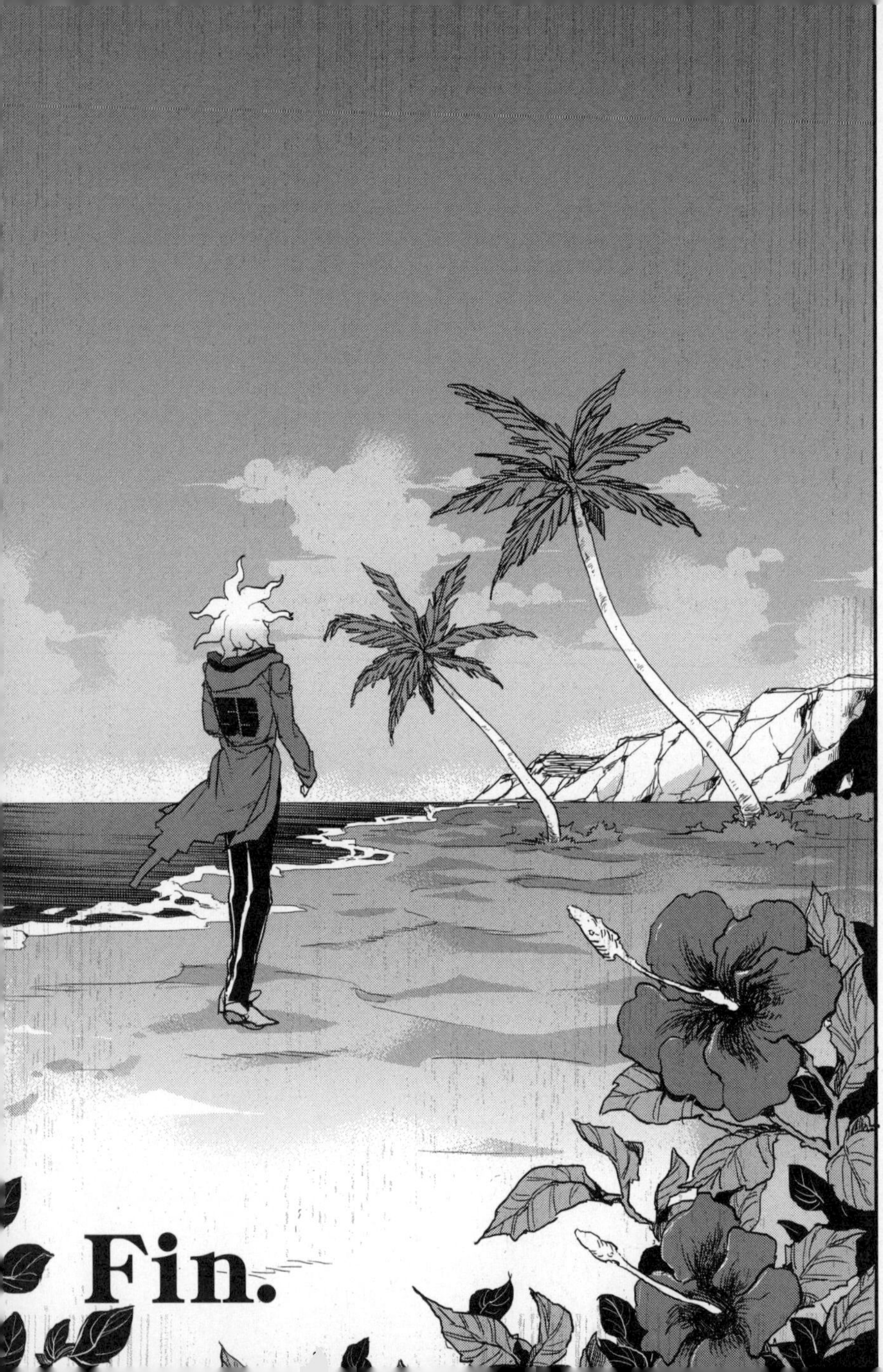
Fin.

Ep.xx

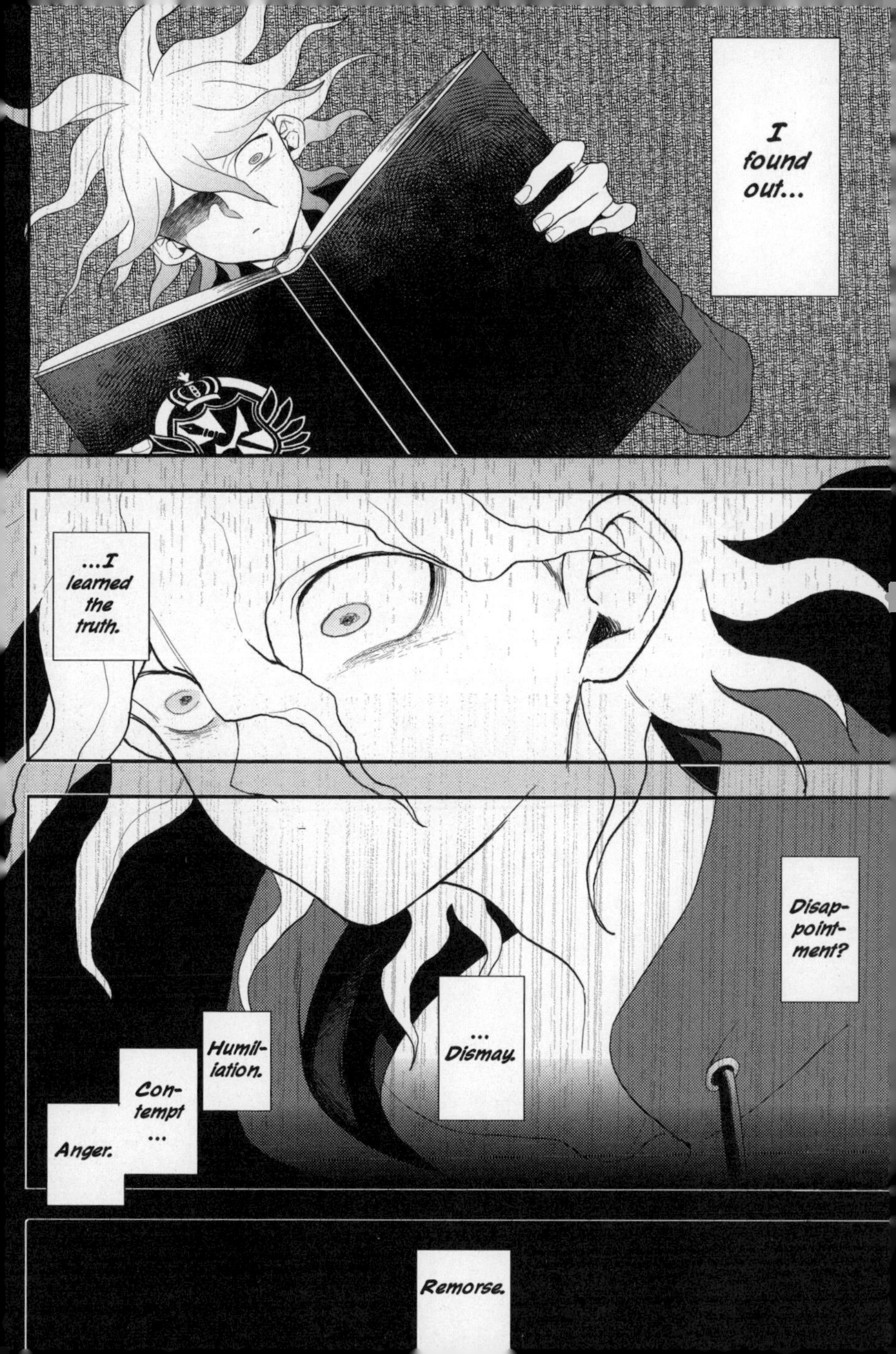
I found out...
...I learned the truth.
Disappointment?
... Dismay.
Humiliation.
Contempt ...
Anger.
Remorse.

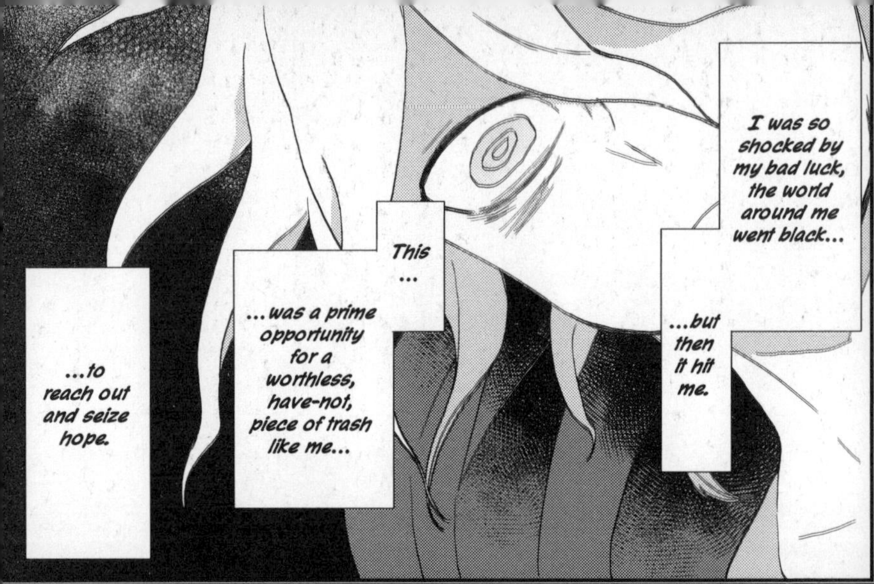
I was so shocked by my bad luck, the world around me went black...
...but then it hit me.
This...
...was a prime opportunity for a worthless, have-not, piece of trash like me...
...to reach out and seize hope.
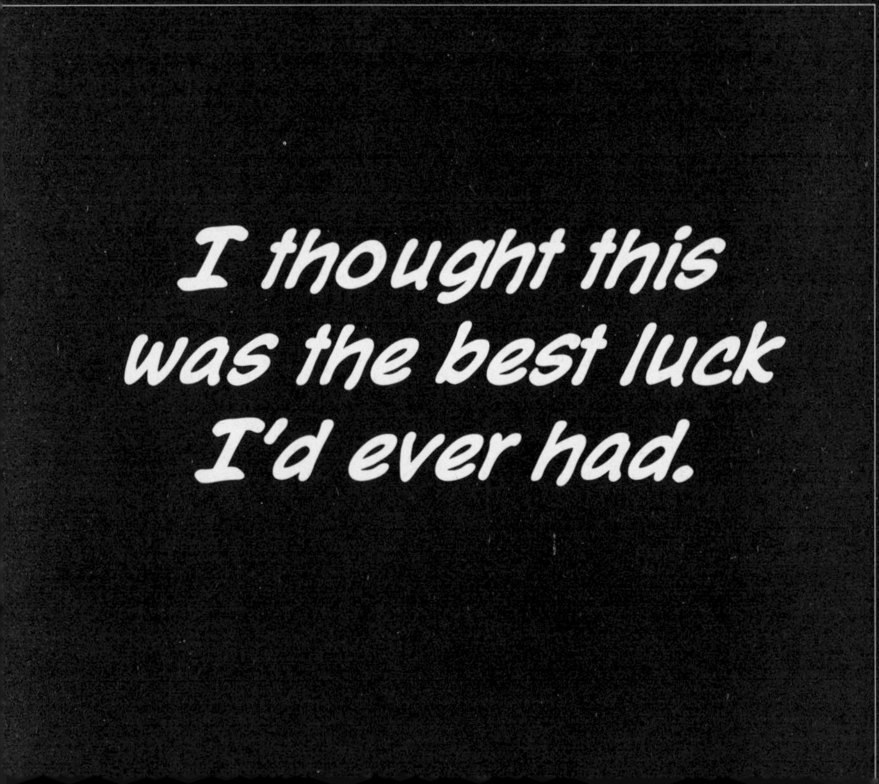
I thought this was the best luck I'd ever had.

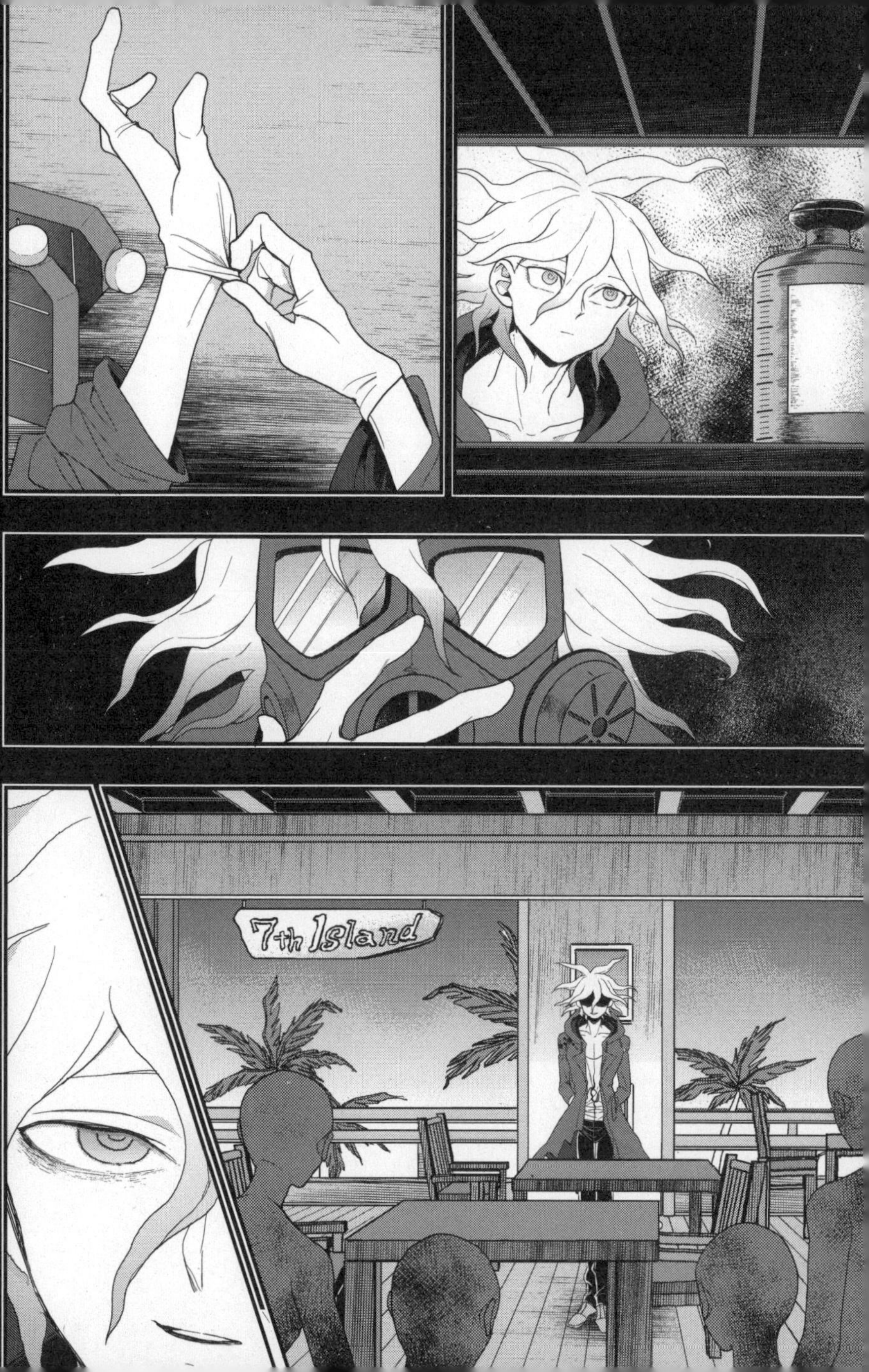
7th Island

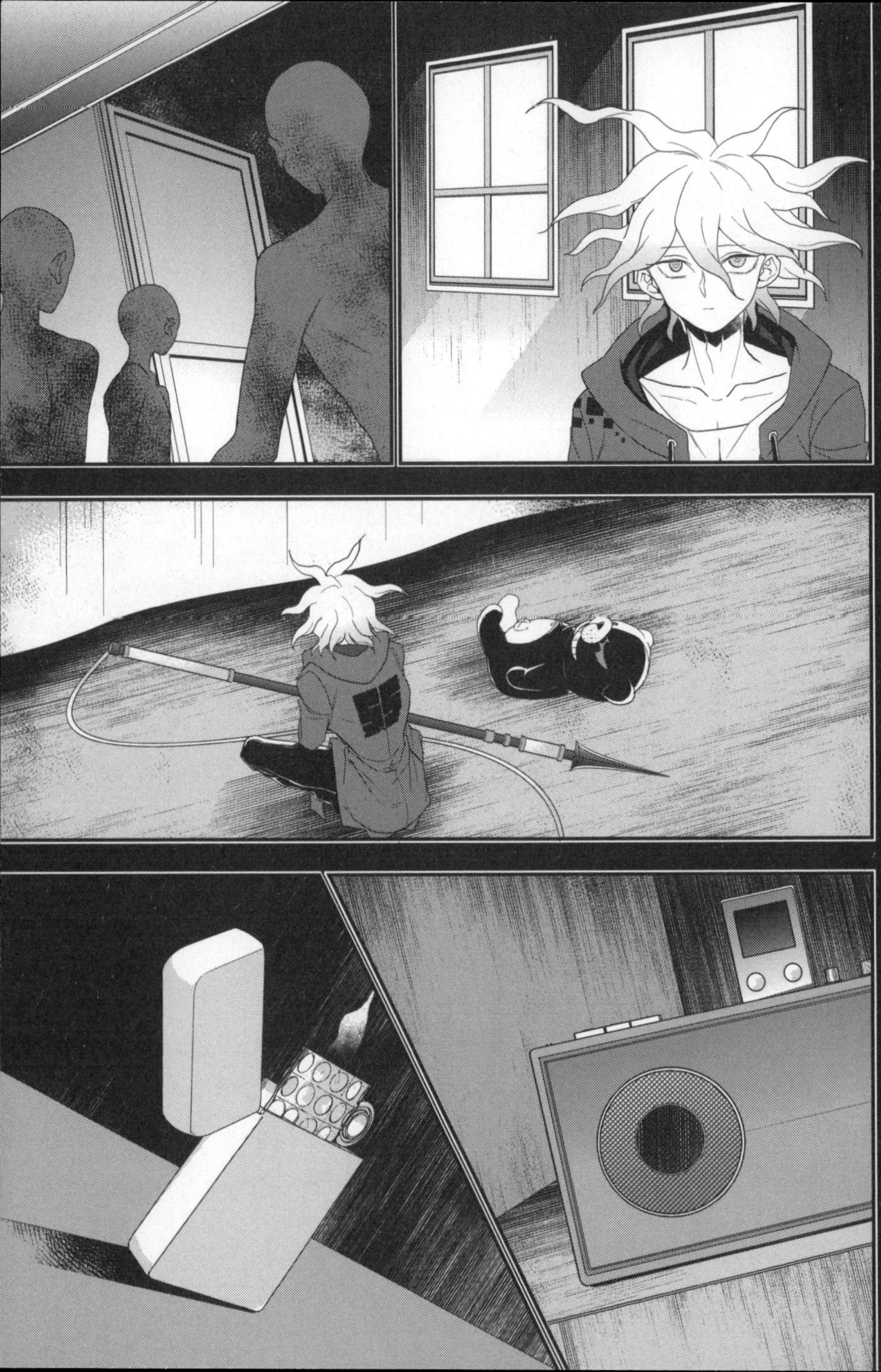

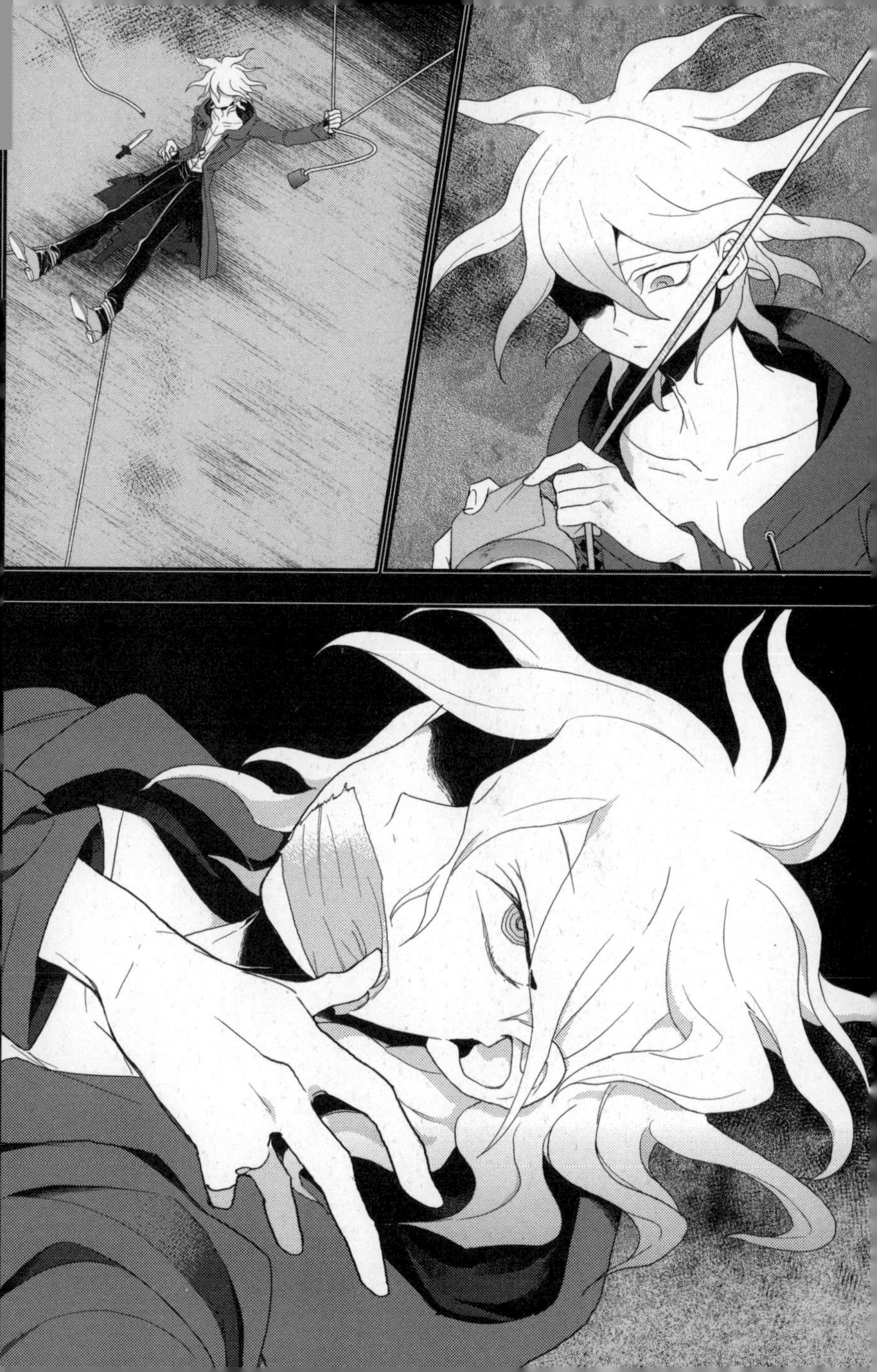

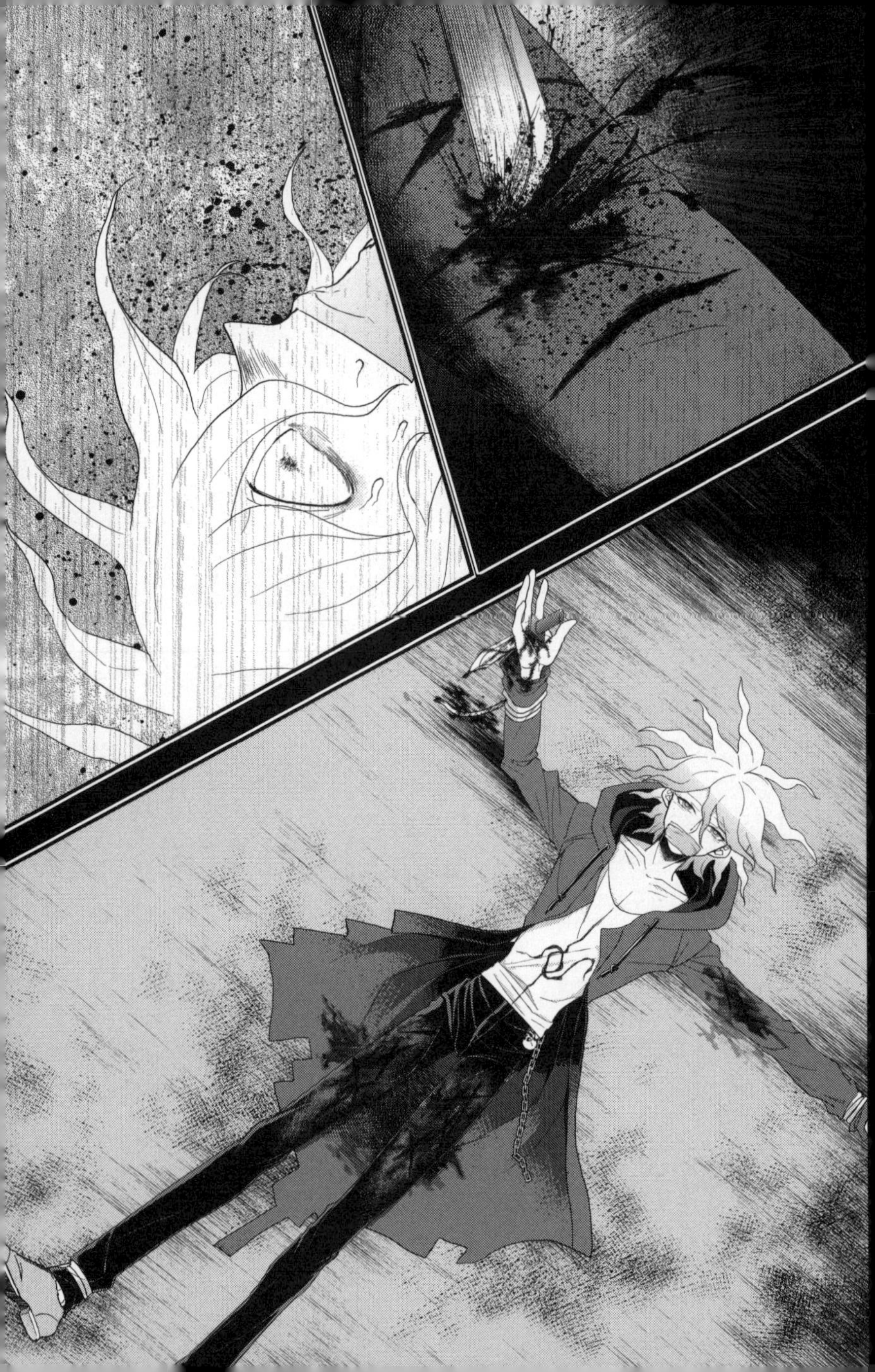

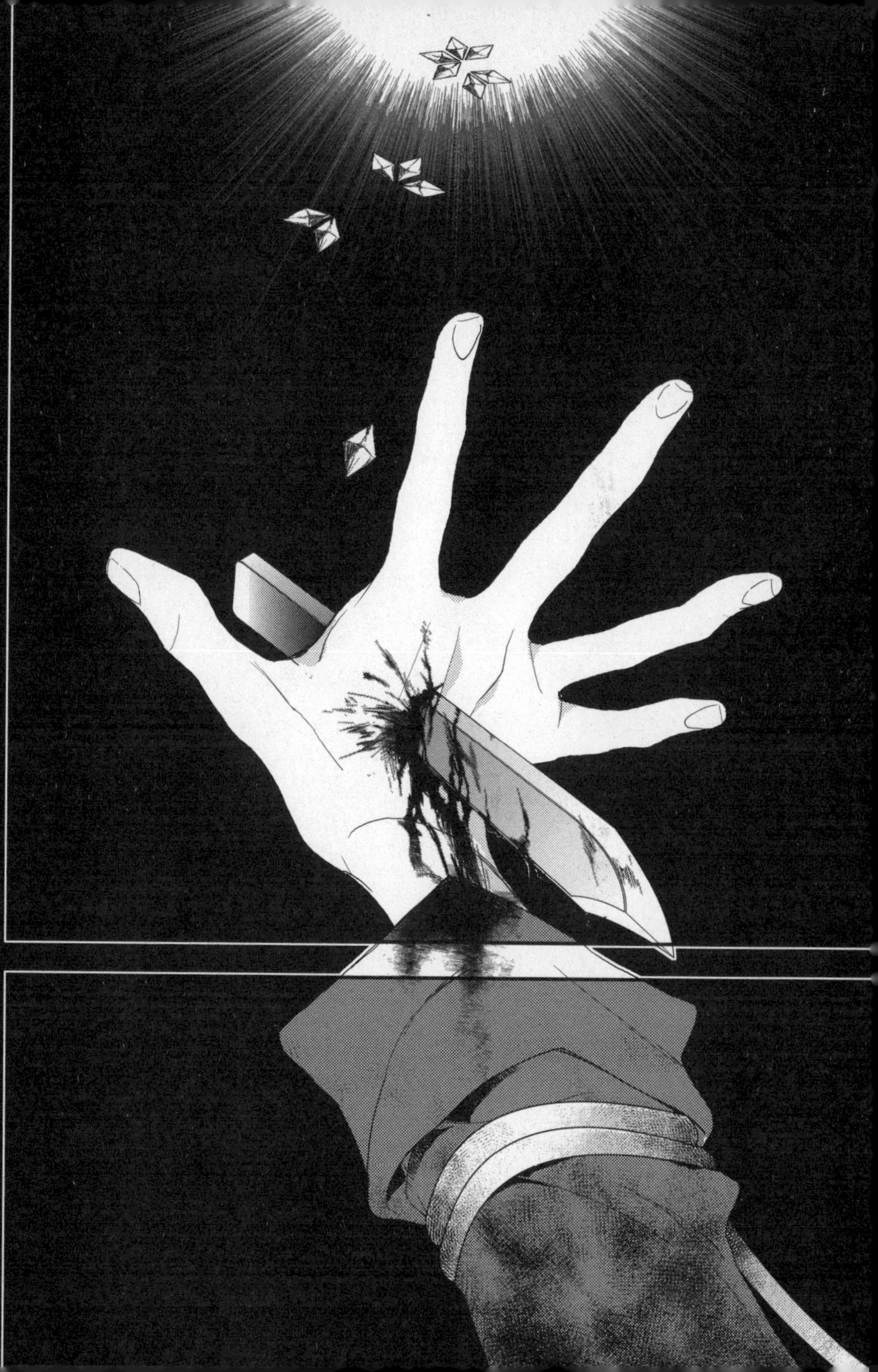

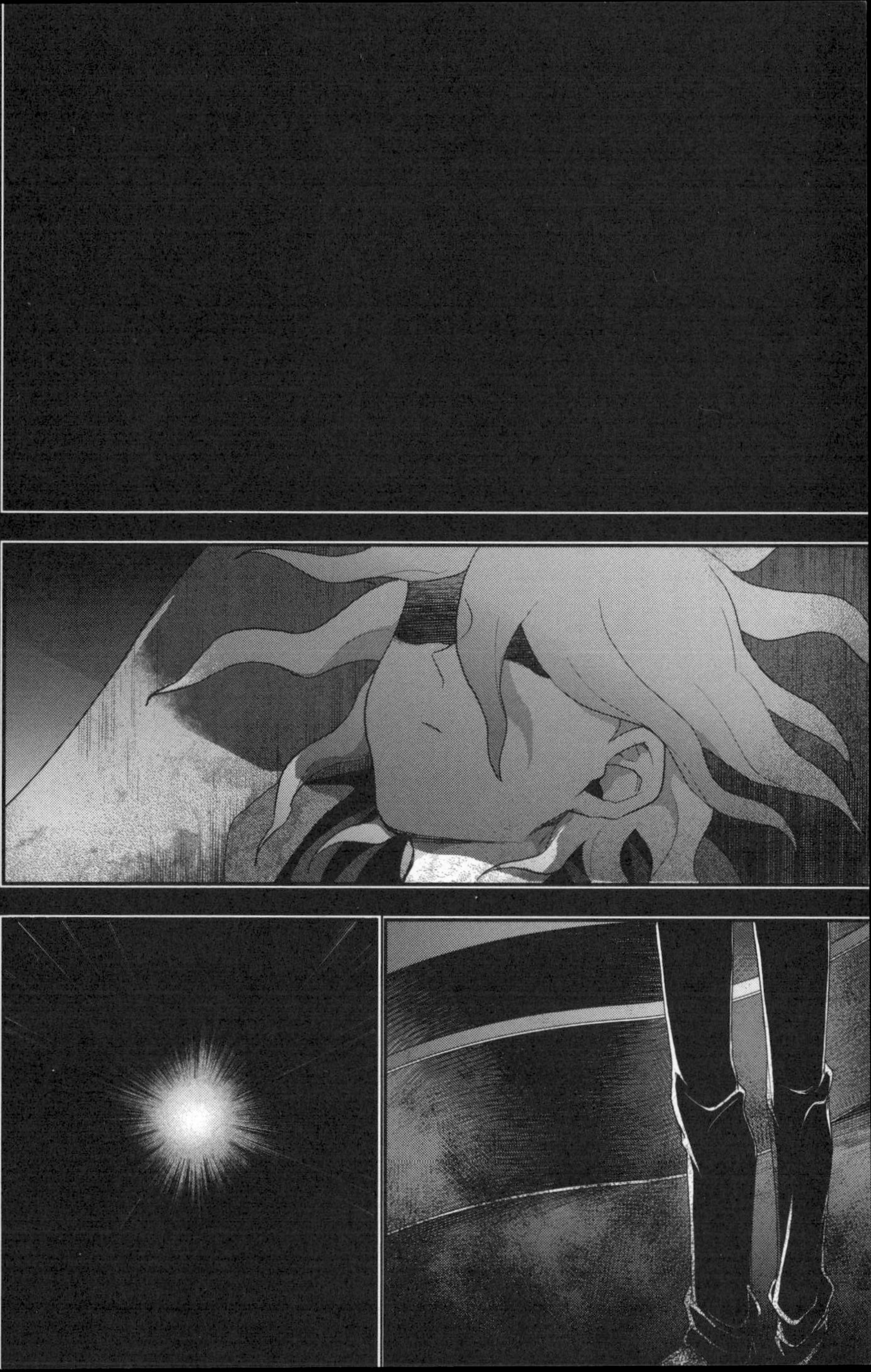

Long time, no see. It's Kyousuke Suga. This is the final volume of **Danganronpa 2: Ultimate Luck and Hope and Despair!** How did you like this manga spinoff focusing on the perspective of Komaeda…?

Although it doesn't have a very big page count, I put a lot of love into the extra chapter at the end. I know I still have a lot to learn as a manga-ka, but I put my best foot forward the whole way through. I'd be tickled pink if you enjoyed yourself along the way, even if just a little.

This serialization wound up taking a super long time due to some complications, but I will always treasure the time and experience of getting to draw the manga adaption of a game I love, from the viewpoint of my favorite character…! It was wonderful getting to draw this from beginning to end.

Although I feel a bit sad to be done, I've always loved the **Danganronpa** series and characters, and will continue to love them…! I'd like to extend a big thank you to the staff at Spike Chunsoft, all of my assistants, everyone associated with this manga, and to you, the readers!

This brings the manga adaption of the story from Komaeda's view to an end, but I hope maybe we'll meet again someday with some other series…! Goodbye, and once again, thank you!

Kyousuke Suga
twitter: akeri00

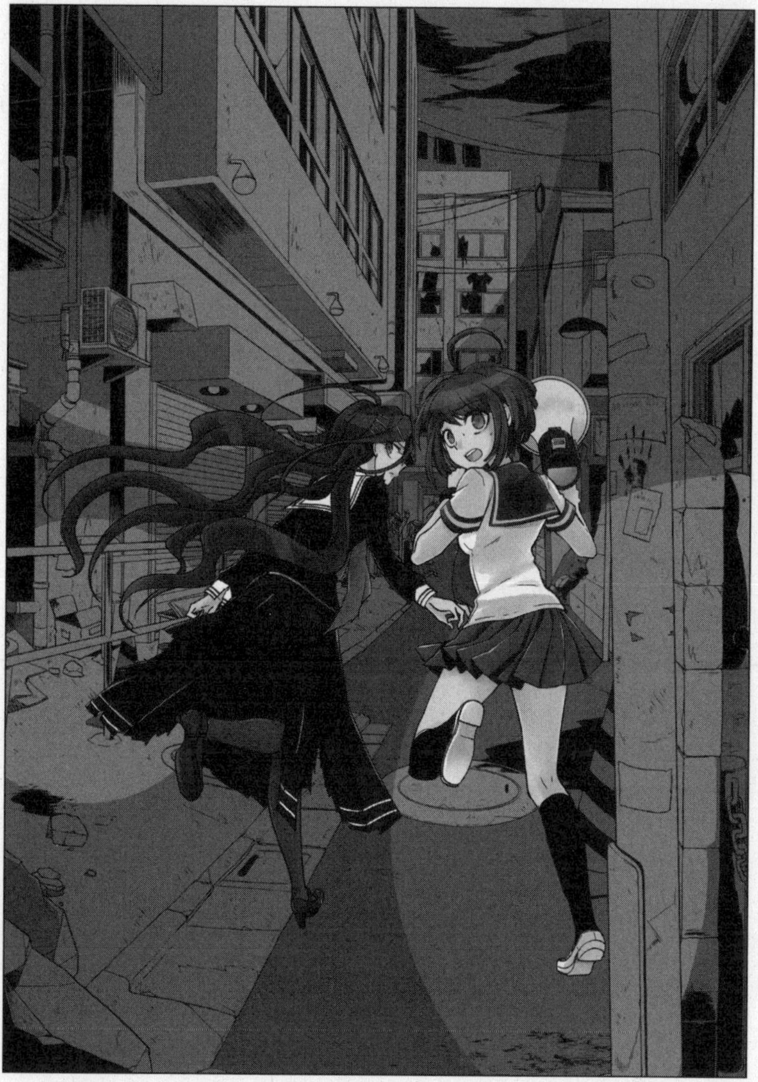

COMING SOON! *DANGANRONPA ANOTHER EPISODE: ULTRA DESPAIR GIRLS*

Girls on the run! Based on the game between the events of *Danganronpa* and *Danganronpa 2*, *Ultra Despair Girls* tells the story of Komaru Naegi, the younger sister of Makoto Naegi. Caught between the factions fighting to control the post-apocalyptic world, Komaru's best chance for survival is the least likely one of all—pair up with Toko Fukawa . . . aka the crazed serial killer, Genocide Jack (Jill)!

VOL. 1 OF *DANGANRONPA ANOTHER EPISODE: ULTRA DESPAIR GIRLS* IS OUT IN AUGUST 2019!

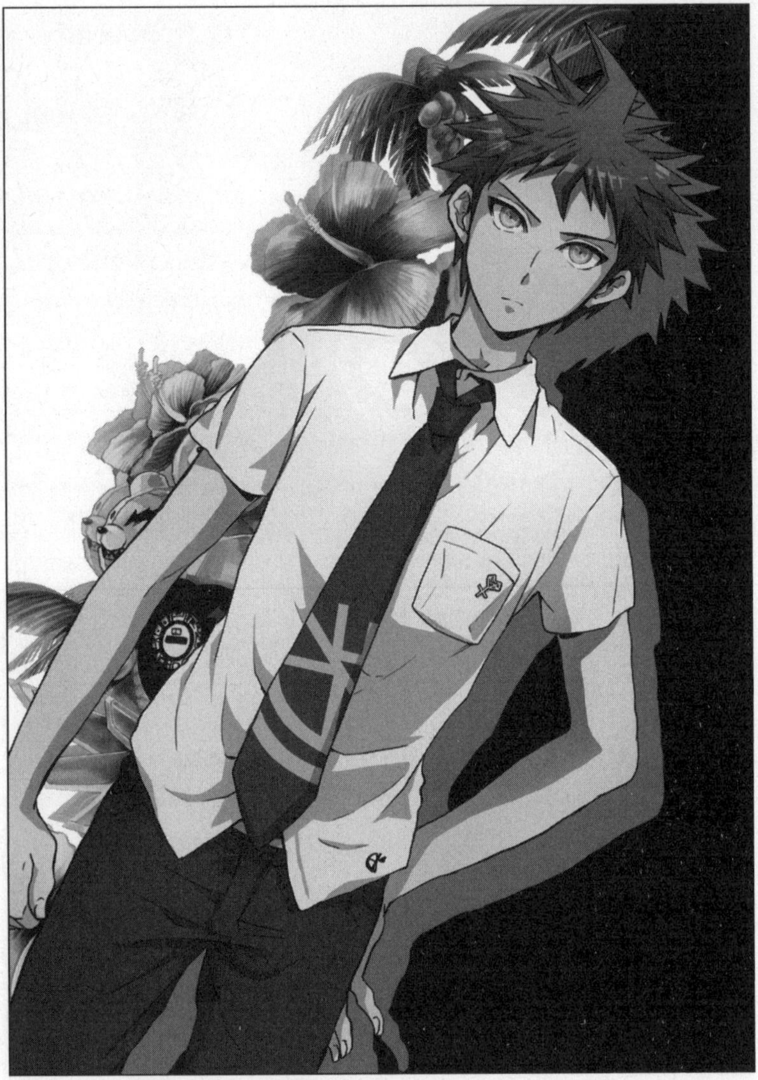

COMING SOON! *DANGANRONPA 2: GOODBYE DESPAIR*

Replay the ultimate murder game with *Danganronpa 2: Goodbye Despair*! You've seen Komaeda's version of events in *Ultimate Luck and Hope and Despair*—now in *Goodbye Despair*, manga artist Kuroki Q gives you the perspective of his arch-rival (?) Hajime Hinata! Things are seen at a different angle when you're the Ultimate . . . ???

VOL. 1 OF *DANGANRONPA 2: GOODBYE DESPAIR* IS OUT IN NOVEMBER 2019!

president and publisher
MIKE RICHARDSON

designer
SARAH TERRY

ultimate digital art technician
SAMANTHA HUMMER

English-language version produced by Dark Horse Comics

DANGANRONPA 2: ULTIMATE LUCK AND HOPE AND DESPAIR VOLUME 3

SUPER DANGANRONPA 2 CHOU KOUKOUKYU NO KOUUN TO KIBOU TO ZETSUBOU Volume 3 © Spike Chunsoft Co., Ltd. All Rights Reserved. © Kyousuke Suga 2017. Originally published in Japan in 2017 by MAG Garden Corporation, Tokyo. English translation rights arranged with KADOKAWA CORPORATION, Tokyo through TOHAN CORPORATION, Tokyo. This English-language edition © 2019 by Dark Horse Comics LLC. All other material © 2019 by Dark Horse Comics LLC. Dark Horse Manga™ is a trademark of Dark Horse Comics LLC. All rights reserved. No portion of this publication may be reproduced or transmitted, in any form or by any means, without the express written permission of Dark Horse Comics LLC. Names, characters, places, and incidents featured in this publication either are the product of the author's imagination or are used fictitiously. Any resemblance to actual persons (living or dead), events, institutions, or locales, without satiric intent, is coincidental.

Published by
Dark Horse Manga
A division of Dark Horse Comics LLC
10956 SE Main Street I Milwaukie, OR 97222

DarkHorse.com

To find a comics shop in your area, visit comicshoplocator.com.

First edition: June 2019
ISBN 978-1-50670-735-8
Digital ISBN 978-1-50670-738-9

7 8 9 10

Printed in the United States of America

NEIL HANKERSON Executive Vice President **TOM WEDDLE** Chief Financial Officer **RANDY STRADLEY** Vice President of Publishing **NICK MCWHORTER** Chief Business Development Officer **DALE LAFOUNTAIN** Chief Information Officer **MATT PARKINSON** Vice President of Marketing **VANESSA TODD-HOLMES** Vice President of Production and Scheduling **MARK BERNARDI** Vice President of Book Trade and Digital Sales **KEN LIZZI** General Counsel **DAVE MARSHALL** Editor in Chief **DAVEY ESTRADA** Editorial Director **CHRIS WARNER** Senior Books Editor **CARY GRAZZINI** Director of Specialty Projects **LIA RIBACCHI** Art Director **MATT DRYER** Director of Digital Art and Prepress **MICHAEL GOMBOS** Senior Director of Licensed Publications **KARI YADRO** Director of Custom Programs **KARI TORSON** Director of International Licensing **SEAN BRICE** Director of Trade Sales

DESPAIR MAIL

c/o Dark Horse Comics | 10956 SE Main St. | Milwaukie, OR 97222 | danganronpa@darkhorse.com

As you just saw a few pages ago (and as has been hinted at for a while now . . .) this is not the end of Dark Horse's Danganronpa manga, and we have two more series on the way: Danganronpa Another Episode: Ultra Despair Girls, and Danganronpa 2: Goodbye Despair. That means we'll also be continuing DESPAIR MAIL, so we'd love to receive more of your thoughts, fan art, cosplay, etc., on all things Danganronpa! Remember to use high resolution if possible (300 dpi or better) for your photos or images, so it'll look its best in print.

However, in this final volume of Ultimate Luck and Hope and Despair, we are going to try to catch up with all the fan submissions that haven't appeared yet. What's a trip is that everything you see here in vol. 3, we received before February, whereas the book doesn't even come out until June! As you may know, in commercial book publishing a lot of things have to be done months in advance ^_^" So if you don't see your submissions here, please look for them in the new manga series.

Well, let's begin with the person whose—shall we say, unique—perspective has guided us here, Nagito Komaeda, depicted by Rhiannon Blattel, who says, "I have been a fan of the series for a few years now and most recently completed V3. Although I love and support all of the games/manga/anime, Danganronpa 2 has got to be my favorite. I just tend to love and connect with the characters a lot more. I hope (no pun intended heh) that you all continue to make more manga and exciting content. I will continue to support you all anyway I can! Thanks." Thank you, Rhiannon—and we'll do our best!

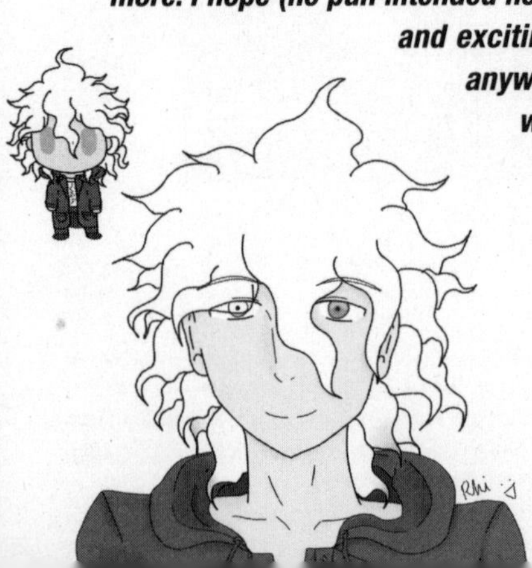
Rhi :)

"Hey! I'm Kerri. (@nanette_fanclub on Instagram) I've been reading the *Danganronpa* manga recently. I've played the game and watched the animation, and it's my favorite thing ever. Toko is my favorite character, because she reminds me of myself. We both wear our socks the same, both have long hair put back in braids, and we both love writing. Most importantly, she helped me accept my 'blemishes'. Toko and I have a beauty mark in the same spot. Seeing a character that looked like me really boosted my confidence and self-esteem."

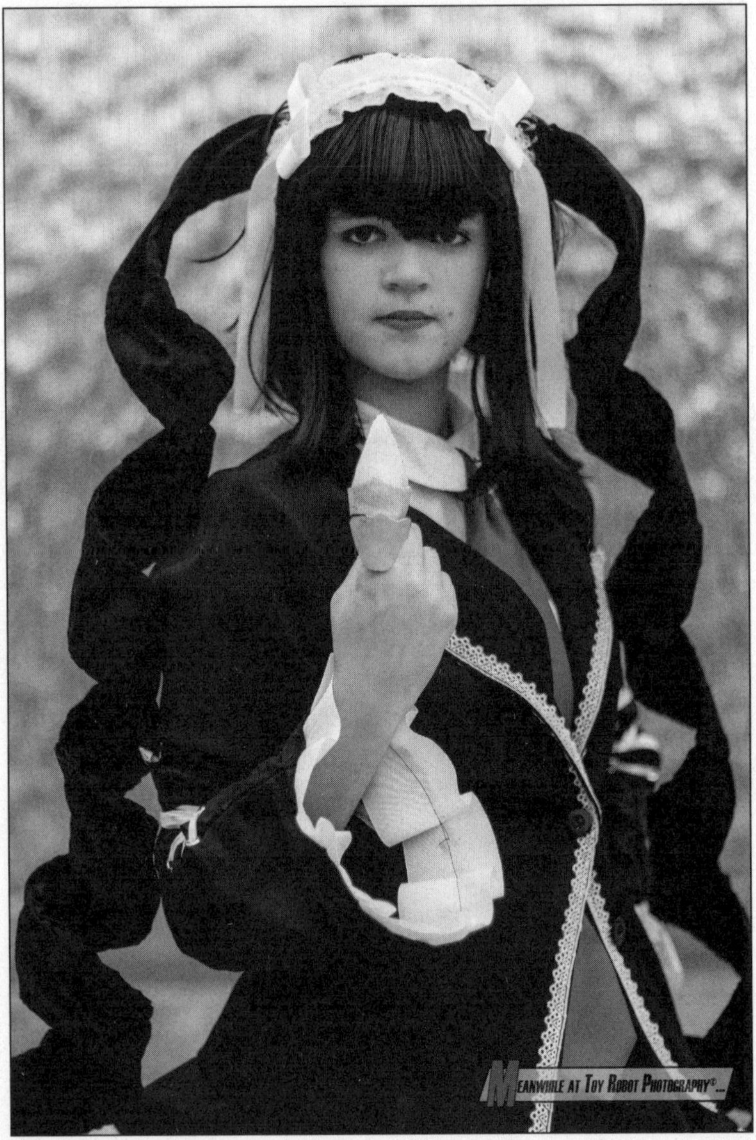
MEANWHILE AT TOY ROBOT PHOTOGRAPHY®...

Kerri (who has been waiting patiently since, like, Christmas 2017—I told you we had a lot of letters to catch up with!) updated us a few months later to add, "This is gonna sound absolutely wild, but I just got accepted to a private high school dedicated to art as a literary student. I'm glad I don't have an alternate personality, lol . . . (I also cosplayed Celestia Ludenberg/Taeko Yasuhiro because aaaa she's so pretty)."

Ultimate Cosplayer
Fuyuko Haruna

Maya Sturmer writes DESPAIR MAIL to say, "I'm a big fan of the *Danganronpa* series, and decided to make my own original character! Her name is Fuyuko Haruna and she is the Ultimate Cosplayer! She dresses in lolita fashion, and has part of her hair dyed. She is inspired by myself, me being really into cosplay (though I just started), and wanting to dye my hair. I hope to cosplay as Celestia (Celeste) Ludenberg in the near future! Thank you for being wonderful people, and creating *Danganronpa* for the world! Sincerely, Maya Sturmer (Ultimate *Danganronpa* Fan.)"

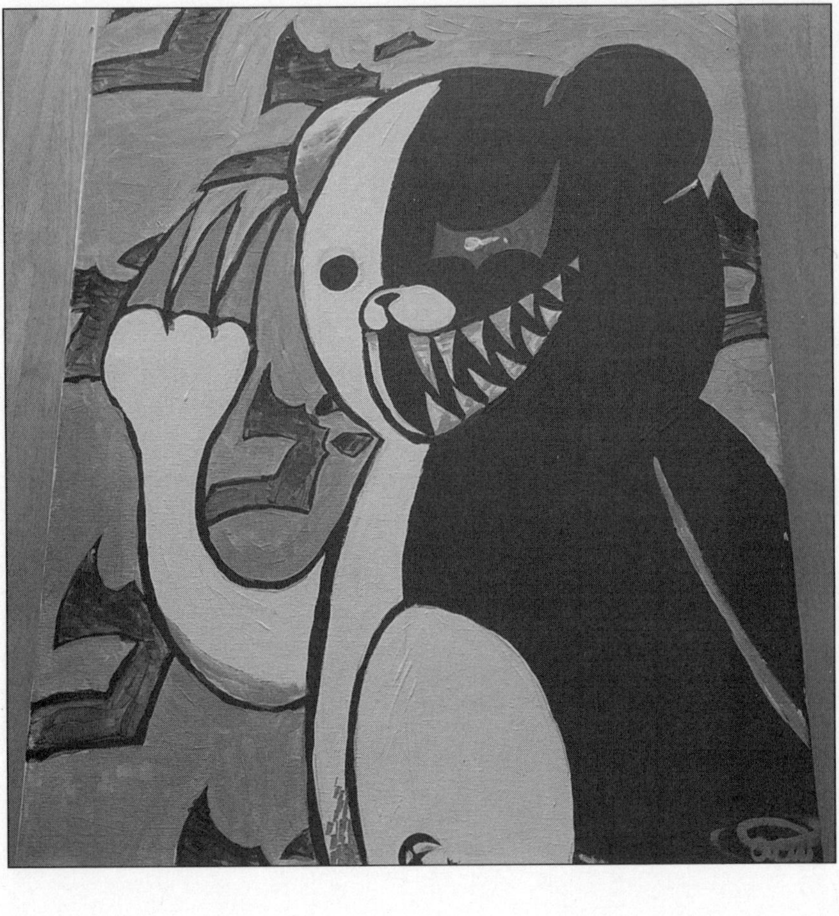

Uh-oh, looks like Monokuma is getting disgusted with all the positivity around here, and has decided to do his best Logan impression. This SNIKT! comes to you courtesy of artist Alexandria (Alex) Willardsen, who says "After buying the first volume of *Danganronpa* and seeing DESPAIR MAIL, I wanted to send in a painting I made of Monokuma! My boyfriend and I are huge *Danganronpa* fans and I was super happy to find out you guys were making a manga for it! I'm looking forward to the next issue as well as other stuff you guys put out!"

(In a high-pitched Monomi voice) "Now that wasn't very nice, Monokuma!" Actually, artist Neil Smith here is referencing the famous Spider-meme of them pointing at each other. Neil explains, "I picked up all the *Danganronpa: The Animation* manga about six months ago and loved them, so I was freaking excited to see they were making another series! I bought it release day, and I saw they were doing the submission things again (which is an awesome thing to include), so I decided on my first day off I would send in a drawing! It would be a dream come true :) for my art to be shown, and thanks for releasing another amazing book!"

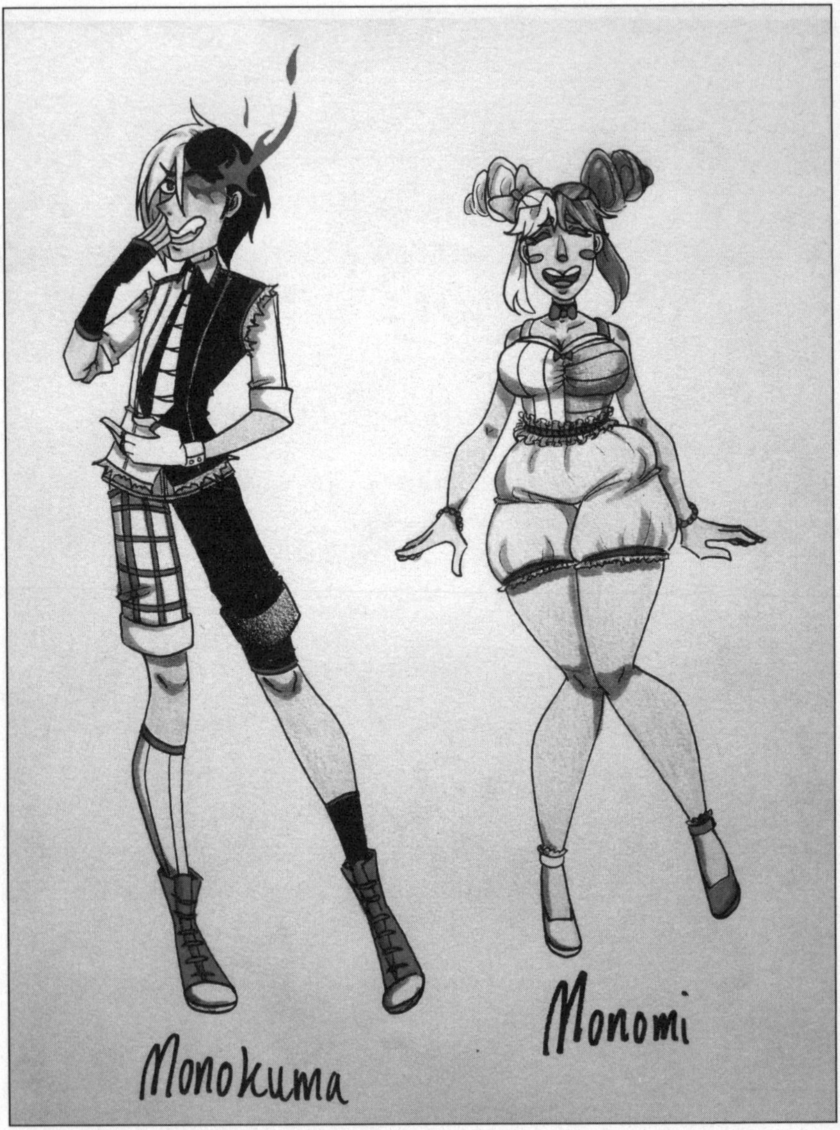
Monokuma
Monomi

And while we've got the both of them here . . . Jason Minton sent in this intriguing illustration with the comment, "I just wanted to show how much I love and appreciate *Danganronpa* and its characters! It's one of my favorite series (anime, manga, and games), so I drew what I thought Monokuma and Monomi would look like as people!"

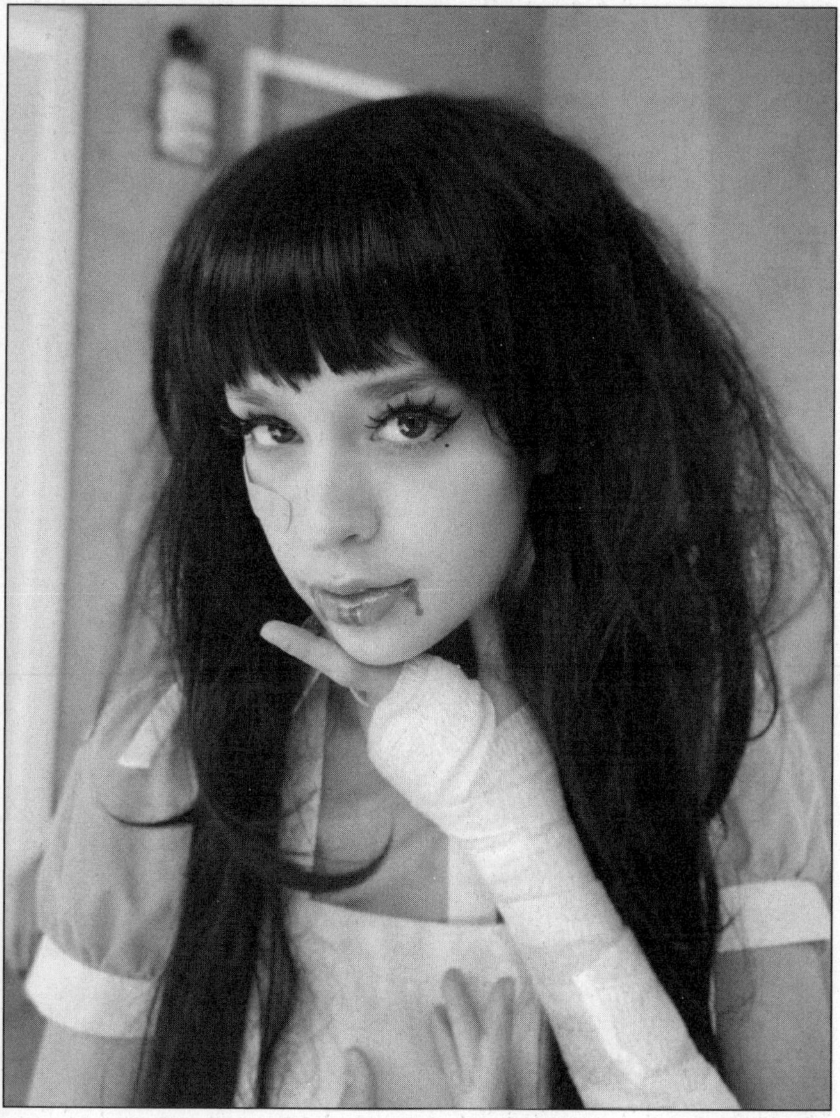

Here's Charlize Lawson (Fizzory on Instagram) as *Danganronpa*'s dedicated health care professional, Mikan Tsumiki. It's just one of her several cosplays from the series, as you can see on the next page . . .

. . . as Charlize chills in Junko mode on the right, while Mukuro beside her on the left is played by Charlize's real-life sister Savannah (Amoribun on Instagram)!

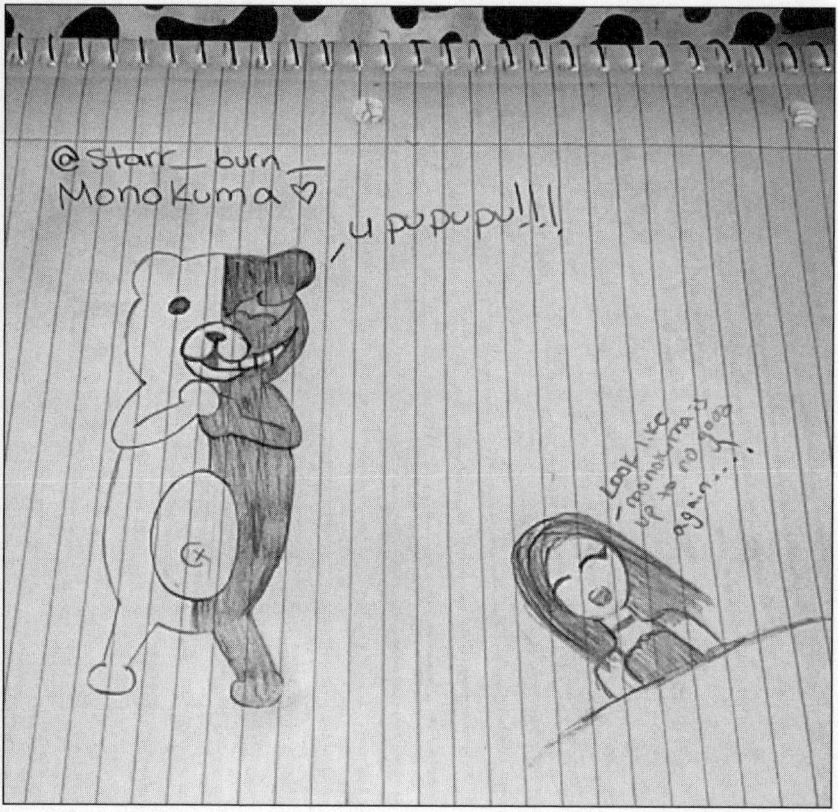
@Starr_burn_
Monokuma♡
upupupu!!!
Look like monokuma's up to no good again...

Baby Pikachu writes in to say, "I've been a fan of *Danganronpa* for a while now, and I love this series! I decided to draw Monokuma, and me saying 'Looks like Monokuma is up to no good again . . . !' Thank you so much, can't wait for future series!" Thank *you* for your patience, Baby Pikachu! ^_^

Chiaki Nanami

At last, someone brings a calming presence to DESPAIR MAIL, as Michael Silveira contributes this drawing of the Ultimate Gamer, Chiaki Nanami.

It's said that her hair clip is inspired by the ship from *Galaga*. As editor, I'd like to say that when my own twin sister and I were kids, we lived near Jack London Square in Oakland, and there was this bar we used to sneak into so we could play the *Galaga* game in there. It was the "cocktail" kind of arcade cabinet where you sat down to play it, and we thought we were sooooo smooth to have accomplished this feat. Looking back after all these years, I want to thank the bartenders for pretending they didn't see us each time ^_^

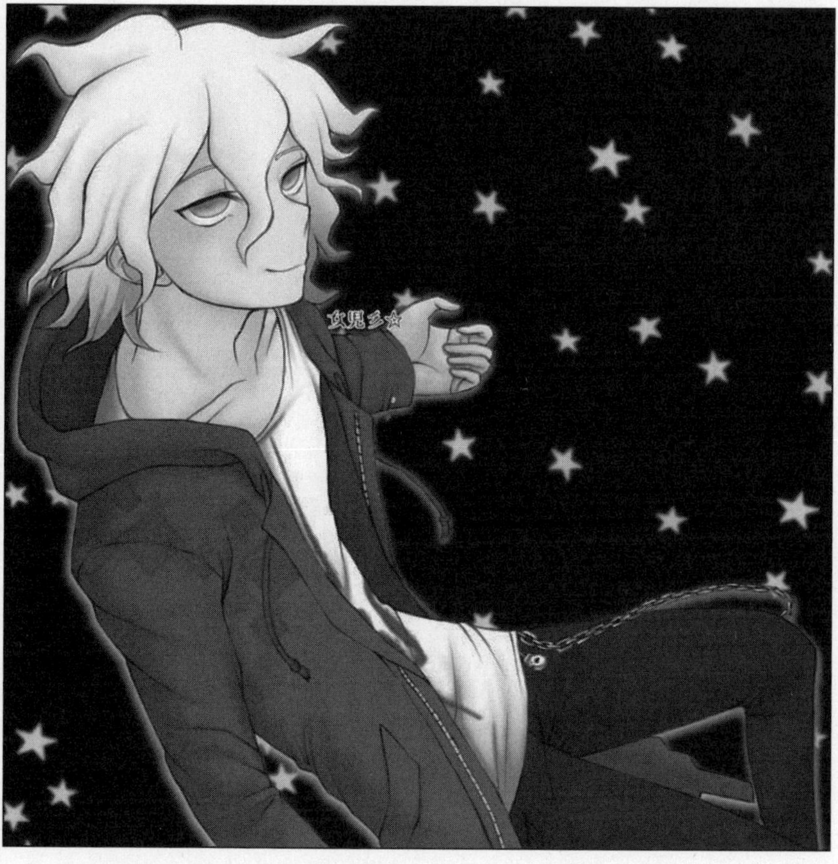

From calming hoodie to crazy hoodie—once again, it's everyone's favorite cracked pepper grinder of hope, Nagito-kun. Would you care for some freshly-ground hope on your salad, sir? A little more? MORE . . . ?

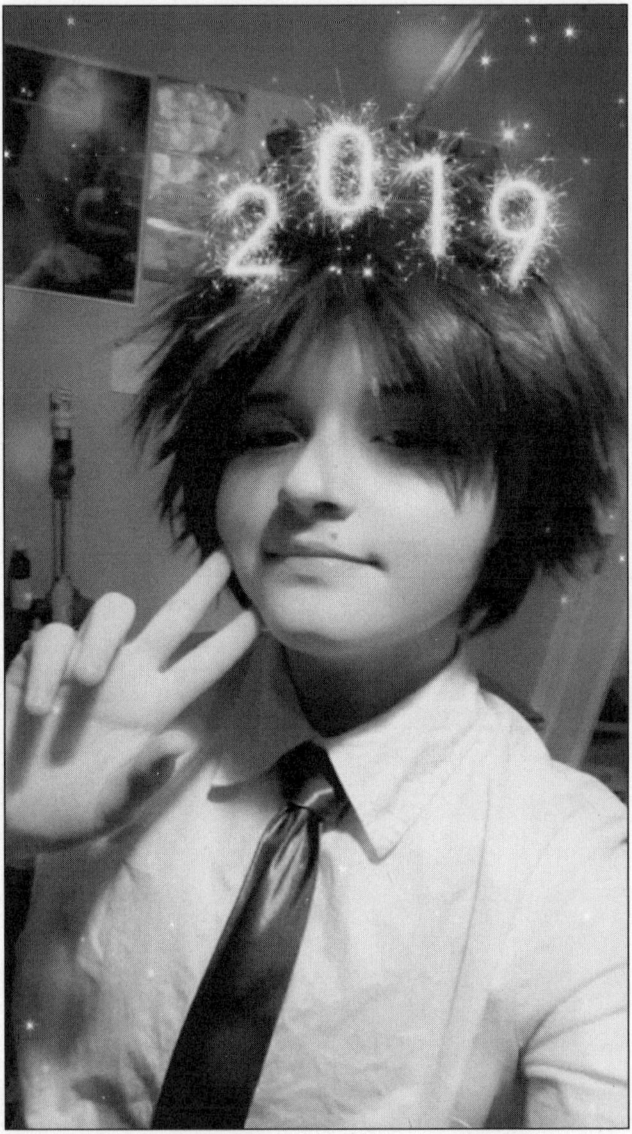
2019

The artist of the Nagito on the right, Tatum Serrette, is pictured here greeting the new year (well, it was January when we got this ^_^) cosplaying as Hinata-kun. Tatum unsurprisingly says, "Nagito has been my favorite since I got into the series, and I absolutely love the characters. I think my least favorite has to be Chiaki, and I plan on cosplaying Mikan and Makoto!" Even the least favorite is absolutely loved—that's the *Danganronpa* spirit!

The contributing artist of this piece says, "Yo! My name's Krisner, also known as Krizeros or @Futurexhope on Twitter and Instagram. I've been a fan of this series since before there was even an official English release for the first game! *Danganronpa* has heavily influenced my art style, and has even helped me grow as an artist. For that, I am forever grateful. Here I drew my favourite *Danganronpa* character in the entire franchise, Twogami! He's been my favorite for years, and I'm so happy they gave him so much love in *D3*. Also, thank you Dark Horse for publishing this manga, it looks great in my bookcase."

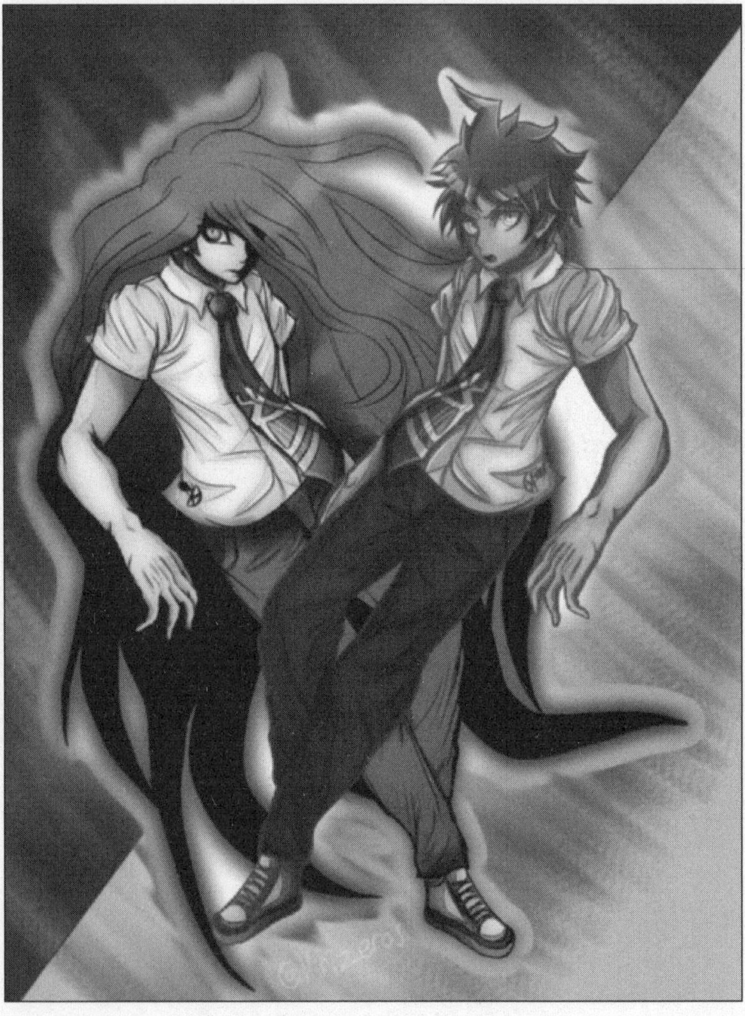

Krisner is another one of the fans who's been patiently waiting so long that they sent in another piece while they were waiting ^_^ "Some Hajime art for his birthday . . . I've known about 'Despair Mail' since the very first volume of *Danganronpa: The Animation*, I just had never gotten around to sending in my art. Though since *Danganronpa 2* is my favorite game of all time, I knew I wouldn't want to miss this opportunity!"

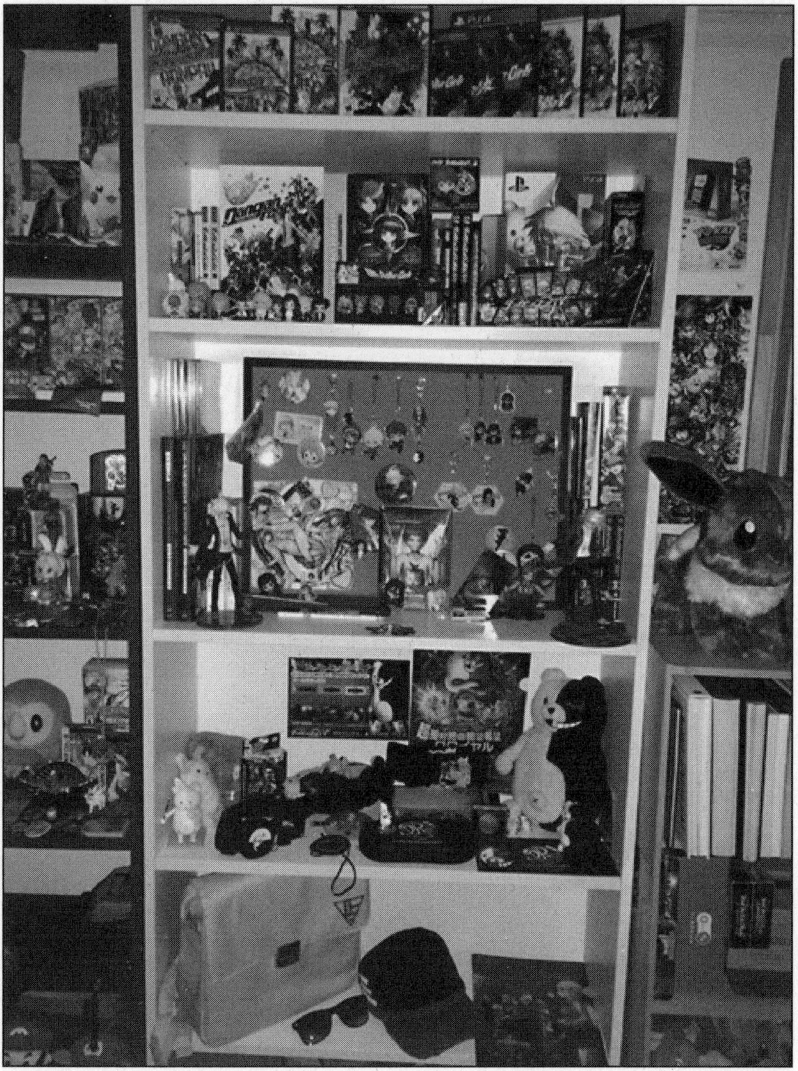

By the way, this is the bookcase Krisner was referring to. I spotted the manga on the bottom right of the center shelf.

Since no one has brought up his name before ^_^ isn't it definitely time for us all to give thanks and praise to Rui Komatsuzaki, who is the original *Danganronpa* character designer? I've read that he was trained as a sculptor, and I think you can see that three-dimensional quality and sense of form in the *Danganronpa* designs. I like the idea that other forms of art besides drawing can enhance and inspire your style as a character designer.

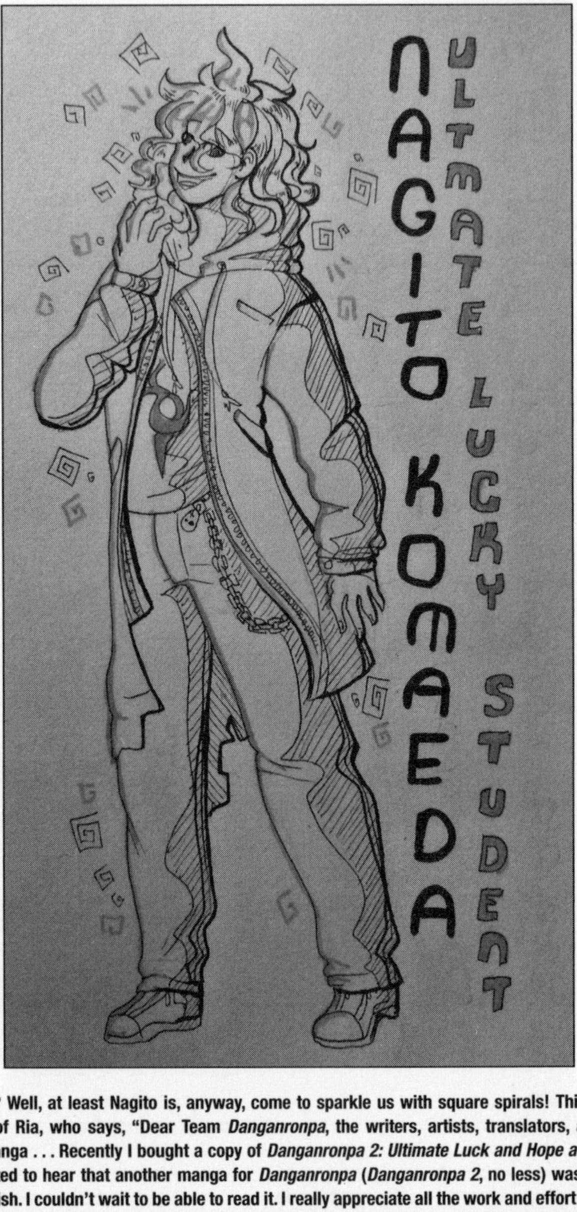
NAGITO KOMAEDA
ULTIMATE LUCKY STUDENT

Aren't we lucky? Well, at least Nagito is, anyway, come to sparkle us with square spirals! This time the drawing is courtesy of Ria, who says, "Dear Team *Danganronpa*, the writers, artists, translators, and crew for the *Danganronpa* manga . . . Recently I bought a copy of *Danganronpa 2: Ultimate Luck and Hope and Despair*. I was honestly so excited to hear that another manga for *Danganronpa* (*Danganronpa 2*, no less) was being published over here in English. I couldn't wait to be able to read it. I really appreciate all the work and effort you guys put into this manga so that we can all enjoy it! I always have wanted to draw Nagito and I thought it was a perfect time to since the most recent manga focused on his viewpoint instead of Hajime's. I really hope you enjoy it!"

At last, some people with practical talents have shown up! Think of the successful farm you could run with Soda to handle the tractor, the thresher, and the baler, and Tanaka to take care of the livestock. The photo came with this greeting: "Hi! My name is Arcadia (the Soda), and my friend Jerry is the Gundham. I'm such a big fan of the series and I'm excited for you guys to put the second game into manga form! *Danganronpa* has honestly changed my life in many good ways, like meeting amazing friends who also share a love for it! Thanks for taking the time to check out our cosplays! May des-bear be with you all!"

This is another time when I wish DESPAIR MAIL was in color, because I love the color in the original drawing here from Mokyu Moguyu, who says, "Something I drew to give Kazuichi and Ibuki some love! I was going to make Kazuichi have tears in his eyes because Ibuki's earrings are sharp, but I decided against it because I didn't want people to think that he's actually hurt (he's just a crybaby). Also, it was hinted that the *Despair Girls* manga might be translated; if that's true, I'm excited! I love the kids and can't wait to see them in a manga, especially Monaca!" As you saw earlier, *Ultra Despair Girls* is coming soon! It occurs to me sometimes that since Kazuichi Soda has those shark's teeth, he may just by accident get lip piercings to match Ibuki's ^_^

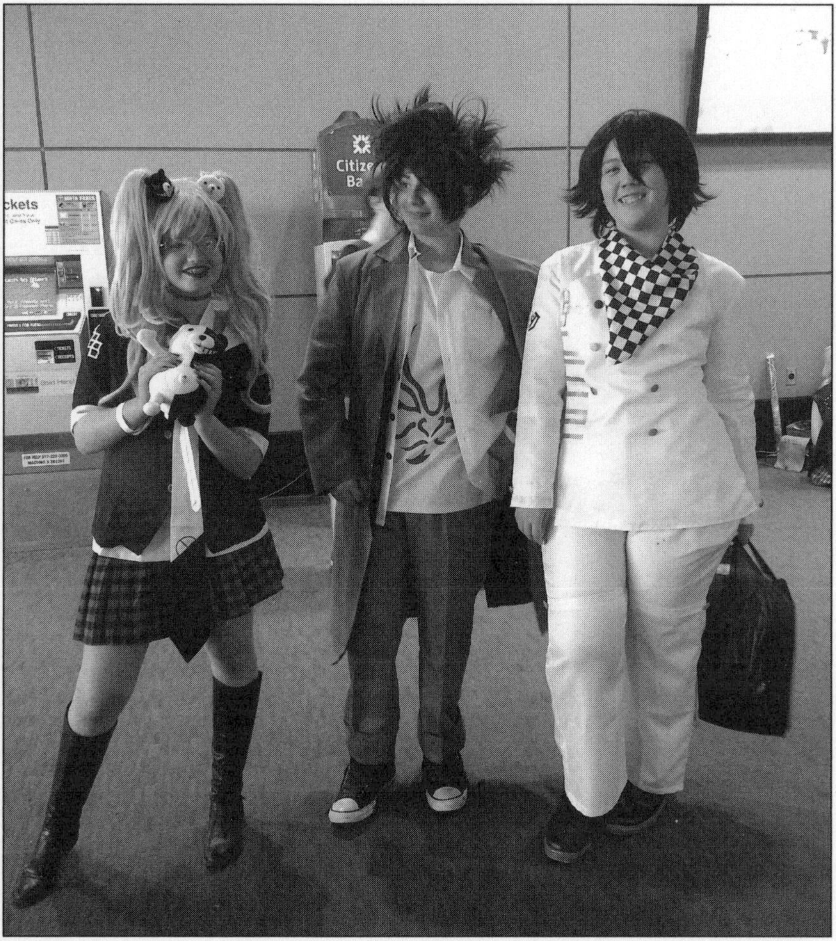
Citize
Ba
ckets

"Hiya! My name is Cat and I'm a HUGE fan of *Danganronpa* (all of the games, manga, and the animation)! I know I'm probably super late to this, but I don't even care if I get in the *DR2* manga. As long as you guys see it, I'll be happy :) I went to Boston Fan Expo as our favorite despair queen, JUNKO ENOSHIMA!!! . . . This is me with a Kokichi Ouma and Kaito Momota cosplayer (They said it's ok for me to send this and possibly be in the manga owo) Thank you guys so much if you can read this! Please respond if you do (^^)"

We're glad you could make it, Cat! In the photo, I spotted the vending machine for "T" tickets and guessed this was a Boston event. I went to Anime Boston a few years ago and stayed in Cambridge while I was there, commuting to the con by subway. The best part was that on Friday morning, the train headed there was half cosplayers and half businesspeople ^_^

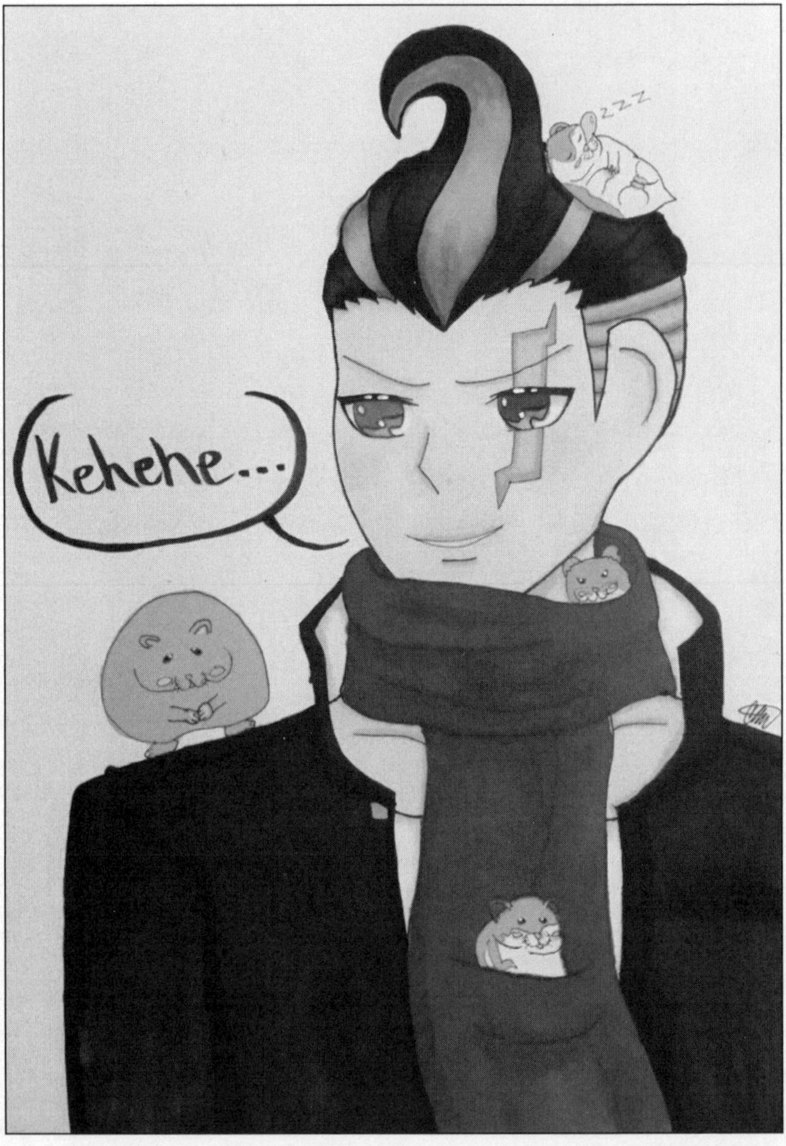
Z Z Z
Kehehe...

"Hi! My name is Charlotte K. and I am a huge fan of the *Danganronpa* series! I found out about *Danganronpa* after picking up Volume 1 of *Danganronpa: the Animation* at the bookstore. I am also an artist, and I have an art account on Instagram which is @charchar12_12. My favorite character of the entire franchise is Gundham Tanaka, and I would love to submit my fan art of him! Thank you so much for publishing more *Danganronpa* books!"

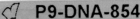
P9-DNA-854

And finally (but just until next time!), all the way from the Netherlands! "I'm Kellodrawsalot. I'm on Twitter and Tumblr. Been a *Danganronpa* fan since I watched the first anime series and started playing the games. Now collecting the manga! Wanted to share a cover I drew for a very shippy wip fancomic I'm creating with my friend Kamenmango! We're both major *DR* fans. Hope that Dark Horse keeps releasing more *Danganronpa* manga! We love them here in the Netherlands!"

Thank you, Kelly! I know how the Netherlands has such a long history with Japan. As those of you who've studied Japanese history already know :) during most of the Tokugawa era, they were only Western country permitted to trade with Japan, and knowledge of modern technology and science was known as "Dutch learning" to the samurai! One of the first pop culture books I ever read about Japan, *Behind the Mask*, was written by a Dutch author, Ian Buruma. He was writing about things like yakuza movies, Takarazuka theatre, and manga years before they became well known outside Japan.

See you again soon in the next *Danganronpa* manga from Dark Horse!

—CGH